FLASH MATH CREATIVITY

DAVID HIRMES
JD HOOGE
KEN JOKOL
TY LETTAU
LIFAROS
JAMIE MACDONALD
GABRIEL MULZER
PAVEL KALUZHNY
KIP PARKER
KEITH PETERS
PAUL PRUDENCE
GLEN RHODES
MANNY TAN
JARED TARBELL
BRANDON WILLIAMS

FLASH MATH CREATIVITY

First Published 2002

Trademark Acknowledgments

Published by friends of ED
30 Lincoln Road, Olton, Birmingham. B27 6PA. UK.

Printed in USA

ISBN: 1-903450-50-0

CREDITS

AUTHORS
DAVID HIRMES
JD HOOGE
KEN JOKOL
TY LETTAU
LIFAROS
JAMIE MACDONALD
GABRIEL MULZER
PAVEL KALUZHNY
KIP PARKER
KEITH PETERS
PAUL PRUDENCE
GLEN RHODES
MANNY TAN
JARED TARBELL
BRANDON WILLIAMS

CONTENT ARCHITECT
BEN RENOW-CLARKE

DESIGNER
KATY FREER

EDITORS
DAN BRITTON
BEN RENOW-CLARKE

TECHNICAL REVIEWERS
KRISTIAN BESLEY
JOHN FLANAGAN
MATTHEW B. HEIN

AUTHOR AGENTS
JEZ BOOKER
CHRIS MATTERFACE

PROJECT MANAGER
JENNIFER HARVEY

PROOFREADER
KRISTIAN BESLEY

MANAGING EDITORS
DAVE GALLOWAY
MEL ORGEE

CONTENTS

1 JAMIE MACDONALD 1

2 GLEN RHODES 19

3 DAVID HIRMES 37

4 LIFAROS 63

5 GABRIEL MULZER 79

6 PAUL PRUDENCE 97

7 KIP PARKER 115

8 JARED TARBELL 133

9 KEITH PETERS 151

10 KEN JOKOL 169

11 TY LETTAU 189

12 PAVEL KALUZHNY 207

13 JD HOOGE 221

14 MANUEL TAN 237

15 BRANDON WILLIAMS 255

TANGENTS 265

Most people don't find creating scripted graphics in a regular programming language that easy. I remember starting C at university and being struck dumb with disbelief that the drawing commands that I knew and loved in BASIC just didn't exist any more. The only thing that we had was a sub-simple graphics library built by the lecturers that was intentionally impossible to use. They didn't want us to breathe images, they just wanted us to bubble-sort our dreams. Flash was a godsend because it made this simple again by allowing me to create graphics in a standard drawing interface, code in a standard coding interface, and combine the two by simply placing the code on the graphic. Suddenly it all made sense. This ease of use has led to many other people tinkering with programming who wouldn't normally do so, and many programmers and mathematicians finding better ways of modeling and displaying what's in their heads. It's a scene reminiscent of the bedroom programming craze of the 80s, and a lot of the math that was being explored then is being brought back to life now.

I moved house a while back, and one of the things I uncovered was a box of old Beebug magazines for the BBC Micro computer, and looking through them I found various programs for creating fractal trees, Lorenz attractors, and function modeling in 3D – all things that turn up in this book. Of course now the resolution's a bit better and they don't take six hours to plot, but the basic principles are the same.

But creation's not all that it's about. Once you've fashioned your masterpiece, you have to change it (save it somewhere first if you like). Art is rarely perfect, there's always something more to add, or something more to take out. In Flash this is the easiest thing in the world to do. Change one variable and you change the whole piece, sometimes subtly, and sometimes astronomically. This is really where the whole book started, with the idea of change.

I love tinkering with code, I love the differences I can make with a quick change here or there, and I can spend hours with the simplest things just changing the same variable over and over again and being mesmerized by the results. Call it simple-minded, but that's me. I'd just spent a few hours doing exactly this when I had a Victor Kiam moment: I loved it so much, I wrote the book. Except I didn't, I just had an idea, the hard writing work was done by the 15 fantastic authors whose passion for the project surprised even me. It's changed a bit since its inception (at one stage I just wanted hundreds of experiments and nothing else), but the basic idea has remained the same – a collection of small experiments with a few iterations each to get you started, and an explanation of what the main variables do so that you'll have a good idea of what to change. To be honest though, I'd almost prefer you to ignore all of this, just grab the files from the site, open them in Flash, and do your best to break them. Once you've done that then go to the chapter and work through the iterations there, gaining a better understanding of the processes that make them tick, then finally go back into Flash and break them again – that's where the fun is, and I think where the majority of the learning is.

The book is split informally into two parts. The first part of the book deals with the smaller experiments, each with an average of ten iterations, and each inviting you to delve into the code and start fiddling. The second section of the book consists of the final three authors; these guys' experiments are more complete applications with interfaces to alter the variables within them. That's certainly no reason to not go into the code and adapt it though, it just means that you can try new things without having to go back into Flash every time.

Most of all though, for me this book is about inspiration. I only did Math at the most basic level at school, but that doesn't stop me being amazed and intrigued by the experiments in this book. I think I must have almost spent as much time going into the files and messing with them as I did editing the material, and I now have a lot more Flash knowledge than I started out with. Working on this book has inspired me to create and experiment a lot more in Flash, and given me more of the information that I needed to translate some of my more esoteric ideas into reality.

The book's filled with ideas to get you started, do with them what you will, but when you're done be sure to post them up on the dedicated forum on our site at **www.friendsofed.com/fmc**. There's nothing I like more than having new code to mess about with.

Ben

Get all the FLAs from here: www.friendsofed.com/fmc/downloads

Break them in a good way.

Re-post them here: www.friendsofed.com/fmc

I'm English and I work doing interface stuff at Relevare (www.relevare.com) in London as well as maintaining my own site, www.nooflat.nu. Before that I worked in a credit card factory and did most of an MA in critical studies in the film department at UCLA. I enjoy the challenge that Flash offers, and I like the fact that it allows you to create systems with limits, combining motion and interaction.

Inspiration is hard to pin down. I guess it necessarily comes from the environment around you in one way or another. For me, that consists of a number of things: music is a big factor, and I listen to a wide range of stuff such as Lee Hazelwood, things on the Scape label, Safety Scissors, Antonelli Elect, and Mike Ladd. Films are another influence; off the top of my head I like Verhoeven a lot, and anything with Warren Oates in it. On top of that, there are more mundane things, such as the problems that I have to solve at work. I'm interested in certain types of interaction and user experience, and I find that a lot of the time I'm driven by sheer frustration, where an inability to do something pushes me to either work it out, or end up with something else. Sometimes these different solutions borne out of mistakes are better than what I'd originally envisaged, but then of course sometimes they're not.

jamie macdonald

nooflat.nu

THE BASIC EFFECT

All of my experiments here start from the same base file, so rather than typing out the same thing four times, I'll just do it this once.

The pieces that I've made are all pretty simple. None of them took more than a couple of hours to put together, but I think they all have possibilities, and the effect on each piece of changing a few parameters is striking. What the pieces have in common is that they work with sine and cosine curves to produce various types of motion, so if you're going to work with these files it's useful to have an idea of how these curves behave. Both curves oscillate. If you look at the two diagrams you'll see that between 0 and 360 degrees they vary between 1 and -1 (for example: sin 90 =1 and sin 270 = -1). The cosine curve is the same as the sine curve except it's moved along, or translated.

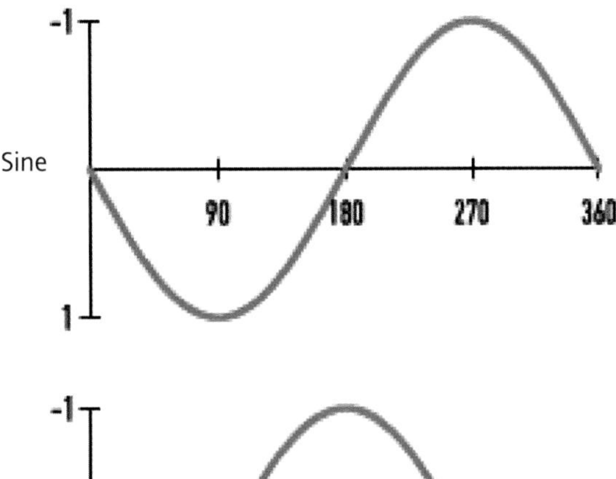

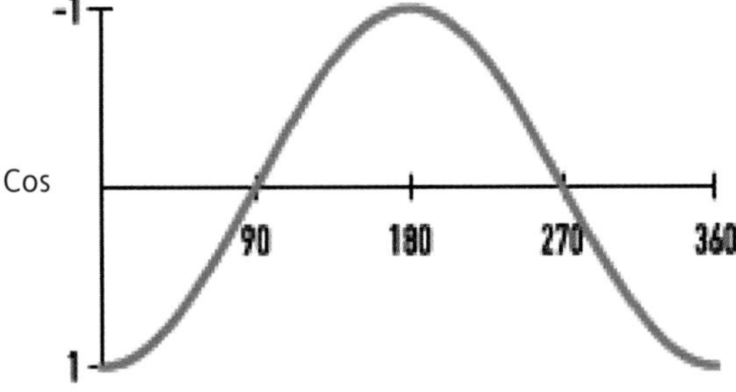

So from this we can say that if we want an oscillation between 10 and -10, then we would just multiply the sine degree by 10. For an oscillation between 0 and 40 we would use 20 multiplied by the sine degree, and then add 20 to the result. It's worth noting that these functions accept values above and below the 360 degree range – beyond this they continue oscillating in the same way, so the numbers 10, 370, 730 and so on will all have the same sine values.

When we're dealing with these functions within Flash we have to remember that they don't work with degrees, but with radians – a different unit of measurement. Before we use Flash's math functions we need to convert our values from degrees to radians, which is a relatively simple procedure:

360 degrees equals 2*PI radians
180 degrees = PI radians
1 degree = pi/180 radians

So to convert a value in degrees to radians we use this formula:

radians = degrees*Math.PI/180

That's the basic math out of the way, now we'll look at making the template file that all of the experiments start from. On the first frame we have simple variables for the height and width of the stage, which we'll use for centering, and letting us know where the boundaries are:

```
stageWidth=550;
stageHeight=400;
```

Now we need a movieclip called `ball`, which consists of a 42 x 42 pixel red circle in the center of the stage. This movieclip is exported with the Identifier `ball` from the Library. There is also another movieclip called `events`. This clip doesn't contain anything, it's just the anchor on which we'll place all of the clip event code. Drag an instance of `events` into the `ball` movieclip, and place the following actions on it:

```
onClipEvent(enterFrame){
   _parent.myfunc();
}
```

These will be used to call a function in `ball`, which will take care of all its actions. We'll define the function later on, as it will be different for each experiment. Finally, drop another instance of `events` onto the main stage and add the following actions:

```
onClipEvent(enterFrame){
   _parent.control();
}
```

This control function will be defined on the main timeline and will be used to add and remove movieclips, define their parameters, and other such things.

That's it for the objects, but one further thing that I added was a function to enable us to dynamically change a movieclip's brightness. This works using the `setTransform` method and we can use it with any color object that we set up. It's worth noting that this is only set up to accept brightness values above zero. Add this code to the first frame on the main timeline:

```
color.prototype.setBrightness=function
  ➥(brightness){
   var anum=100-brightness;
   var bnum=255/100*brightness;
   this.setTransform({ra:anum,ga:anum,ba:anum,
  ➥rb:bnum,gb:bnum,bb:bnum,aa:100,ab:0});
}
```

That's the template file complete. The only changes that need to be made for each file now will be to add actions to the first frame on the main stage.

towardsUs

The first effect involves movieclips that originate in the center of the stage and expand, oscillating around the center point until they appear to hit the viewer's screen and then fade out. The heart of the experiment is made up of two main functions: the `control` function is used to instantiate the movieclips and the `expand` function is used to make them grow. Remember that all of the code for these experiments goes on the first frame of the main movie. Here's the code in its entirety:

```
scaleMax=800;
fadeOut=0.93;
frequency=10;
colMin=0;
colMax=40;
colVariance=colMax-colMin;

function hRad(){return 4+Math.random();}
function vRad(){return 4+Math.random();}
function vRadInc(){return 0.1;}
function hRadInc(){return 0.1;}
function lrSpeed(){return 5+Math.random()*40}
function scaleUpSpeed(){return 1.02;}
function nooCol(){return colMin+random(colvariance);}

function control(){
    if(random(frequency)==0){
      depth++;
      _root.attachMovie("ball","ball"+depth,depth);
      noo=_root["ball"+depth];
      col=new Color(noo);
      col.setBrightness(nooCol());
      noo._x=-50;
      noo._y=-50;
      noo._xscale=noo._yscale=10;
      noo.scaleSpeed=scaleUpSpeed();
      noo.lrSpeed=lrSpeed();
      noo.hRad=hRad();
      noo.vRad=vRad();
      noo.hRadInc=hRadInc();
      noo.vRadInc=vRadInc();
      noo.myFunc=_root.expand;
    }
}

function expand(){
    lr+=lrSpeed;
    hRad+=hRadInc;
    vRad+=vRadInc;
    _x=_root.stageWidth/2+hRad*Math.sin(lr*Math.PI/180);
    _y=_root.stageHeight/2+vRad*Math.cos(lr*Math.PI/180);
    _yscale=_xscale*=scaleSpeed;
    this.swapDepths(Math.floor(_xscale));
    if(_xscale>_root.scaleMax){
      _alpha*=_root.fadeOut;
      if(_alpha<3){
        this.removeMovieClip();
      }
    }
}
```

You'll notice that I try and keep a lot of the separate parts of my code wrapped up in functions, as I find that it's easier to find, understand, and modify things when they are in discreet, functionality-driven, components. It also means that we can return different values depending on the situation, making the math in the main control function a bit neater and easier to digest.

The key variables and functions

scaleMax = the maximum scale before fading out
fadeOut = the speed of the fade out
frequency = how often a new movieclip is created
colMin = the minimum brightness
colMax = the maximum brightness
colVariance = the variation in brightness
lr = the value which we use to determine whereabouts on the sine or cosine curve the ball is; the faster it increases, the faster the oscillation
hRad = the amount of horizontal oscillation either side of the center
vRad = the amount of vertical oscillation either side of the center
vRadInc = the speed at which the amount of horizontal oscillation increases
hRadInc = the speed at which the amount of vertical oscillation increases
lrSpeed = left-right speed: the speed of oscillation
scaleUpSpeed = the speed at which the object expands
nooCol = the brightness of each movieclip
noo = the name of the current object

Now, I'll run through the running of the **control** and **expand** functions. The **control** function is executed every frame, and it creates a random number between 0 and the **frequency** variable that we set earlier. If the random number equals zero, then it creates another movieclip using **attachMovie**. It then goes through calling each of our parameter functions and uses the values returned by these functions to set variables inside the **ball** movieclip. The final thing that this function does is set **myFunc** inside the movieclip to equal **expand**, which is the function that we'll turn to next. Now if you remember earlier when we created the template **ball** movieclip we put another clip inside it that called **myFunc** every frame. What we've done here is set **myFunc** to refer to a function on the root called **expand**, so that when it's executed it will behave as though it were actually within the movieclip. This means that whenever we refer to **_x** in the function, we're actually referring to the **x** position of the instance of whichever ball that it's called from.

The **expand** function is where the main math of the movie is carried out. Firstly we increment our oscillation variables, lr, hRad, and vRad. The lines that set the **_x** and **_y** properties are where the sine and cosine curves come into play. We set these values to be at the middle of the stage plus hRad or **vRad** multiplied by the sine or cosine of **lr**. As we saw earlier the sine of any value will be somewhere between -1 and 1, so here we're setting the x position to somewhere between stageWidth minus hRad, and **stageWidth** plus **hRad**, and it will move between those two values. We then multiply the scale of the object by **scaleSpeed** to increase the size of the object, and then finally we check whether it has reached its maximum size, in which case we decreases its alpha until it's low enough to remove it without it noticeably blinking away.

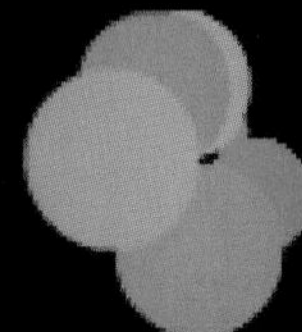

wardsUs2

this iteration I decided to change the file so that stead of oscillating around the center point, they t rushed straight at the viewer. I also made them a bit faster for better effect; the other changes I de were cosmetic. Here's the list of variables that hanged:

```
scaleMax=600;
frequency=5;
colMax=90;
function hRad(){
  return 0;

function vRad(){
  return 0;

function vRadInc(){
  return 0;

function hRadInc(){
  return 0;

function scaleUpSpeed(){
  return 1.2;
```

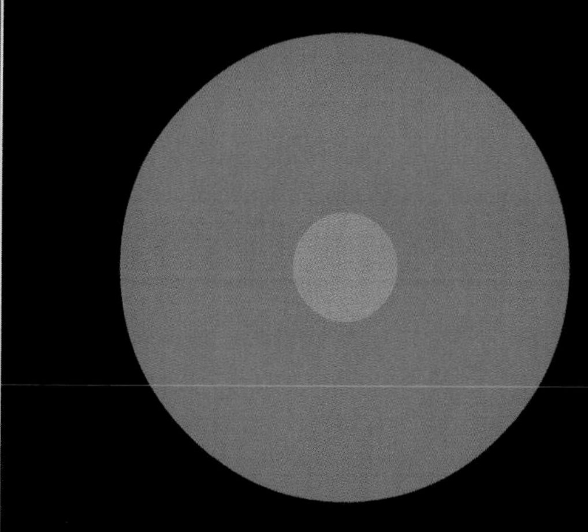

wardsUs3

this iteration, I gave the circles a set, rather than incremental, oscillation, and shortened the time akes them to fade out to give a fast spinning ect.

```
fadeOut=0.7;
function hRad(){
  return 40;

function vRad(){
  return 40;
```

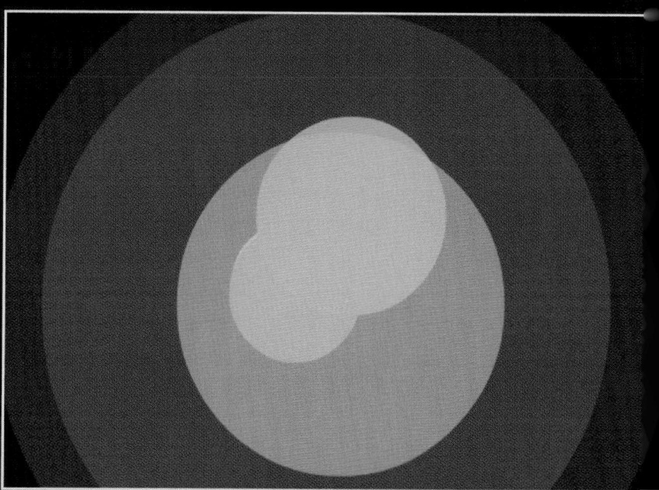

wardsUs4

hanged this one so that the circles began from thing, but then rapidly spiral out of the screen.

```
scaleMax=400;
function hRad(){
  return 0;

function vRad(){
  return 0;

function vRadInc(){
  return 5;

function hRadInc(){
  return 5;
```

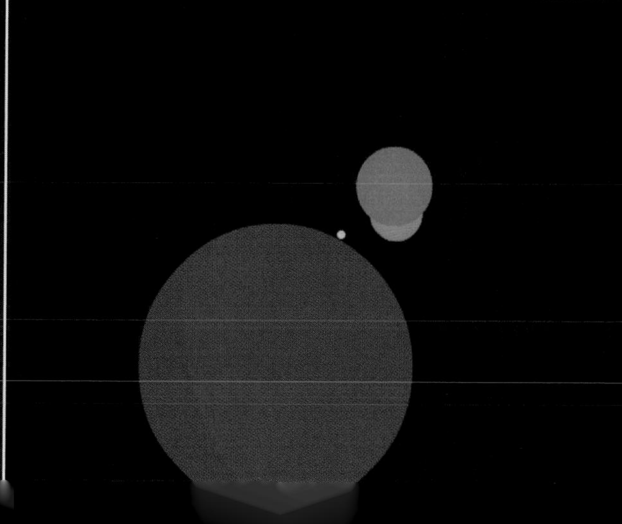

towardsUs5
Here, I decided to just oscillate the movieclips on one plane, with a more constant stream of them attacking from both sides of the screen.

```
frequency=2;
function vRadInc(){
  return 0;
}
function hRadInc(){
  return 20;
}
```

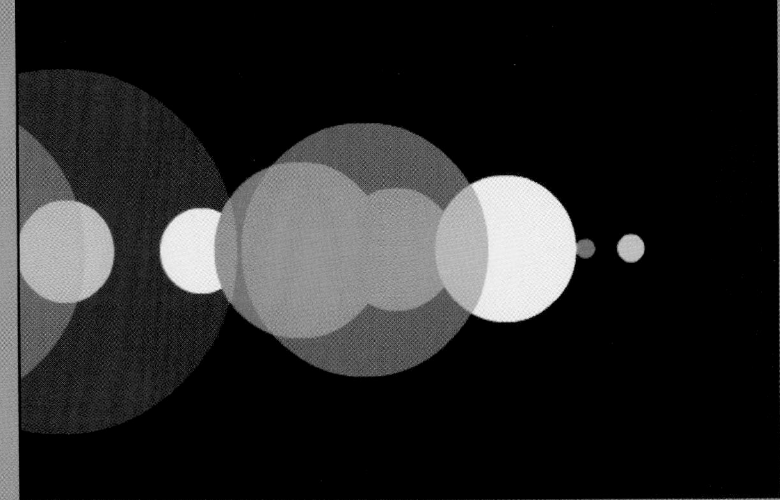

towardsUs6
I decided to down the tempo again for this experiment, the circles remind me of a bubble-gun lazily moving from side to side firing bubbles out and just watching them pop.

```
function hRadInc(){
  return 5*Math.random();
}
function lrSpeed(){
  return 3+Math.random()*3;
}
function scaleUpSpeed(){
  return 1.05;
}
```

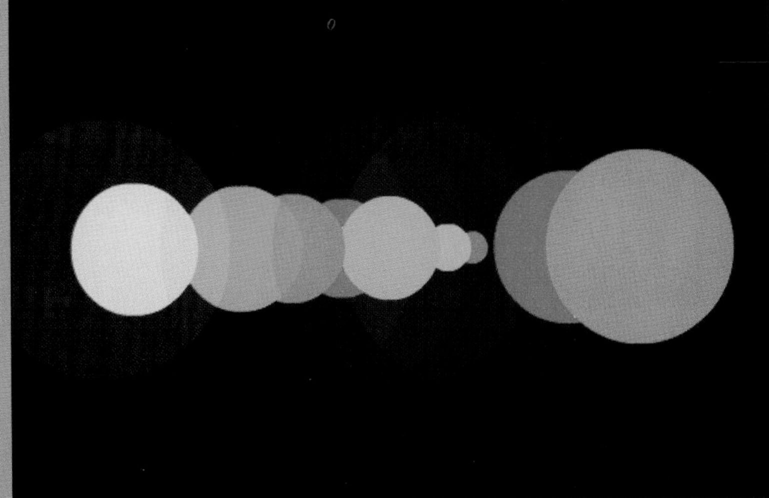

towardsUs7
Back to spinning again now, but this time with a controlled increment meaning that all of the bubbles pop at the same place.

```
scaleMax=900;
frequency=10;
colMax=20;
function vRadInc(){
  return 1.5;
}
function hRadInc(){
  return 1.3;

function lrSpeed(){
  return 10;
}
function scaleUpSpeed(){
  return 1.1;
}
```

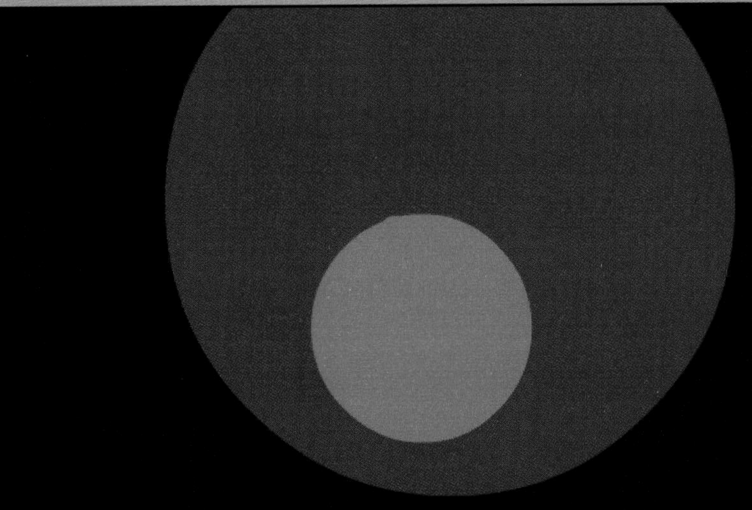

towardsUs8

Here, the circles bounce towards us rapidly in a tight oval.

```
colMin=70;
colMax=90;
function hRad(){
  return 5;
}
function vRad(){
  return 25;
}
function vRadInc(){
  return 0;
}
function hRadInc(){
  return 0;
}
function lrSpeed(){
  return 40;
}
```

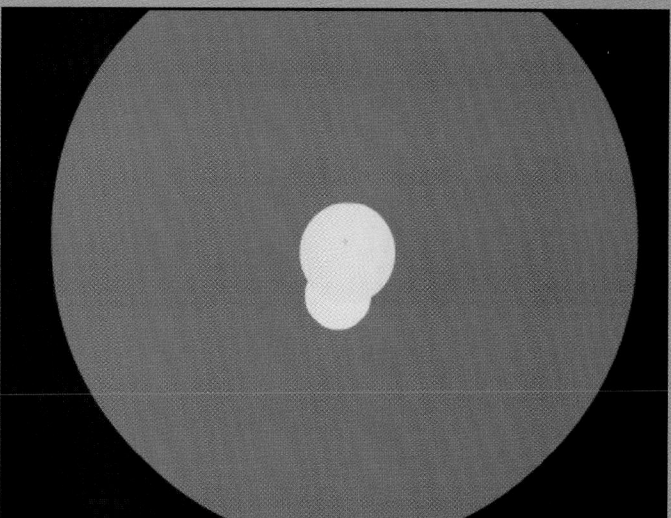

towardsUs9

In this experiment I've massively increased the horizontal oscillation, and given them a small vertical one so that it looks as though the circles are coming out of 3 vertical guns, rather than one horizontal one.

```
function hRad(){
  return 300;
}
function vRad(){
  return 9;
}
function lrSpeed(){
  return 60;
}
```

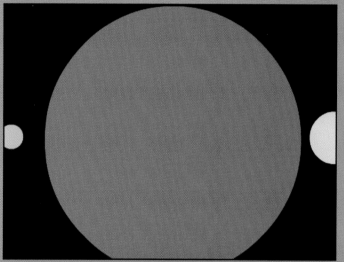

towardsUs10

In this final experiment, I pulled the horizontal oscillation back a little to remove the strange effect of last time, and also changed the increment and oscillation speed to smooth out the wide spiral.

```
function hRad(){
  return 200;
}
function vRadInc(){
  return 1;
}
function hRadInc(){
  return 1;
}
function lrSpeed(){
  return 10+random(10);
}
```

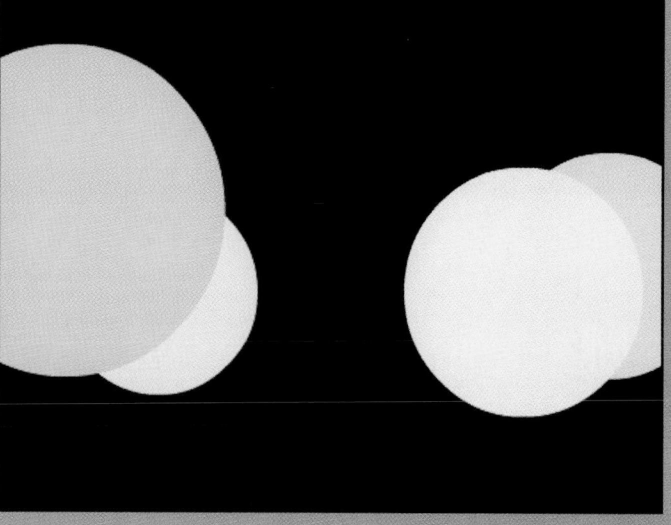

There are a number of ways you could change this movie. First of all there are a lot of variations that can be created just by changing the parameters. The oscillation could expand on the x-axis, but not the y, the speed of oscillation could vary more wildly, the clips could fade out earlier, or scale up slower, and so on. Beyond that, you could try swapping around the sine and cosine methods, or dropping in tan instead, and seeing what effect that has.

inLine

For this effect we're going to place the circles in a line, and then each circle is going to expand and contract using a sine curve to set its value. We'll use each circle's distance from the center to determine the degree it starts with (and thus its position on the sine curve), giving the effect of a wave moving along the line from the center. This will all become much clearer once you see it in motion. To give you some idea of it, it reminds me a bit of the light on the front of KITT in Knight Rider, that or the Cylons from Battlestar Galactica, just that mine doesn't sweep from side to side as much... though I'm sure it could do with a bit of tweaking.

Once again we'll start from our base movie template, with all of the following code on the first frame of the root:

```
hsp=4;
total=70;
twidth=(total-1)*(hsp);
brmin=0;
brmax=40;

function inc(val){return 3;}
function colinc(val){return 4;}
function yMag(val){return 1;}
function minScale(val){return 1;}
function maxScale(val){return 12;}
function startDegree(val){return 3*val;}

for(i=0;i<total;i++){
    _root.attachMovie("ball","ball"+i,i);
    var offset=Math.abs((total/2)-i);
    noo=_root["ball"+i];
    noo._y=stageHeight/2;
    noo._x=(stageWidth-twidth)/2+hsp*I;
    noo.baseY=stageHeight/2;
    noo._xscale=noo._yscale=minScale();
    noo.inc=inc(offset);
    noo.colinc=colinc(offset);
    noo.col=new Color(noo);
    noo.brmin=brmin;
    noo.brmax=brmax;
    noo.degree=noo.coldegree=startDegree(offset);
    noo.brvariation=noo.brmax-noo.brmin;
    noo.yMag=yMag(offset);
    noo.minscale=minScale(offset);
    noo.maxscale=maxScale(offset);
    noo.variation=noo.maxscale-noo.minscale;
    noo.myFunc=oscillate;
}

function oscillate(){
    degree+=inc;
    value=Math.sin(degree*Math.PI/180);
    _xscale=_yscale=minscale+(variation/2)+(variation/2)*value;
    coldegree+=colinc;
    value2=Math.sin(coldegree*Math.PI/180);
    brightness=brmin+(brvariation/2)+ (brvariation/2)*value2;
    col.setBrightness(brightness);
    _y=baseY+value2*yMag;
}
```

The key variables and functions

hsp = the spacing on the x-axis
total = the total number of circles
twidth = the total width of the line of circles
brmin = the minimum brightness
brmin = the maximum brightness
inc = the speed of oscillation in scale
colinc = the speed of oscillation of brightness
yMag = the amount of vertical oscillation
minScale = the minimum scale of an object
maxScale = the maximum scale of an object
variation = the difference between **minScale** and **maxScale**
brvariation = the difference between **brmin** and **brmax**
startDegree = the degree at which each circle starts
offset = how far the current position is from the center position
noo = the name of the current object
degree and **coldegree** = counters
value = the sine value of degree
value2 = the sine value of **coldegree**

You'll notice that some of these functions are passed an argument, **val**, which will represent how many positions away from the center each ball is placed. The variable that is passed as this argument is **offset**, so most of the time you can think of these as being synonymous. For this experiment we don't need a control function, because we're just setting the clips up at the start and then leaving them to take care of themselves, so you can remove the events clip from the main stage if you like. We just run a loop to position all of the movieclips initially, and then set **myfunc** to the **oscillate** function at the end. In this function we increment our two counters, **degree** and **coldegree**, and then calculate the sine values of those two values and use them to set the scale and brightness respectively, of the ball.

inLine2

The following changes give a thicker, faster, and more elastic dough-like result.

```
hsp=3
function inc(val){
    return 10;
}
function colinc(val){
    return 40;
}
function minScale(val){
    return 10;
}
function maxScale(val){
    return 24;
}
```

inLine3

I've made this one a bit thicker and bouncier still, and also changed the **startDegree** function to create something resembling a strange Victorian moustache generator.

```
function yMag(val){
    return 3;
}
function minScale(val){
    return 20;
}
function maxScale(val){
    return 30;
}
function startDegree(val){
    return 9*val;
}
```

inLine4

Here, I changed **inc** to give a smoothly pulsing result; I also removed the bouncing effect as it was getting a bit much.

```
function inc(val){
    return 3*val;
}
function yMag(val){
    return 0;
}
function startDegree(val){
    return 5*val;
}
```

inLine5

In this iteration, I created a great, and initially completely different seeming, effect. I increased the bounce massively, but also increased the **startDegree** so that each object is now far more spread out so that you start to lose the impression that it's a line.

```
function inc(val){
    return 10*val;
}
function yMag(val){
    return 3*val;
}
function minScale(val){
    return 10;
}
function maxScale(val){
    return 20;
}
function startDegree(val){
    return 35*val;
}
```

inLine6

Another completely different effect was created here by dividing rather than multiplying **val** to give **startDegree**, and also changing **yMag** similarly.

```
hsp=4 ;
total=50 ;
function yMag(val){
    return 30/(val/3);
}
function startDegree(val){
    return 35/val;
}
```

inLine7

Back to a straight line again, but with a new rhythmically pulsing wave.

```
function yMag(val){
    return 0;
}
function maxScale(val){
    return 30+10/(val/3);
}
function startDegree(val){
    return val;
}
```

As with the previous effect, just changing the values of the parameters can produce many variations. You might also try using each ball's distance from the left of the line instead of the center of the line as the value affecting how fast the scale oscillates.

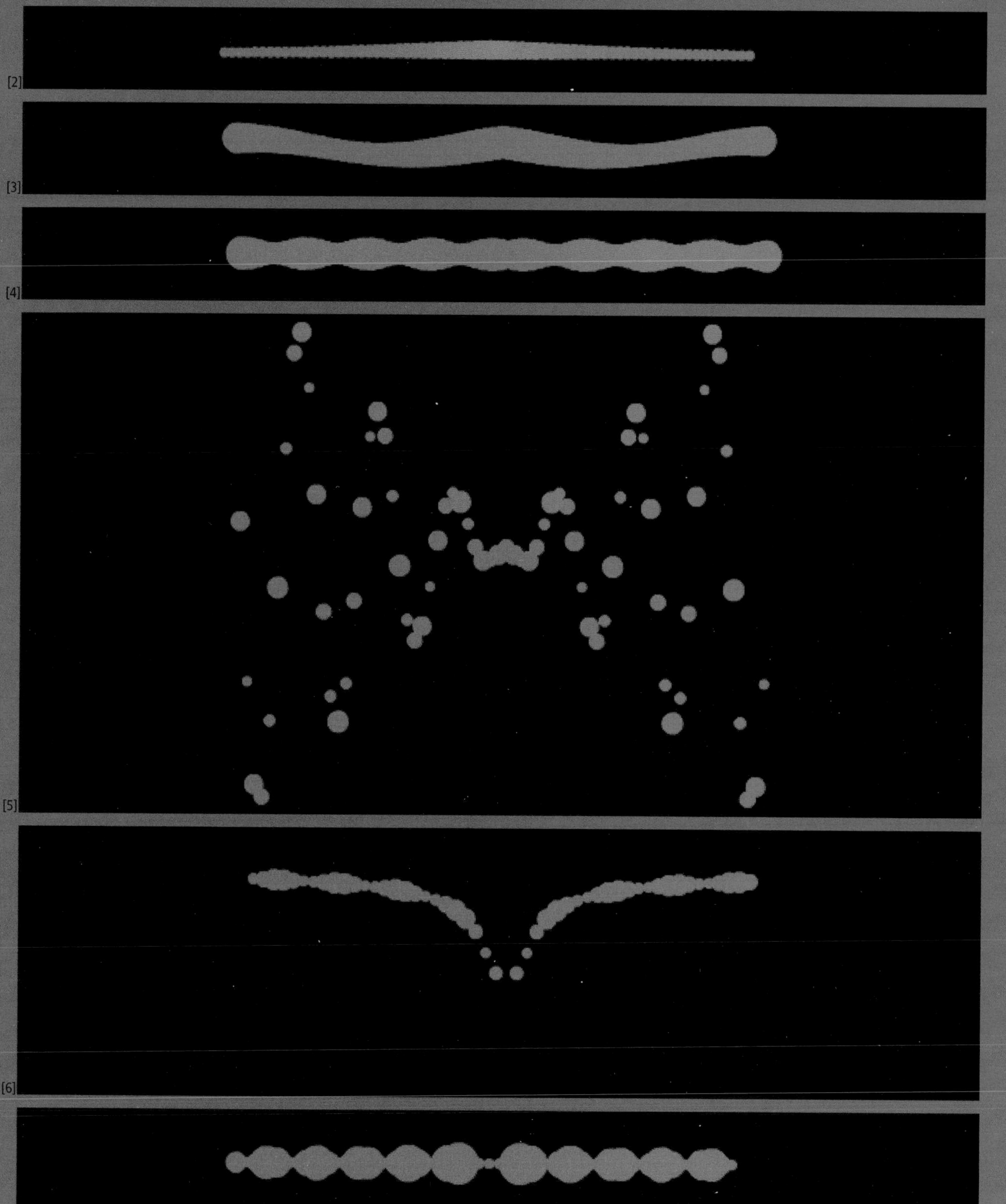
[2]
[3]
[4]
[5]
[6]
[7]

rightToLeft

This effect involves creating circles that orbit a central point that moves across the screen from right to left, while also oscillating up and down. The vertical motion will be taken care of in the same way as with the previous effect, incrementing a value and calculating the sine of that value to create the oscillation. For the orbiting we need to use sine and cosine in a different way. For any given circle we can calculate the **x** and **y** positions of a point on the circumference if we are given the radius, and the angle at which the point is to the center. We can calculate this by making a right angle triangle from the center of the circle to the point on the circumference as in this diagram:

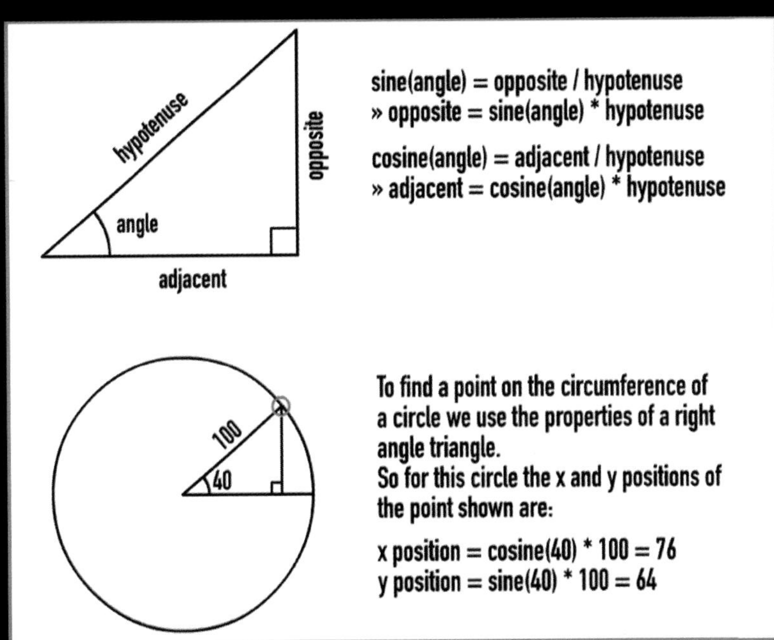

hypotenuse
opposite
angle
adjacent
sine(angle) = opposite / hypotenuse
» opposite = sine(angle) * hypotenuse
cosine(angle) = adjacent / hypotenuse
» adjacent = cosine(angle) * hypotenuse
100
40
To find a point on the circumference of a circle we use the properties of a right angle triangle.
So for this circle the x and y positions of the point shown are:
x position = cosine(40) * 100 = 76
y position = sine(40) * 100 = 64

So, in Flash the two formula we need are:

```
xposition = radius * Math.cos(degrees*Math.PI/180)
yposition = radius * Math.sin(degrees*Math.PI/180)
```

Now we can move on to creating the effect. Here's the code to add to the first frame of the template file:

```
frequency = 30;
colMin = 0;
colMax = 50;
colVariance = colMax-colMin;

function leftRightSpeed () {return -2;}
function maxScale () {return 120;}
function minScale () {return 60;}
function leftRightRadius () {return 150;}
function circlingSpeed () {return 5;}
function circleStartPoint () {return 0;}
function upDownRange () {return 10;}
function yFreqInc () {return 12;}
function nooCol (val) {
    val *= 30;
    return colMin+colvariance*0.5+(0.5*colVariance) * Math.sin(val*Math.PI/180);
}
```

```
function control () {
    if (g>frequency) {
      g = 0;
      depth++;
      _root.attachMovie("ball", "ball"+depth, depth);
      noo = _root["ball"+depth];
      noo._y = stageHeight/2;
      noo.fulcrumX = noo._x=stageWidth+30;
      noo.maxScale = maxScale();
      noo.minScale = minScale();
      col = new Color(noo);
      col.setBrightness(nooCol(depth));
      noo.variance = noo.maxScale-noo.minScale;
      noo.acrossRadius = leftRightRadius();
      noo.upDownRange = upDownRange();
      noo.degree = circleStartPoint();
      noo.degreeInc = circlingSpeed();
      noo.yFreqInc = yFreqInc();
      noo.leftRightSpeed = leftRightSpeed();
      noo.myFunc = shootMeAcross;
    }
}
function shootMeAcross () {
    fulcrumX += leftRightSpeed;
    degree += degreeInc;
    _x = fulcrumX+Math.cos(degree*Math.PI/180)*acrossRadius;
    _xscale = _yscale=minScale+(variance*0.5)+(variance*0.5) * Math.sin(degree*Math.PI/180);
    yfreq += yFreqInc;
    _y = _root.stageHeight/2+upDownRange*Math.sin(yfreq*Math.PI/180);
    this.swapDepths(Math.floor(_xscale));
    if (_x<-40) {
      this.removeMovieClip();
    }
}
```

The key variables and functions

`frequency` = how often circles are created
`colMin` = the minimum circle brightness
`colMax` = the maximum circle brightness
`colVariance` = the range of brightness
`leftRightSpeed` = how fast the circles move across the screen
`maxScale` = the maximum circle scale
`minScale` = the minimum circle scale
`leftRightRadius` = the radius of the circle that the ball moves around
`circlingSpeed` = the speed at which the ball moves around the circle
`circleStartPoint` = the degree at which the ball starts on the circle
`upDownRange` = the range of the ball's up/down motion
`yFreqInc` = the speed at which the ball moves up and down
`nooCol` = sets the brightness for each ball, increasing the `val` multiplier means the colors will oscillate more
`noo` = the name of the current object
`fulcrumX` = the center point that a circle orbits around, so by moving this we move the circle

The main math goes on in the `shootMeAcross` function, which is called inside each circle. We start off by moving the fulcrum across the screen and we then increment the `degree` value, which takes our circle around its orbit, and the `yfreq` value, which controls the `y` position of the circle. We set the `x` position of the circle using the cosine of our `degree` value, and then the scale using its sine value (we're using this instead of `y` in order to simulate depth – we have effectively flipped the circle on its side). After that we set the `y` position using the sine of our `yfreq` variable so that it oscillates up and down. The final thing to do is to remove the movieclip when it goes off screen.

rightToLeft2
In this iteration I've made the `upDownRange` a lot greater, giving more of an impression of 3D movement.

```
function leftRightRadius(){
    return 50;
}
function circlingSpeed(){
    return 10;
}
function upDownRange(){
    return 70;
}
function yFreqInc(){
    return 4;
}
```

rightToLeft3
In this iteration I increased the number of balls appearing to create an almost constant stream, and also changed the path that they oscillate around.

```
frequency=3;
function leftRightSpeed(){
    return -3;
}
function maxScale(){
    return 180;
}
function leftRightRadius(){
    return 60;
}
function circlingSpeed(){
    return 8;
}
```

rightToLeft4
Here I altered the scaling and the `upDownRange` to produce a more concentrated, almost flat line with pulses along it.

```
frequency=4;
function minScale(){
    return 0;
}
function leftRightRadius(){
    return 30;
}
function upDownRange(){
    return 20;
}
function yFreqInc(){
    return 1;
}
```

rightToLeft5
I changed the `upDownRange` and `yFreqInc` here to produce a nice looping motion.

```
colMax=100;
function maxScale(){
    return 60;
}
function upDownRange(){
    return 60;
}
function yFreqInc(){
    return 10;
}
```

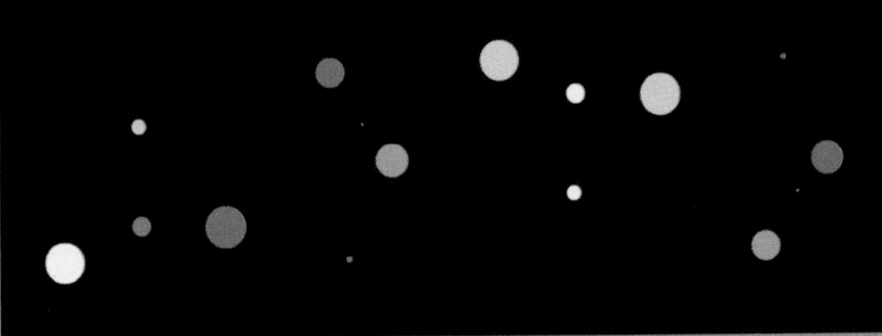

rightToLeft6
This iteration creates another really nice, wide looping pattern.

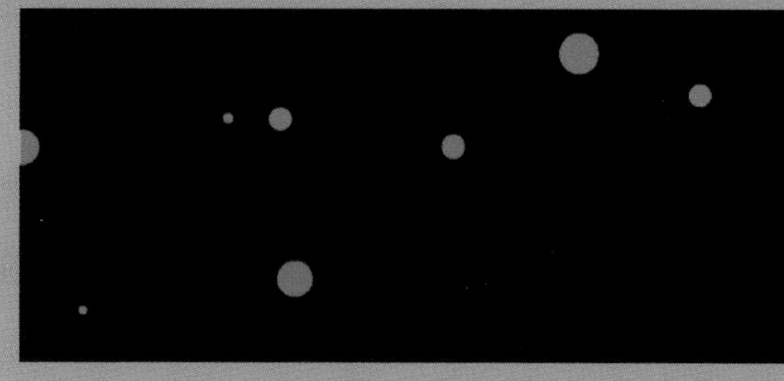

```
colMax=20;
function leftRightRadius(){
    return 50;
}
function upDownRange(){
    return 120;
}
function yFreqInc(){
    return 5;
}
```

rightToLeft7

Here I've decreased the `upDownRange` significantly, and widened the loop to produce this effect with a really deep and pronounced 3D feel to it.

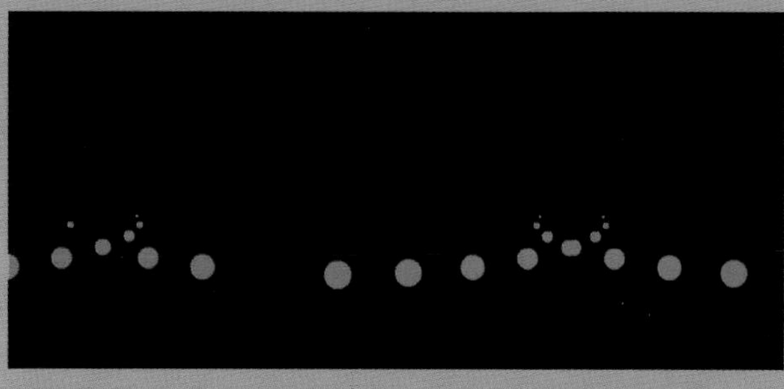

```
frequency=1;
function leftRightSpeed(){
    return -4;
}
function maxScale(){
    return 40;
}
function leftRightRadius(){
    return 80;
}
function circlingSpeed(){
    return 5;
}
function upDownRange(){
    return 19;
}
```

rightToLeft8
In this example I've changed the code to produce a single loop, but with a pronounced wobble in it.

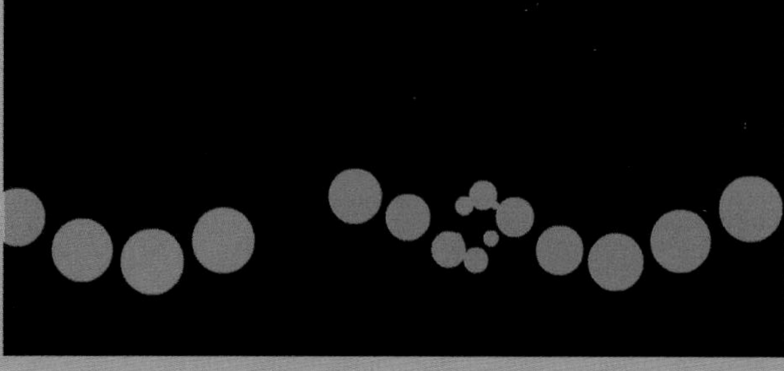

```
frequency=2;
function leftRightSpeed(){
    return -3;
}
function maxScale(){
    return 90;
}
function circlingSpeed(){
    return 3;
}
function yFreqInc(){
    return 10;
}
```

rightToLeft9
The addition of some random elements in this final iteration give a really nice chaotic-but-still-familiar feel to it.

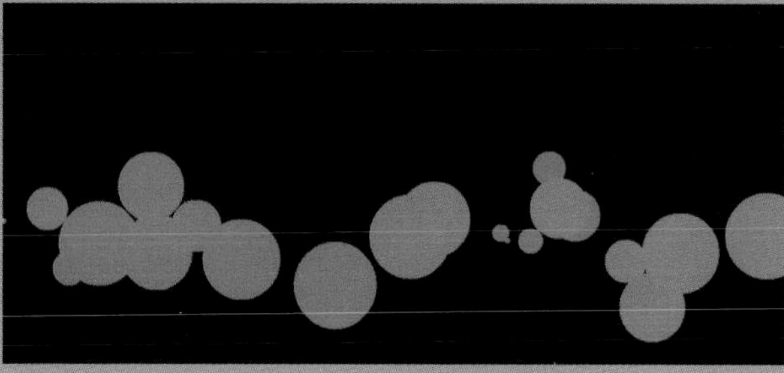

```
frequency=3;
function leftRightSpeed(){
    return -2-Math.random();
}
function maxScale(){
    return 120;
}
function upDownRange(){
    return random(50);
}
```

There are many different effects that can be created here by altering the parameters, for instance varying the speed of circling and the speed of motion across, which can produce a snaking form or various spirals. Also try changing the shape of the object it's possible to have messages scrolling across the screen along strange looping paths. Certainly beats a boring old news ticker.

sinGrid

This final effect positions a number of circles in a grid and then uses a sine wave to alter their color and brightness. Within this grid we can create the effect of a wave by starting each circle off with a degree value slightly offset from the one next to it. We can calculate this offset in a number of ways, but the basic thing we need to do is to divide 360 by the total number of circles. Say, for instance we have ten objects – we can start them off at 36, 72, 108, 144, 180, 216, 252, 288 and 324 degrees, and so on. With these start values, each circle will be placed somewhere between the minimum and maximum scales (as the sine values oscillate between 1 and -1). As each degree value increases, the gap between them will be maintained and it will appear that a wave is moving across the grid, starting from the bottom right and moving up row by row. If we change this offset so the values vary between 0 and 180, then this will appear as only half of a sine wave.

Once again we'll start off by adding all of the code into the first frame of our template. You can also remove the `events` movieclip that's sitting on the main stage, as we won't need that in this experiment.

```
across=10;
down=10;
total=across*down;
hsp=20;
vsp=20;
degInc=360/total;
numberOfOscillations=1;

bx=(stageWidth-hsp*across)/2;
by=(stageHeight-vsp*down)/2;

function increment(offset){return 30;}
function minScale(){return 3;}
function maxScale(){return 54;}
function minBrt(){return 0;}
function maxBrt(){return 50;}

for(i=0;i<total;i++){
     _root.attachMovie("ball","circ"+i,i);
     noo=_root["circ"+i];
     noo._x=bx+column*hsp;
     noo._y=by+row*vsp;
     noo.col=new Color(noo);
     var offset=Math.abs(total/2-i);
     noo.myInc=increment(offset);
     noo.minScale=minScale();
     noo.maxScale=maxScale();
     noo.variance=noo.maxScale-noo.minScale;
     noo.minBrt=minBrt();
     noo.maxBrt=maxBrt();
     noo.colVariance=noo.maxBrt-noo.minBrt;
     noo.myFunc=undulate;
     noo.degree=i*deginc*numberOfOscillations;
     column++;
     if(column==across){
       column=0;
       row++;
     }
}

function undulate(){
     degree+=myInc;
     sinVal=Math.sin(degree*Math.PI/180);
     _xscale=_yscale=minScale+(variance*0.5)+(variance*0.5)*sinVal;
     brightness=minBrt+(0.5*colVariance)+(0.5*colVariance)*sinVal;
     col.setBrightness(brightness);
}
```

The key variables and functions

`across` = the number of circles across
`down` = the number of circles down
`total` = the total number of circles
`hsp` = the horizontal spacing
`vsp` = the vertical spacing
`degInc` = the number of degrees per circle to span one complete oscillation
`numberOfOscillations` = how much of a complete curve to display at once
`bx` = the starting x position
`by` = the starting y position
`increment` = how fast the wave moves across - we pass this an offset value which represents how many positions away form the center the current circle is (we're not using this initially, but it can be implemented)
`minScale` = the minimum scale
`maxScale` = the maximum scale
`minBrt` = the minimum brightness
`maxBrt` = the maximum brightness
`column` and `row` = the current column and row

The `for` loop sets up the grid initially, and it's then updated constantly by the `undulate` function that contains the majority of the math. This function's fairly simple, just incrementing our `degree` value and then using that to set the scale and brightness as we have before.

sinGrid02
This simple change gives a nice diagonal pulse.

```
numberOfOscillations = 12;
```

sinGrid03
Increasing the value again gives a more rapid, steeper diagonal pulse.

```
numberOfOscillations = 21;
```

sinGrid04
By decreasing the value to less than one, we get a single, strong bottom-to-top pulse.

```
numberOfOscillations = 0.5;
```

sinGrid05
By changing the `increment` to a random value, we start off with the single pulse, but then rapidly descend into chaos.

```
function increment(offset){
     return 10+Math.floor(5*Math.random());
}
```

sinGrid06
Here, I changed the `increment` value again, this time to incorporate the `offset`, to produce a really hypnotic cyclical motion.

```
function increment(offset){
     return 4+offset;
}
```

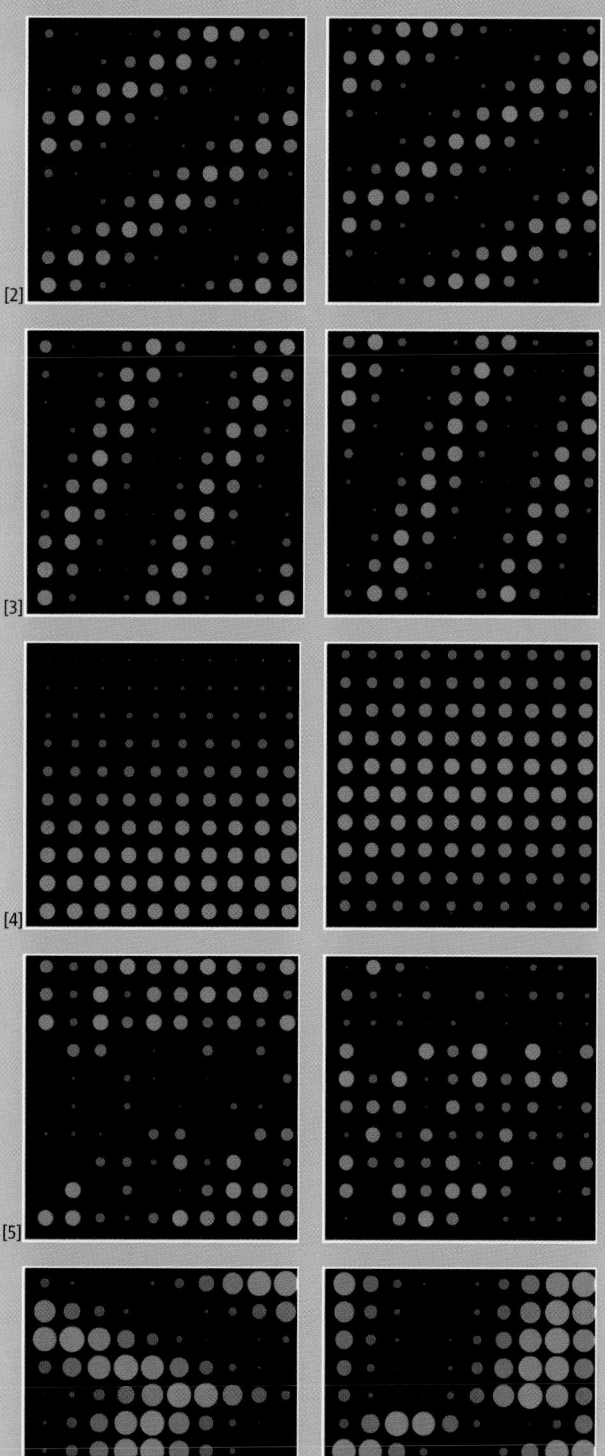
[2]
[3]
[4]
[5]
[6]

...decided to change the shape of the grid here, creating a ... rectangle with an interesting wave motion that rewards patient viewing.

```
across=7;
down=14;
numberOfOscillations=100;
function increment(offset){
    return 14+offset/20;
}
```

sinGrid08

For this experiment I kept the main formulae the same, but changed the shape of the grid to a really long thin rectangle.

```
across=5;
down=25;
```

sinGrid09

Back to the square pulsing grid again, but this time with a different brightness in the pattern.

```
across = 10;
down = 10;
numberOfOscillations = 3;
function minScale(){
    return 15;
}
function maxScale(){
    return 60;

function maxBrt(){
    return 100;
}
```

By decreasing the spacing between the circles, but at the same time increasing the scale of them, they begin to lose their individuality and morph into oscillating blocks of color.

```
hsp=7;
vsp=7;
numberOfOscillations= 0.33;
function minScale(){
    return 45;
}
function maxScale(){
    return 130;
}
```

With this effect you might try implementing the `offset` value so that the speed of oscillation is determined by how far each ball is from the center, or you could change this so it's affected by how far it is from the corner, and so on. Altering the `numberOfOscillations` variable can also produce different types of waves. It's also worth noting that you can reverse the direction of any wave by subtracting the increment from 360 – so an increment of 320 will move in the opposite direction to an increment of 40.

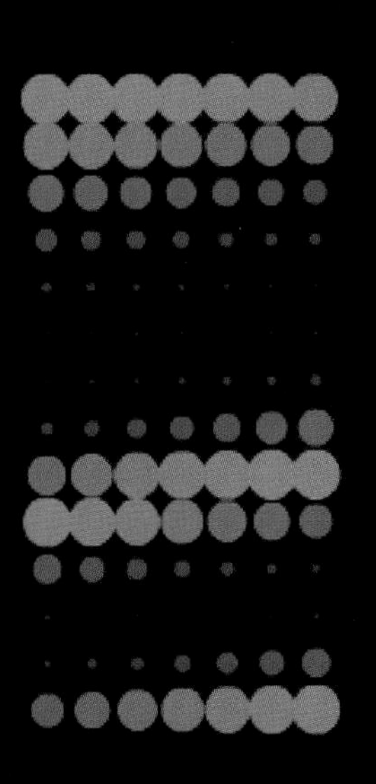

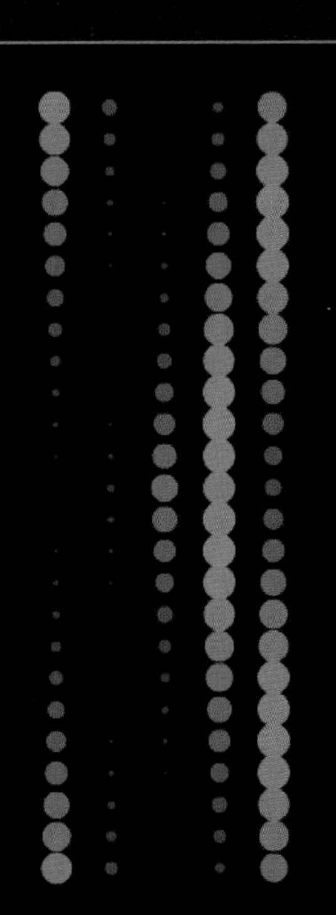

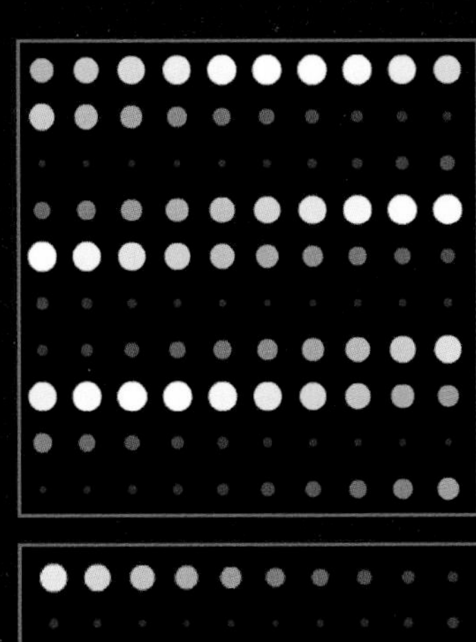

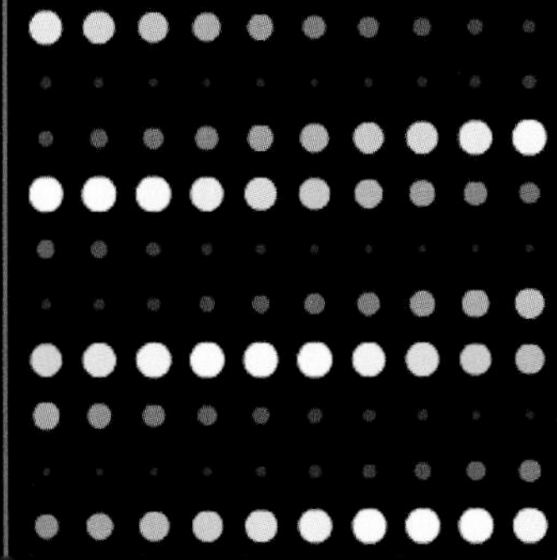

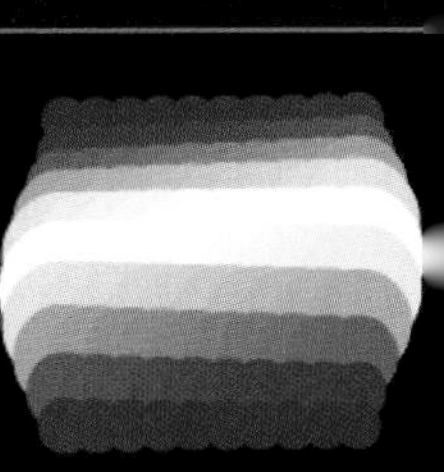

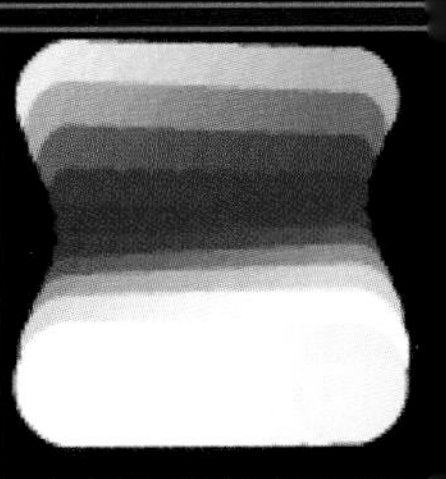

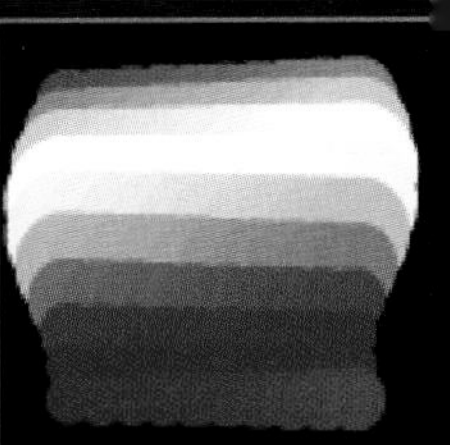

When I walk down the street, lie in bed, drive my car, stare at the city skyline or play piano my mind is always running away in a crazy mathematical spiral. I'm always looking for patterns. No, I'm not insane; my mind just works like that.

So, in this particular mathematical quest, I found myself looking for the patterns and beauty in everything I saw. You know what I discovered? That everything is beautiful in some way, or another. The grid of window lights in the city skyline, the streak of after-images left by looking at the sun, the rolling of waves or the swaying of branches; they're all beautiful – and they're all driven by numbers.

Naturally, life isn't a plain grid, so I found myself adding lots of randomization to the mix. Also, as the experiments went on and I modified, shifted and adjusted the values, I found that I did stray somewhat from the original idea, but that's because the beauty left the real world, and entered the just-as-beautiful digital, numeric, mathematical realm.

I started my mind going early in life when I was about 4 years old. At that age, I began playing the piano, which was sitting unused in our house. I've been playing ever since then. Later, in 1997, I co-wrote a full-length musical called Chrystanthia. Somewhere along the way, I picked up game programming as a hobby, and eventually ended up making games professionally for home console systems. Then, in 1998, I discovered how I could take all my experiences and combine them when I discovered Flash. The rest is history. I share my ideas on my web site, www.glenrhodes.com.

glen rhodes

www.glenrhodes.com

Flowers

```
onClipEvent (load) {
     for (i=0; i<120; i++) {
          nm = "petal" + i;
          duplicateMovieClip (_root.petal, nm, i);
          _root[nm]._rotation = Math.random()*360;
          _root[nm]._xscale = _root[nm]._yscale=Math.random()*_root.petal._xscale+20;
     }
}
```

'Flowers' consists very simply of the above code, which is attached to a movieclip on the main timeline called **controller**. This code makes copies of a movieclip on the main timeline called **petal**. The copies are placed in a circle around each other, much like the petals of a rose are arranged. This creates a simple virtual flower.

The key variables

i = The main counter variable which is used in a loop to count through the copies as they are made.
nm = A temporary string variable used to store the name of the new petal (**petal1**, **petal2**, **petal3**, and so on)
s = a counter used for scale (will appear in **flower3.swf**)
rot = a counter used for rotation (will appear in **flower3.swf**)
dr = a variable attached to each petal copy, which is used as an increment for increasing the **_rotation** of the petal every frame (will appear in **flower6.swf**)

Iterations

In **flower2.swf**, one line of code has been added to the main loop:

```
_root[nm].swapDepths(2000-_root[nm]._xscale);
```

This will place petals that are smaller, on top of the larger petals in the background. This is more accurate to the way a real flower's petals are arranged.

In **flower3.swf**, instead of using random variables for scale and rotation, I'm using a fixed set of variables:

```
_root[nm]._rotation = rot+=15;
_root[nm]._xscale = s;
_root[nm]._yscale = s;
s+=1;
```

This creates a radial patterned effect, somewhat like a seashell.These use the new variable **s**, which I've set to 10 before the **for** loop.

In **flower4.swf**, **rot** is being increased by 7 instead of 15 with each copy, and the flower itself has been changed to a creamy gradient color – creating another cool seashell look.

In flower5.swf, s is increased by 2 with each copy instead of 1, and rot is increased by 14. The contents of petal have been changed to a shape-tweened black and white gradient, so that when it's fully formed, the 'seashell' has a cool color scrolling effect.

flower6.swf is identical to flower5.swf, except that the shape tween is slightly different, and I've added the following code to the petal object itself:

```
onClipEvent(enterFrame){
    _rotation+=dr;
}
```

and within the controller, there's a new line in the duplication loop:

```
_root[nm].dr = (Math.random() * 4 - 2);
```

This will make each petal rotate by dr each frame.

In flower7.swf, the petal has been changed to be a long, slim oval petal, and the code attached to the petal has been changed to include:

```
_xscale+=2;
_yscale+=2;
_rotation++;
if (_xscale > 300) {_xscale = 10;}
```

This will make the flower grow towards us every frame, and eventually, when the petal gets too big to be seen, it will become small again and reappear in the center of the flower with a really cool and strange effect. I also changed the _rotation line in the controller clip back to Math.random() * 360 to make the flower more random again.

In flower8.swf, everything is the same except the petal is now purple/blue and when _xscale is greater than 300, I'm now taking the petal and setting its _xscale and _yscale to be 10. This creates a perpetual sinking effect – like we're flying into the flower, or that petals are flying towards us.

flower9.swf looks very much like fireworks. All the petals start out at a random _xscale and _yscale between 0 and 10, and then they expand quickly out from the middle. As they expand, each petal's _alpha is being decreased, so they're fading out. When the petals have faded out, they are moved back to the middle, and shrunk. The process then repeats. To achieve this I changed s on controller to:

```
s = Math.random() * 10;
```

And changed the code on petal to:

```
onClipEvent (enterFrame) {
    if (_name != "petal") {
      _xscale += 2;
      _yscale += 2;
      _alpha–;
      if (_xscale>200) {
        _xscale = 10;
        _yscale = 10;
        _alpha = 100;
        _rotation = Math.random()*360;
        s = Math.random()*20;
        _xscale = s;
        _yscale = s;
      }
    } else {
      _visible = false;
    }
}
```

[5]

[6]

[7]

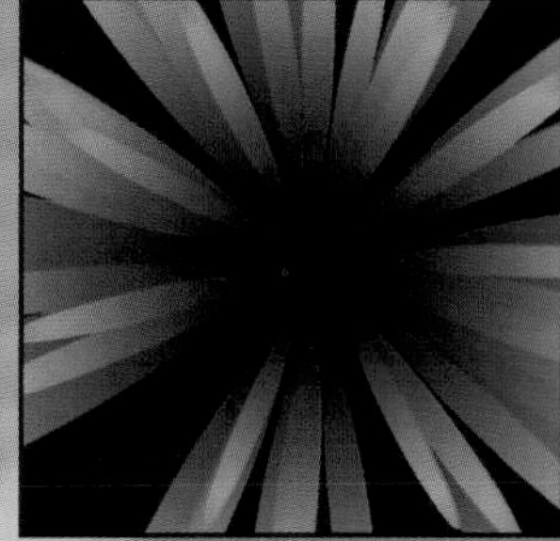
[8]

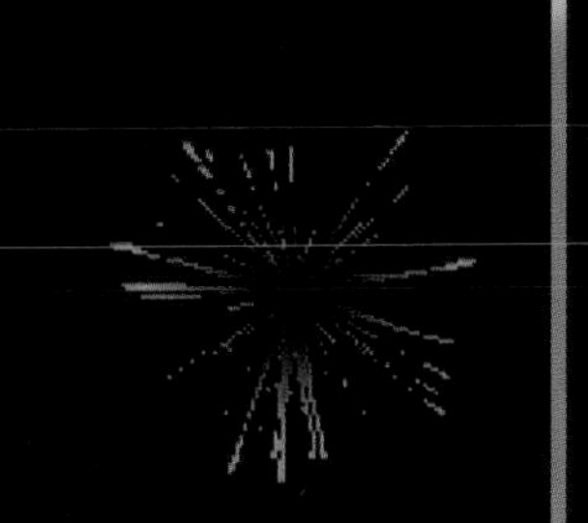
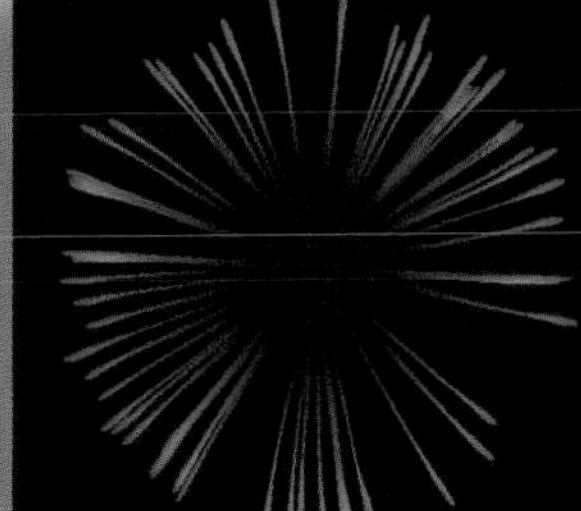
[9]

In `flower10.swf`, the effect is almost that we are flying through space, and stars are streaking past us. It's just like `flower9.swf` except that the `_xscale` and `_yscale` of each petal begins at a random value between 0 and 100, instead of 0 to 10.

In `flower11.swf`, I'm using almost the same code as `flower10.swf`, and the graphic has been changed to be a single tear shaped white dot. This is near where the end of the petal would have been, so now it really looks like stars streaking towards us. The code changes are – I've increased the number of stars from 30 to 60, and I've taken out the alpha fade from the petal clip.

I thought that I'd taken the starfield angle to its logical conclusion, so I decided to return to the roots. `flower12.swf` takes us back to the original flower images code using the code from `flower3` to create static flower images. The petal image has been changed to be a smooth red gradient with a white tip and a purple base.

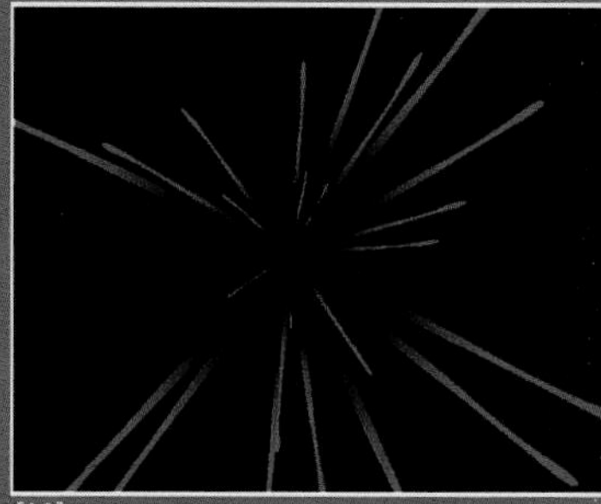

[10]

[11]

`flower13.swf` is identical to `flower12.swf`, except that in the duplication loop, `s` is being calculated like this:

```
s = (Math.random() * 5);
```

...and the _xscale / _yscale of each petal is being calculated like this:

```
_root[nm]._xscale = _root[nm]._yscale = (s * s * s) + 10;
```

This creates an exponential separation of petals as they move outward – the inner petals are much closer together than the outer petals. This is more consistent with real flowers. I also added some code to `petal` to make the original petal invisible.

`flower14.swf` is identical, except the shape of the petal has been changed slightly.

In `flower15.swf`, rather than calculate a random `s`, instead `s` is incremented like this:

```
s+=0.04;
```

...and the rotation of the copy is calculated like this:

```
_root[nm]._rotation = r+=6;
```

[12]

I also increased the number of petals to 220, this creates an exponential spiral, which fades from red to black in the middle, and is lined with a white edge.

In `flower16.swf`, `s` is incremented by 0.02 with each copy, and `_rotation = r+=27`. Also added, is this line:

```
_root[nm]._alpha = a-= 0.5;
```

`a` is a new variable that I set to 100 before the `for` loop. This creates a tight spiral of copies, which fade as they go outward. The effect here looks like anelectron micrograph of a pollen spore, with digital coloring.

`flower17.swf` uses the same code, except each petal has an `enterFrame clipEvent`, with one line of code in it:

```
_xscale--;
```

[13]

I've also added a spike to the tip of the petal graphic itself. This creates a pollen spore, which implodes and then expands slowly like some sort of headless blowfish.

In `flower18.swf`, the code is identical to `flower16.swf`, except the image of the petal has changed and rather than black at the inner end of the petal, it fades instead to a creamy white. When run, this SWF generates an image like a flower with a glowing light at the center.

`flower19.swf` sees the same code, with a slightly different image for the flower, and therefore a different looking final image. The effect is somewhat like an alien tropical flower of unknown origin.

[14]

The effects of Flower can be further expanded to make better use of the random functions, to create much more wild and varied looking flowers. Perhaps, the flowers could be combined with the tree effect to produce completely organic, computer-generated images.

Trails

```
onClipEvent (enterFrame) {
     if (_name == "master") {
          _x += dx;
          _y += dy;
          _rotation += dr;
          if (_x>550) {
               _x = 550;
               dx *= -1;
          }
          if (_x<0) {
               _x = 0;
               dx *= -1;
          }
          if (_y>400) {
               _y = 400;
               dy *= -1;
          }
          if (_y<0) {
               _y = 0;
               dy *= -1;
          }
          nm = "copy" + _root.counter;
          duplicateMovieClip (this, nm, _root.counter++);
     } else {
          _alpha *= _root.fade;
          if (_alpha<=3) {
               removeMovieClip (this);
          }
     }
}
```

This code is attached to one movieclip with the instance name, `master`, which is a white rounded square sitting on the main timeline. to frame 1 of the main timeline, we have the following code:

```
_quality = "LOW";
_root.master.dx = 4;
_root.master.dy = 4;
_root.master.dr = 1;
fade = 0.9;
```

Now, the master code basically moves `master` around the stage, and bounces it off the walls. As it moves, it spawns copies of its frame, with the instance names `copy1`, `copy2`, `copy3`, etc. When a copy is created, it will inherit the properties (`_rotation`, `_x`, `_y`, of `master`. Finally, the copy will then stay exactly where it is and fade out. This creates a very smooth set of trails behind the `master` movieclip. These effects are based on a motion effect.

The key variables

`dx` = the horizontal speed at which master is moving
`dy` = the vertical speed at which master is moving
`dr` = the speed at which master is rotating every frame
`fade` = the rate at which the copies fade out
`counter` = a variable that keeps track of which copy of master we're creating (so that unique names are given to each copy)
`nm` = temporary variable used to create the string which is the name of the copy ("copy" + counter)

Iterations

For `trails2.swf`, I decided to change the motion of `master` to sine and cosine formulas, like so:

```
_x = 275+Math.cos(2*ang)*200;
_y = 200+Math.sin(3.2*ang)*170;
ang += 0.05;
```

The fading copy is the same, except that I set `_yscale` to be equal to `_alpha`, so that the copy will fade out and squash vertically as it does so. With the position now being set a by sine and cosine curve, I am now able to remove all of the code checking to see if the movieclip had left the screen.

`trails3.swf` is identical to `trails2`, except when the copy fades out, it now squashes horizontally, and rotates away as it fades by adding `_rotation += 5` to the `else` clause. The image has also been changed to a rainbow box.

`trails4.swf` is identical to `trails3.swf` except we have two movieclips on the main timeline, `master` and `master2`. These move with the same sine and cosine formulas except that `Math.sin(3.2*ang)` is on `_y` on master, and to `_x` on `master2`. They are opposite so that the two masters (and their trails) will dance about in mirroring curves.

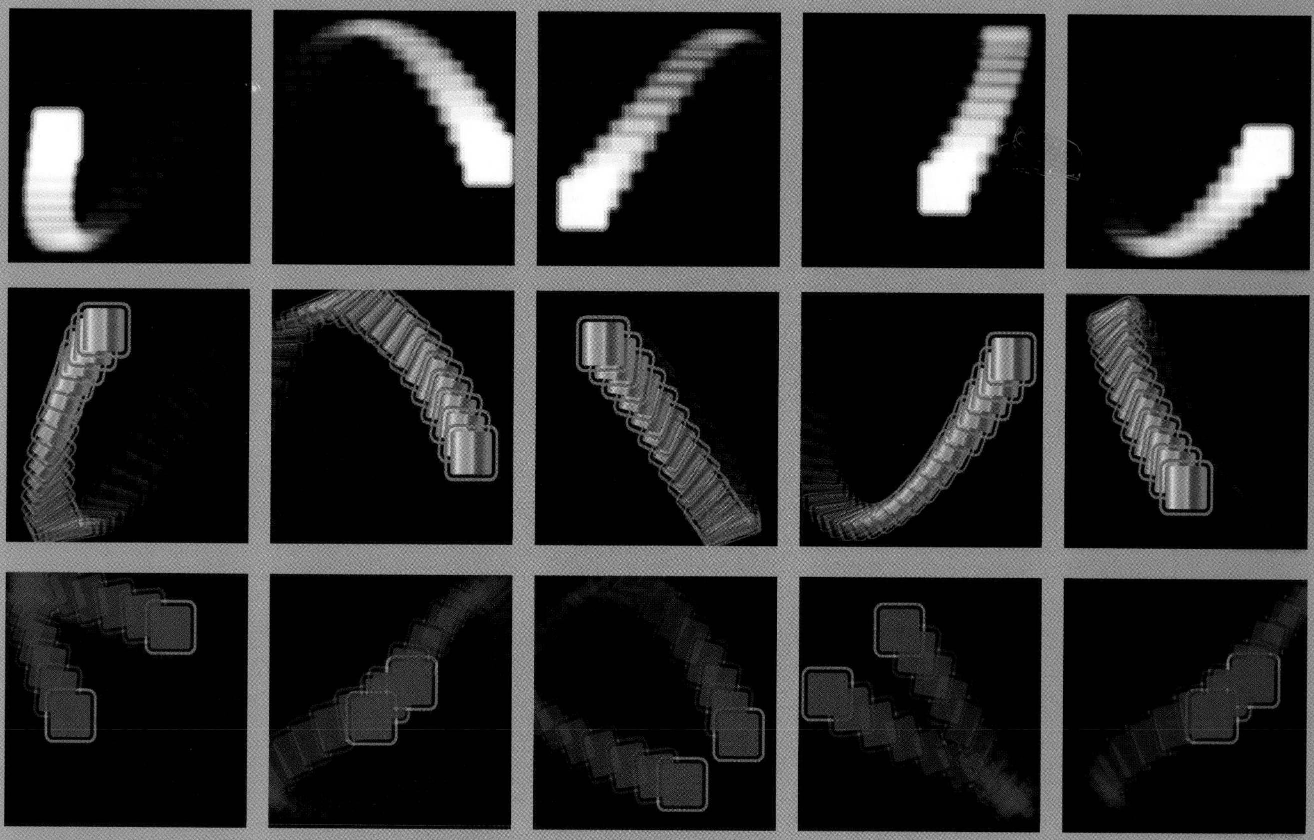

trails5.swf uses the same motion, except the **master** object is rotating as it moves, and it's moving faster. I've also changed the image to be a dumbbell shape, which creates a trail that looks like a DNA strand. I also incorporated code to create a **Color** object and dynamically change the color of the master (and hence the copy) based on its **_x** and **_y** position, like so:

```
r = 250 - (_x / 2);
g = _y / 2;
b = 80;
c.setRGB ((r << 16) + (g << 8) + b);
```

And I added the **Color** object definition to the actions on frame 1:

```
_root.master.c = new Color(_root.master);
```

trails6.swf is identical to **trails5.swf** except that the center point of the **master** movieclip has been moved to the left circle on the dumbbell, which creates a cool lopsided swinging effect as it moves around. I also changed the color algorithm a bit:

```
r = 0;
g = 250 - (_y / 2);
b = (_x / 2);
```

trails7.swf is identical to **trails5.swf**, except the rotation of **master** is now a function rather than a fixed amount:

```
_rotation += Math.cos(ang) * 5;
```

This has the effect of making **master** look like it's swooping like a bird, rather than just spinning haphazardly. I also changed **ang** to 0.03.

trails8.swf uses the same motion as **trails7.swf**, but the image in **master** has been changed to look like some sort of strange dragon or bird. When run as a trail, this looks like a long flying dragon swooping around the screen – very cool. It also moves slower than **trails7**.

Finally, **trails9.swf** looks like **trails8.swf** except it uses the **Color** object to make the dragon all black, evil and ominous looking. The copies also scale away on x and y to look like the tail is receding into the distance. To enhance this effect, I added in a background of mountains and an orange sky.

You could easily make the dragon keyboard or mouse-controlled and create a game of some sort, or perhaps create a fleet (flock?) of dragons.

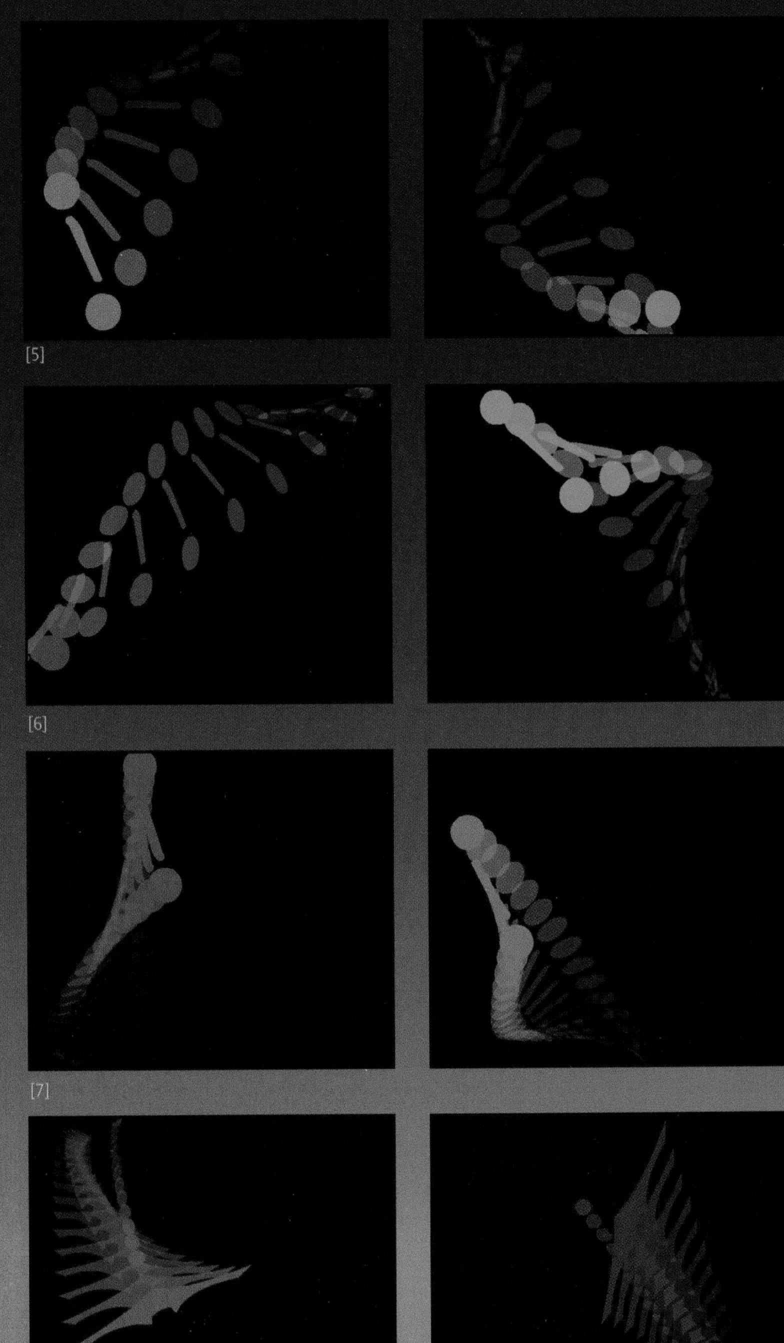
[5]
[6]
[7]
[8]

Trees

```
onClipEvent (enterFrame) {
     if (destr<-180) {
          destr += 360;
     }
     if (destr>180) {
          destr -= 360;
     }
     if (_rotation<-180) {
          _rotation += 360;
     }
     if (_rotation>180) {
          _rotation -= 360;
     }
     if (_rotation>destr) {
          _rotation--;
     }
     if (_rotation<destr) {
          _rotation++;
     }
     _rotation = Math.floor(_rotation);
     if (_rotation == destr && _root.numsticks<_root.maxsticks && dead != true) {
          nm = "st" + _root.numsticks;
          duplicateMovieClip (_root.stick, nm, _root.numsticks++);
          ra = _rotation*(Math.PI/180);
          dx = Math.cos(ra)*20;
          dy = Math.sin(ra)*20;
          _root[nm]._x = _x-dx;
          _root[nm]._y = _y-dy;
          _root[nm]._rotation = _rotation;
          _root[nm].destr = _rotation-_root.da;
          nm = "st" + _root.numsticks;
          duplicateMovieClip (_root.stick, nm, _root.numsticks++);
          _root[nm]._x = _x-dx;
          _root[nm]._y = _y-dy;
          _root[nm]._rotation = _rotation;
          _root[nm].destr = _rotation+_root.da;
          dead = true;
     }
}
```

This code is attached to a single movieclip on the main timeline with the instance name `stick`. This is simply a 20-pixel long vertical line, with the center point at the bottom.

This code is then attached to frame 1 of the main timeline:

```
stick.destr = 90;
stick._rotation = 90;
numsticks = 0;
maxsticks = 200;
da = 20;
```

When this movie is started, `stick` is on the stage, and it will spawn two copies of itself (`stn, st(n + 1)`), creating new sticks which branch off at `da` degrees on either side of the parent. Then, those branches will each create two more copies in exactly the same way, and so on until the shrub is complete. When a new branch is created, it is given a `_rotation`, equal to that of its parent. It is also given a `destr` or, destination rotation. This is where it wants to be when it spawns its own branches. This process has the effect of making the tree appear to grow out of itself. You may also notice that some of the branches have the annoying habit of rotating almost full circle before coming to a rest, I'll be dealing with this later.

The key variables

destr = The destination rotation that stick must be at before it spawns its two child branches. The _rotation of the stick will be subtracted or added-to to slowly to get to its destination
numsticks = A global counter which keeps track of the number of sticks copied. This increments each time a copy is made
maxsticks = The maximum number of sticks allowed before spawning is halted. Otherwise, the tree would grow infinitely, and crash the computer
dead = This is a flag which determines whether or not the code of a stick needs to be run anymore. Once a stick has reached its destr and it has spawned its child branches, its code no longer needs to be run, so its dead value is set to true
nm = Temporary variable used to create the string which is the name of the child stick ("st" + _root.numsticks)
ra = A variable which is the _rotation of this stick converted from degrees to radians, to be used with Math.cos and Math.sin
dx = The x offset from the base of the stick to the tip, to determine where to place the starting point of the child stick
dy = The y offset from the base of the stick to the tip, to determine where to place the starting point of the child stick
da = A global variable which is the amount of angle to add/subtract from the current _rotation in order to set the child's destr. If the parent is at 60 degrees, and da was 20, then the destr of the two children will be 40 and 80

treemake2.swf is identical except that the calculation of branch length has been adjusted to look like this:

```
len = (Math.random() * 10) + 10;
```

...so that len is going to be a number between 10 and 20. This line goes just before the dx and dy calculations, and the dx and dy lines were also changed so that they are now multiplied by len instead of 20. Also, another new piece of code has been added:

```
randa = Math.floor(Math.random() * _root.da);
```

This goes just after the first _root[nm]._rotation = _rotation line. I've also changed the two _root[nm].destr = _rotation lines, replacing the final _root.da with our new randa. This means that rather than set the destr of stick to _root.da, it will be set to a random number between 0 and _root.da. This iteration makes the tree take on a much more random organic appearance. Finally, I changed da on the first frame to 45 to make the tree more open and spread out.

In treemake3.swf I introduced a variable for stick length (called sticklen) to frame 1 and set it to 40. So, whereas in the above example the stick length was between 10 and 20, in this iteration the stick length is now between 10 and _root.sticklen, by changing this code:

```
len = (Math.random() * (_root.sticklen - 10)) + 10;
```

In order to make this work, I also lengthened the actual graphic of the movieclip to 40 pixels to allow for a length greater than 20 without creating strange gaps between the branches (due to len being greater than the actual length of the stick graphic, so the child branches are spawned beyond the end of the parent).

In treemake4.swf, I decided on a radical change and removed the real time rotation of the stick (using destr). Instead, the _rotation of each child is simply set to _rotation + randa to start with. This speeds up the process, and takes care of some situations where sticks were rotating completely around the circle to get back to their destr. To do this, I first removed all of the initial set of if statements up to and including the line _rotation = Math.floor(_rotation). Then I removed this clause from the long if statement (_rotation == destr &&). The final pieces to remove are the two lines beginning _root[nm].destr, and then add -randa and +randa respectively to the end of the _root[nm]._rotation = _rotation lines. I also added a semi-transparent circle at the end of each stick to highlight the joint.

treemake5.swf is identical to treemake4.swf, except I've added a vertical linear brown gradient to each stick to give it a 3D feel. This makes the tree appear more lifelike.

In treemake6.swf, I've added two green leaves to the stick to give a more fully-fledged tree. Try tweening the leaf growth here.

treemake7.swf is identical to treemake6.swf, except the leaves have been turned to pink blossoms, and I changed _root.da to 20 and the len from '10 to _root.sticklen' to '20 to _root.sticklen' (by changing both 10s to 20s), to give a much more vertical tree.

In treemake8.swf, I added two small branches to the graphic of the stick. This creates a tree with a much fuller look, with many more branches.

In treemake9.swf, I added some greenery to these small branches, creating a very lush tree, and changed len back to 10.

treemake10.swf shows the removal of all the random elements, and a greater concentration on the patterns, so len = _root.sticklen - 10, and randa = _root.da. Now that's the case you can just as easily take out the line entirely and then replace all occurrences of randa with _root.da. On the first keyframe _root.da has been set to 25, and _root.sticklen to 45. The stick image has also been changed to a gradient filled blue gem, just for fun.

In treemake11.swf, I've done a couple of things. First, I changed the shape to a simple green line with a little white X on the end, and I also set _root.da to 45. This creates some very interesting mathematical patterns, based on 45-degree angles. Finally, I've added code to make each successive generation fade out a bit, with this:

```
_root[nm]._alpha = _alpha - 10;
```

In treemake12.swf, I've changed _root.da to be 66.66 degrees. This creates a lovely hexagonal pattern. I've also changed the image on the stick to be a red to black gradient, with white tips.

In treemake13.swf, _root.da is a simple 90 degrees. The image of the stick has been changed to a horizontal brown to black gradient, and this creates a cool basket weaving effect.

treemake14.swf is the chessboard of the future! _root.da is still 90 degrees, but the image has been changed to a radial filled black to white gradient, with a gray square drawn next to it. _root.sticklen has been changed to 65.

In treemake15.swf, _root.da has been changed from 90 to 88. This creates the appearance of the chessboard starting to collapse chaotically from the middle.

In treemake16.swf, the colors have been changed – the background is white and the stick is black with a softened edge. _root.da is 76 and _root.sticklen is 45. This creates something that looks like an X-Ray photograph of a crystallized molecule.

This could be used to create many cool and interesting background images. Try making the image of the stick more or less complicated, and just play around with the different values for _root.da, _root.sticklen and _root.maxsticks. You could also make some of the position determination a math function, to change the look of the positioning.

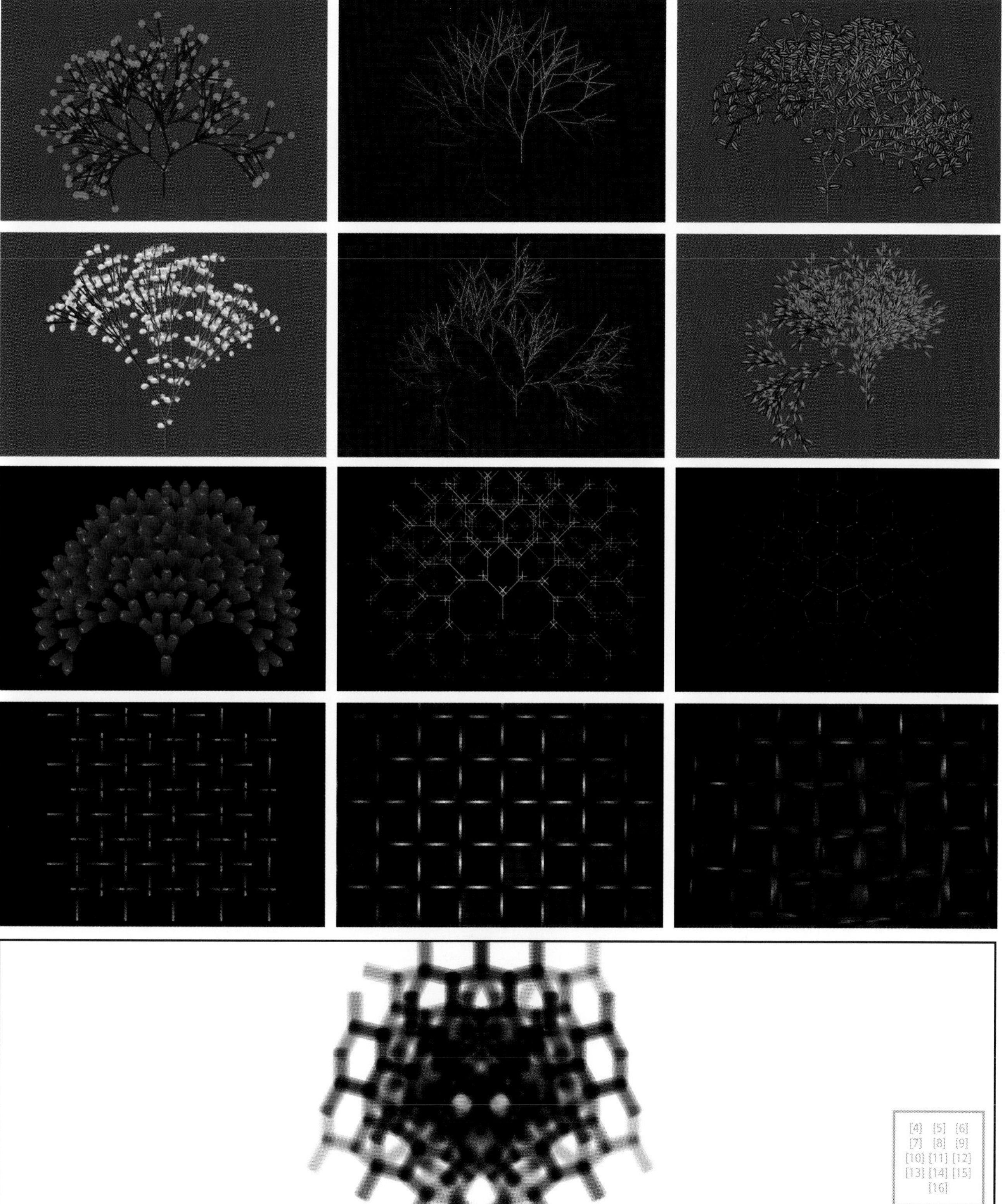
[4] [5] [6]
[7] [8] [9]
[10] [11] [12]
[13] [14] [15]
[16]

Circles

The following code is attached to a movieclip on the main timeline called `circle`. This movieclip consists of a single black circle about 62 pixels in diameter.

```
onClipEvent (load) {
     sx = _x;
     sy = _y;
     ang = 0;
}
onClipEvent (enterFrame) {
     _x = sx+(Math.sin(ang)*(mynum));
     _y = sy+(Math.sin(ang)*(mynum));
     ang += 0.1;
}
```

There is also another movieclip on the main timeline called `controller`. This is responsible for duplicating and laying out the circles. The following code is attached to it:

```
onClipEvent (load) {
     num = 0;
     for (i=0; i<10; i++) {
          for (j=0; j<10; j++) {
               nm = "cir" + num;
               duplicateMovieClip (_root.circle, nm, num);
               _root[nm]._x = i*_root.circle._width;
               _root[nm]._y = j*_root.circle._height;
               _root[nm].mynum = num;
               num++;
          }
     }
}
```

Essentially what we're doing is creating a grid of circles on screen. The theory behind this experiment is that we can do different things with the circles in this grid and achieve very cool results.

The key variables

`sx` = The starting `_x` location of each circle. Contained within the circle itself, and stored on load
`sy` = The starting `_y` location of each circle. Contained within the circle itself, and stored on load
`ang` = A variable which is used as a counter in a circular loop. This is an angle that is fed into various trig functions, and then incremented. Each circle copy has its own `ang`
`mynum` = A unique number given to each circle in the order that it's created. This number is stored in the circle copy itself
`i` = An outer counter for the loop which positions the circle – `i` is used to determine the copy's `_x`
`j` = An inner counter for the loop which positions the circle – `j` is used to determine the copy's `_y`
`num` = a temporary counter used during the loop to determine which circle we're currently creating

In circ1.swf, the grid of circles simply pulses along a diagonal line, each circle along pulsing a bit more than the previous one. The amount of motion it possesses is determined by the value of its mynum. This uses a Math.sin function on _x and _y of each circle to create this pulse.

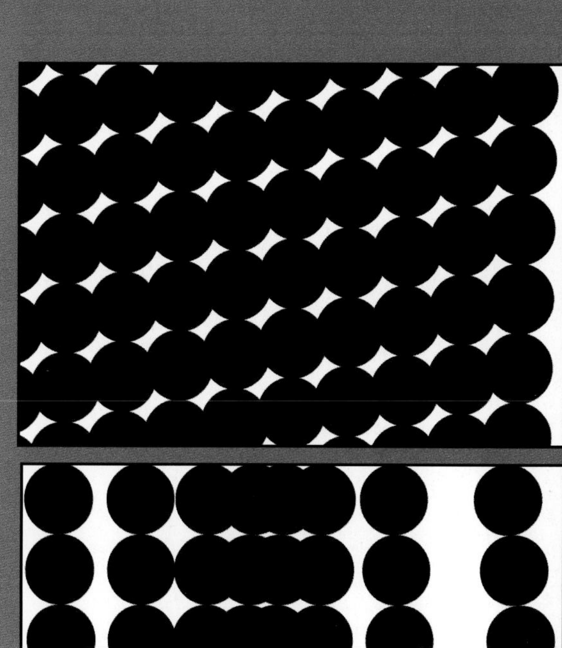

In circ2.swf, we're only pulsing along _x, not _y. Also, the line which increments ang: (ang+=0.1) has been changed to ang+=(mynum / 450). This will mean that each circle will pulse at a slightly different rate, and a very cool wave-like motion is created, as all the circles move of their own accord.

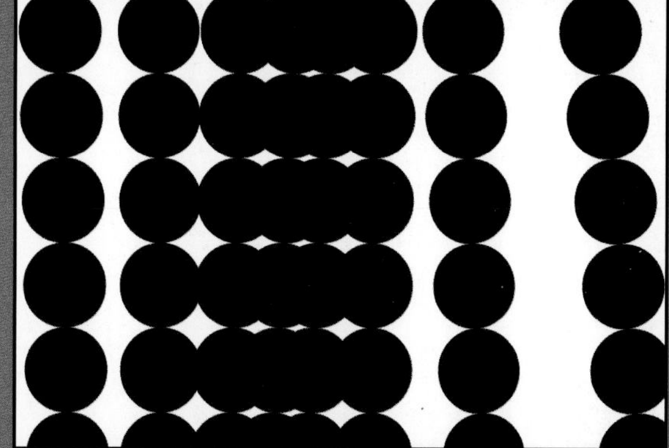

In circ3.swf, the line '_x =' in the circle movieclip has been changed to '_yscale = _xscale = sx + (Math.sin(ang) * (mynum))'. Also sx and sy have been changed to equal _xscale and _yscale as well. This means that each circle will not pulse in position, but rather in size. This creates a very cool set of patterns as areas of light and dark move across the screen, as if we were looking close up at a printed newspaper. Watch this one for a while and you'll be entranced.

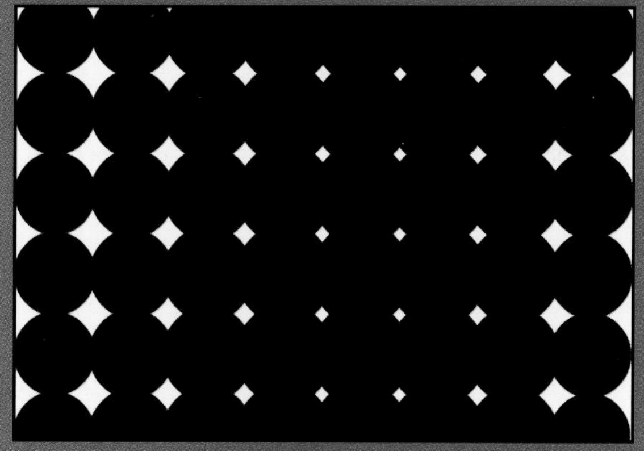

In circ4.swf, I've added the '_x = sx + (Math.sin(ang) * (mynum))' back in, which creates a cool horizontal lava lamp effect as the circles resize and move left and right.

In circ5.swf, I've added a color object to each circle, with the following lines of code within the load clip event:

```
c = new Color(this);
r = _x;
g = 0;
b = _y;
c.setRGB((r << 16) + (g << 8) + b);
```

As you can see, I'm setting the r, and b components of the circle based upon its _x and _y position. I've also rewritten the enterFrame event so only this code remains in it:

```
_x = _yscale = _xscale = sx + (Math.sin(ang) * (mynum * 2));
ang+=(mynum / 450);
```

This creates a different horizontal lava lamp effect, which uses a rainbow of blues and reds.

Next in circ6.swf I set each circle with:

```
_y = sy + (Math.sin(ang) * (mynum));
_xscale = sy + (Math.cos(ang) * (mynum * 2));
```

This effect creates the appearance of a hanging wind chime or something similar which is twirling and bobbing in a strong breeze..

In circ7.swf, I've added the color code to the enterFrame clip event, so the colors of the circles are changing based on the position of each circle as it moves, and altered the colors slightly to this:

```
r = _x / 3;
g = 127 + (Math.cos(ang) * 127);
b = _y / 2;
```

The motion of each circle is also now based on a very simple _x = sin, _y = cos equation:

```
_y = sy + (Math.sin(ang) * (mynum));
_x = sx + (Math.cos(ang) * (mynum));
```

Meaning that each circle moves in a circular motion. The overall effect is a large wave effect, which eventually descends into chaos.

In circ8.swf, I've added this line of code to the enterFrame:

```
_alpha = 50 + (Math.cos(ang) * 50);
```

This means that some circles will vanish and reappear in a sweeping motion.

In circ9.swf, I changed the shape from a plain circle to a square with a circle hidden behind. This has a neat flowing-changing-morphing grid effect.

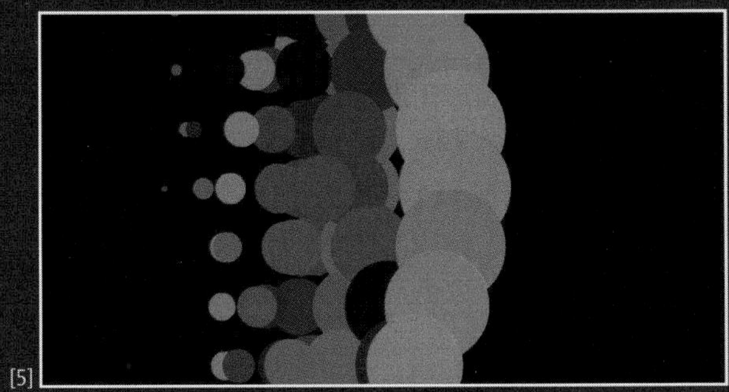

[5]

[6]

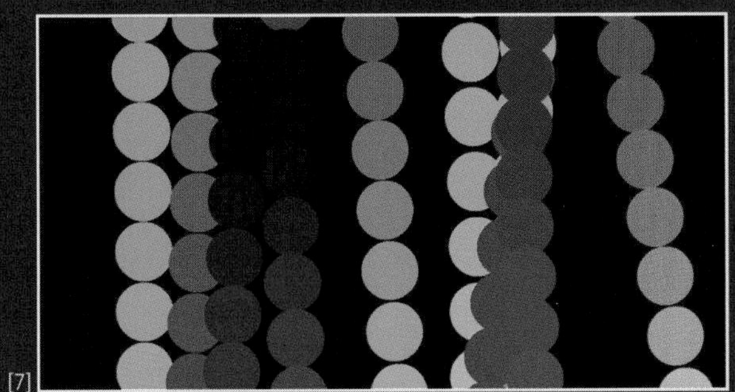

[7]

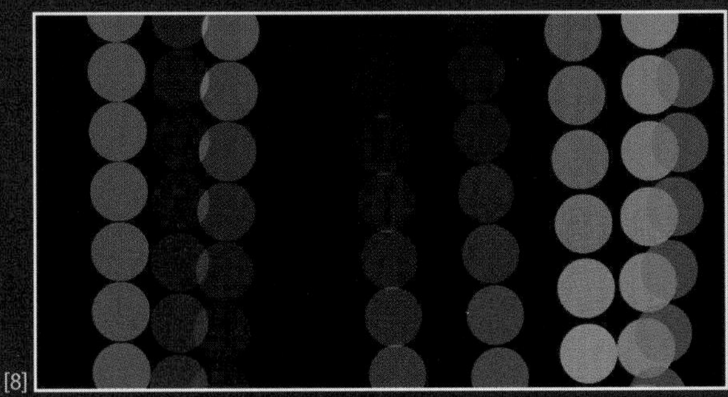

[8]

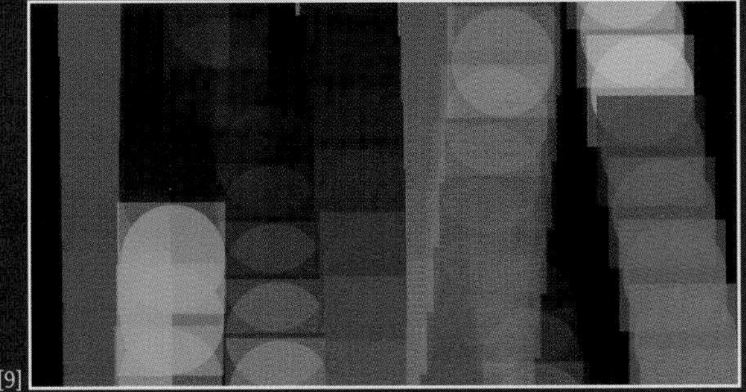

[9]

In circ10.swf, there's a stunning visual difference, but a very small code difference. Rather than use sx and sy as the pivot point for the circle, I'm using 275 and 200, like this:

```
_x = 275 + (Math.cos(ang) * (mynum));
_y = 200 + (Math.sin(ang) * (mynum));
```

This has the effect of creating a really cool spiralling effect. Watch it for a few minutes and you'll see some amazingly mesmerizing patterns emerge. Also try taking out the alpha changing line to make it run quicker, and playing about with the colors.

In circ11.swf, I've changed the incrimination of ang to this:

```
ang += (mynum / 100);
```

Which means ang will increment quicker. Above that though, I've also added this line of code:

```
mynum+=Math.cos(ang);
```

This has the effect of changing the mynum value of each circle up and down in a wave.

circ12.swf sees one modification:

```
mynum+=(Math.cos(ang2+=0.1) * 7);
```

This crazy line of code makes the spiraling shape expand and shrink, as if it were breathing. I also changed the color code to make the circle blue. In circ13.swf, I changed the _x code to look like this:

```
_x = 275 + (Math.cos(ang) * (mynum * 2));
```

By multiplying mynum by 2, the spiral takes on a horizontally stretched look. It looks like a spiraling blue galaxy.

In circ14.swf, I've replaced the 275 in the _x code with (mynum * 2), changed the final mynum in the _y code to mynum * 2, taken out the mynum+= line, and added this line instead:

```
_alpha = 100 - (mynum);
```

This makes the circles fade out depending on their number. I also changed ang to equal mynum/450 rather than 100. The color code has also been altered to make it a purple shade:

```
r = mynum;
g = 0;
b = mynum*2;
```

In circ15.swf, the following line has been added:

```
mynum+=(Math.cos(ang2+=0.2) * 7);
```

This is similar to the code used in circ12.swf, and it creates a pulsing, and spiraling look. The colors are now green.

In circ16.swf, I put the sx and sy back into the _x and _y code:

```
_x = sx+(Math.cos(ang)*(mynum*2));
_y = sy+(Math.sin(ang)*(mynum*2));
```

I also took out the _alpha line to make the shapes more visible. The color has been changed to a kind of peach. This looks like a slew of strange dancing snakes.

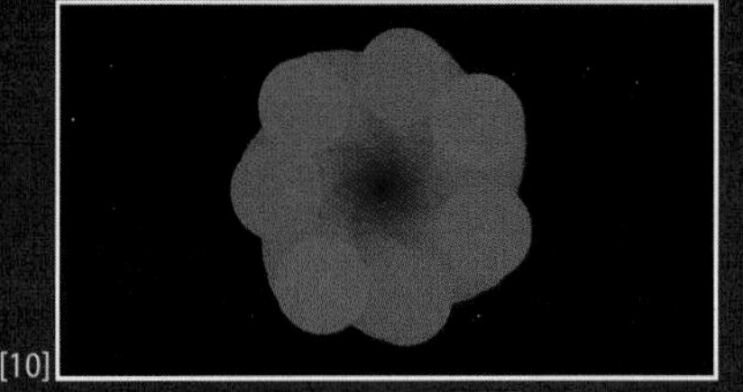
[10]

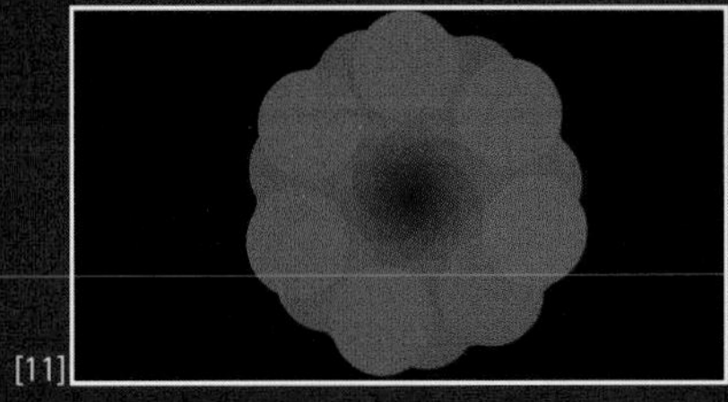
[11]

[12]

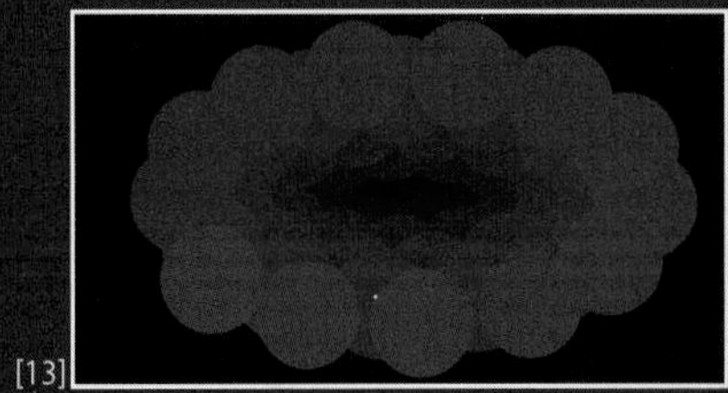
[13]

[13]

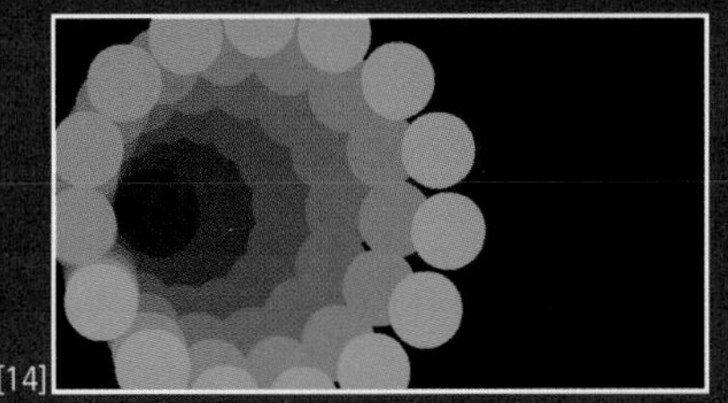
[14]

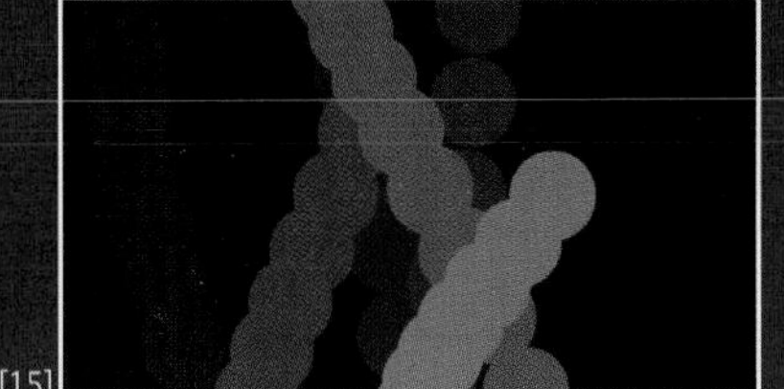
[15]

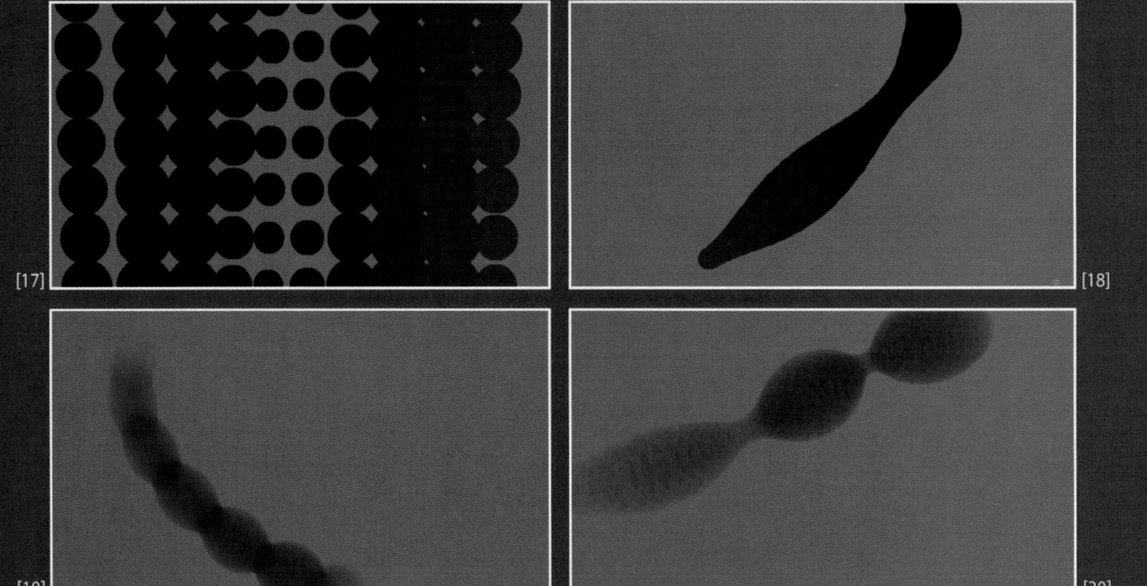

[17] [18] [19] [20]

In circ17.swf, the grid effect is revived by changing sx and sy back to equaling _xscale and _yscale, and replacing the enterFrame code with this:

```
_yscale = _xscale = sx + (Math.sin(ang) * ((mynum + 40) / 2));
_x += (Math.sin(ang));
ang += (mynum / 450);
```

The circles now pulse in _xscale, _yscale, and along _x giving a very mesmerizing and organic effect. I also changed the changed the color code so that r=mynum*2, and g=mynum.

In circ18.swf, I added the following line to the load clip event code:

```
ang2 = mynum / 50;
```

And the position and scale code has been changed slightly to this:

```
_yscale = _xscale = sx + (Math.sin(ang) * ((mynum + 40) / 2));
_x = 275 + (Math.cos(ang2 * 1.2) * 200);
_y = 200 + (Math.sin(ang2 += 0.1) * 200);
```

With this, we have a very strange looking worm which flies around the screen, and has a lumpy segmented look.

circ19.swf is identical to circ18.swf, except that in the load clip event, I've added this code:

```
_alpha = (mynum + 1) / 4;
```

This makes the worm fade out toward the ends.

In circ20.swf, I've changed the _x code to look like this:

```
_x = 275 + (Math.tan(ang2 * 1.5) * 200);
```

Using the Math.tan function, the worm will appear to loop around from right to left, creating the appearance of lots of worms swimming past the screen.

There are three main effects here – the spirals, the grid and the worm – all of which have emerged out of the same experiment. You could try changing some more of the variables, or try different functions – tan, and sqrt can produce interesting effects.

First I wanted to be a fireman, then an astronaut, then a car mechanic, then an architect. Then I wanted to make dioramas for the Museum of Natural History. Then I wanted to be a rock star, then a writer, a 3D animator, a carpenter, and then a writer again. Then for a while all I wanted to do was ride the F train drinking Tecate from a can. Then I wanted to be a web designer, then an artist, then a roof gardener. Now I'm back to fireman.

Like many things in the universe, I try to get the most done with the least amount of work. Creating simple instructions like "1. Draw a line for a while, and then change direction. 2. Repeat 1000 times" is easy to say, but might give you a hand cramp if you actually tried it. This may have been why the artist Sol LeWitt had the bright idea to just write up instructions and then have other people actually produce the artwork. I have a tough time telling people what to do, so I prefer to boss a computer around.

I almost always start out with a specific goal in mind and fail at it miserably. Luckily, the detritus I wind up with is often more interesting than my original goal. Today's discarded failure is tomorrow's friends of ED book chapter.

(Oh, and you might notice that I often take an idea, algorithm, or function from one set of experiments and try to apply it to other sets. Cross-pollination is a great productivity tool, it's not because I'm lazy.)

david hirmes

hirmes.com

Lines

The idea behind this piece is pretty simple: Draw a series of connected lines of random length within the bounds of a rectangular area. Open up `lines01.swf` to see it in action. As the movie plays out, both random patterns, and the rectangle that bounds the patterns, are revealed. I think that this piece is a useful place to start out exploring the wide world of algorithmic drawing – that is, random and/or semi-intelligent pattern formation.

There are two movieclips in this piece: `line` and `container`. The `line` clip is just the standard 100x100 pixel diagonal hairline sitting in the Library. This clip has been set up to export as a linked symbol named `line`. The `container` clip is empty and is just used to hold the code. The `container` clip also acts as the registration point for the movie, so be sure to place it in the top-left hand corner of the stage. Here is the code that lives on top of `container`:

```
onClipEvent (load) {
  leftBounds = x = 20;
  topBounds = y = 20;
  rightBounds = 380;
  bottomBounds = 380;
  baseMax = 20;
  randomMax = 10;
  maxLines = 500;

  function makeLineFunction () {
   counter++;
   this.attachMovie("line", counter, counter);
   line = this[counter];
   line._x = x;
   line._y = y;
   maxDistance = baseMax*random(randomMax);
   minDistance = 2;
   direction = random(2) ? -1 : 1;
   xEnd = x+(direction*(minDistance+random(maxDistance)));
   direction = random(2) ? -1 : 1;
   yEnd = y+(direction*(minDistance+random(maxDistance)));
   if (xEnd<leftBounds) {
    xEnd = leftBounds;
   }
   if (xEnd>rightBounds) {
    xEnd = rightBounds;
   }
   if (yEnd<topBounds) {
    yEnd = topBounds;
   }
   if (yEnd>bottomBounds) {
    yEnd = bottomBounds;
   }
   line._xscale = xEnd-x;
   line._yscale = yEnd-y;
   x = xEnd;
   y = yEnd;
   if ( counter > maxLines ) {
    makeLine = null;
   }
  }
  makeLine = makeLineFunction;
}
onClipEvent (enterFrame) {
  makeLine();
}
```

The key variables

the Bounds – set the boundaries that the lines will be drawn within. My movie is a 400x400 square with the container clip in the top-left corner, so I set the Bounds to be just within this square.
x and y – the current starting position of the line
baseMax – the base length of a line
randomMax – a random number which baseMax is multiplied by to obtain the final possible line length
maxLines – the maximum number of lines drawn
maxDistance – the final possible line length
minDistance – the minimum line length
direction – a direction flag, either 1 or –1, used as a multiplier to reverse the direction. This is worked out quite cleverly by taking a random number (returning either 0 or 1) and using this to determine a Boolean state check with the little-employed ?: conditional operator. If the Boolean check is true then the first expression (following the ?) is returned, and if it's false then the second expression (following the :) will be returned.
xEnd and yEnd – the target end position of the line to be drawn

Alrighty, let's take this thing apart.

The function makeLineFunction is where it all happens. First we add 1 to the counter, which keeps track of the number of lines we've created, and then we use attachMovie to create a new instance of the line clip. The name and the depth of the clip are set to be counter (officially Macromedia cautions against using numbers as the names of clips, but it produces cleaner code and I've never had a problem with it). To make the code clearer, we next setup the variable line to point to the line clip we've just created. Next, the x and y values of the line are set. We start to determine how long the line will actually be and in what direction it will go, first by setting the minimum and maximum line length variables, then by choosing whether the direction will be left or right and up or down, and finally randomly choosing a distance within these parameters and adding that distance to the existing x and y position.

The set of four if statements make sure that the line doesn't go past the bounds that we've set up. To finish drawing of the line, we change the scale of the line object to the end positions (xEnd and yEnd) minus the starting positions (x and y). Finally, we set the x and y variables to equal the end positions so the next time we run this function, the line will start where the last one ended, thus creating the illusion of a single continuous line.

The last part of the function checks to see if we've gone over the limit of the total number of lines we set out to create. If we have gone over the limit, the makeLine function is set to null. Why? Because if you take a look at the enterFrame clip event, you'll notice the only code in it is makeLine(). makeLine has been set to point to the makeLine Function at startup, so on every enterFrame clip event the makeLineFunction is executed. When makeLine is set to null, the function is no longer called during enterFrame clip events, freeing up your CPU to do other tasks. This is one of the reasons it is often more efficient to create loops using functions and clip events than two frame loops within a timeline.

Iterations

lines 02

Here I've introduced a new simple movieclip of a filled circle and exported it from the Library with the linkage name circle. By adding the following code to makeLineFunction:

```
this.attachMovie("circle", counter+maxLines,
counter+maxLines);
```

I've created the circle and ensured that it appears above the lines by adding maxLines to the depth count. I've also changed the two line._ lines to this:

```
line._x = this[counter+maxLines]._x = x;
line._y = this[counter+maxLines]._y = y;
```

These set the circle to be at the same position as the start of each line.

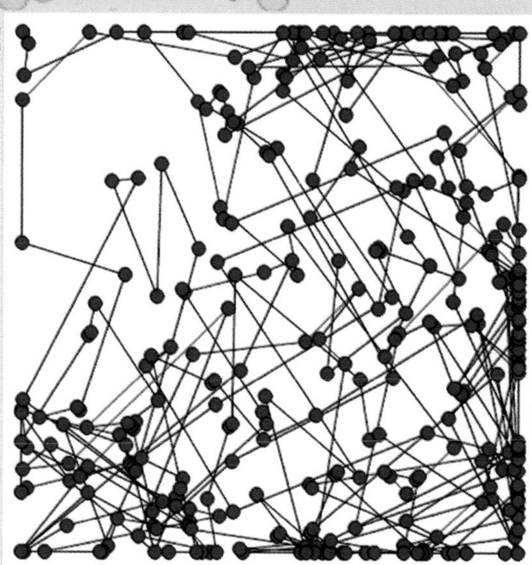

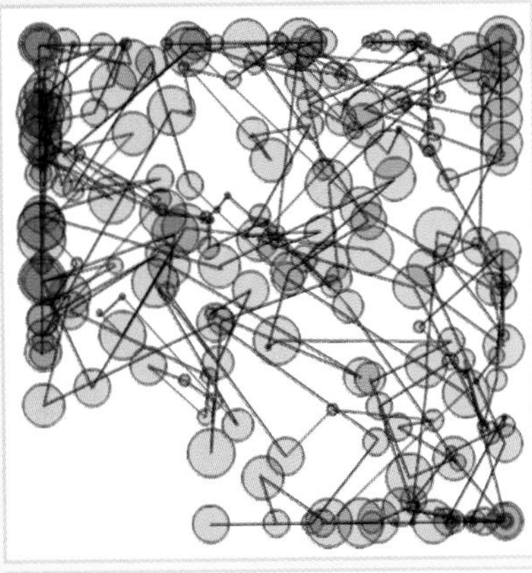

lines 03
This time I've changed the code to make the circles appear beneath the lines. Here's the new `line` and `circle` positioning code:

```
this.attachMovie("line", counter+maxLines, counter+maxLines);
this.attachMovie("circle", counter, counter);
line = this[counter+maxLines];
circle = this[counter];
line._x = circle._x = x;
line._y = circle._y = y;
```

I also changed the size of the `circle` clip with the following new lines:

```
circle._xscale = maxDistance * .4;
circle._yscale = maxDistance * .4;
```

lines 04
Here I reduced the length of the lines by changing `baseMax` and `randomMax` to 6. I also removed the random element in determining the line distance by changing the following lines to:

```
xEnd = x+(direction*(minDistance+maxDistance));
yEnd = y+(direction*(minDistance+maxDistance));
```

By doing this, I've reduced the possible angles to four. You'll notice that there's a slight exception to this rule at the corners because of the position being overridden by the bounds checking code.

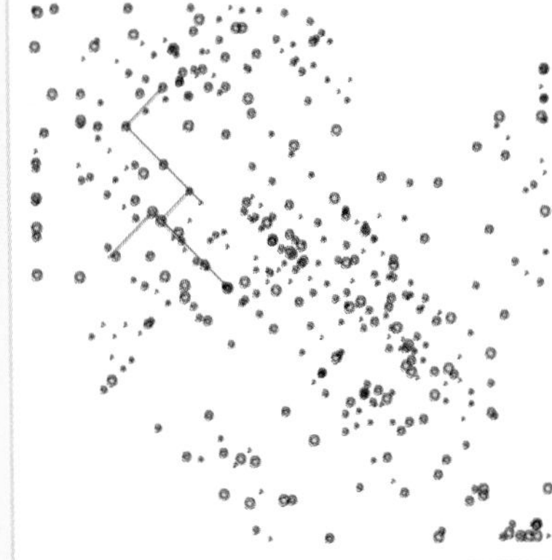

lines 05
I created this interesting effect by adding just one line of code to the end of the function, just before the `if` statement:

```
this[counter+maxLines-10].removeMovieClip();
```

Now the lines are continuously removed leaving only 10 on the screen at any one time, but the circles remain.

lines 06
I decided to go right back to the original code again and play with some different effects. Here I added a basic alpha component with the following new lines in the function:

```
alpha++;
if ( alpha > 100 ) {
    alpha = 0;
}
line._alpha = alpha;
```

This creates a simple illusion of depth.

lines 07
I went back to the base file again and changed `line` from a simple line to a filled rectangle. I also added a piece of code to allow the user to pause, and restart, the drawing by pressing any key:

```
onClipEvent (keyDown) {
   makeLine = (typeof(makeLine) == "function") ? null : makeLineFunction;
}
```

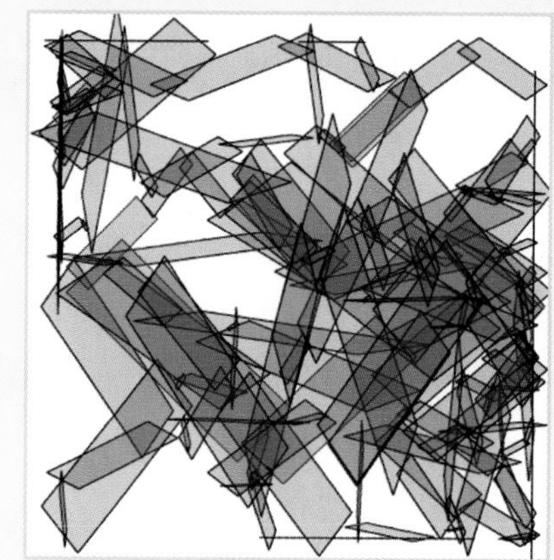

lines 08
Returning to the original file, I now decided to play about with masking. I added a circular mask over the container layer, then another layer over the top of both of those with a line drawn around the edge of the mask so that the boundary is visible. The other graphic I changed was the `line` clip, which is now a thin rounded rectangle at 20% alpha. I also changed the `Bounds` and starting position of the line to keep it more within the confines of my mask:

```
x=150;
y=150;
leftBounds = 50;
topBounds = 50;
rightBounds = 315;
bottomBounds = 315;
```

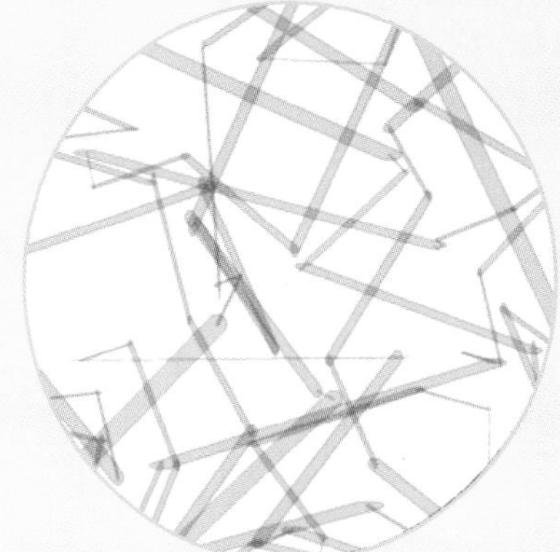

lines 09
Here I changed the shape of the mask again, and altered the `Bounds` to keep them within my new shape. To further enhance the mask effect, I added this line to the `enterFrame` clip event:

```
_rotation++;
```

I reduced `maxLines` to 300 to stop the movie from slowing down too much with the new rotation, and I also set the movie quality to low for the same reason.

lines 10
Returning to the original again, I decided to go down a completely different route. This time I wanted to try and draw curves instead of just straight lines. I achieved this by using sine and cosine to determine the line end point, but the addition of the random element in the `maxDistance` variable gives the whole thing a strangely childlike appearance. Here are the new end point lines:

```
xEnd = x + (Math.cos(counter*0.1) * maxDistance);
yEnd = y + (Math.sin(counter*0.1) * maxDistance);
```

I also changed the initial constants to keep the line size small, and to set it to start drawing from the middle:

```
leftBounds = 20;
topBounds = 20;
x = leftBounds + rightBounds / 2;
y = topBounds + bottomBounds / 2;
baseMax = 4;
randomMax = 4;
```

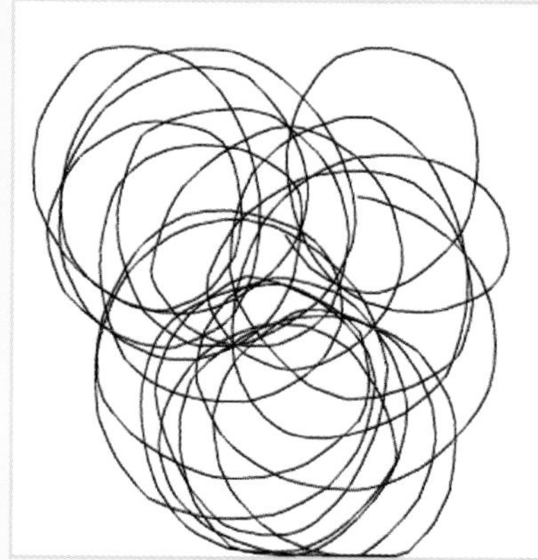

lines 11

I went back to the original once more and decided to animate the line drawing. To do this, I first took the line scaling code out of the main code by changing these lines:

```
line.xNew = xEnd-x;
line.yNew = yEnd-y;
```

I then added some code to the `line` clip itself. To do this I converted the line into another movieclip called `innerLine` inside the original `line` clip. I then attached the following code to `innerLine`:

```
onClipEvent(load) {
     _parent._xscale = 0;
     _parent._yscale = 0;
     x = _parent.xNew;
     y = _parent.yNew;
     steps = 20;
}

onClipEvent(enterFrame) {
     if ( steps > 0 ) {
       _parent._xscale = x / steps;
       _parent._yscale = y / steps;
       steps--;
     }
}
```

lines 12

In this iteration the main code is the same, but I changed the `innerLine` code to make the lines grow at an even rate:

```
onClipEvent(load) {
     _parent._xscale = 0;
     _parent._yscale = 0;
     x = _parent.xNew / 20;
     y = _parent.yNew / 20;
     c = 20;
}
onClipEvent(enterFrame) {
     if ( c > 0 ) {
       _parent._xscale += x;
       _parent._yscale += y;
       c--;
     }
}
```

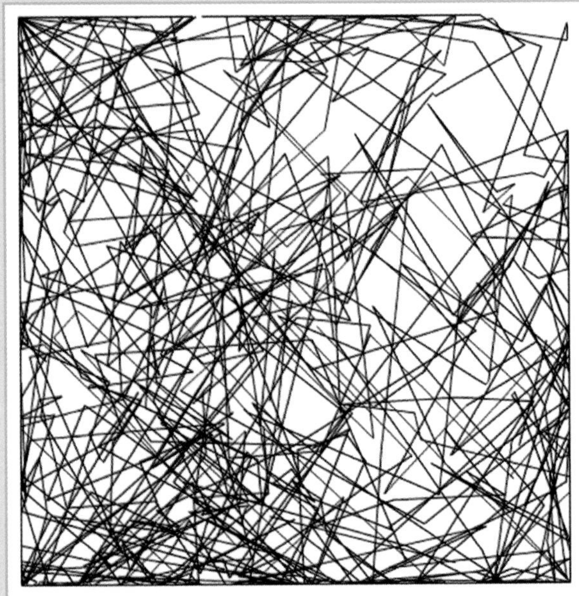

lines 13

I now wanted to try and get the lines to draw one at a time, so it would look like they were being hand drawn in one continuous line. To achieve this I had to add an `if` statement around the code in `makeLineFunction`:

```
if ( this[counter].done == 1 || counter < 1) {
```

This sets a flag to tell the program whether the current line has finished drawing or not, and then I pick up and act on this flag in the `innerLine` code:

```
onClipEvent (load) {
     _parent._xscale = 0;
     _parent._yscale = 0;
     c = 10;
     x = _parent.xNew/c;
     y = _parent.yNew/c;

     function growFunction () {
       if (c>0) {
         _parent._xscale += x;
         _parent._yscale += y;
         c--;
       } else {
         _parent.done = 1;
         grow = null;
       }
     }
     grow = growFunction;
}

onClipEvent (enterFrame) {
     grow();
}
```

lines 14

After creating the effect in code, I realized that it could probably be done just as well with a simple tween. So for this experiment I stepped right back to the beginning again and did just that.

lines 15

This uses exactly the same code as the last one, I just changed the tween for a more dramatic effect.

lines 16

I changed the tween again so that this time there is an alpha fade as well as some movement to give the line the appearance of sliding into place from nothingness.

IN AND OUT OF THE GRID

Why grids? Why "In and Out of the Grid"? Well, for one thing, I often find it useful to start with a simple structure and play off it, eventually getting so far away that the original structure is barely recognizable. I think there's just a pleasure in seeing form dissolve into chaos and back to form.

Let's take a look at the first piece. It has three clips in the Library: as with most of my pieces, `container` is an empty clip where the main code loop goes. All other clips are dynamically created inside `container`. The only purpose of `atomContainer` is to hold `atom` inside it. This structure will become useful in the more sophisticated pieces where we want to put clip events on each of the objects. This is explained more fully in my `Springs` experiment. For now, just consider it good practice to put a "wrapper" clip around the clip that has your art. Speaking of the art, you'll notice that the `atom` clip is a simple translucent rectangle. The alpha is kept down around 25% so that more complex patterns can emerge when many clips are overlapping. The other important thing to notice about the clip is that its registration point is at one end of the rectangle.

In this first grid piece, all of the code lives on the clip `container`:

```
onClipEvent (load) {
   _highquality = false;
   xNumber = 7;
   yNumber = 7;
   total = xNumber*yNumber;
   gridSpacing = 21;
   rotationAmount = 3;

   for (y=0; y<yNumber; y++) {
     for (x=0; x<xNumber; x++) {
       counter++;
       this.attachMovie("atomContainer", counter, counter);
       this[counter]._x = x*gridSpacing;
       this[counter]._y = y*gridSpacing;
       this[counter]._rotation = random(180);
       this[counter]._xscale = 100;
       this[counter]._yscale = 10+random(90);
     }
   }
}

onClipEvent(enterFrame) {
   counter = total+1;
   while( counter-- ) {
     this[counter]._rotation += rotationAmount;
   }
}
```

The key variables

`xNumber` – the number of clips we'll create on the x-axis (horizontal)
`yNumber` – the number of clips for the y-axis (vertical)
`total` – the total number of objects
`gridSpacing` – how far apart each clip will be from each other
`rotationAmount` – the amount that the clips rotate every frame

We use a similar method to that described in the `Lines` experiment to create each object: use a counter variable to keep track of the number of clips and use the same variable to name them and set their depth. We also set a random `rotation` and `yscale` value for each object.

OK, everything is set up, now for the most difficult part: putting it in motion. For every `enterFrame` clip event, we cycle through all of the clips and increase the `rotation` parameter by the amount specified in the `rotationAmount` variable.

Okay so I lied about the difficulty, that's all there is to it. Check out `grid 01`.swf to see it in motion.

Iterations

grid 02

After running the first example, you'll probably be wondering what this has got to do with grids; hopefully this'll make it a bit clearer. In this iteration things get a little more griddy. I started with the addition of two new variables to hold the hard-coded values of my stage size:

```
canvasWidth = 600;
canvasHeight = 600;
```

I then changed the `xNumber`, `yNumber`, and `gridSpacing` to 20. I removed the `rotationAmount` variable and changed the `for` loop to look like this:

```
for (y=0; y<yNumber; y++) {
    for (x=0; x<xNumber; x++) {
      counter++;
      this.attachMovie("atomContainer", counter, counter);
      this[counter]._x = x*gridSpacing;
      this[counter]._y = y*gridSpacing;
    }
}
```

Lastly, I removed the whole `enterFrame` clip event and added these two lines after the `for` loop:

```
_x = (canvasWidth-(gridSpacing*xNumber))/2;
_y = (canvasHeight-(gridSpacing*yNumber))/2;
```

By subtracting the size of the grid by the size of the stage and dividing it by 2, we're able to center the whole grid on the stage. I also changed the `atom` graphic to be a simple 20x20 pixel filled circle.

grid 03

Now things start to get more interesting. In this iteration I added a few lines to the end of the `for` loop:

```
scale = random(150);
this[counter]._xscale = scale;
this[counter]._yscale = scale;
```

This creates a complex pattern by simply randomly setting the scale of each circle.

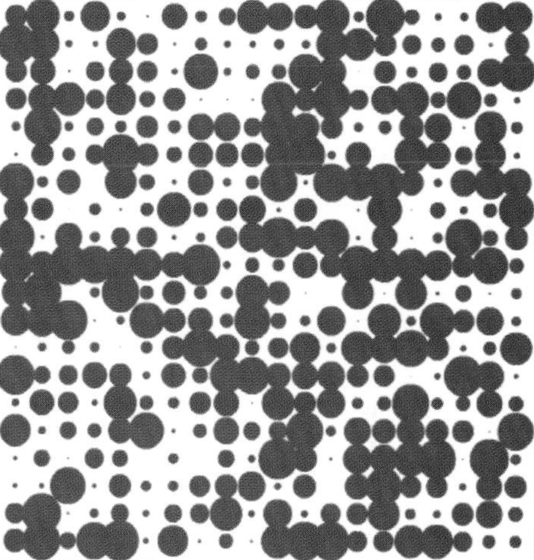

grid 04

In this iteration I started to add some animation with a new `enterFrame` clip event:

```
onClipEvent(enterFrame) {
    counter = total+1;
    while( counter-- ) {
      if ( this[counter]._xscale < 200 ) {
        this[counter]._xscale++;
        this[counter]._yscale++;
      }
    }
}
```

Here we create a simple animation by incrementing the scale of each circle, stopping when the scale equals 200. In effect here, we're going from a random pattern back into a standard uniform grid.

grid 05

I played about a bit with the animation again to create this interesting effect that starts off looking a bit like one of those old flashing-light computers in 70s sci-fi shows, and morphs through strange optical illusions (look out for the white dots appearing inside the circles after you've been staring at it too long) and into a wobble-skinned square before coming to rest as the grid of circles that we all know and love. How did I achieve this? Quite simply really...

First I removed the initial random factor, taking out the `scale = random` line and replacing the following two lines with these:

```
this[counter]._xscale = 1;
this[counter]._yscale = 1;
```

Next, I altered the `enterFrame` code to this:

```
counter = total+1;
sizer++;
while( counter-- ) {
   if ( this[counter]._xscale < 200 ) {
     scale = sizer + random(40);
     this[counter]._xscale = scale;
     this[counter]._yscale = scale;
   }
}
```

Rather than steadily increasing the scale here, I've added a random element. The key is that the `sizer` variable is constantly increasing so that ultimately the scale of every circle will be 200.

grid 06

The code is exactly the same, but I changed the graphic from a filled circle to an empty one with just an outline to create new patterns.

grid 07

In this example, the grid structure itself becomes much harder to identify because of the rotation of the circles, but it's still there. I moved the circle away from its registration point to give the movie a semi-chaotic orbital feel. The first thing I did was to change `xNumber` and `yNumber` to 10 and brought back the old `rotationAmount = 3` line. I brought the scaling code back in to the `for` loop as well:

```
for (y=0; y<yNumber; y++) {
   for (x=0; x<xNumber; x++) {
     counter++;
     this.attachMovie("atomContainer", counter, counter);
     this[counter]._x = x*gridSpacing;
     this[counter]._y = y*gridSpacing;
     scale = random(150);
     this[counter]._xscale = scale;
     this[counter]._yscale = scale;
     this[counter]._rotation = random(360);
     this[counter].rotation = rotationAmount;
     this[counter].rotation *= random(2) ? -1 : 1;
   }
}
```

Here I've given each circle a random starting rotation, and a random rotation direction. I also changed the `enterFrame` code to this:

```
onClipEvent(enterFrame) {
   counter = total+1;
   while( counter– ) {
     this[counter]._rotation += this[counter].rotation;
   }
}
```

grid 08

In this iteration I decided to try using letters instead of shapes. I changed `atom` into a dynamic text box, set to the variable name `text`, with a capital 'A' in it initially. I then added the following code to the `atom` clip:

```
onClipEvent(keyDown) {
   text = String.fromCharCode( Key.getCode() );
}
```

This code waits for a key press and then changes the dynamic text field to show the character that was just typed. Try it out to see what I mean, different characters can produce some wildly different patterns. You may also want to remove the random element from the scale of each clip to allow for more uniform patterns.

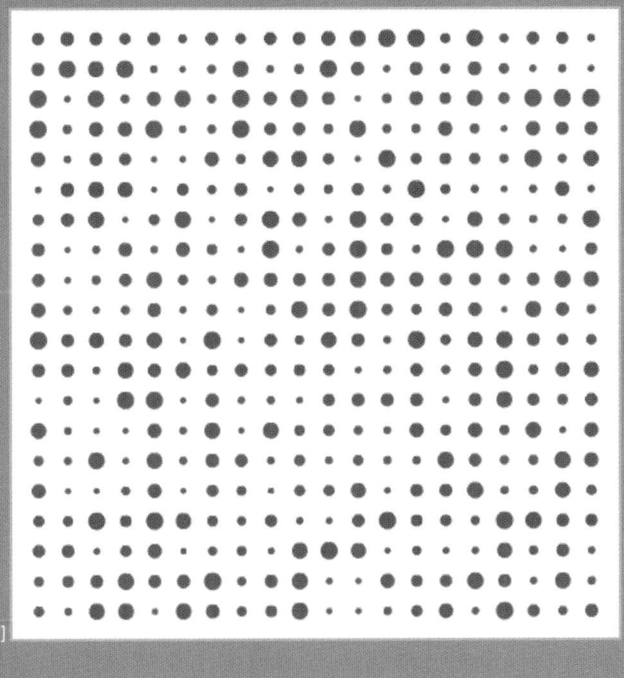

[5]

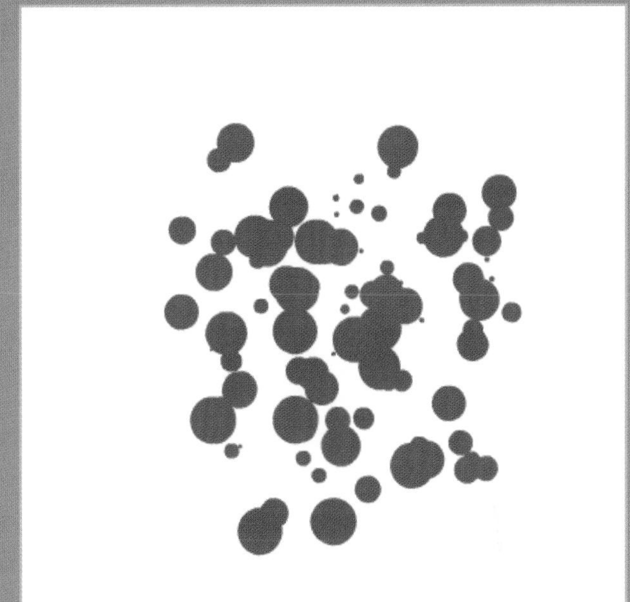

[7]

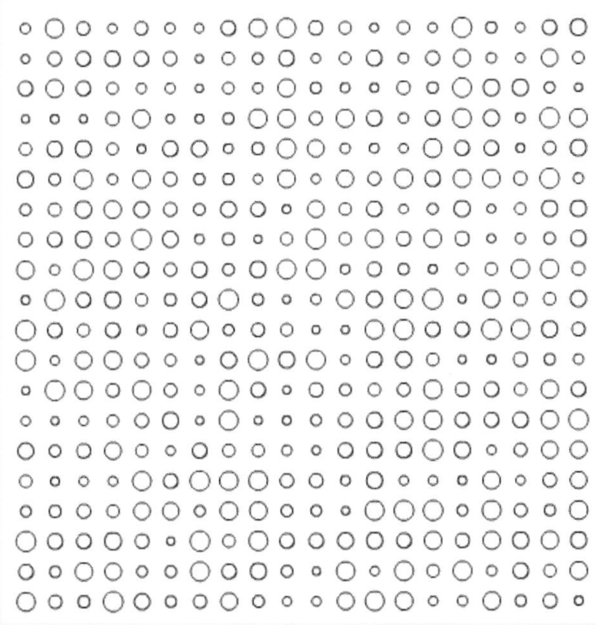

[6]

[8]

grid 09

This experiment gives completely different results, but it's based on exactly the same code. By changing a few lines, we've now got a movie that reacts to mouse movements, and attaches an almost anti-magnetic effect to the mouse pointer. To start with I changed the graphic back to a simple off-center circle, and removed the script on the `atom` clip, then I turned back to the `container` code. Firstly, I took all of the code relating to rotation out of the `load` clip event. Next, I added a line to the end of the `enterFrame` clip event, and changed the following line to get this:

```
rotation=(Math.atan2(_yMouse-this[counter]._y,_xMouse-this[counter]._x)/Math.PI)*180;
this[counter]._rotation = rotation;
```

This finds the rotation value that would be used to point the clip to the mouse position, but because the clips are off-center, they instead appear to recoil away from the mouse. Try this with different shapes and positions, as it can create some very strange patterns.

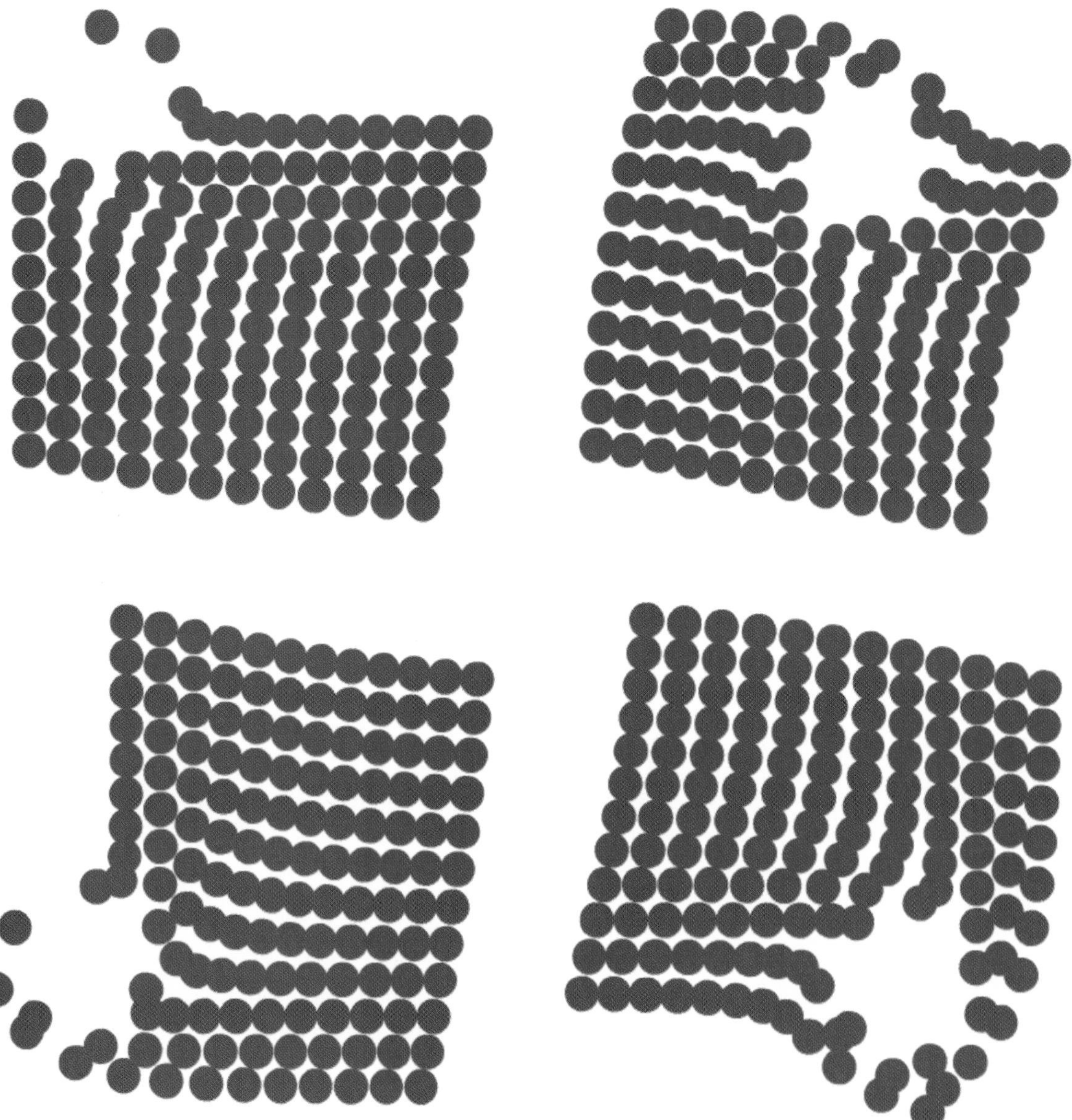

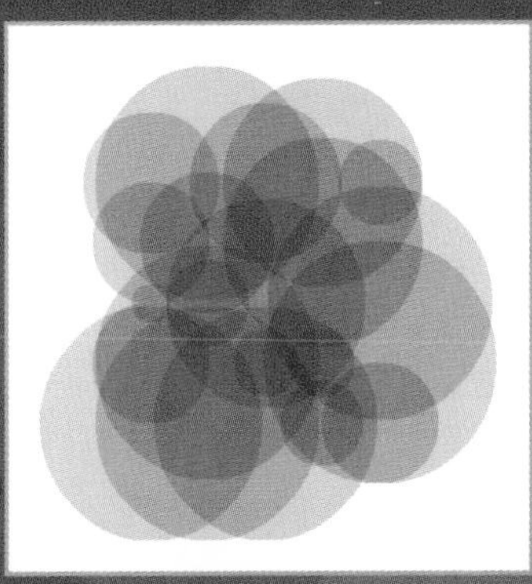

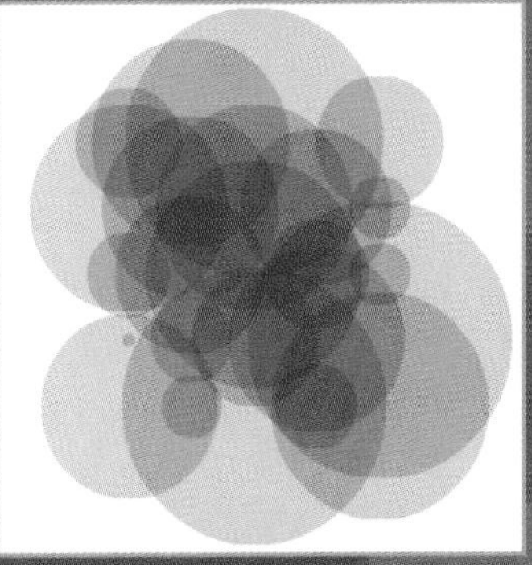

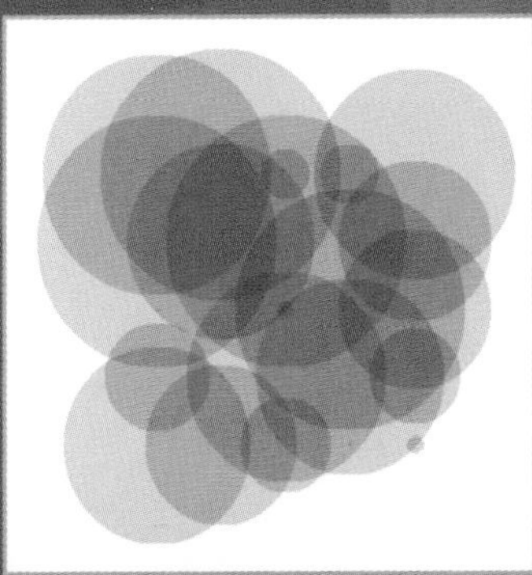

grid 10

Back to basics again for this one, removing all of those mouse activated shenanigans. I've reduced the **xNumber** and **yNumber** to 5, and raised the **gridSpacing** to 40 to allow for the larger circles that I'll be making. The main change is in the **atomContainer** wrapper clip, but I also changed the main **enterFrame** clip event to this:

```
onClipEvent(enterFrame) {
    i++;
    _root.mamaSin = Math.sin(i*(Math.PI/180));
}
```

In this code we're just continuously running a sine wave and storing the value in a variable on the root called **mamaSin**. This value is then picked up by the code on the **atom** clip itself:

```
onClipEvent (load) {
    permV = random(15)+1;
}
onClipEvent (enterFrame) {
    v = permV*_root.mamaSin;
    i += v;
    angle = Math.cos(i*(Math.PI/180));
    // turn value from -1 to 1 range into 0 to 1 range
    angle++;
    angle *= 0.5;
    _xscale = angle*100;
    _yscale = angle*100;
}
```

Here we start off by initializing a new variable, **permV**, this is our random factor that makes each circle different from the others. We then multiply our random number by the current **mamaSin**, and use this to set the scale of **atom**.

Try experimenting with different shapes with this one, it can produce some exceptionally interesting results.

SPRINGS

People seem to take some sort of inherent pleasure in watching objects oscillating. There's something about that chaos coming to rest in harmony and structure that fits with the psyche. Humans like to find patterns in things, and it's even better when those things find patterns for themselves. In this set of pieces, we'll create, and explore, a simple implementation of spring motion.

The movie consists of 3 clips: `container`, `atomContainer`, and `atom`. `container` holds the code that dynamically creates all the other clips, `atomContainer` holds the code that controls the spring motion for each atom, and contains `atom` as well. `atom` is the actual clip that you will see in motion. This structure may seem a little convoluted at first, but you'll see later on how useful it can be. We could have simply had a single clip that controlled everything in a two-frame loop on the main timeline, but I think this solution is a bit more elegant, and certainly more portable since everything happens inside a single `container` clip.

Let's first look at the code on top of `container` that creates the grid of objects:

```
onClipEvent (load) {
  canvasWidth = 550;
  canvasHeight = 550;
  xNumber = 5;
  yNumber = 5;
  total = xNumber*yNumber;
  gridSpacing = 40;

  for (y=0; y<yNumber; y++) {
    for (x=0; x<xNumber; x++) {
      counter++;
      this.attachMovie("atomContainer", counter, counter);
      this[counter]._x = x*gridSpacing;
      this[counter]._y = y*gridSpacing;
    }
  }

  _x = (canvasWidth-(gridSpacing*xNumber))/2;
  _y = (canvasHeight-(gridSpacing*yNumber))/2;
}
```

The code above has already been described in the "In and Out of the Grid" section, so let's instead take a closer look at the code that lives in `atomContainer`:

```
onClipEvent (load) {
  xHome = _x;
  yHome = _y;
  zHome = 100;
  springiness = .2;
  decay = .8;
}
onClipEvent (enterFrame) {
  y = ((yHome-_y)*springiness)+(y*decay);
  _y += y;
  x = ((xHome-_x)*springiness)+(x*decay);
  _x += x;
  z = ((zHome-_xscale)*springiness)+(z*decay);
  _xscale += z;
  _yscale += z;
  _alpha = z+100;
}
onClipEvent (keyDown) {
  _x = random(550)-225;
  _y = random(400)-200;
  z = random(200)-100;
}
onClipEvent (mouseDown) {
  _x = random(550)-225;
  _y = random(400)-200;
  z = random(200)-100;
}
```

The key variables

xHome and yHome – the coordinates that this clip will always come back to. Since we've set up the grid already, the place where this clip resides is where we want it to always come back to, so we'll set xHome and yHome to the current x and y position of this clip
zHome – represents the "depth" of the clip, or how far forward and backwards the clip will travel in space.
springiness – how tightly wound the spring action will be, and therefore how quickly the spring moves
decay – determines how quickly the spring will get back to its original position (xHome and yHome), that is, the amount of oscillations it will make. Note that decay must be a number less than 1 or the spring motion will go on forever (not necessarily a bad thing, but I just thought you should know)

Now we get to the meat of the code. For every enterFrame clip event, we determine the new x, y, and z coordinates of the object. Since the computer screen is a two-dimensional surface, we've got to fake a z or depth coordinate by scaling the clip as well as altering its alpha setting – the further back we send the object, the more we'll reduce the scaling and alpha settings of the clip.

The formula we use to create the spring motion is the same for each dimension. Before the formula is explained let's take a quick look at the keyDown and mouseDown clip events. They both have the same code in them, when you click your mouse or hit the keyboard the object is sent to a random destination in every dimension. This is the equivalent of pulling the end of a spring and letting go. Now we're ready to see how the formula works. It looks like this:

```
change = ((home position - current position) * springiness) + (last change * decay)
```

Once the change is determined, we add it to the current position. By the nature of the formula, the current position will eventually wind up back at the home position. If you feel like the formula is too complicated to understand, don't freak out. I've included an extra flash file for download (springgraph.fla) to help visualize how the formula works.

Iterations

spring 02

Here I changed the shape of the atom clip to be a square instead of a circle. The container code is the same, but I made a few alterations to the atom code to allow for some rotation. I removed the x and y code from all of the clip events, leaving only z, xscale and yscale, and alpha. I then added this line to the load clip event:

```
rotationDirection = random(2) ? -1 : 1;
```

...and this line to the enterFrame clip event:

```
_rotation = rotationDirection * z;
```

This means that now when the user starts the oscillations going, instead of the shape moving pendulously, it now rotates back and forth on the spot. I also changed the springiness to .3 and the decay to .9 for aesthetic effect.

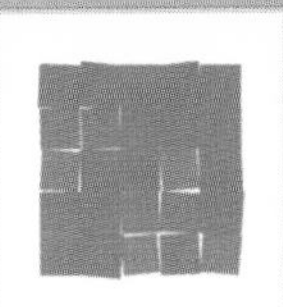

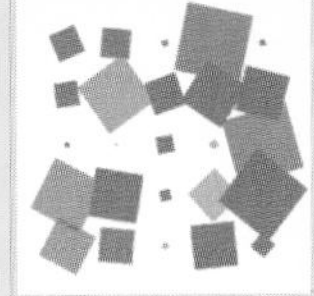

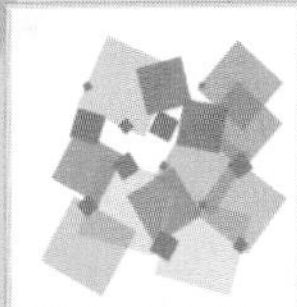
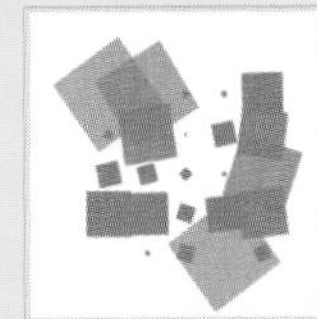

spring 03

For this experiment I changed the graphic again, this time to a pentagon. I also added a color object to give each atom a random color when they first appear. I set gridSpacing to 45 to give a larger gap between the shapes. The main change though is the addition of the color object code to the end of the inner for loop; I also added a line to set the initial rotation to a random value:

```
this[counter]._rotation = random(360);
this[counter].c = new Color(this[counter]);
this[counter].c.setRGB(Math.floor(Math.random() * 0x1000000));
```

The last line of this code is a little tricky – Math.random produces a number between 0 and 1; since setRGB expects a 6 digit hex value, then to get a random color from the entire range of colors available, we multiply the random value by a hex value equal to the max color value.

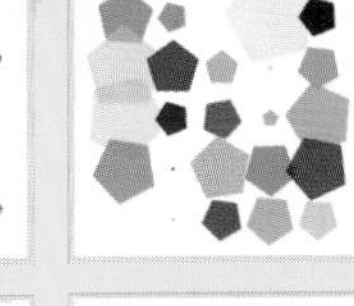
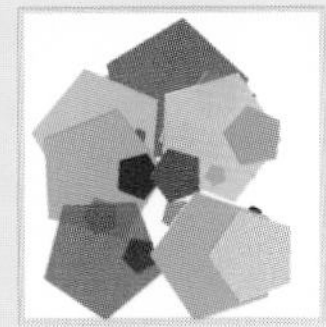
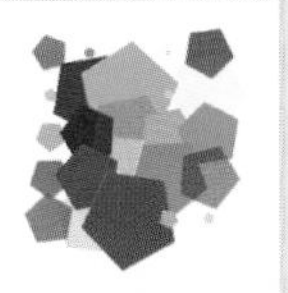
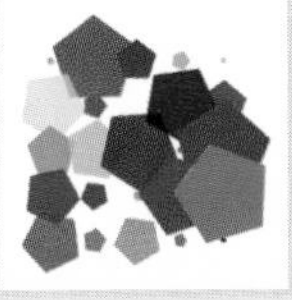
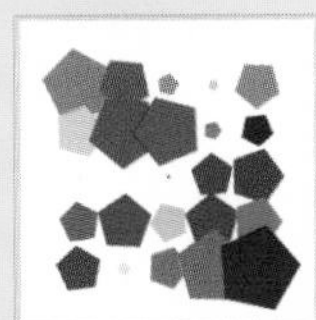

spring 04
Back to circles again. In this iteration I decided to lose the grid altogether, and instead placed all of the objects at the same `x` and `y` position. The `container load` clip event code now looks like this:

```
onClipEvent (load) {
  canvasWidth = 550;
  canvasHeight = 550;
  counter = 25;

  while (counter--) {
    this.attachMovie("atomContainer", counter, counter);
  }

  _x = canvasWidth/2;
  _y = canvasHeight/2;
}
```

For the `atom` code, I returned to the original `spring01` code, but made a couple of small alterations. I removed the `alpha` line, and changed the `key-` and `mouse` events so that everything equals `random(200)-100`.

spring 05
Here I spiced up the graphic a bit more again, and this time I rotated it by a set amount each time to give it a bit of variety. I changed the `container` code by altering the `counter` line to read:

```
total = counter = 25;
```

I also added this line to the while loop to set the initial rotation of the clips:

```
this[counter]._rotation = (360/total)*counter;
```

The only change that I made to the `atom` code was to put the `alpha` line back in.

spring 06
Following on the gridless theme, I decided to try adding in the Blobs code, and structure, from my earlier experiments. The `container` code is pretty similar, the only major additions being a `for` loop rather than a `while` loop with the following code in it:

```
for(counter=1; counter<=total; counter++) {
  this.attachMovie("edgeContainer", counter, counter);
  this.attachMovie("atomContainer", counter+(total+1), counter+(total+1));
}
```

...and a change to the line before it to just `total = 25`, as there's no need to define `counter` here anymore. There is also not much change to the `atom` code, I changed `decay` to be `.9`, and removed the last 3 lines of `z` code from the `enterFrame` clip event. We then have the new `edgeContainer` symbol containing `edge` with the following code on it:

```
onClipEvent(load) {
  me = Number(_parent._name);
  me += _root.container.TOTAL;
  me++;
}
onClipEvent(enterFrame) {
  _x = _root.container[me].atom._x;
  _y = _root.container[me].atom._y;
}
```

spring 07
In this iteration I simply commented out the first two lines of the `atom enterFrame` code that control the `y` positioning, everything else is the same:

```
//y = ((yHome-_y)*springiness)+(y*decay);
//_y += y;
```

This gives the whole thing a nicely different vertical column effect.

[04]

[05]

[06]

[07]

spring 08

In this experiment I returned to the same code from `spring02.fla`. I changed the graphic to add a dynamic text box over the square set to the variable, `text`. The only amendment that I made to the `container` code was to set the `gridSpacing` to `50`, the rest of the changes all come on the `atom` code. I removed both of the rotation lines, changed the `springiness` to `.2`, and the `alpha` to `z+50`. I added the following line to the `enterFrame` clip event:

```
text = Math.ceil(_xscale);
```

This simply sets the dynamic text boxes to show the scale of their parent squares. The other big change that I made was to the behavior of the squares themselves, rather than returning back to their original size when the user takes an action, they now go to a random size set in `zHome`. I achieved this by altering the code in the `key-` and `mouseDown` clip events to equal this:

```
zHome = random(250) - 175;
```

spring 09

Here I decided to go in a completely different direction again, but following the same theme of re-using old code from my earlier experiments. This time I decided to take the line drawing code from the Lines experiment. Instead of atoms, we've now got lines, but the structure is exactly the same. Here's the code that's now on the `container` clip:

```
onClipEvent (load) {
  _highquality = false;

  function paintFunction () {
    counter++;
    this.attachMovie("lineContainer", counter, counter);
    maxDistance = 15*random(10);
    minDistance = 2;
    dir = random(2) ? 1 : -1;
    xEnd = x+(dir*(minDistance+random(maxDistance)));
    dir = random(2) ? 1 : -1;
    yEnd = y+(dir*(minDistance+random(maxDistance)));
    this[counter]._xscale = xEnd-x;
    this[counter]._yscale = yEnd-y;
    x = xEnd;
    y = yEnd;
    if (counter>50) {
      paint = null;
    }
  }
  paint = paintFunction;
}
onClipEvent (enterFrame) {
  paint();
}
onClipEvent(mouseMove) {
  _rotation = _root._xmouse;
}
```

I won't go over it again, as it's already been explained in the Lines section. All of our springy code is now contained on the `line` clip. This code is almost exactly the same as that on the `spring01 atom` clip, the only changes being the addition of these two lines to the end of the `load` clip event:

```
_xscale = 0;
_yscale = 0;
```

...and the alteration of the x and y positioning code in the user action sections. These are now both set to this:

```
_x = random(550);
_y = random(400);
```

spring 10

There's no code difference in this example, but by changing the graphic from a rectangle to a small off-center circle, you get an effect that's almost like a pseudo reflective pool.

spring 11

Here I went back to the original code once more, and then added the ability to draw your own patterns with the mouse. Have a play with it to see what I mean. The main change to the code is on the `container` clip, where I added all of the extra functionality to the end:

```
onClipEvent (enterFrame) {
  if (down == 1) {
    this[record]._x = _xmouse;
    this[record]._y = _ymouse;
    record++;
    if ( record > total) {
      record = 1;
    }
  }
}
onClipEvent(mouseUp) {
  down = 0;
}
onClipEvent(mouseDown) {
  down = 1;
}
```

This code simply places the atom at the current cursor position when the mouse is pressed, and cycles round replacing old clips when it comes reaches the `total` limit. The only other modification that I made was in the `atom` code. Here I just removed the `mouseDown` clip event because I was already using the mouse to draw with, and I didn't want it springing all over the place while I was trying to draw. All of the spring triggering is now done with the keyboard.

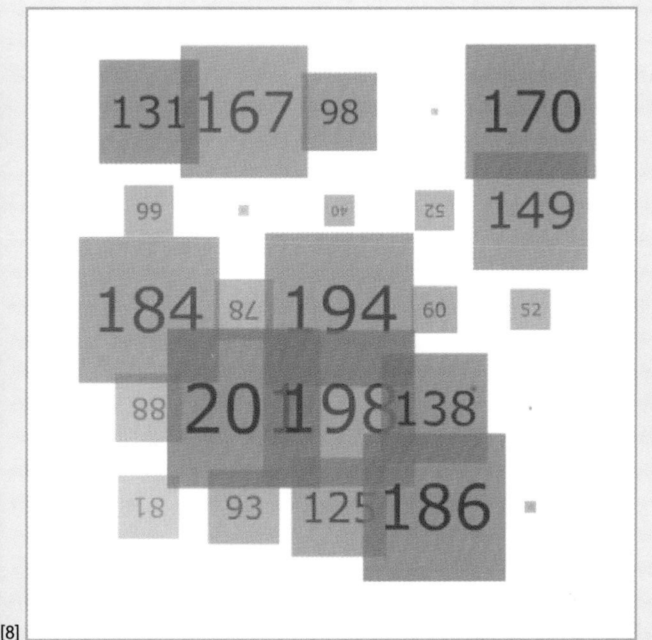

[8]

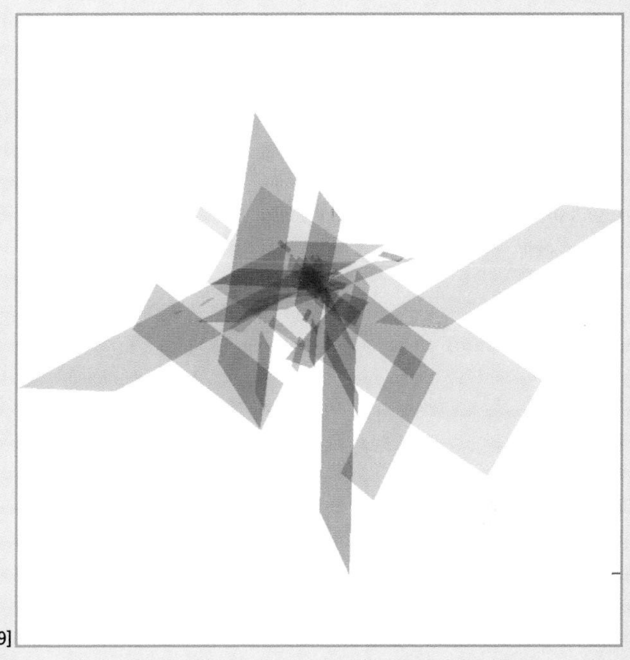

[9]

[10]

[11]

BLOBS

In this experiment, I used a relatively simple technique to create the illusion of individual clips merging with each other. In this first piece, the circular objects move horizontally in fits and starts, creating "new" objects as they merge with each other.

The piece consists of three clips: the now familiar `container`, `ball`, which is simply a white circle placed in the center of the clip, and `edge`, which is a slightly larger sized circle, the edge of which will become the "visible" portion of the piece.

All of the code lives on `container`:

```
onClipEvent(load) {
  canvasWidth = 500;
  canvasHeight = 400;
  total = 20;
  for(i=1; i<=total; i++) {
    this.attachMovie("ball",i+total,i+total);
    ball = this[i+total];
    ball._x = random(canvasWidth);
    ball._y = random(canvasHeight/2)-(canvasHeight/4);
    ball.vx = random(60);
    this.attachMovie("edge",i,i);
    this[i]._x = ball._x;
    this[i]._y = ball._y;
  }
  leftBounds = this[1]._width * -1;
  rightBounds = this[1]._width + canvasWidth;
}

onClipEvent(enterFrame) {
  for (i=1; i<=total; i++) {
    ball = this[i+total];
    ball._x += ball.vx;
    if ( ball._x > rightBounds ) {
      ball._x = leftBounds;
    }
    this[i]._x = ball._x;

    ball.vx *= 0.8;
    if ( ball.vx < 0.00001 ) {
      ball.vx = random(60);
    }
  }
}
```

After setting up the width and height of the canvas and determining how many clips we'll use, we create the clips inside a `for` loop. Notice that the `ball` clip is created at a higher depth than the `edge` clip, and then the `edge` clip is placed in the same x and y position as the `ball` clip. This is the main component to creating the "blobs" effect – because all of the `ball` clips are at a higher depth than all of the edge clips, the `ball` clips will always cover any of the edges that they come in contact with.

Notice the unique `vx` variable (short for velocity of x) that is created for each ball. This random value determines how quickly the clip will travel. Looking at the `enterFrame` clip event, we see that for every ball object, we increase its `x` value by it's own `vx` variable and then check to see if it's off screen. (When the left and right boundaries were set up at the end of the `load` clip event, the width of the object was taken into account so that the object is fully off-screen before it is moved to the other edge of the screen.) Once the bounds are checked, the `edge` clip (`this[i]`) is moved to the same position as the `ball`. Finally, the velocity variable is multiplied by a number smaller than 1 (.8 in this case) so as to create a cheap ease-out motion effect. The `if` statement checks to see when `vx` gets very low, and when it does it sets a new velocity for the clip.

n this iteration I introduced some new shapes for the blobs. I did this by creating new frames in the ball ınd edge clips with the new shapes in them, and then randomly choosing a frame in the code to display he different shapes. This is a really easy way to experiment with new shapes and forms without having o go in and change any of the code. I changed both instances of the `vx` variable to equal `random(100)` ather than `random(60)` so that the shapes would shift quicker across the screen. The only additions hat I made to the code are in the `load` clip event where I added the shape selection script, and also ome code to give the shapes a random rotation. These actions go at the end of the `for` loop in the oad clip event:

```
ball._rotation = random(360);
this[i]._rotation = ball._rotation;

ball.gotoAndStop(random(ball._totalFrames)+1);
this[i].gotoAndStop(ball._currentFrame);
```

ou can play around and add as many different shapes as you like now and the code will automatically ccommodate this and randomly select them to display. The only thing to remember to do is the edge or your shape as well as the shape itself.

blobs 03

Here I decided to go a different way and allow the shapes a complete run of the screen rather than just etting them go from left to right. I also went back to only using circles, so I removed the rotation and rame selection code that I added last time. I'll go through the changes that I made to the code split between the two clip events, starting with `load`. First of all, I changed `total` to 25 because I was using nore of the screen so I wanted more shapes to fill it with. Next, in the `for` loop, I changed `ball._y` to equal `random(canvasHeight)` because I wanted them to occupy the whole screen rather than just a ixed portion of it. Following this, I altered the `ball.vx` line and added a new `ball.vy` line to get this:

```
ball.vx = random(3) + (random(2) ? -1: 1);
ball.vy = random(3) + (random(2) ? -1: 1);
```

Here we simply give each ball a random `x` and `y` speed: The final changes that I made to the `load` clip event came right at the end where I added top and bottom boundaries to the existing left and right ones:

```
topBounds = this[1]._height * -1;
bottomBounds = this[1]._height + canvasHeight;
```

Now onto the `enterFrame` clip event code. Here I simply added `y` code the same as the existing `x` code, and new bounds checking code for the balls' new movement. I also removed the lines that changed the ball speed, giving it a smooth, rather than an easing, motion. The new `for` loop code looks like this:

```
for (i=1; i<=total; i++) {
  ball = this[i+total];
  ball._x += ball.vx;
  ball._y += ball.vy;
  if ( ball._x > rightBounds ) {
    ball._x = leftBounds;
  }
  if ( ball._x < leftBounds ) {
    ball._x = rightBounds;
  }
  if ( ball._y > bottomBounds ) {
    ball._y = topBounds;
  }
  if ( ball._y < topBounds ) {
    ball._y = bottomBounds;
  }
  this[i]._x = ball._x;
  this[i]._y = ball._y;
}
```

blobs 04

In this experiment I made all the balls start from the center of the canvas and explode out of it at a greater speed than last time. Here are the simple changes that I made; they're all in the `load` clip event code:

```
ball._x = canvasWidth/2;
ball._y = canvasHeight/2;
ball.vx = random(6) + (random(2) ? -1: 1);
ball.vy = random(6) + (random(2) ? -1: 1);
```

blobs 05

I radically changed the code in this iteration to distribute the clips evenly in a line across the canvas and have them rotating depending on mouse position. This gives the effect of two morphing lines where the shapes themselves begin to become indistinct. This could be made more so by covering one half of the canvas with a blank shape on a higher level leaving only one line morphing away merrily. Here's the complete code for this experiment:

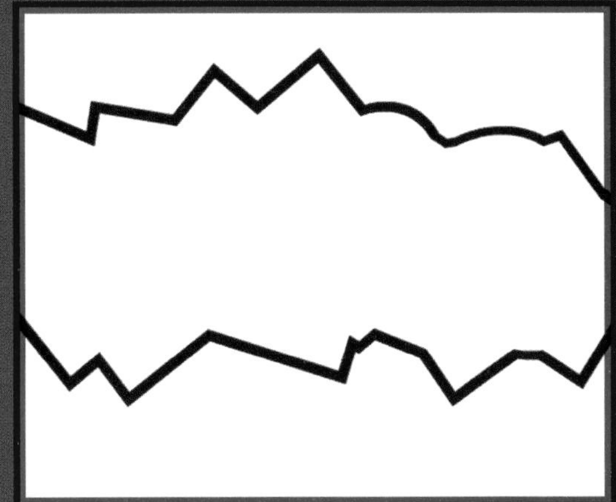

```
onClipEvent(load) {
  canvasWidth = 500;
  canvasHeight = 400;
  total = 25;
  for(i=1; i<=total; i++) {
    this.attachMovie("ball",i+total,i+total);
    ball = this[i+total];
    ball._x = i * 20;
    ball._y = random(100)-50;
    this.attachMovie("edge",i,i);
    this[i]._x = ball._x;
    this[i]._y = ball._y;
    ball.direction = random(2) ? -1 : 1;
    ball._rotation = random(360);
    this[i]._rotation = ball._rotation;
    ball.gotoAndStop(random(ball._totalFrames)+1);
    this[i].gotoAndStop(ball._currentFrame);
  }
}

onClipEvent(enterFrame) {
  for (i=1; i<=total; i++) {
    ball = this[i+total];
    ball._rotation += (((_root._xmouse-200)*.05)*ball.direction);
    this[i]._rotation = ball._rotation;
  }
}
```

Most of this code should be self-explanatory, and you'll notice that I brought back the frame selection code for choosing new shapes from `blobs02`. One new addition worth pointing out is the new `ball.direction` code, which just sets the direction of the shape rotation depending on which side of the center of the canvas that the mouse cursor is in.

blobs 06

This is similar to the last experiment, but rather than having the clips in a line, I distributed them randomly around the screen, and they now spin uniformly rather than being based on mouse position. I also added a new feature where the user can just click the mouse to reposition the shapes instead of having to rerun the entire movie. The only changes that I made to the `load` clip event were to remove the `ball.direction` code, and to change the `x` and `y` lines to set a random starting position:

```
ball._x = random(canvasWidth);
ball._y = random(canvasHeight);
```

Again, there was very little change to the `enterFrame` clip event, where I simply set the shape rotation to an increment rather than being mouse based:

```
ball._rotation++;
```

The major change comes with the addition of a new clip event for when the user presses the mouse button. The code in here is very similar to the `load` clip event code, so it shouldn't need explaining:

```
onClipEvent(mouseDown) {
   for(i=1; i<=total; i++) {
     ball = this[i+total];
     ball._x = random(canvasWidth);
     ball._y = random(canvasHeight);
     this[i]._x = ball._x;
     this[i]._y = ball._y;
     ball._rotation = random(360);
     this[i]._rotation = ball._rotation;
     ball.gotoAndStop(random(ball._totalFrames)+1);
     this[i].gotoAndStop(ball._currentFrame);
   }
}
```

blobs 07

In this iteration I decided to leave rotation and motion and play about with scaling instead. The shapes now constantly grow in fits and starts. To stop them from just growing out of proportion and out-growing the canvas, I added a toggle so that when the user clicks the mouse they will begin to shrink instead, then grow again when the user next clicks the mouse, and so on, and so on. There is one thing to note here, when the shapes shrink into negative numbers then they start to grow again, because a negative shrink is a grow. I decided to leave this in, as I liked the effect of the pulsing to nothing, and then back out again. The other user control that I added was that instead of having random shapes, every clip is now the same shape and the user swaps between shapes by hitting a key on the keyboard.

With all of this new functionality, there are some major changes to the code. I'll start with the relatively little-changed `load` clip event, and then move on to the major new stuff. I changed `total` to 20 to cut down on over crowding, and below it I added this new line:

```
grow = 1;
```

This new variable is the toggle for whether the shapes are growing or shrinking, we begin with it set to 1 making all of the shapes grow. I changed the `y` position of the shapes to be within a smaller band rather than the whole canvas. They still spread over quite a large area, but the whole thing feels somehow much more manageable and less chaotic like this:

```
ball._y = random(canvasHeight/2)-(canvasHeight/4);
```

Under this, I brought back the old `vx` variable, but this time rather than controlling motion speed, it will control the speed at which the shapes scale.

```
ball.vx = random(70);
```

I removed the rotation code from the loop, and altered the shape selection code so that it started from the first frame instead of a random one:

```
ball.gotoAndStop(1);
this[i].gotoAndStop(1);
```

Now onto the big changes, the `enterFrame` clip event had a major overhaul and now looks like this:

```
onClipEvent(enterFrame) {
   for (i=1; i<=total; i++) {
     ball = this[i+total];
     ball._xscale += (ball.vx*.1);
     ball._yscale += (ball.vx*.1);
     if ( ball._xscale > 400 ) {
       ball._xscale = 400;
       ball._yscale = 400;
     }
     if ( ball._xscale < 1 && vx < 0) {
       ball._xscale = 1;
       ball._yscale = 1;
       vx = 0;
     }
     this[i]._xscale = ball._xscale;
     this[i]._yscale = ball._yscale;

     ball.vx *= 0.8;
     if ( Math.abs(ball.vx) < 0.001 ) {
       ball.vx = random(70) * grow;
     }
   }
}
```

Here I have simply replaced the motion/rotation code with scale code, and added some similar code to our original easing motion code to make the shapes grow in random spurts.

The `mouseDown` clip event has been reduced to just this one line:

```
grow *= -1;
```

This simply toggles the variable `grow` between 1 and -1 whenever the mouse is clicked, which is then used in the easing code above to make the shape grow, or shrink. Finally we have another new clip event to change shapes whenever a key is pressed:

```
onClipEvent(keyDown) {
   for(i=1; i<=total; i++) {
     if ( this[i+total]._currentFrame ==
   ➥this[i+total]._totalFrames ) {
       this[i+total].gotoAndStop(1);
     } else {
       this[i+total].nextFrame();
     }
     this[i].gotoAndStop(this[i+total]._currentFrame);
   }
}
```

This uses fairly straightforward code, just moving along the frames when a key is pressed until it reaches the final frame, and then it loops back to the beginning and starts again.

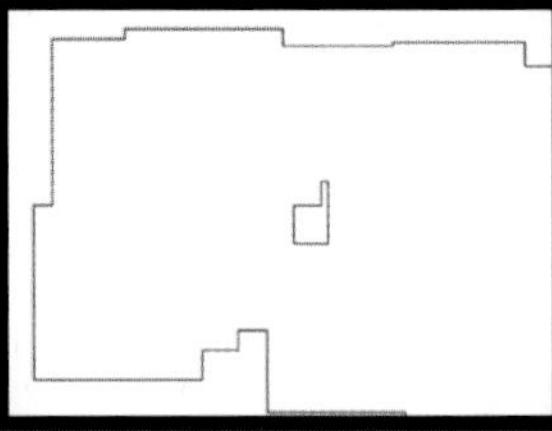

blobs 08

This iteration is similar to the last one, but I've added some simple tweening animation to a couple of the shapes, and started them off set to a random rotation again with these lines at the end of the initial `for` loop:

```
ball._rotation = random(360);
this[i]._rotation = ball._rotation;
```

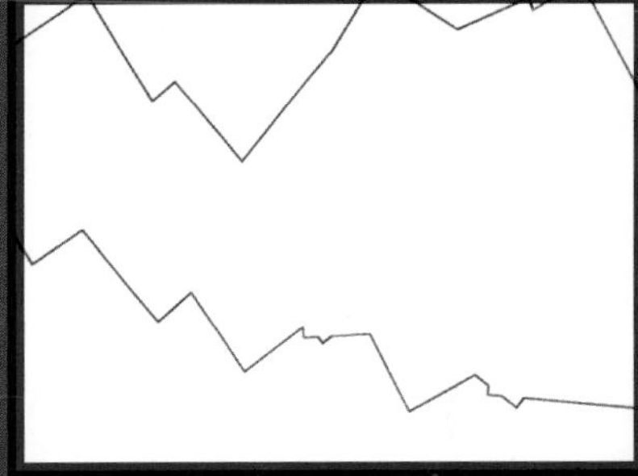

blobs 09

This piece should look familiar if you've been through some of my other experiments, as the code is based on (and is very similar to) the first piece in the `Grids` section. It's basically the same, but with the added code to control the `edge` clip as well as the main shape. Here it is in full:

```
onClipEvent (load) {
  xNumber = 5;
  yNumber = 5;
  total = xNumber*yNumber;
  gridSpacing = 21;
  rotationAmount = 3;
  for (y=0; y<yNumber; y++) {
    for (x=0; x<xNumber; x++) {
      counter++;
      this.attachMovie("atomContainer", counter+total, counter+total);
      this[counter+total]._x = x*gridSpacing;
      this[counter+total]._y = y*gridSpacing;
      this[counter+total]._rotation = random(360);
      this[counter+total]._xscale = 100;
      this[counter+total]._yscale = 70+random(30);
      this[counter+total].velocity = random(4)+1;
      this.attachMovie("edge",counter,counter);
      this[counter]._x = this[counter+total]._x;
      this[counter]._y = this[counter+total]._y;
      this[counter]._rotation = this[counter+total]._rotation;
      this[counter]._xscale = this[counter+total]._xscale;
      this[counter]._yscale = this[counter+total]._yscale;
    }
  }
}

onClipEvent(enterFrame) {
  for(counter = 1; counter<=total; counter++ ) {
    this[counter+total]._rotation += this[counter+total].velocity;
    this[counter]._rotation = this[counter+total]._rotation;
  }
}
```

blobs 10

This final experiment is a mix of most of the experiments we've been looking at: it uses a grid structure with a spring function on each clip, and the blobs method to display it all. Because of this, there is now code in three separate places: on the main `container` clip, on the `atom` clip within `atomContainer`, and on the `edge` clip within `edgeContainer`.

This is the code on `container`. It's basically just the grid layout code:

```
onClipEvent (load) {
  canvasWidth = 550;
  canvasHeight = 550;
  xNumber = 5;
  yNumber = 5;
  total = xNumber*yNumber;
  gridSpacing = 60;
  for (y=0; y<yNumber; y++) {
    for (x=0; x<xNumber; x++) {
      counter++;
      this.attachMovie("edgeContainer", counter, counter);
      this.attachMovie("atomContainer", counter+(total+1), counter+(total+1));
      this[counter]._x = x*gridSpacing;
      this[counter]._y = y*gridSpacing;
      this[counter+total+1]._x = x*gridSpacing;
      this[counter+total+1]._y = y*gridSpacing;
    }
  }
  _x = (canvasWidth-(gridSpacing*xNumber))/2;
  _y = (canvasHeight-(gridSpacing*yNumber))/2;
}
```

The `atom` code is pretty much the same as the code in the `Springs` section, and its explanation can be found there:

```
onClipEvent (load) {
  xHome = _x;
  yHome = _y;
  springiness = .2;
  decay = .9;
}
onClipEvent (enterFrame) {
  y = ((yHome-_y)*springiness)+(y*decay);
  _y += y;
  x = ((xHome-_x)*springiness)+(x*decay);
  _x += x;
}
onClipEvent (keyDown) {
  _x = random(200)-100;
  _y = random(200)-100;
}
onClipEvent (mouseDown) {
  _x = random(200)-100;
  _y = random(200)-100;
}
```

The final code is on the `edge` clip, which basically just makes sure that each `edge` is set to the same `x` and `y` position as its respective `atom`:

```
onClipEvent(load) {
  me = Number(_parent._name);
  me += _root.container.TOTAL;
  me++;
}
onClipEvent(enterFrame) {
  _x = _root.container[me].atom._x;
  _y = _root.container[me].atom._y;
}
```

Andrés Sebastián Yáñez Durán (...lifaros)

I'm an ActionScripter from Chile. There aren't many of us AS coders here, and there aren't many ActionScript jobs either, so I started searching for clients on the Internet instead, developing some applications, and participating on Flash forums.

I have a lot of hobbies – sometimes I work as an electronics engineer on satellite communications and networking, sometimes I work as a painter and sculptor. As you can see, I love both art and math.

Nowadays I work as a freelance ActionScripter for people from the USA and United Kingdom, and I also develop educational Flash math work for a company in Norway.

I enjoy playing with math, and I'm always trying to simulate physical phenomena using ActionScript. The main source of inspiration for me is nature: Physical parameters such as sound, light, temperature, and pressure – all different natural energies that can be measured and plotted, and all heavily centered in math.

Another source of inspiration are Flash math forums, and books regarding math and electronics. I have a lot of books, some of them concerning satellite communications, signals and systems, digital circuits, microprocessors, and so on, and a lot of math books regarding algebra, vectors, geometry and Fourier transformations, and I only have to pick up and dip into any of them to be inspired.

As you already know ActionScript is a powerful tool that can be used to develop cool interactive websites and applications by successfully combining science and design. We don't need to be engineers to deal with engineering, it just takes a little patience and passion. One man's "boring" math is another man's amazing creation.

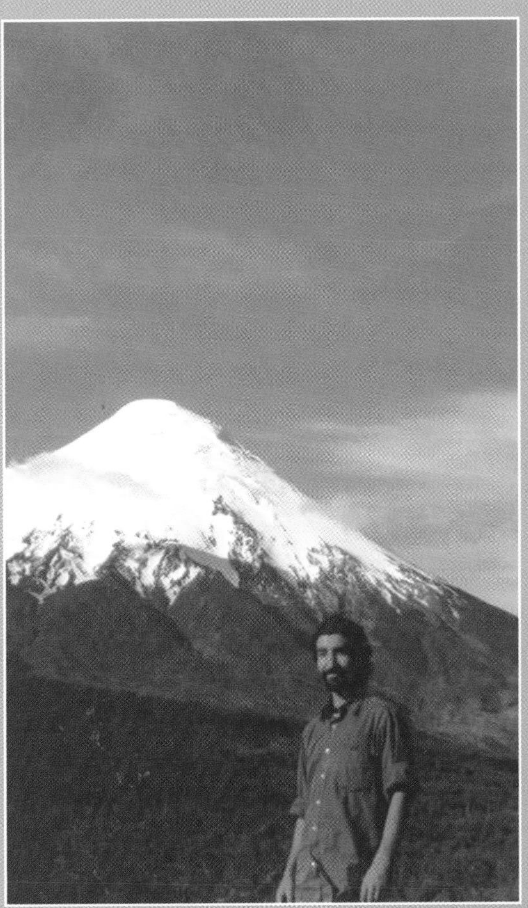

lifaros

The Alien Message

This application combines randomization and symbol design to generate a strange alien message. To accomplish this task, we're going to develop a tiled pattern on the screen, where each alien letter will fit together perfectly with every adjacent letter.

We have three basic types of letters: lateral, corner, and inner, in movieclips with those instance names on the main stage. You can see all of these shapes in the FLA. Notice that I created them all as tessellating shapes, with different shapes as different frames within each of these three main movieclips.

 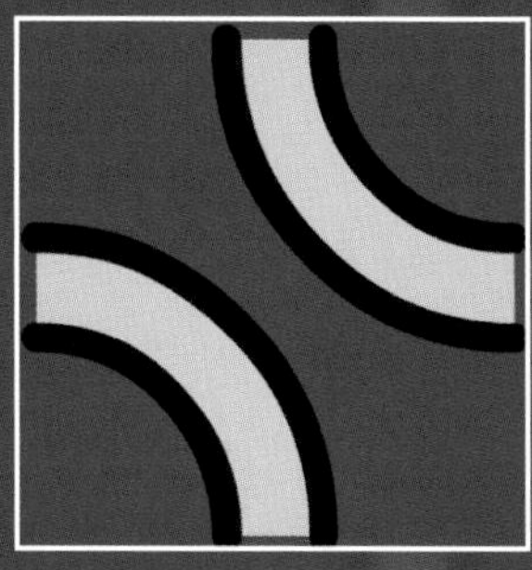 

After creating all of the shapes, the code is used to position them on the stage, and to change them when the user moves the mouse over them. I have a short three-frame loop in my movie to check whether it has all loaded before it displays it. This isn't necessary for the movie however, so I haven't detailed it here. If you're interested you can take a look in the FLA, otherwise all of the following code just goes on the first frame of the root.

```
inner._visible=0;
corner._visible=0;
lateral._visible=0;
columns = 14;
rows = 8;
xpos = 50;
ypos = 60;
width = 39;
cornersymbols=8;
lateralsymbols=15;
innersymbols=9;
q = 1;
for (row=0; row<=rows-1; row++) {
    for (column=0; column<=columns-1; column++) {
     duplicateMovieClip ("inner", "alien"+q, q);
    this["alien"+q].gotoAndStop(random(innersymbols+1));
     if (row == 0) {
       duplicateMovieClip ("lateral", "alien"+q, q);
       this["alien"+q].gotoAndStop(random(lateralsymbols));
     }
     if (row == rows-1) {
       duplicateMovieClip ("lateral", "alien"+q, q);
       this["alien"+q]._rotation = 180;
       this["alien"+q].gotoAndStop(random(lateralsymbols+1));
     }
     if (column == 0) {
       duplicateMovieClip ("lateral", "alien"+q, q);
       this["alien"+q]._rotation = -90;
       this["alien"+q].gotoAndStop(random(lateralsymbols+1));
     }
     if (column == columns-1) {
       duplicateMovieClip ("lateral", "alien"+q, q);
       this["alien"+q]._rotation = 90;
       this["alien"+q].gotoAndStop(random(lateralsymbols+1));
     }
     if (row == 0 && column == 0) {
```

```
        duplicateMovieClip ("corner", "alien"+q, q);
        this["alien"+q]._rotation = 0;
        this["alien"+q].gotoAndStop(random(cornersymbols+1));
       }
       if ((row == rows-1) && column == 0) {
        duplicateMovieClip ("corner", "alien"+q, q);
        this["alien"+q]._rotation = -90;
        this["alien"+q].gotoAndStop(random(cornersymbols+1));
       }
       if (row == 0 && column == columns-1) {
        duplicateMovieClip ("corner", "alien"+q, q);
        this["alien"+q]._rotation = 90;
        this["alien"+q].gotoAndStop(random(cornersymbols+1));
       }
       if (row == rows-1 && column == columns-1) {
        duplicateMovieClip ("corner", "alien"+q, q);
        this["alien"+q]._rotation = 180;
        this["alien"+q].gotoAndStop(random(cornersymbols+1));
       }
       this["alien"+q]._x = width*column+xpos;
       this["alien"+q]._y = width*row+ypos;
       q++;
      }
  }
  stop ();
```

Each of the different shapes within the three main movieclips are on buttons with the following code on:

```
  on (rollOver) {
      gotoAndStop(random(_parent.lateralsymbols)+1);
  }
```

Note that you'll have to enter the name of the correct parent movieclip, so if they're inside the `lateral` movieclip then it's `_parent.lateralsymbols`, if they're in the `corner` clip then it's `_parent.cornersymbols`, and if they're in the `inner` clip, then it's `_parent.innersymbols`. This code just means that when the user runs their mouse over the shape, then another random shape will be chosen to replace it.

The key variables

`columns` = the number of columns of letters
`rows` = the number of rows of letters
`xpos` and `ypos` = the starting position in the top-left hand corner of the screen
`width` = the width of each shape, I set this to one less than their actual width so that they tesselated perfectly
`cornersymbols` = the number of different frames of corner symbols to chose from
`lateralsymbols` = the number of different frames of lateral symbols to chose from
`innersymbols` = the number of different frames of inner symbols to chose from
`q` = a loop counter

After setting the initial variables, the main code sits within two nested `for` loops – one for rows and one for columns. It just loops through this code assigning a random shape of the correct type in the correct place.

Iterations

alien01
First of all, I experimented with different layouts. Here I made a thin vertical message.

columns = 2;
rows = 8;

alien02
Then I went the other way and made a thin horizontal message.

```
columns = 14;
rows = 2;
```

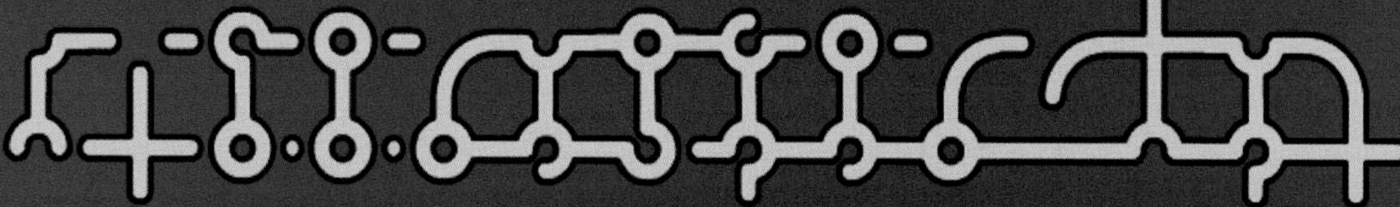

alien03
I settled on a good-sized shape that I've kept for all of the rest of the experiments and set about playing with the numbers of different letters. To start with, I set them all to having only one of each, which gave a nice static pattern.

```
columns = 14;
rows = 4;
cornersymbols = 1;
lateralsymbols = 1;
innersymbols = 1;
```

alien04
I decided to carry on just slowly increasing the number of symbols to see what the different effects were. This one's with two of each symbol. You can make some nice long lines that remind me of those steady-hand coordination games where you have to move a metal ring along a piece of twisting wire with an alarm that goes off if they make contact.

```
cornersymbols = 2;
lateralsymbols = 2;
innersymbols = 2;
```

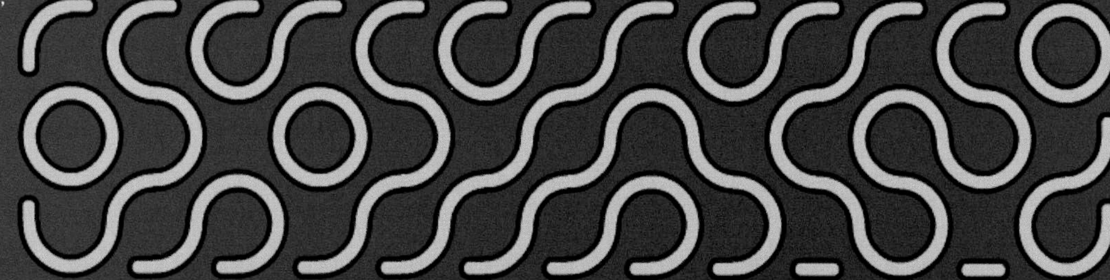

alien05
This one's with three of each symbol.

```
cornersymbols = 3;
lateralsymbols = 3;
innersymbols = 3;
```

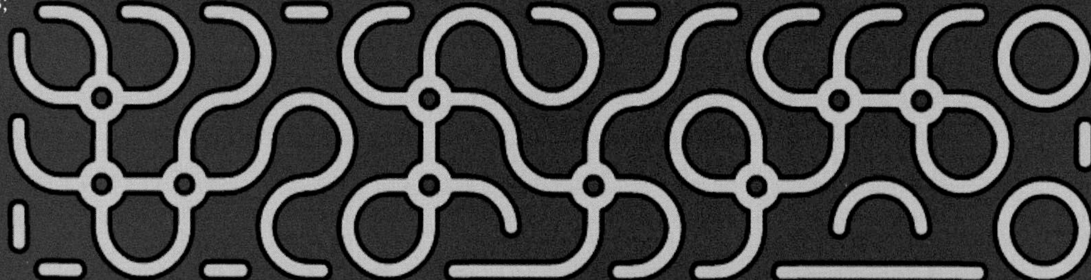

alien06
And this one's with 4 of each symbol.

cornersymbols = 4;
lateralsymbols = 4;
innersymbols = 4;

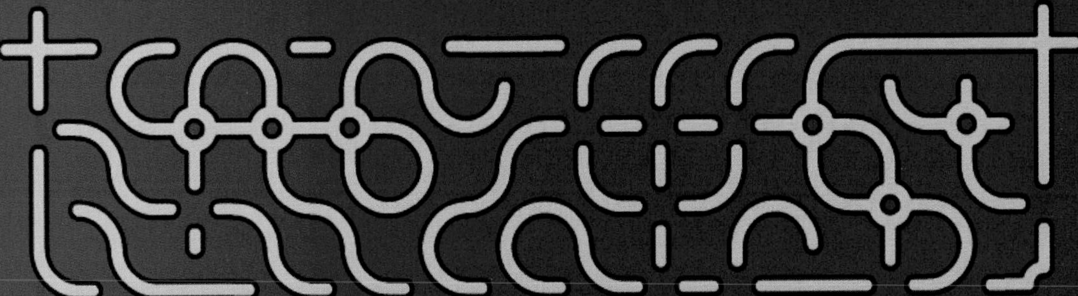

alien07
For the next three experiments I tried out setting two of the letter types to their maximum numbers, but keeping the third at 1, and therefore unchangeable. First of all I tried it with the `innersymbols` set in stone.

cornersymbols = 8;
lateralsymbols = 15;
innersymbols = 1;

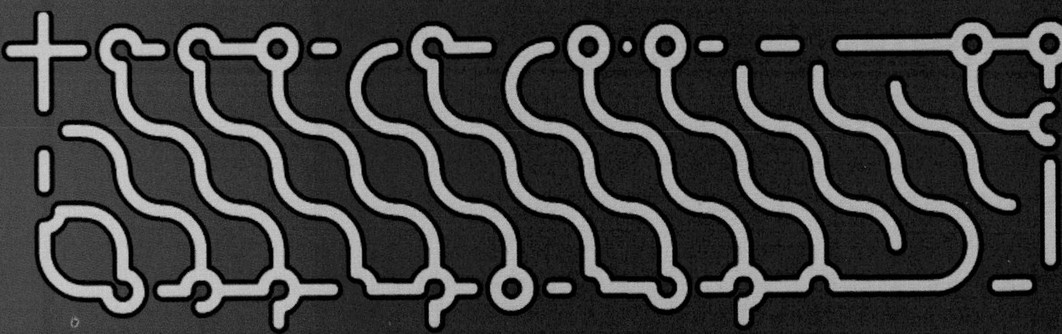

alien08
Next I tried the effect with the corners set so they always remained curved.

cornersymbols = 1;
lateralsymbols = 15;
innersymbols = 9;

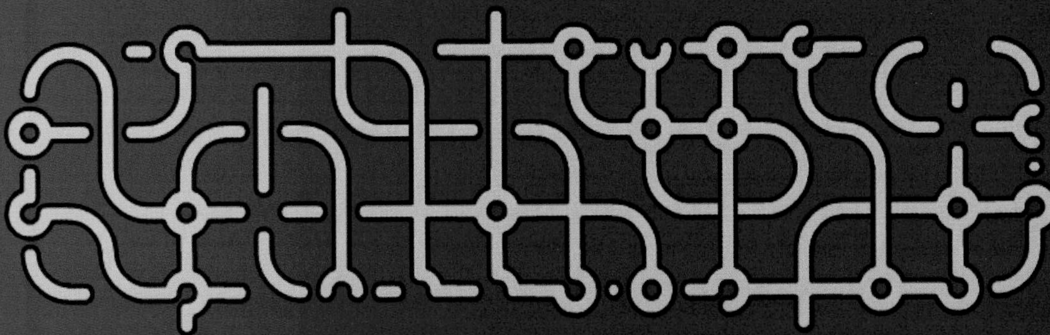

alien09
Finally, I tried leaving the outer lines as curves and letting the user change the inner characters and the corners.

cornersymbols = 8;
lateralsymbols = 1;
innersymbols = 9;

Other things you could do with this would be to play about with some of the other parameters, and of course modify the shape and color of the letters and background to create some cool designs.

The Flag Effect

In this set of experiments we're going to use masking to cut a source image into slices so that we can then control those slices independently. If we use a lot of slices, then we can obtain a soft wave movement like a flag flapping in the wind.

The basic set-up is this: On the main stage there is a movieclip with the instance name, `image`. Inside this clip are two layers, a mask layer containing a simple square graphic, and a masked layer which contains a movieclip with the instance name, `picture`. The `picture` clip simply contains the image that we're going to be working with. Back in the `image` clip, the mask has its center at the center point of the clip, and the `picture` clip has its top-left hand corner at the center point of the clip. That's the main parts in place, the only other thing to add is the code. By the way, I've also added a couple of sliders to my movie to dynamically control the frequency and amplitude. These are simply tied to the `fx` and `fy`, and `ampx` and `ampy` variables on the main stage. They aren't essential to the running of the movie, but you can find the code to them in the FLA if you'd like to add them yourself.

Here's the main code that sits on the first frame of the root:

```
ycenter = 200;
xcenter = 275;
scale = 1;
mode = 0;
slices = 30;
w = 10;
width = scale*image.picture._width;
height = scale*image.picture._height;
if (mode==0){
columns = slices;
rows = 1;
} else{
columns = 1;
rows = slices;
}
cellxsize = width/columns;
cellysize = height/rows;

for (n=0; n<rows*columns; n++) {
  duplicateMovieClip ("image", "image_"+n, n);
  row = int(n/columns);
  column = n%columns;
  myname = this["image_"+n];
  with (myname) {
    picture._width = 100*columns;
    picture._height = 100*rows;
    picture._x = -100*column-50;
    picture._y = -100*row-50;
  }
  myname.row = row;
  myname.column = column;
  myname._x = xcenter+(-width/2)+cellxsize*column+width/(2*columns);
  myname._y = ycenter+(-height/2)+cellysize*row+height/(2*rows);
  myname._xscale = cellxsize+0.3;
  myname._yscale = cellysize+0.3;
}

image._visible = 0;
_quality = "low";
fx = 1;
fy = 1;
ampy = 20;
ampx = 20;
stop ();
```

The other section of code is attached to the **image** clip on the main stage:

```
onClipEvent (load) {
  dtr = Math.PI/180;
  t = 0;
  y0 = _y;
  x0 = _x;
}
onClipEvent (enterFrame) {
  if (_parent.mode == 0) {
    f = _parent.fx*column*(360/_parent.columns);
    _y = y0+_parent.ampy*Math.sin(dtr*(f+_parent.w*t++));
  } else {
    f = _parent.fy*row*(360/_parent.rows);
    _x = x0+_parent.ampx*Math.sin(dtr*(f+_parent.w*t++));
  }
}
```

The key variables

ycenter = the vertical center of the stage
xcenter = the horizontal center of the stage
scale = the scale of the image on screen, setting this to 2 will double the size of the image, and so on
mode = the mode flag, 0 gives horizontal waves, 1 gives vertical waves
slices = the number of sections that the image is sliced into
w = the speed of oscillation
width = the source image width
height = the source image height
columns = the number of columns
rows = the number of rows
cellxsize = the slice width
cellysize = the slice height
fx and **fy** = the wave frequency
ampx and **ampy** = the wave amplitude
dtr = a degrees to radians conversion constant
t = a counter for our position on the sine curve

It works by duplicating the image and the mask, and then repositioning and resizing them respectively. The code on the movieclip then dynamically positions the clip along the sine curve to give a wave effect.

flag01
First of all, I experimented with the number of slices, initially I dropped it to 10 to see what difference a smaller number would make, and got this chunky effect.

```
slices = 10;
```

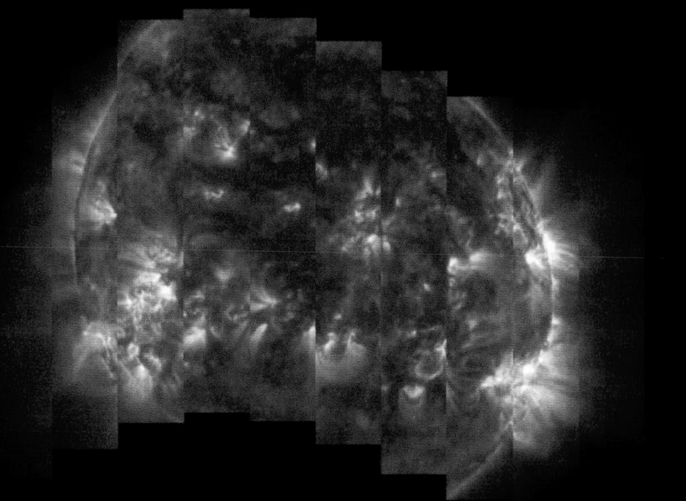

Next I set the number of slices to double its initial value to see how it ran, and how smooth the wave was.

```
slices = 60;
```

flag03
Seeing how smoothly and well the last experiment ran, I decided to double it again and check the effect. This gave a beautifully smo
but the animation was too slow, and Flash began to drop frames.

```
slices = 120;
```

flag04
This time I decided to go the other way, changing to a horizontal wave and increasing the speed.

```
slices = 30;
w = 30;
mode = 1;
```

flag05
In the next series, I played about with the frequency variable to see what difference that made.

```
fy = 2;
```

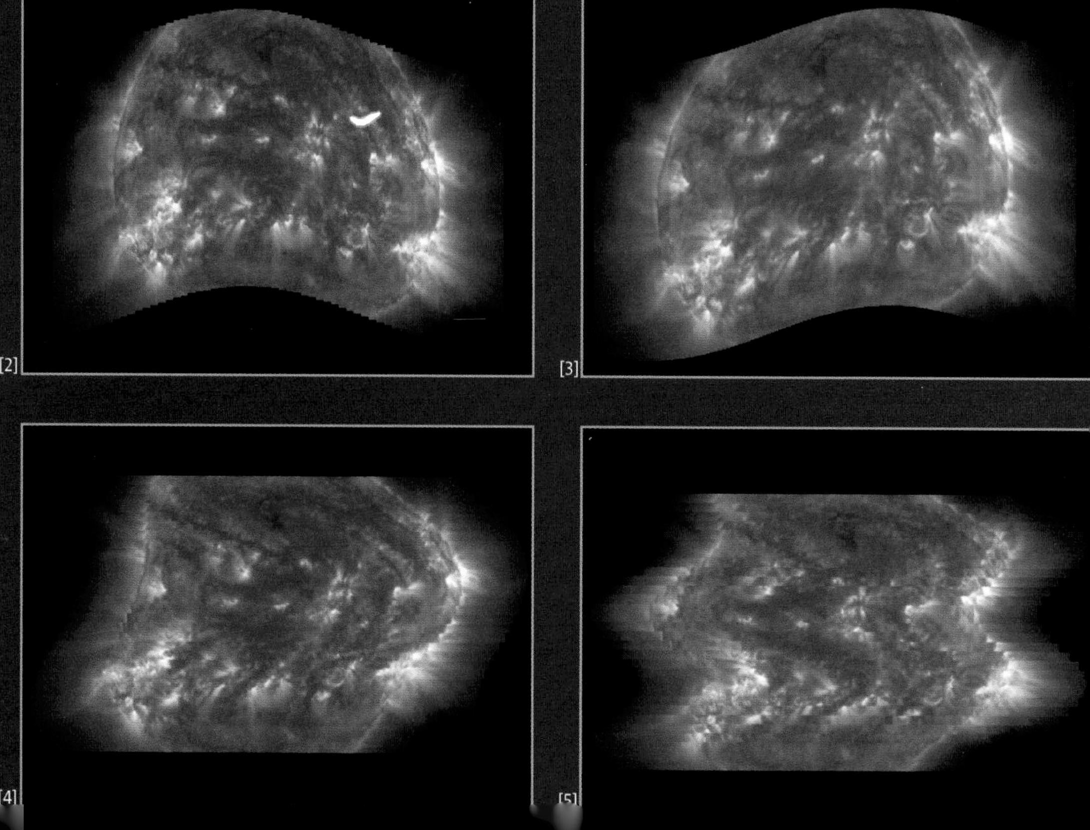

[2] [3]

[4] [5]

flag06

I carried on with the frequency experiment gradually incrementing to see the effect of an increased number of waves.

```
fy = 3;
```

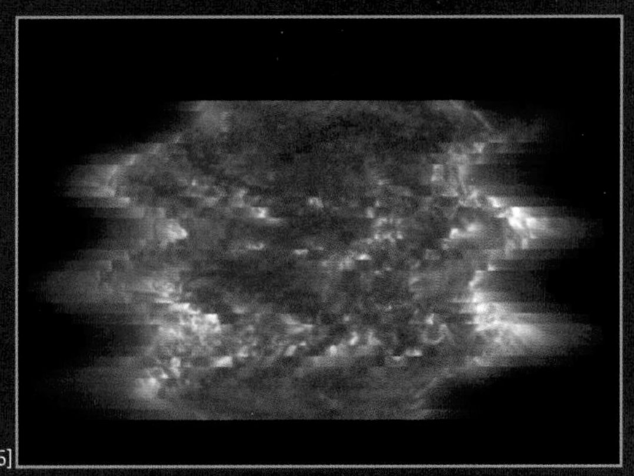

[6]

flag07

Here I set the frequency to 4, and we begin to really lose the shape of the image behind it.

```
fy = 4;
```

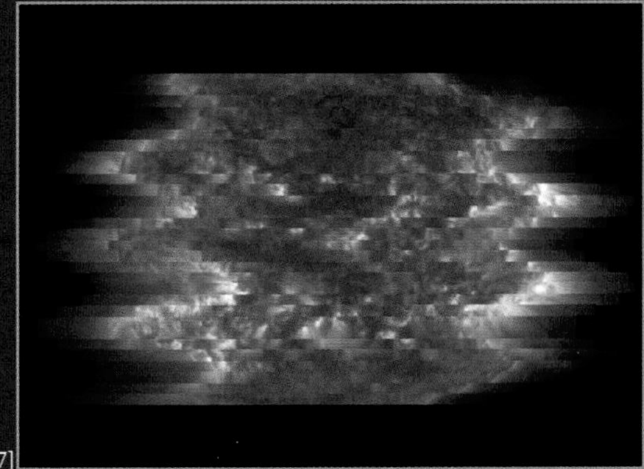

[7]

flag08

After playing with the frequency, I decided to finish up by seeing the effect of changing the amplitude. Setting it low gives the impression of a flag flapping in a stiff breeze.

```
slices = 60;
mode = 0;
fy = 1;
ampx = 5;
```

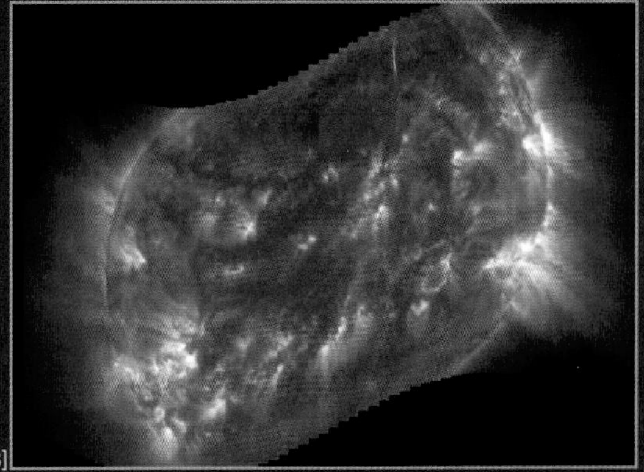

[8]

flag09

Setting the amplitude a lot higher gives the impression of a stronger gale, or someone shaking out a carpet.

```
ampx = 40;
```

There are a lot more things that can be changed, try altering the shape of the mask or the image, you can get some really interesting effects from skewed parallelograms. Another thing to try is changing the formula on the `enterFrame` clip event. By using `tan` instead of `sin` you can achieve some interesting results almost like pages flipping.

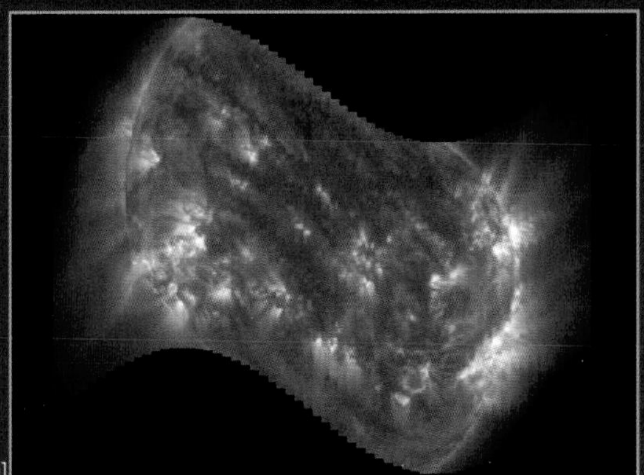

[9]

The Rainbow Flower

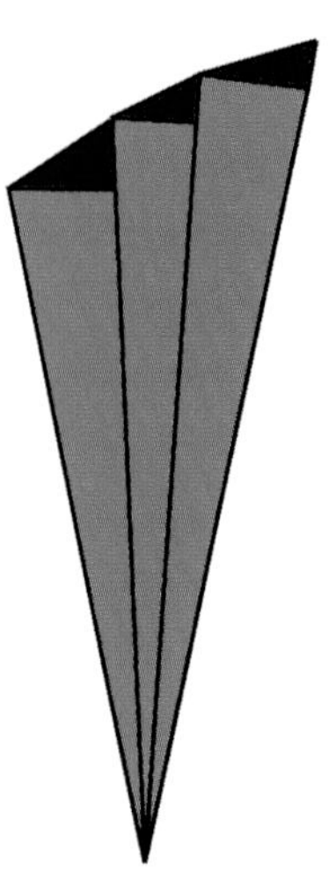

This series of experiments combines two effects – random shape generation and color cycling – to produce some interesting psychedelic flowers. These radial shapes were developed using a Fourier series, and then adding sine waves to achieve a smooth random shape. We then apply a series of color transforms to it to enable the cyclical hue change. The strange shapes are created by using two triangles, resized and placed next to each other to give a smooth outline:

The movie consists of 4 frames: the first creates the shape, the second sets up the color information, and the third and fourth loop to cycle the colors. If you wish to, you can run the movie with just the first frame if you only want to create the shapes and not include the color cycling. If you look in my FLA, you'll also find that I included an initial two-frame loop to check that the movie has fully loaded before displaying it, this isn't essential for the effect, so I haven't described it here, but check my FLA if you'd like to see how it's done.

The movie has two layers, one with four keyframes with all of the code on, and the second containing the graphics. As I said earlier, the graphics consist of two simple 100x100 pixel right-angle triangles inside their own movieclips: one with the instance name `myatriangle`, the inner triangle, and the other called `mybtriangle`, which is the outer triangle. That's it for the graphics layer, now for the code. The code on the first frame looks like this:

```
points = 120;
N = 10;
frequency = 2;
dtr = Math.PI/180;
y = [];
x = [];
amplitude = [];
phase = [];
xcenter = 275;
ycenter = 175;
df = 360/(points-1);
sum = [];
amplitude[0] = 120;
for (i=1; i<=N; i++) {
     amplitude[i] = 50/i;
     phase[i] = -180+random(360);
}
for (i=0; i<points; i++) {
     angle = (i*df-180);
     pointangle = frequency*angle;
     sum[i] = amplitude[0];
     for (j=1; j<=N; j++) {
          sum[i] += amplitude[j]*Math.sin(dtr*(j*pointangle+phase[j]));
     }
     sum[i] = -sum[i];
     x[i] = sum[i]*Math.cos(dtr*angle);
     y[i] = -sum[i]*Math.sin(dtr*angle);
}
for (i=0; i<points-1; i++) {
     mybtriangle.duplicateMovieClip("mybtriangle"+i, i);
     myatriangle.duplicateMovieClip("myatriangle"+i, i+1000);
     sk = Math.abs(sum[i])>Math.abs(sum[i+1]) ? 1 : -1;
     sj = Math.abs(sum[i])>Math.abs(sum[i+1]) ? 1 : 0;
     this["myatriangle"+i]._x = xcenter;
     this["myatriangle"+i]._y = ycenter;
     this["myatriangle"+i]._xscale = -sum[i+sj]*Math.cos(dtr*df);
     this["myatriangle"+i]._yscale = -sk*sum[i+sj]*Math.sin(dtr*(df+0.2));
     this["myatriangle"+i]._rotation = -df*(i+!sj);
     this["mybtriangle"+i]._xscale = sum[i+!sj]-sum[i+sj]*Math.cos(dtr*df);
     this["mybtriangle"+i]._yscale = -sk*sum[i+sj]*Math.sin(dtr*df);
     this["mybtriangle"+i]._rotation = -df*(i+!sj);
     this["mybtriangle"+i]._x = x[i+!sj]+xcenter;
     this["mybtriangle"+i]._y = y[i+!sj]+ycenter;
}
mybtriangle._x=-10000;
myatriangle._x=-10000;
```

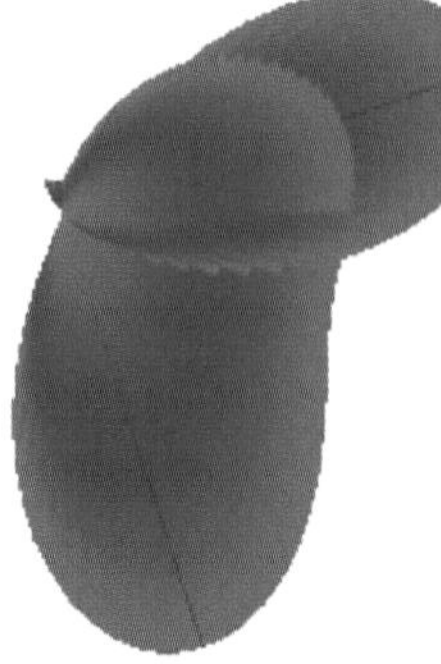

That's all of the clip duplication, data calculation, and drawing done. The second frame has this code on:

```
redstep=10;
bluestep=5;
blueoffsetstep=15;
redoffsetstep=5;
greenoffsetstep=10;
greenstep=15;
red=random(100);
blue=random(100);
blueoffset=random(255);
redoffset=random(255);
greenoffset=random(255);
green=random(100);
```

This just sets up the initial color values. The third frame contains this...

```
play();
for (i=0; i<points-1; i++) {
    myColor = new Color(this["myatriangle"+i]);
    myColorTransform = new Object();
    myColor.setTransform({ra:red, rb:redoffset, ga:green, gb:greenoffset, ba:blue, bb:blueoffset});
    myColor = new Color(this["mybtriangle"+i]);
    myColorTransform = new Object();
    myColor.setTransform({ra:red, rb:redoffset, ga:green, gb:greenoffset, ba:blue, bb:blueoffset});
}
red += redstep;
redstep *= red>100 || red<0 ? -1 : 1;
redoffset += redoffsetstep;
redoffsetstep *= redoffset>255 || redoffset<0 ? -1 : 1;
blue += bluestep;
bluestep *= blue>100 || blue<0 ? -1 : 1;
blueoffset += blueoffsetstep;
blueoffsetstep *= blueoffset>255 || blueoffset<0 ? -1 : 1;
green += greenstep;
greenstep *= green>100 || green<0 ? -1 : 1;
greenoffset += greenoffsetstep;
greenoffsetstep *= greenoffset>255 || greenoffset<0 ? -1 : 1;
```

...which updates the colors using the values that were initialized in the previous frame. Finally the last frame just has this code:

```
prevFrame();
```

This just loops back to the previous frame to carry on updating the colors.

The key variables

`points` = the number of segments
`N` = the number of waves along the outside of the shape
`frequency` = the number of 'petals' that are repeated to make the shape
`dtr` = the degrees to radians conversion constant
`y` = the vertical coordinate array
`x` = the horizontal coordinate array
`amplitude` = the size array
`phase` = the phase array, used in calculating the shape
`xcenter` = the horizontal center
`ycenter` = the vertical center
`df` = the angular amount of drawn shape, so 360 is the full shape, 180 is half the shape, and so on
`sum` = an array for holding various calculations for the drawing of the shape

rainbowflower01
I decided to try a few different sets of settings at different frequencies. First off, I kept everything the same and just altered the frequency. With a setting of 1 you just get a random shape.

```
frequency = 1;
```

rainbowflower02
By increasing the frequency to 3, you can see how each of the petals of the flower repeats itself.

```
frequency = 3;
```

rainbowflower03
Setting the frequency to 5, we begin to get something resembling a flower much more rather than just a blob.

```
frequency = 5;
```

rainbowflower04
I played about with another set of variables, decreasing the number of waves along the edge of the shape, and setting `amplitude[0]` to a negative figure meaning that the flower goes back on itself.

```
frequency = 1;
N = 5;
amplitude[0] = -30;
amplitude[i] = 120/i;
```

rainbowflower05
I then tried these settings again with different frequencies to create some interestingly spiky overlaps.

```
frequency = 3;
```

rainbowflower06
The same settings, but this time with a greater number of petals.

```
frequency = 5;
```

rainbowflower07
In this final series I changed `amplitude` and `N` again, and then ran through another set of `frequency` changes. With `N` and `frequency` set to 1, we get a shape like a kidney bean.

```
frequency = 1;
N = 1;
amplitude[0] = 80;
amplitude[i] = 60/i;
```

rainbowflower08
By setting frequency to 3 we get a simple trifoliate shape, like a clover.

```
frequency = 3;
```

rainbowflower09
Finally, with a frequency of 5, we get a nice basic 5-petalled rainbow flower.

```
frequency = 5;
```

This is just a taster of the shapes that can be created by fiddling with these algorithms. Try experimenting with some of the other variables, or simply just changing the shape and color of the two triangles to give some radically different results.

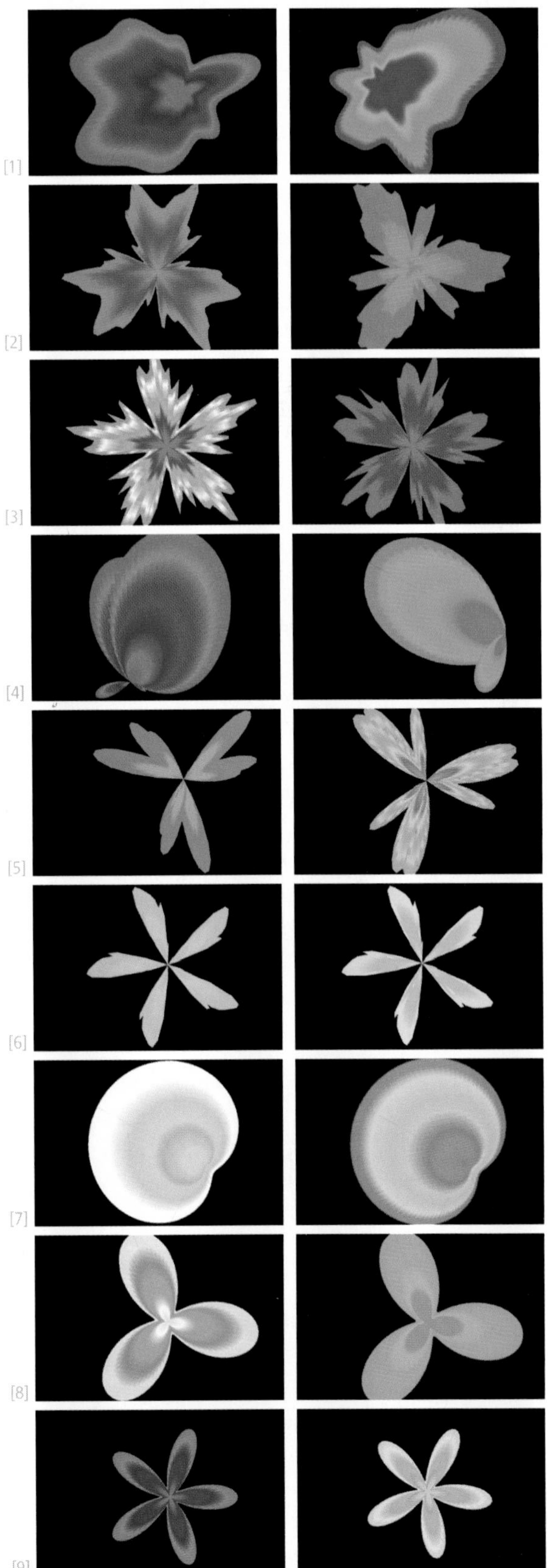
[1] [2] [3] [4] [5] [6] [7] [8] [9]

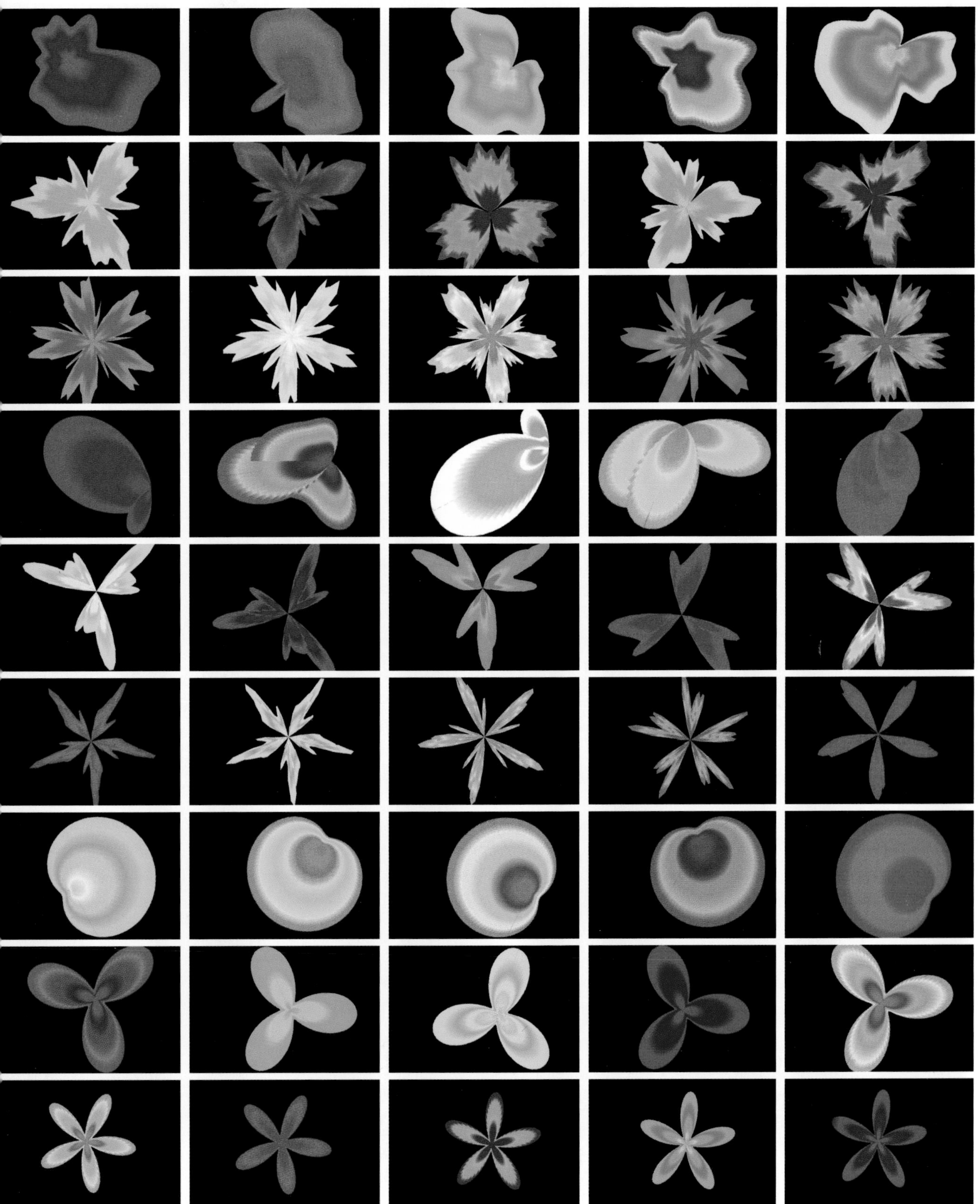

The Stem Generator

This is a nice stem generator developed to simulate natural backgrounds. Rather than using a branching algorithm to create a tree, this generates nice leafy climbers or bamboo shoots. The first thing that I've done is to use my usual two frame loading loop, but if you like you can leave this out and just have everything on one frame. There are three movieclips to make up the effect, and they each have the same instance name as their clip name: **myline**, **myleaf**, and **mybranch**. **myline** is what will be used to create the stems, and it consists of the oft-used 100x100 pixel diagonal line with its registration point in the top-left hand corner, but the line has been replaced with a thin leaf shape to give the stem more structure. **myleaf** is a similar shaped leaf, but this time it's horizontal with its registration point on the far left hand side. **mybranch** is just a container for the other two movieclips, and it will also hold some code on its first frame. **mybranch** is then placed on the main stage of the movie and we're ready to code.

The following script is placed on the first frame of the root:

```
branches = 10;
xcenter = 275;
xoffset = 225;
for (i=0; i<branches; i++) {
   mybranch.duplicateMovieClip("mybranch"+i, i);
   this["mybranch"+i]._x = xcenter+random(2*xoffset)-xoffset;
   this["mybranch"+i]._y = 400;
}
mybranch._visible = 0;
stop ();
```

This sets up some initial variables and uses them to duplicate and position the branches on the screen, governing the number of separate plants that there are. The remaining code sits on the first frame of the **mybranch** movieclip and looks like this:

```
points = 30+random(40);
leaves = 13;
y = [];
x = [];
dy = 5;
offset = 0.007;
y[0] = 0;
x[0] = 0;
for (i=1; i<=points; i++) {
   y[i] = -dy*i;
   x[i] = x[i-1]+i*offset*(random(21)-10);
}
for (i=0; i<points; i++) {
   myline.duplicateMovieClip("myline"+i, i);
   this["myline"+i]._x = x[i];
   this["myline"+i]._y = y[i];
   this["myline"+i]._xscale = x[i+1]-x[i];
   this["myline"+i]._yscale = y[i+1]-y[i];
}
for (i=0; i<leaves; i++) {
   myleaf.duplicateMovieClip("myleaf"+i, i+1000);
   myColor = new Color(this["myleaf"+i]);
   myColorTransform = new Object();
   myColorTransform.ga = 70+random(30);
   myColorTransform.ba = 0;
   myColorTransform.ra = 0;
   myColor.setTransform(myColorTransform);
   this["myleaf"+i]._x = x[points-2*i];
   this["myleaf"+i]._y = y[points-2*i];
   this["myleaf"+i]._xscale = 30+1*i;
   this["myleaf"+i]._yscale = 10+1*i;
   this["myleaf"+i]._rotation = random(180)-180;
}
myline._visible = 0;
myleaf._visible = 0;
stop ();
```

This code is used to create each individual plant. It contains two loops, one for the number of points that make up the stem, and one for the number of leaves on each plant. These loops contain number, position, scale, and color information for leaves and stem.

The key variables

`branches` = the number of separate plants
`xcenter` = the horizontal center of the screen
`xoffset` = the maximum distance from the center that branches will be placed
`points` = the number of segments making up each stem
`leaves` = the number of leaves on each branch
`dy` = the distance between each point, and thus the length of each segment
`offset` = a multiplier used to determine the width (and therefore also the zigzag) of each segment

[2]

Iterations

stem02

First of all, I experimented with a couple of iterations of just increasing the number of branches to see the difference in appearance and loading time. Increasing the number to 30 gives us a nicely populated screen with a manageable loading time.

```
branches = 30;
```

stem03

Here I increased the number of branches again to 60. This gives a much denser jungle, but it takes a little too long to load.

```
branches = 60;
```

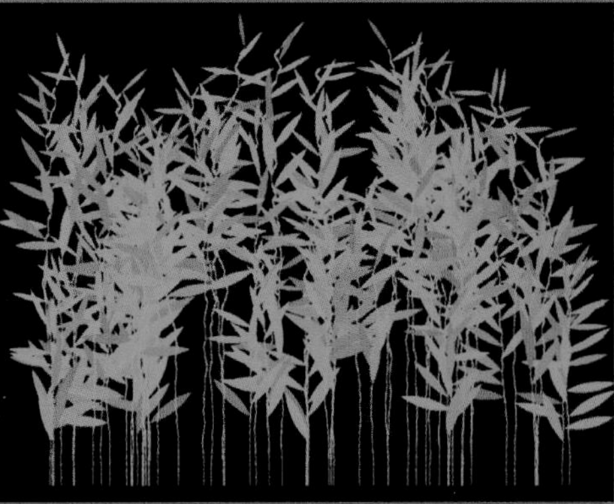

[3]

stem04

I settled on 30 branches as the best medium and moved on to experimenting with different variables. First I looked at the `xoffset`, trying a much smaller value to achieve a tight shrub in the center of the screen.

```
branches = 30;
xoffset = 50;
```

stem05

I preferred a more spread out plant, so I tried an `xoffset` of 100, which gave some space between stems, but also still allowed a good sense of depth and cluster from the overlapping leaves. This is the value that I decided to stay with for the rest of the iterations.

```
xoffset = 100;
```

[4]

[5]

stem06

Next, I turned my eye to the number of leaves on the plant. First I tried a much smaller number, giving a simpler plant.

```
leaves = 5;
```

stem07

I quite liked this simplicity, so I tried adding just a couple more leaves to see the effect.

```
leaves = 7;
```

stem08

Next I decided to increase the number of leaves to 30 to see what difference that would make. By including leaves all the way down the plant, it completely changed its appearance. Now we have a much heavier shrub.

```
leaves = 30;
```

stem09

I set the number of leaves back to its original 13, and experimented instead with the `points` value, and the scale of the leaves. This gives a nice creeper with well-distributed, wide leaves.

```
leaves = 13;
points = random(70);
this["myleaf"+i]._yscale = 40+1*i;
```

stem10

I liked the effect of the stubbier leaves, so I played with the scale a bit more to accentuate it.

```
this["myleaf"+i]._xscale = 15+1*i;
this["myleaf"+i]._yscale = 45+1*i;
```

There are numerous things that you can do here to create different plants. First of all, the actual graphical elements can be changed to suit your botanical tastes. You can also experiment with different amounts for the variables I've looked at here, or others that I haven't such as the Color object, or the `dy` and `offset` values.

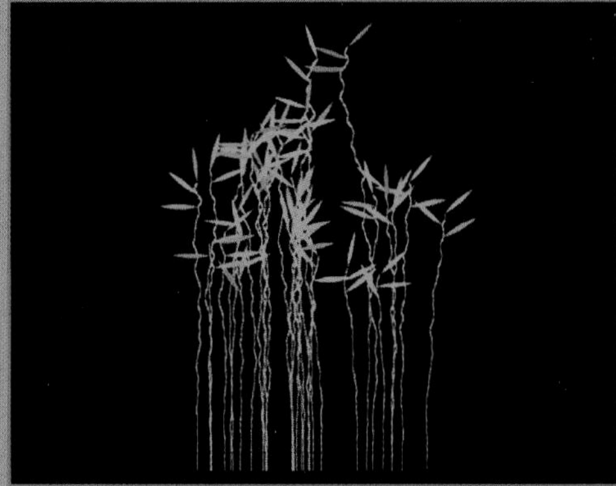

[6]

[7]

[8]

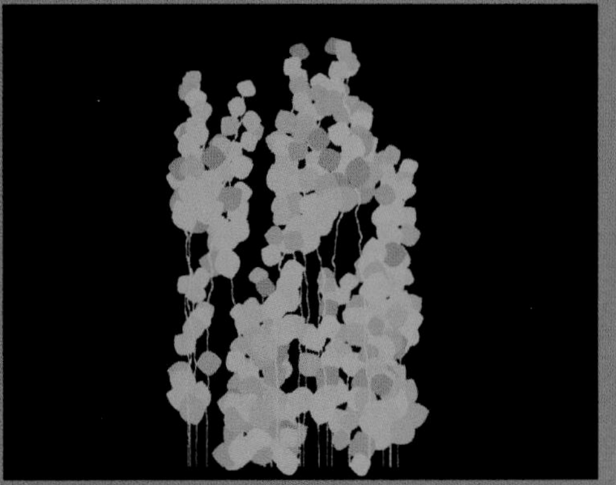

[9]

[10]

I was born last century in southern Germany and currently live in Berlin. I work as a freelance media/motion designer, and at the moment, this means working a lot with Flash on conceptual designs. I also lecture on occasion, and write a bit sometimes too.

I started playing with "programming" as a child – first of all on a computer that didn't even have a monitor, but was connected to an outdated Teletype printer instead. My skills were very limited and the results weren't too impressive, and I quickly got bored with it.

A computer or so later on, I learned how to move blocks and sprites around on the screen, and things became more interesting. Also around this time people started showing me other fascinating stuff, like fractals and their like, which were very popular then. Playing around with these, and other things helped my understanding and influenced the way I approached problems.

Today this drawing and moving things by math and programming is part of my job – but I still don't consider myself a programmer or a math whizz. I just need this stuff to bring my designs and visions to life. Not that I do everything in code, the beauty of Flash is that it also lets me animate things manually whenever the feeling takes me, but sometimes when I'm working on scripted animations or games, things seem to take on a strange life of their own, and this is what absolutely fascinates me.

gabriel mulzer

voxangenlica.net

Fibonacci flower

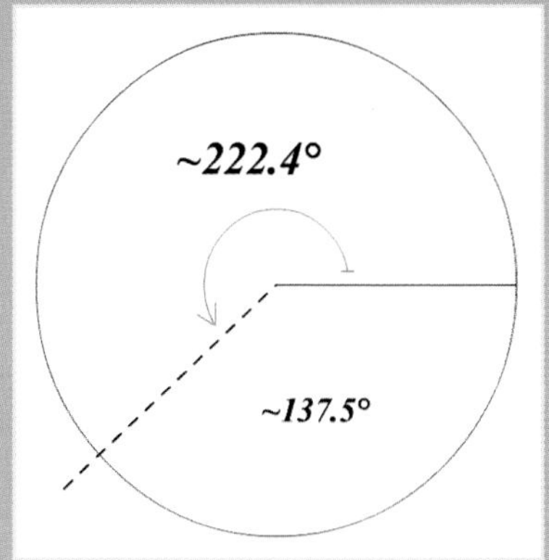

If you're a designer you've probably heard of the Golden Section, Golden Ratio, and Fibonacci series before – ratios that are very common in nature, and therefore regarded as divine proportions for things since time began. They're also very useful in giving programmed images the appearance of natural harmony.

A Fibonacci sequence runs like this:

1, 2, 3, 5, 8, 13, 21, 34, 55, 89, 144, 233, 377, 610, 987, 1597, 2584, 4181, ...

Each number in the series is the sum of the previous two. The further you go on, the more the ratio between two successive numbers will converge to the Golden Ratio which is approximately 1:1.6180339, or 0.6180339 in decimal form.

What's special about this ratio is that if you divide anything by it, the ratio between the bigger part and the original is the same as the ratio between the smaller section and the bigger section. This is the Golden Section. Ive done a diagram here to illustrate it. If you cut the white plane *a* at the dotted line (the Golden Section), then *c* is in a Golden Ratio to *b*, *b* is in a Golden Ratio to *a*, and *a* is in a Golden Ratio to *a+b*.

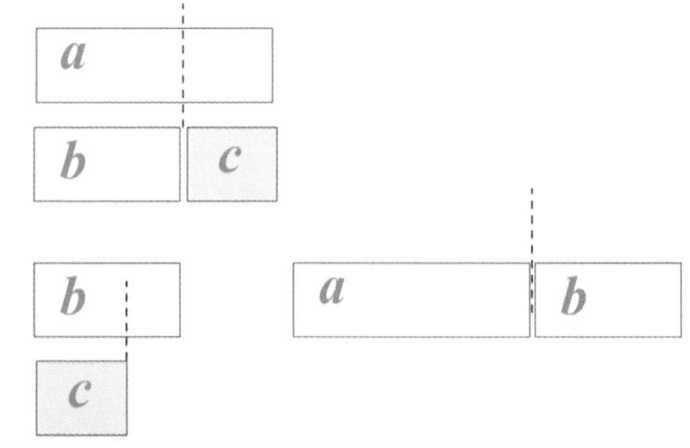

This gets really interesting if you divide the 360 degrees of a circle this way, and use this *Golden Angle* to repeatedly offset something. Due to the nature of the Golden Section we can use either the bigger or the smaller of the resulting angles.

We're going to create a movie that consists of two movieclips. The first one is the `viewer` movieclip, which is a simple rectangle on the stage that I use as a container for all of my code. The second is the graphic that we'll actually be duplicating, and it's called `leaf`. In this first example it consists of a small black dot. Set this to be exported from the Library with the linkage name `leaf`. Next, attach the following code to the `viewer` movieclip on the stage:

```
onClipEvent (load) {
  function init () {
    maxleaves = 300;
    //
    G = 1/1.618033989;
    GA =360- 360*G;
    //
    rad = 20;
    rgrowth = 1.005;
    //
    cur = maxleaves;
  }
  init();
}
onClipEvent (enterFrame) {
  if (cur) {
    cur-;
    //
    rot += GA;
    rot -= int(rot/360)*360;
    //
    rad *= rgrowth;
    x = Math.cos(rot*Math.PI/180)*rad;
    y = Math.sin(rot*Math.PI/180)*rad;
    //
    this.attachMovie("leaf", "l"+cur, cur);
    mc = this["l"+cur];
    //
    mc._x = x;
    mc._y = y;
    mc._rotation = rot;
  }
}
```

The key variables

`maxleaves` = the number of iterations, and therefore the number of leaves that will be attached
`G` = the golden ratio
`GA` = the golden angle in degrees
`rad` = the initial radius
`rgrowth` = a factor by which the radius will grow with each iteration
`cur` = the current iteration. In this case I start counting backwards, because I want to use this as the depth level for the attached movieclips, and I always want the clips that are attached first to be the ones on top
`rot` = the angle that the clip should be offset and rotated by. `rot` is increased by `GA` for each iteration

We start off by defining the initial values and constants in the `load` clip event. I placed these in an extra function called `init` so that we can reset them to the initial values at any time.

In the `enterFrame` handler we start by checking if the value of `cur` is greater than zero. If it is, then there are still iterations to be done. The value of `cur` is then decreased by one at the start of each iteration until it falls below zero and the loop comes to an end.

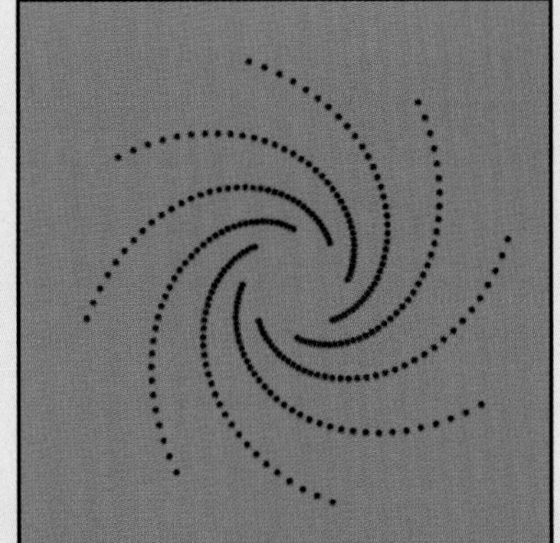

We then increase `rot`, ensuring that it's in the range of 0 to 360 with the following line:

```
rot -= int(rot/360)*360;
```

This is done because the results might become less accurate if `rot` gets really high when there are a large number of iterations.

After defining the new radius we calculate an `x` and `y` location rotated by `rot` and with a distance of `rad` from the center. We then attach a new movieclip and place it at that location. The clip is also rotated by the same angle. Of course, this won't be noticeable at the moment because we're using a circular graphic, but change this and you'll see the difference it makes. You can see the result of this code in `fibon0.swf`.

If you're the doubting kind, you can quickly prove that this sunflower-type distribution is only due to our special angle with the following: add or subtract 2 or 3 degrees to `GA` in the `init` function, and you'll find that even with such slight changes, the even distribution disappears.

Iterations

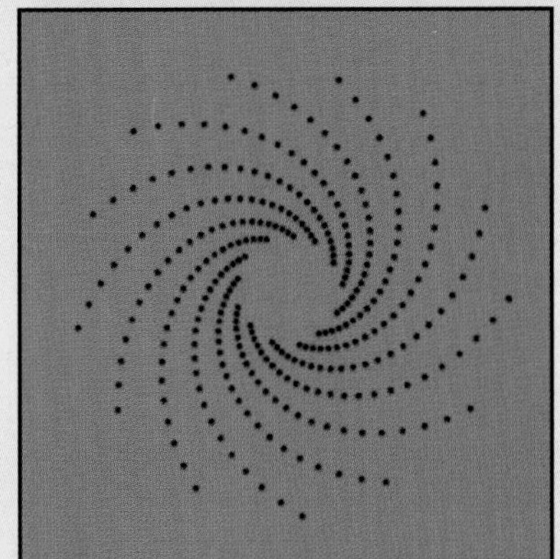

fibon0a

To prove the Golden Ratio, try subtracting 3 from `GA`. The sunflower type symmetry is gone and we're left with a swirl.

```
GA = 360-360*G-3;
```

fibon0b

By changing this to 0.5 we still have a swirl but with a smaller angle resulting in more 'prongs'.

```
GA = 360-360*G+.5;
```

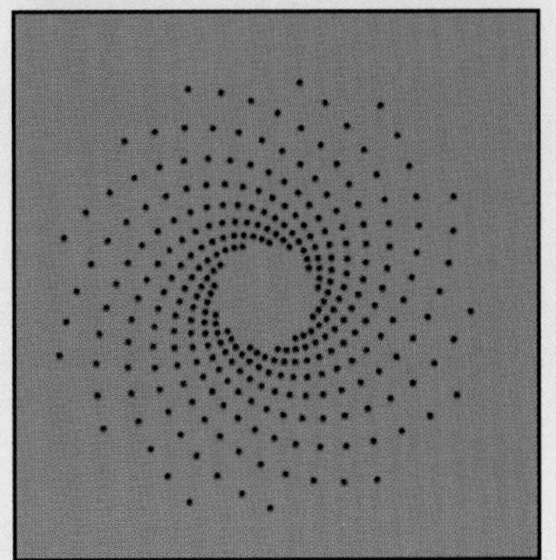

fibon0c

Adding 0.3 we still have a swirl rather than the sunflower type symmetry, but you can see how the pattern gets closer as the value added gets closer to zero.

```
GA = 360-360*G+.3;
```

fibon1a

To create a more flower-like pattern we need to replace the dot graphic with a more leaf-like one, and add growth factors for the `_xscale` and `_yscale` of the clip. Add the following variables into the `init` function:

```
growx = 1.0001;
growy = 1.018;
xscl = 45;
yscl = 19;
```

... and the following code is then added into the `if` loop that creates the iterations:

```
xscl *= growx;
yscl *= growy;

mc._xscale = xscl;
mc._yscale = yscl;
```

I also made some slight aesthetic modifications to the initial `rad` and `rgrowth` values.

It's also possible to make some changes to vary the golden angle over time. To do this, add the following code to the `init` function:

```
degenerate = 1.001;
```

...and this in the iteration loop:

```
GA *= degenerate;
```

Depending on `degenerate`, the golden angle will alter over time at different speeds (for comparison, setting `degenerate` to 1 will not alter the angle). Let's now alter the variables in a few examples to see what the impact is.

fibon1b
To start with we'll leave the initial golden angle as it was originally, but decrease `degenerate`. Note that we've also made the y scaling bigger than the x scaling this time. The various growth values have also been modified slightly.

```
GA = 360-360*G;
degenerate = .9998;
rad = 10;
rgrowth = 1.013;
growx = 1.008;
growy = 1.015;
xscl = 30;
yscl = 100;
```

fibon1c
In this experiment we'll alter both the golden angle and `degenerate`. We'll also change the scaling so that it's back to being equal on both the x and y axis.

```
GA = 360-360*G+5;
degenerate = .9999;
rad = 10;
rgrowth = 1.013;
growx = 1.008;
growy = 1.015;
xscl = 60;
yscl = 60;
```

These are just a couple of examples of what you can do. Try changing the petal shapes and colors to see how many different vibrant flowers you can create.

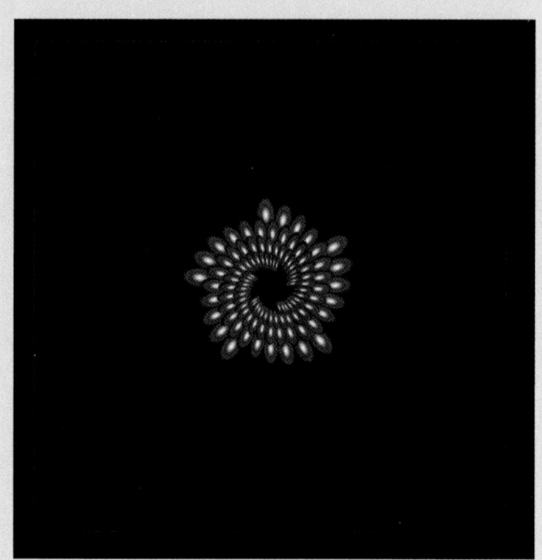

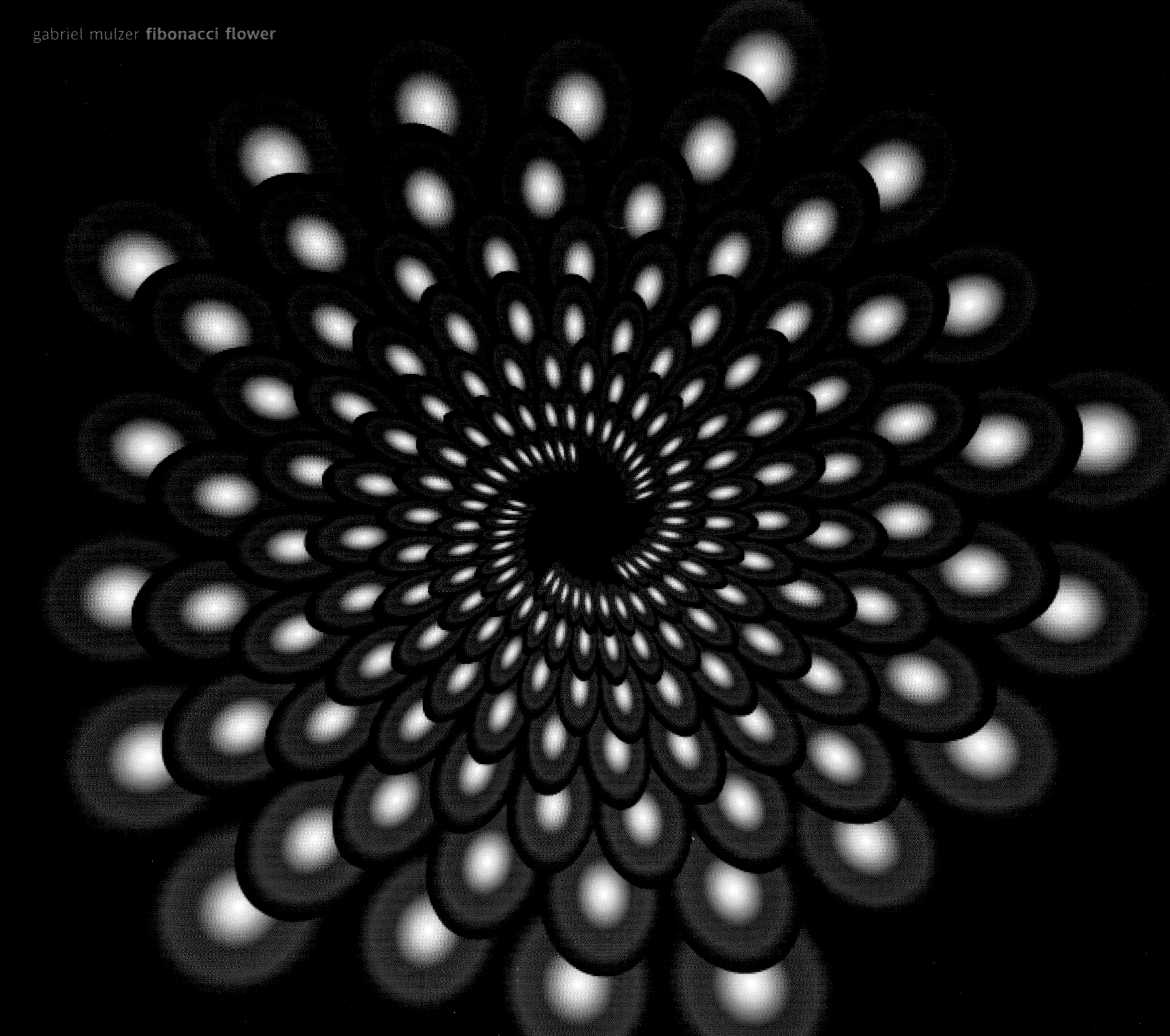

gabriel mulzer **fibonacci flower**

Particles

A particle system consists of a set of tiny objects that all behave under the same set of physical or mathematical laws. This can be additional external forces like general gravity as well as behaviors inherent to the particles themselves. A particle system can get very complex and need a lot of calculating power where particles influence other particles, but even a simple model can develop complex and unpredictable behaviors. Particle systems are used to emulate physical models like clouds, gasses, rain, and crowds, with each purpose needing specific behaviors and laws.

We'll create a basic particle system, consisting of an 'emitter' where the particles are generated, and a 'collector' that attracts the particles. The particles will wander from one to the other and there will be one additional perturbing force which you can think of as a kind of 'wind'. The particles will also have their own individual behavior.

If you look at `particles.fla` you'll see that this experiment has four key movieclips. There is the `dot` movieclip that acts as a particle, which in this example consists of two small lines, but a dot would be just as good if that's what you'd rather use. This clip has been exported from the Library with the identifier `dot`. The `viewer` movieclip acts as the boder for the experiment and has the final two movieclips, `emitter` and `collector`, placed within it.

Let's take a look at the main code for this experiment, which is attached to the `viewer` movieclip:

```
onClipEvent (load) {
    particles = 38;
    pminlife = 20;
    pmaxlife = 50;
    pmass = 40;
    pinitspd = 5;
    // emitter
    em_x = emitter._x;
    em_y = emitter._y;
    em_a1 = -Math.PI/180*45;
    em_a2 = Math.PI/180*30;
    // collector
    coll_x = collector._x;
    coll_y = collector._y;
    coll_m = 15000;
    coll_r = 50;
    // wind
    wind_v = 9;
    wind_a = Math.PI/180*(-45);
    wind_vx = Math.cos(wind_a)*wind_v;
    wind_vy = Math.sin(wind_a)*wind_v;
    wind_fq = Math.PI/180*2;

    function reset (mc) {
      mc._x = em_x;
      mc._y = em_y;
      mc.vx = Math.cos(em_a1+Math.random()*em_a2)*pinitspd;
      mc.vy = Math.sin(em_a1+Math.random()*em_a2)*pinitspd;
      mc.m = pmass;
      mc.life = random(pmaxlife-pminlife)+pminlife;
    }
    for (i=0; i<particles; i++) {
      attachMovie("dot", "p"+i, i);
      reset(this["p"+i]);
    }
}
onClipEvent (enterFrame) {
    wind_ph += wind_fq;
    wind_f = Math.sin(wind_ph);
    wind_x = wind_vx*wind_f;
    wind_y = wind_vy*wind_f;
    for (i=0; i<particles; i++) {
      mc = this["p"+i];
      if (mc.life) {
        mc.life--;
        dx = coll_x-mc._x;
        dy = coll_y-mc._y;
        d = Math.sqrt(dx*dx+dy*dy);
        grav = (mc.m*coll_m)/(d*d);
        mc.vx += (wind_x-mc.vx+(dx/d)*grav)/mc.m;
        mc.vy += (wind_y-mc.vy+(dy/d)*grav)/mc.m;
```

```
            mc._x += mc.vx;
            mc._y += mc.vy;
            if (d<coll_r) {
                mc.life = 0;
            }
        } else {
            reset(mc);
        }
    }
}
```

The key variables

`particles` = the number of particles. Don't set this too high if you've got a slow machine
`pminlife`, `pmaxlife` = the minimum and maximum number of frames a particle will live for. Afterwards it will be reset and used to represent a new particle
`pmass` = the virtual mass of a particle
`pinitspd` = the initial speed of a particle
`em_x`, `em_y` = the location of the emitter. This is read from the `emitter` clip's properties, so that you can change them more intuitively
`em_a1`, `em_a2` = two angles (in radians) at which particles will leave the emitter. The first is absolute and the second will mark a range within which a random number is added to this angle
`coll_x`, `coll_y` = the location coordinates of `collector`
`coll_m` = the mass of `collector`. Particles are artracted according to the gravitational pull of this mass
`coll_r` = a radius around `collector`. If a particle falls into this range it will disappear and be reset as a new particle
`wind_v` = a maximum velocity for the 'wind' that will affect the particles and interfere with their motion towards `collector`
`wind_a` = the angle that the wind blows at
`wind_vx`, `wind_vy` = vectors calculated from the wind angle and the velocity. You can set this to dynamically cange, but you'll need to re-calculate it every time in the clip's frame loop if you do so. We'll start with a fixed direction for this exercise
`wind_fq` = the frequency at which the wind will increase and decrease in a tidal manner. The wind will actually blow back and forth in the direction we specify, with periodical increases and decreases in force. This frequency is specified as an angle, and it will later be added to the wind phase for each frame
`mc.vx`, `mc.vc` = a horizontal and vertical vector resulting from the wind's initial speed, and the angle at which it is emitted. The angle here is worked out with `em_a1` plus a random value from 0 up to `em_a2`. If `em_a2` is set to zero, then all particles will leave at the same angle, if it's a full circle they will leave randomly in any direction, and if it is a quarter circle they will be emitted randomly within a quarter circle
`mc.life` = the lifespan in frames for each particle, set to a random value between `pminlife` and `pmaxlife`

`wind_f` = amplitude value calculated using the wind phase that periodically changes between 1 and –1
`wind_vx`, `wind_vy` = the actual horizontal and vertical velocities for this phase

There is a short function in the `load` clip event to initialize and reset our particles, called `reset (mc)`. `mc` is our shortcut reference to the `dot` movieclip instances named `p0`, `p1`, and so on.

The `load` handler ends with a loop that attaches the defined number of particles and initializes then using the `reset` function. On its own, this would leave all the clips on one spot, so we use the `enterFrame` code to make them move.

The next step in the code is the `for` loop that moves the particles. The horizontal, vertical, and absolute distances to the collector are then calculated and stored as `dx`, `dy`, and `d`. The Gravitation force is then calculated using the principle that:

```
gravity = (mass1*mass2)/(distance*distance)
```

The horizontal and vertical components of the gravity on the particle (`dx/d*grav` and `dy/d*grav`) are used toward the x and y velocities of the particle (`mc.vx` and `mc.vx`). The wind is also a contributing factor here, so we add the difference between the wind speed and the particle speed to the gravitational force. Finally we take `inertia` into account:

```
inertia = force/mass
```

When we've put our variable names into these equations we're left with:

```
mc.vx += (wind_x-mc.vx+(dx/d)*grav)/mc.m;
```

The horizontal speeds are added to the clip's former _x and _y location to represent its new location. Our final check in the loop is to see if the distance is smaller than the radius of `collector`, in which case the particle is reset.

I've also added an invisible button to `emitter` and `collecter` in my file so that they can be dragged around the screen.

The motion in this experiment varies greatly depending on the masses: higher masses on the particle will increase gravity, but also increase inertia, so the wind doesn't move them as much, and so on. You will also find that gravity decreases quickly with distance. And with certain angles, gravity can speed up the particles so much that they escape `collector` completely.

If you only need vertical gravity, you can skip all the `collector` stuff, distances, and individual gravity, and use a much simpler model instead such as this:

```
mc.vx  +=(wind_x-mc.vx)/mc.m;
mc.vy  +=(wind_y-mc.vy)/mc.m+grav;
mc._x  += mc.vx;
mc._y  += mc.vy;
```

Here `grav` is simply set to a constant such as 1 in the beginning. You can also set the mass of the particles randomly, or reset them at a random position, scale them, or fade them dependent on any of their properties.

Let's now try some variations to see the effects of simple changes. In the example SWFs you'll see that I've changed the graphics slightly on some of them, and set `emitter` and `collector` in different places to get different effects (remember that I set them both to be draggable). Don't forget to go back to the original `particles.fla` code for each variation.

Iterations

p1

For this experiment our particles will have a shorter minimum life, but the same maximum. The angles of projection from the emitter are also being changed. Our maximum wind speed is being decreased, so the impact of the wind will not be as great, and I've also set it to hit our particles from a different angle. The tidal motion in which our wind increases and decreases has been increased though.

```
pminlife = 5;
em_a1 = Math.PI/180*60;
em_a2 = Math.PI/180*180;
wind_v = 3;
wind_a = Math.PI/180*(-30);
wind_fq = Math.PI/180*5;
```

p2

The initial mass of the particles is much heavier here, which will affect the gravitational force on them. The mass of `collector` is also much lighter, which affects its gravitational pull. The maximum wind speed is faster here too. We're also adding variance to the mass when the `reset` function is called.

```
pminlife = 40;
pmaxlife = 120;
pmass = 4800;
pinitspd = -3;
em_a1 = Math.PI/180*45;
coll_m = 3000;
wind_v = 180;
wind_a = Math.PI/180*(-30);
wind_fq = Math.PI/180*5;
mc.m = random(pmass/2)+pmass/2;
```

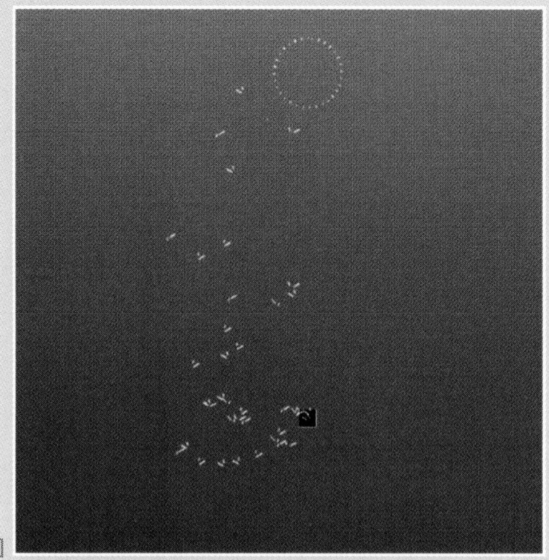

[1]

[2]

p3

Here we're going to make the angle that the particles leave `emitter` change from left to right, and back again. `collector` will have a strong gravitational pull here due to an increased mass.

```
pmaxlife = 100;
pmass = 10;
pinitspd = 0;
em_a1 = -Math.PI/180*65;
em_a2 = Math.PI/180*90;
coll_m = 20000;
wind_v = 4;
wind_a = Math.PI/180*(10);
wind_fq = Math.PI/180*3;
```

p6

If you look at the final file here you'll see that our particles move in a circle around `collector`. Note the changes to `em_a1` and `em_a2`, as they have a big impact on the effect.

```
pminlife = 40;
pmaxlife = 120;
pmass = 2000;
pinitspd = 10;
em_a1 = Math.PI/180*90;
em_a2 = Math.PI/180*5;
wind_v = 10;
wind_a = Math.PI/180*(-30);
wind_fq = Math.PI/180*5;
```

p8

In our final experiment the fading and color change are simply animated in the movieclip, not scripted. This animation also contains a change in size. The initial particle speed and maximum wind speed here are low and particle mass high, which helps us create a smoke effect.

```
pminlife = 55;
pmaxlife = 80;
pmass =180;
pinitspd = 2;
em_a1 = -Math.PI/180*65;
em_a2 = Math.PI/180*10;
coll_m = 1000;
wind_v = 3;
wind_a = Math.PI/180*(60);
wind_fq = Math.PI/180*1;
```

So, these files demonstrate the ways we can make artificial climatic conditions, such as wind, gravity, and mass, affect the movement of objects. The principles could be very useful in creating a real life scene in Flash, but with the added benefit of providing us with the control of those elements that we'll never have in real life.

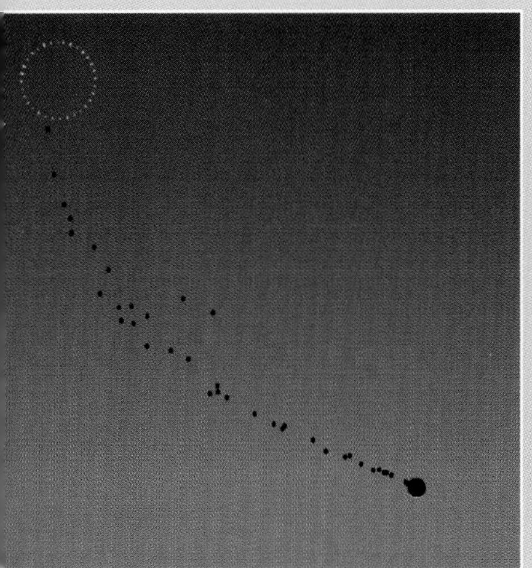

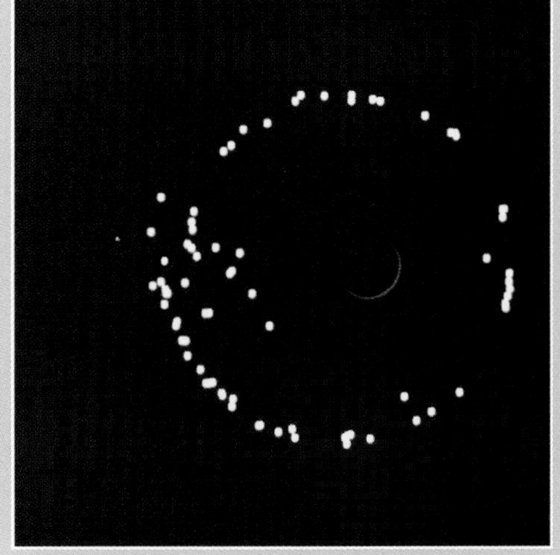

[6]

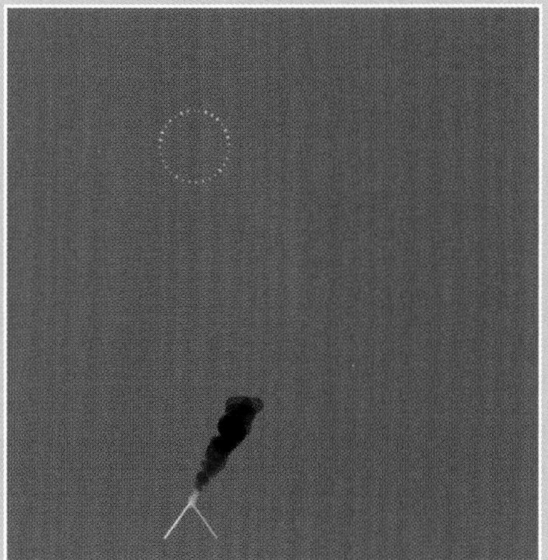

[8]

Recursive patterns

Recursion is often needed when you have to calculate approximations for limits, like the Golden Section, in fractal sets, or for algorithms that need repetitive steps until a condition is met.

We'll use this to create simple self-repetitive patterns where we'll just attach movieclips, and then rotate and scale them relative to each other, over and over again.

You'll need a movieclip with the linkage name `dot`, which is preferably a simple graphic like a 100x100 pixel dot so that it can be percentage-scaled. We'll attach the following code to a second movieclip, `viewer`, which is just a rectangular outline within which the recursive effect will occur.

```
onClipEvent (load) {
   angmax = 360*Math.PI/180;
   dimin = .382;
   maxchild = 3;
   maxrec = 4;
   dep = 1;

   function addthing (x, y, scl, ang, child,
sub) {
      dep++;
      attachMovie("dot", "d"+dep, dep);
      var mc = this["d"+dep];
      mc._x = x;
      mc._y = y;
      mc._yscale = mc._xscale=scl;
      mc._rotation = ang/(Math.PI/180);
      if (sub) {
         var cang = angmax/child;
         while (child) {
            var nx = x+Math.cos(ang)*scl;
            var ny = y+Math.sin(ang)*scl;
            var nscl = scl*dimin;
            var nang = ang+cang*child;
            //
            addthing(nx, ny, nscl, nang, maxchild,
sub-1);
            child--;
         }
      }
   }
   addthing(0, 0, 100, 0, maxchild, maxrec);
}
```

The key variables

`angmax` = the maximum angle that subsequent clips will be rotated and placed at. This angle will be divided by the number of clips
`dimin` = a factor we're going to scale subsequent clips by
`maxchild` = how many subsequent "child" clips will be added to each clip
`maxrec` = the maximum recursion depth – how many generations of subsequent clips will be added, before the function quits
`dep` = the depth level at which a new clip is placed

As you'll see, you have to be a little bit careful with the `maxchild` and `maxrec` values, as alterations to these will affect the total number of clips and recursions.

The main bulk of our code consists of the `addthing` function, so we'll take a look at what this consists of now. You'll see that the function has six parameters:

`x` = the _x location of the clip
`y` = the _y location of the clip
`scl` = the scale of the clip
`ang` = the rotation angle of the clip
`child` = how many offspring will be added for the clip
`sub` = how many generations will occur, as in the number of times the function will be called from within itself

The function starts by increasing the depth that the new clip is to be placed on by one. Each clip will be placed at a different depth. We then attach an instance of the `dot` movieclip and name it in relation to its depth. For example, a clip where the depth is equal to 2 will be called `d2`.

For simplicity and typing convenience, we then create a variable `mc` that acts as a shortcut reference to the newly attached clip. The clip's properties are set to the location, scale, and rotation of `x`, `y`, `scl`, and `ang`. Our function will then use an `if` statement to check if there's another generation to follow – which is if `sub` is set to any value other then zero.

If the sub value is not zero, then a `while` loop will run after a new variable `cang` is defined. `cang` is the child angle and is used for the subsequent clips that are produced. If you look at the `while` loop you'll see that the main action is to call the `addthing` function again from within itself – this is how the recursive pattern occurs. The rest of the loop creates some new variables that are then passed as parameters when the function is called. You'll see that these variables have the same names as our original function parameters, except that they have an `n` prefix at the beginning to show that they're new. The loop will run forever if we don't decrease the value of `child` by one every time the statement is looped. When the value of `child` is equal to zero the loop will stop.

To evoke this nested repetition, we add a line that calls the function once with our initial values:

```
addthing(0, 0, 100, 0, maxchild, maxrec);
```

By replacing the line that calls the function with a `for` loop that uses the `maxchild` value, we can call the function more than once and with different values:

```
for (i=0; i<maxchild; i++) {
   var ang = angmax/maxchild*(i+1);
```

```
    var nx = Math.cos(ang)*50;
    var ny = Math.sin(ang)*50;
    addthing(nx, ny, 50, ang, maxchild, maxrec);
}
```

This effect can be found in `recurs_1.fla`.

Let's now play around with the initial values and see what effects can be created.

Iterations

recurs_1b
Here we'll have fewer children, but more recursions. We'll also increase the scaling factor and alter the angle. You'll see that the end effect is very different to our last experiment.

```
angmax = 520*Math.PI/180;
dimin = .6;
maxchild = 2;
maxrec = 5;
```

recurs_1c
We'll now make the number of children and recursions the same. We'll make the angle so that the clips are within a 180 degree area. You'll see in the SWF that they're all located in a semicircle from the dot they're based around.

```
angmax = 180*Math.PI/180;
dimin = .5;
maxchild = 3;
maxrec = 3;
```

You can produce stars by changing the shape in this example to a triangle.

recurs_1d
You might notice that the offset of the next generation always follows one direction, as we are always adding to the angle. For a more homogenous appearance, we can add an offset angle. Add the following line after the `var cang = angmax/child;` line:

```
var angoff = -(angmax+cang)/2;
```

We'll also modify the `nang` variable so that the child clips aren't placed in a range from the maximum to zero, but instead use the range of half the maximum to minus half the maximum.

```
var nang = ang+angoff+cang*child;
```

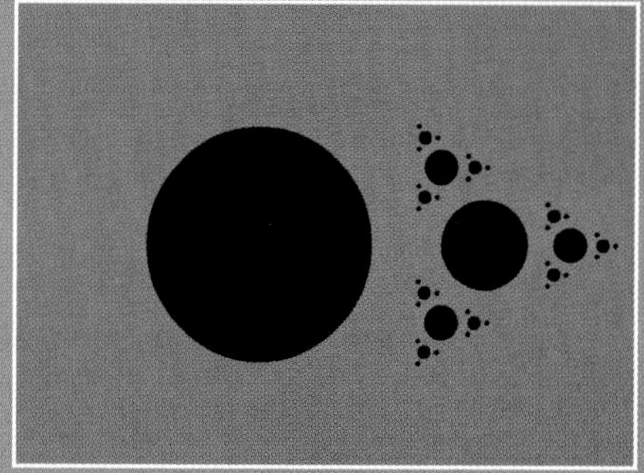
[1a]

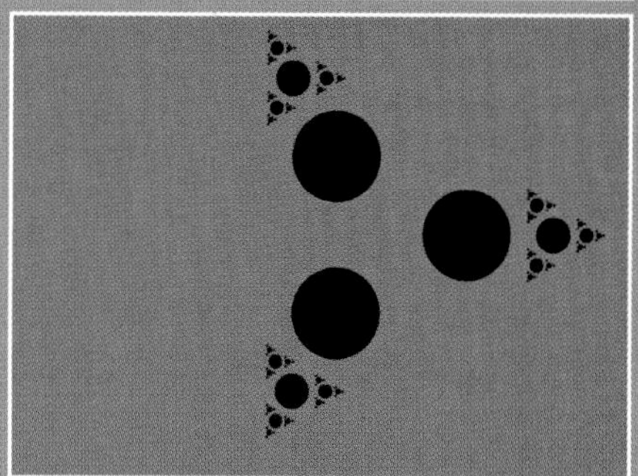
[1]

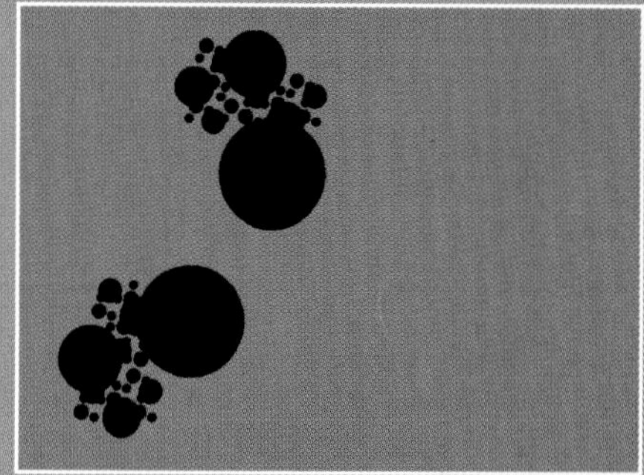
[1b]

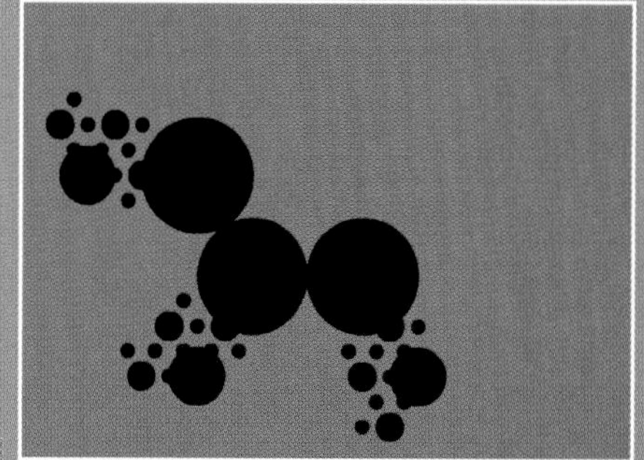
[1c]

[1d]

For the next examples we're going to modify the `dot` symbol. The symbol we're going to use can be found in `recurs_2.fla`. We're also going to revert back to a single call of the function, and an angle of -90°. Replace the `for` loop that you've been using with the following line:

```
addthing(0, 100, 100, -Math.PI/2, maxchild, maxrec);
```

If you turn to `recurs_2.fla` you'll see that this change has already been made. This file has the variables set to:

```
angmax = 270*Math.PI/180;
dimin = .618;
maxchild = 3;
maxrec = 4;
```

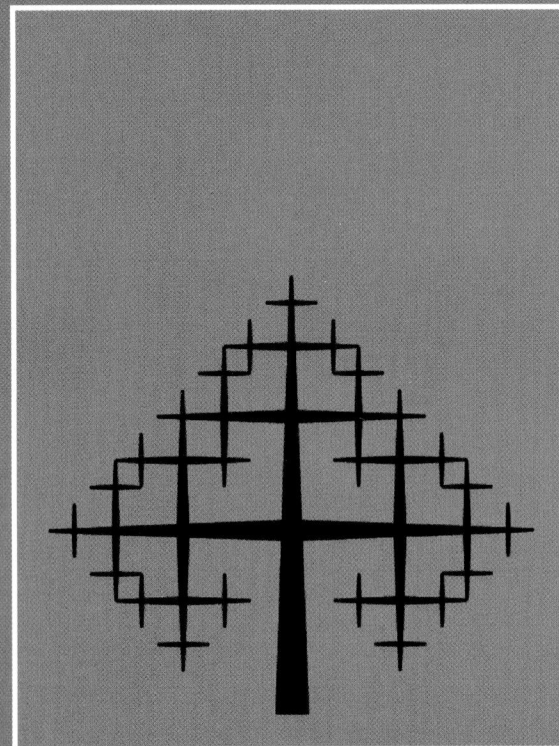

Let's play with the variables again and see what tree effects we can create.

recurs_2a
Here we're decreasing the number of children in each clip. This will give our tree less branches and a more realistic tree form. We're also limiting the angle that the branches appear in. This looks like a bare tree in the winter.

```
angmax = 138*Math.PI/180;
dimin = .618;
maxchild = 2;
maxrec = 4;
```

recurs_2b
We've increased the angle here and our tree looks more like a conifer or Christmas tree. The greater angle is filled by more branches and each branch is more populated. We do this through the recursion and child values. If you look at the tree stump it has three branches going off it. There are three branches going off each of those, and so on. This is where the number of children comes in. If you look at the number of times a branch splits off into three you'll see that it is five times – the number of recursions.

```
angmax = 720*Math.PI/180;
dimin = .5;
maxchild = 3;
maxrec = 5;
```

recurs_2c
We're restricting the angle again in our next experiment. We're also going back to two children. This time we're increasing the number of recursions to seven. So, whilst our branches are thinly populated by children, there are more of them.

```
angmax = 220*Math.PI/180;
dimin = .618;
maxchild = 2;
maxrec = 7;
```

recurs_2d
Our next tree is tall, but its branches are all at the top within a small angle, which is set to 90 degrees. Because of the small angle and a higher number of children, the tree looks more densely populated.

```
angmax = 90*Math.PI/180;
dimin = .5;
maxchild = 3;
maxrec = 5;
```

You can try adding a slight random value to the new `nang` angle and `nscl` scale to create a more natural tree:

```
var nscl = scl*dimin+random(5);
var nang = ang+angoff+cang*child+
  ➥ random(38)*Math.PI/180;
```

recurs_2e
A final idea is to use a graphic clip that aleady contains a self-repetitive pattern for a more complex look.

recurs_2f
You can see from these files how easy it is to make complex looking object from the simplest start point of the basic `dot` movieclip. Try playing around with other shapes and see what objects you can create.

[2a]

[2b]

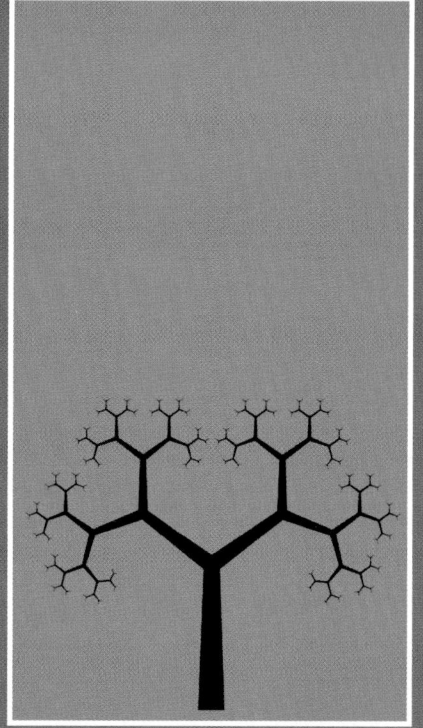
[2c]

[2d]

[2e]

[2e]

sine & co

I use trigonometric functions in nearly every Flash movie that I make. You need them whenever you want to translate angles and vectors to and from a Cartesian coordinate system like the stage of Flash. However, they can also be useful for harmonic value changes of any kind.

I've often heard people complaining that they only faintly remember trigonometry from school and claiming that they never really understood it. The basic relation between the most needed functions, sine and cosine, and their corresponding angles can be easily shown and understood with Flash.

The Flash movie for this experiment consists of two movieclips. The first is a container movieclip that acts as the stage for the experiment. In the `trig1.fla` example file you'll see that this consists of an outline rectangle to define the viewer area, and a circle with a 100-pixel radius that is centered on the stage. The clip has been called `viewer`. The second movieclip, `dot`, consists of a small circle and I've also added a horizontal and vertical line through the center. This clip has been exported from the Library with the linkage name `dot`.

Here is the code we require for this experiment. It should be attached to the `viewer` movieclip:

```
onClipEvent (load) {
   ang = 0;
   angstep = Math.PI/180;
   rad = 100;

   for (i=0; i<3; i++) {
    attachMovie("dot", "dot"+i, i);
   }
}

onClipEvent (enterFrame) {
   ang += angstep;

   dot0._x = dot1._x=Math.cos(ang)*rad;
   dot0._y = dot2._y=-Math.sin(ang)*rad;
   dot0._rotation = -ang*180/Math.PI;
}
```

The key variables

`ang` = an angle measured in radians
`angstep` = a value with which we will increase the angle step by step
`rad` = the radius

The `onClipEvent` handler defines our variables and then goes on to attach the `dot` movieclip three times by means of a `for` loop and the `attachMovie` action. The dots are name `dot0`, `dot1`, and `dot2`.

On the `enterFrame` handler `ang` is increased by `angstep` in each frame. The x locations of `dot0` and `dot1` are set to the cosine of `ang`, multiplied by the radius, and the y locations of `dot0` and `dot2` are set to the sine, and once again multiplied by the radius.

Finally, the rotation of `dot0` is set to equal the negative value of `ang` in degrees.

(Note, I negated the values for _y and rotation, because in Flash _y increases downwards, while in math it usually increases upwards. You don't have to do this though, so just skip the negative signs if they bug you, and the animation will just be flipped.)

So, `dot1` only changes its horizontal position, dependent on the angle's cosine value, while `dot2` only moves horizontally, dependent on sine. `dot0` combines both and moves horizontally like `dot1` and vertically like `dot2`, and moves in a circular line of the radius we specified.

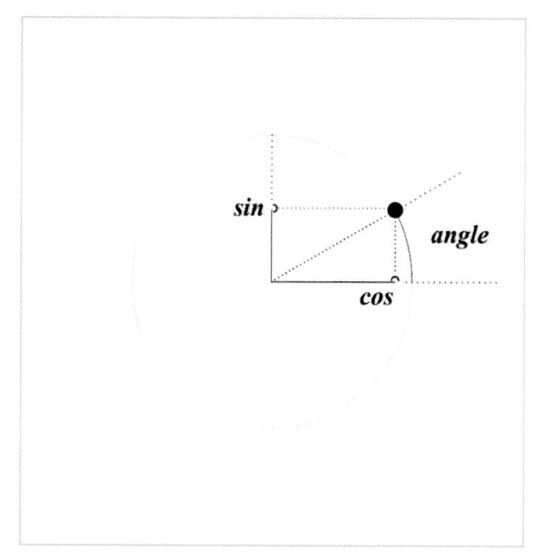

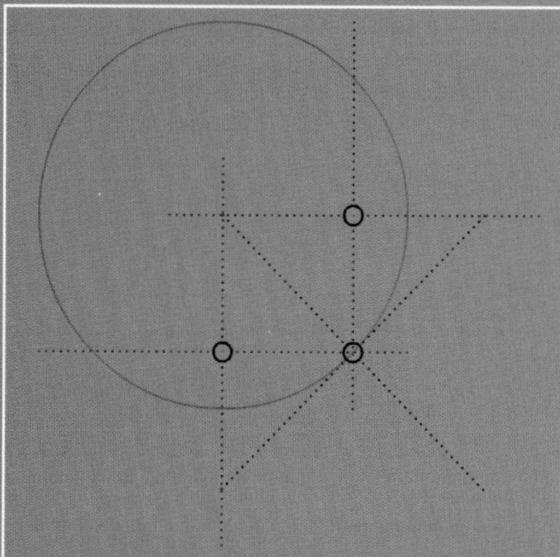

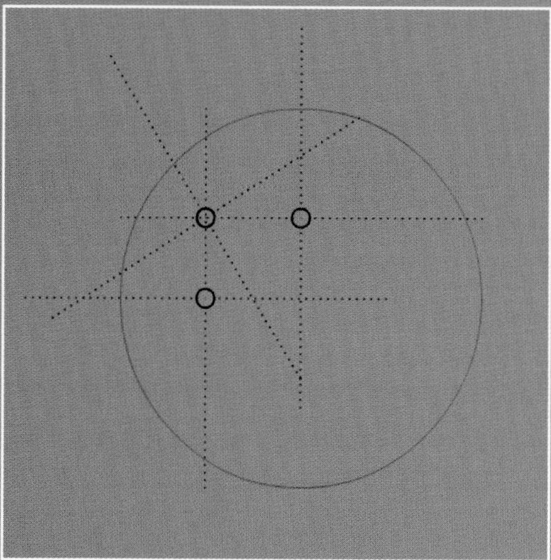

Test `trig1.fla` and watch the effect that this simple code creates.

Changing `rad` will change the circle's size. Changing `angstep` will change the speed and the direction if `angstep` is decreasing `ang`.

If you scale the `sin` and `cos` values with two different values, instead of a uniform radius, it will result in an elliptical motion. Add the following lines into the `onClipEvent(load)` handler and remove the `rad` variable:

```
xscl = 100;
yscl = 50;
```

We'll now use this scaling to affect the radius. Modify the `onClipEvent(enterFrame)` handler by replacing `rad` with our scaling factors:

```
dot0._x = dot1._x=Math.cos(ang)*xscl;
dot0._y = dot2._y=-Math.sin(ang)*yscl;
```

This effect can be seen in `trig1a.swf`.

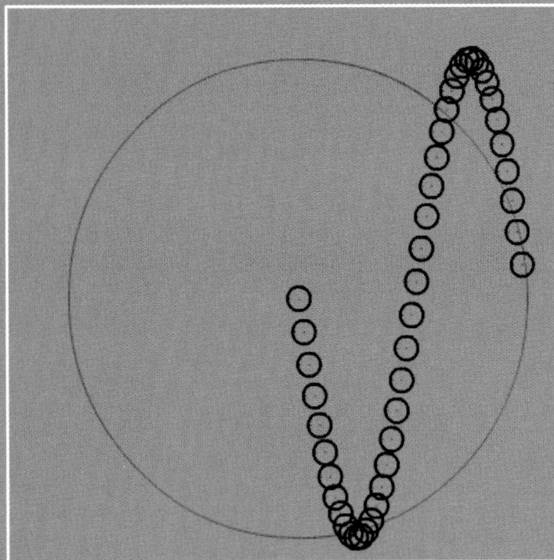

trig1b
We'll start by plotting the sine wave. Firstly, modify the dot movieclip by removing the horizontal and vertical lines. We just want the dot here. We only need the load clip event for now, and this will have one new variable, steps, which is the number of times our loop will run for.

```
onClipEvent (load) {
   ang = 0;
   steps = 45;
   xscl = 100;
   yscl = 100;
//
   for (i=0; i<steps; i++) {
     attachMovie("dot", "dot"+i, i);
     ang = 2*Math.PI/steps*i;
     eval("dot"+i)._x = xscl/steps*i;
     eval("dot"+i)._y = Math.sin(ang)*yscl;
   }
}
```

trig1c
We can animate this effect by now adding an enterFrame clip event:

```
onClipEvent (enterFrame) {
   phaseoffset += Math.PI/180*5;
   for (i=0; i<steps; i++) {
     ang = 2*Math.PI/steps*i+phaseoffset;
     eval("dot"+i)._x = xscl/steps*i;
     eval("dot"+i)._y = Math.sin(ang)*yscl;
   }
}
```

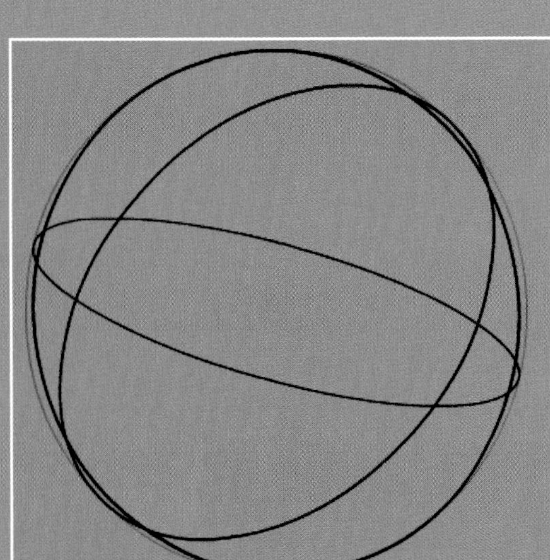

trig1d
Our next experiment requires a couple of changes to the dot movieclip. We want to make the graphical element an outline circle with a radius of 100 pixels. The circle then wants to be centered in the movieclip. The effect we're going to create hinges on changes to the _xscale and _rotation in our code:

```
onClipEvent (load) {
   ang = 0;
   steps = 3;
   xscl = 100;
   yscl = 100;
//
   for (i=0; i<steps; i++) {
     attachMovie("dot", "dot"+i, i);
   }
}

onClipEvent (enterFrame) {
   phaseoffset += Math.PI/180*3;
   for (i=0; i<steps; i++) {
     ang = 2*Math.PI/steps*i+phaseoffset;
     eval("dot"+i)._xscale = Math.cos(ang)*xscl;
     eval("dot"+i)._rotation = ang*180/Math.PI;
   }
}
```

trig1e

The next example creates a similar effect, but with different sized circles. To achieve this effect we make use of the _yscale property:

```
onClipEvent (load) {
   ang = 0;
   steps = 7;
   xscl = 100;
   yscl = 100;
//
   for (i=0; i<steps; i++) {
     attachMovie("dot", "dot"+i, i);
     eval("dot"+i)._yscale = yscl/steps*i;
   }
}

onClipEvent (enterFrame) {
   phaseoffset += Math.PI/180*5;
   for (i=0; i<steps; i++) {
     ang = 2*Math.PI/steps*i+phaseoffset;
     eval("dot"+i)._xscale = Math.cos(ang)*eval("dot"+i)._yscale;
     eval("dot"+i)._rotation = ang*180/Math.PI;
   }
}
```

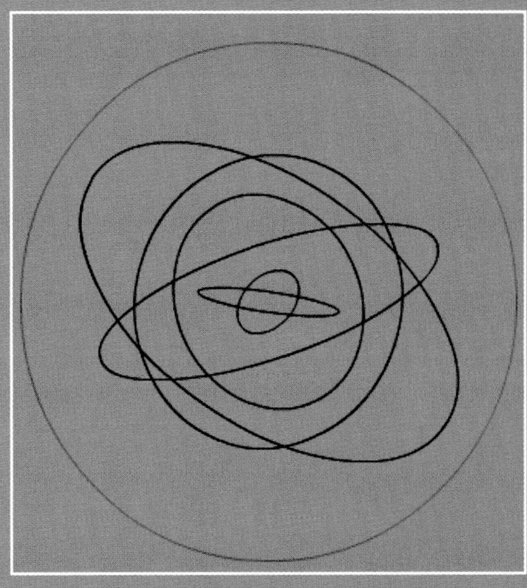

trig1f

Here's the code for our final variation:

```
onClipEvent (load) {
   ang = 0;
   steps = 7;
   xscl = 100;
   yscl = 100;
//
   for (i=0; i<steps; i++) {
     attachMovie("dot", "dot"+i, i);
   }
}

onClipEvent (enterFrame) {
   phaseoffset += Math.PI/180*1;
   for (i=0; i<steps; i++) {
     ang = 2*Math.PI/steps*i+phaseoffset;
     eval("dot"+i)._xscale = Math.cos(ang)*_xscale;
     eval("dot"+i)._yscale = Math.sin(ang)*_yscale;
     eval("dot"+i)._rotation = ang*180/Math.PI;
   }
}
```

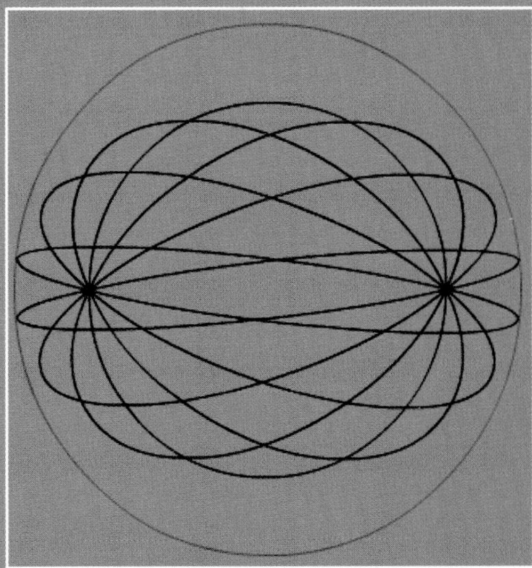

Well, that's the end of our brief look at sine & co. You can see how some great effects can be achieved with very basic modifications to the code. You might even understand some of that trigonometry now!

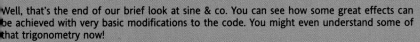

Paul Prudence was born, lives, and works in London, UK. Early years were spent drafting fantastical landscapes in pen and ink. The most formative experience was undoubtedly the stealing of an encyclopedia of surrealism from the local library as a young teenager. Later on a mistake was made studying fine art at Goldsmiths College in London.

After trashing the idea of being part of the 'art world' and being in the enviable position of being unemployable, he spent a few years travelling, then voluntary working as an art therapist in a mental hospital. Spare time was spent staying up until morning painting pictures influenced by altered states of consciousness.

In the last few years he's traded the traditional mediums of paint and paper for photons and the qwerty mnemonic. Since then he's had some graphic work published in magazines and a video work commissioned by UK TV.

The modular nature of Flash lends itself well to the way I like to work. The combined power of ActionScript with the way nested movieclips work gives us a tool that can make an animated system that with a few tweaks can be radically altered from one state to another. This makes it ideal for artistic experimentation. Old code and clips can be reused in new experiments and built into new and often surprising forms; all modules made in Flash remain alive.

Flash is a uniquely beautiful program that allows a perfect merge of both aesthetic concerns and math. One of my ongoing interests is the relationship between art and math or science, and how the two seemingly disparate disciplines can affect and influence one and another. Flash is a brilliant program for examining this relationship.

I've always been interested in self-replicating and repeating systems such as those found in nature, because often simple iterative processes, repeated over and over, can bring about highly complex forms. The building blocks of life, DNA itself, arise out of replication of other DNA strands. Many of the most beautiful forms in nature, shells, radiolarians, plant structures, and nervous systems come into existence through a repeating core element.

Looking through history it's easy to see a huge amount of art and artifacts that also employ repetitive motifs to great effect. They're often geometric, and sometimes paying homage to the kind of repetition found in nature. For example, in Tibet religious paintings called tankas adorn temples, and are often a swirl with repeating motifs. In Islamic art repetition is taken to its zenith. Complex geometric designs, as well as intricate patterns of vegetal ornament (such as the arabesque), create the impression of unending repetition, which is believed by some to be an inducement to contemplate the infinite nature of God. Often when I go to bed after staring at the screen for hours, I close my eyes and continue to see 3D patterns twisting and moving through space!

paul prudence

transphormetic.com

Recursive

For this experiment we need a simple graphic symbol that has its linkage properties set to export and is given the identifier name **`unit`**. With this identifier we can call the clip using the **`attachMovie`** command.

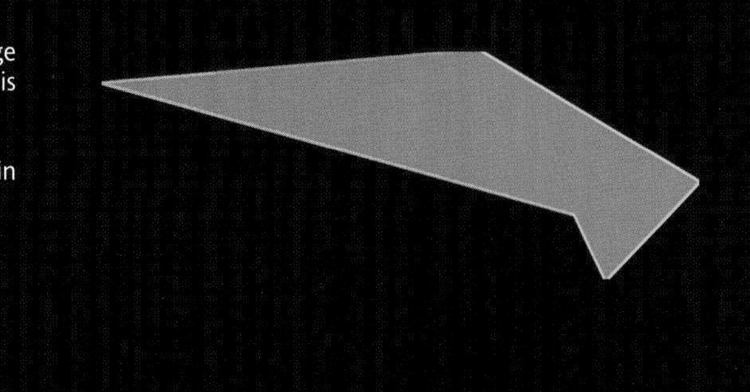

Our basic code for the experiment is attached to frame 1 of the main timeline in a new movie. The code is as follows:

```
a = a + 1;
i = i + 1;
attachMovie ("unit", "unit" + a, i);

_root["unit" + a]._y = Math.sin(i)*300;
_root["unit" + a]._x = Math.cos(i)*600;

if ( a>1000 ) _root.stop();
```

This simple piece of code duplicates the **`unit`** clip in positions across the screen according to a trigonometric function of the variable **`i`**. When a certain amount of duplications have passed the movie stops. The trigonometry plots the duplicates of the clip in sequences that give the final configuration a curved shape.

On frame 2 of the movie we add the simple command **`gotoAndPlay(1)`** to create a loop. The effect that is created can be seen in **`recursive_01.fla`**.

The key variables

`a` = a counter to attach individual instances of the clip onto the screen. As each loop passes, 1 is added to the value of a, and one new duplication of the clip is added to the screen
`i` = another simple counter with 1 being added to its value on each loop. The x and y positions of the newly added clip are then set according to the sin/cosine value of argument **`i`**

Let's look at some examples of how we can modify and build on this starting point. Note that in many of these examples the graphic we're using has been altered to achieve a different effect. Remember to go back to the base file **`recursive_01.fla`** to start each experiment.

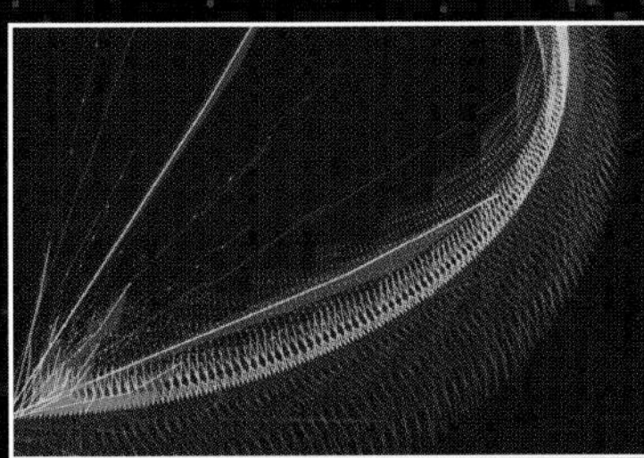

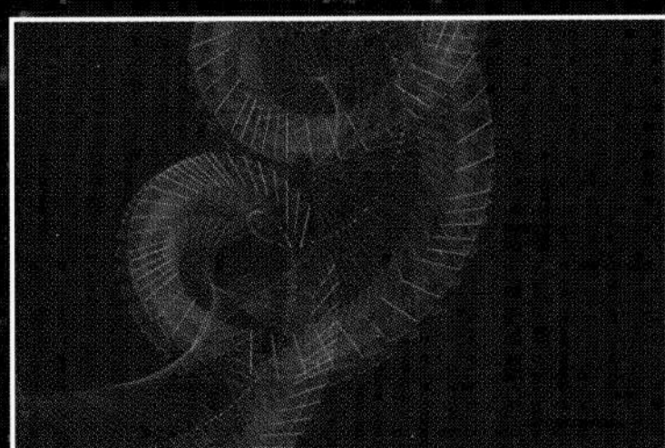

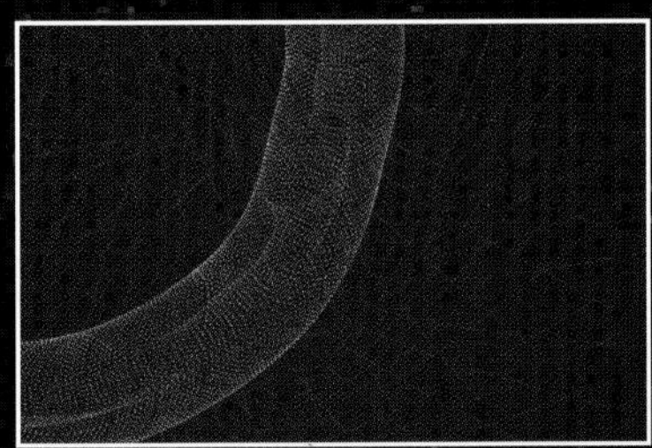

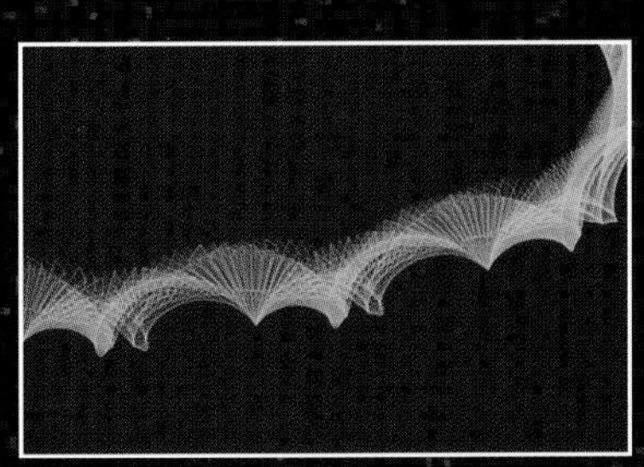

Iterations

recursive_02

For the first experimentation we're going to increase the number of clips attached by replacing 1000 with 2000 in the `if` statement. The value used to calculate the `_x` value has also been changed from 600 to 500. Here are the lines that want modifying:

```
_root["unit" + a]._x = Math.cos(i)*500;
if ( a>2000 ) _root.stop();
```

We're also going to add scaling to the clips is both the x and y directions. The `_xscale` value is based on the counter `i`, which also represents a clips depth. The greater the value of `i`, the larger the scaling factor. Consequently, the later in the effect a clip is draw, the wider it is on the x axis. The y scaling will be the `tan` value of `i`. We're going to add rotation to the clips as well. Again this will be based on the `i` value, and increases as more clips are attached. Here's the code we add to frame 1 to create this effect:

```
_root["unit" + a]._xscale = i/100;
_root["unit" + a]._yscale = Math.tan(i);
_root["unit" + a]._rotation = i/20;
```

recursive_03

We're modifying the `_x` property again, but this time from 600 to 300. The greater this value the greater the area across the screen the effect occurs. All our effect will start at the left of the screen, but how far across they span is dependant on the value we use here. By decreasing the value we're limiting our effect to a smaller area on the left of the screen. Try changing this value that the `cos` output is multiplied by to see the effect of high and low values. Here's the modification we're making in this experiment:

```
_root["unit" + a]._x = Math.cos(i)*300;
```

We're also going to add a rotation value again. By using a sine equation the value of rotation will move up and down in the same way that the sine curve does. Add the rotation code:

```
_root["unit" + a]._rotation = Math.sin(i)*600;
```

recursive_04

In this movie we'll again change the `_x` property to 300 and adding the same rotation value as in the last experiment. The difference between this experiment and the last is that we're increasing the number of clips attached. Here's the code to add/modify:

```
_root["unit" + a]._x = Math.cos(i)*300;
_root["unit" + a]._rotation = Math.sin(i)*600;
if ( a>1500 ) _root.stop();
```

recursive_05

For our next experiment we'll change the `_y` value and once again add rotation. When we changed the `_x` value by multiplying the cosine result by different values we discovered that the higher the value the further across the stage the span of the effect was. All the effects started on the left, and how far across they went was determined by the multiple value. With the `_y` value the principle is similar. All the effects will start at the top of the screen, but how far down the screen they span is affected by the multiple we use on the sine value. We're basing the rotation factor on a multiple of the cosine value this time. Add/modify the following lines:

```
_root["unit" + a]._y = Math.sin(i)*200;
_root["unit" + a]._rotation = Math.cos(i)*1000;
```

recursive_06

We'll now add an alpha effect to our existing variables to add a transparent effect. Another new variable that changes the color will also be added. We'll use the color object to set the RGB transformation value, which is determined by the value of `a`. Here's that has been added or modified to create the `recursive_06.swf` effect:

```
_root["unit" + a]._y = Math.sin(i)*200;
_root["unit" + a]._rotation = a;
_root["unit" + a]._alpha = 60;
var newcol = new color(_root["unit"+i]);
newcol.setRGB(a*(16777215/2));
```

recursive_07

Let's now make the rotation conditional. It will only happen when the value of a gets over 750. If you watch the effect you should be able to see where this occurs. Here's the code that deviates from our base clip:

```
if ( a>750 ) _root["unit" + a]._rotation = Math.cos(i)*60;
if ( a>1500 ) _root.stop();
```

recursive_08

Here we're replacing the cosine value with the sine value to calculate the `_x` value, and we're making a smaller number of instances by limiting the `if` statement to 200. Add or modify this code:

```
_root["unit" + a]._x = Math.sin(i)*600;
_root["unit" + a]._rotation = i;
_root["unit" + a]._yscale = Math.sin(i)*200;
if ( a>200 ) _root.stop();
```

recursive_09

This file reintroduces the `_yscale` factor. We once again are using the sine function to calculate the `_x` positioning with the following code:

```
_root["unit" + a]._y = Math.sin(i)*900;
_root["unit" + a]._x = Math.sin(i)*600;
_root["unit" + a]._rotation = i;
_root["unit" + a]._yscale = Math.sin(i)*300;
if ( a>900 ) _root.stop();
```

recursive_10

Let's now make the math used to calculate the `_x` and `_y` positions a bit more complex. We'll use the square root value in addition to the sine and cosine functions that we've been using previously to calculate these values.

```
_root["unit" + a]._y = Math.cos (a)*(200- Math.sqrt(a)*30)+Math.cos(a)+400;
_root["unit" + a]._x = Math.sin (a)*(100- Math.sqrt(a)*30)+Math.sin(a)+200;
if ( a>900 ) _root.stop();
```

recursive_11

We'll again make use of the code in the last example with slight changes in the numbers. We'll also now add in our other variable that we've made major use of: `_rotation`, `_yscale`, and `_xscale`.

```
_root["unit" + a]._y = Math.cos (a)*(200-Math.sqrt(a)*30)+Math.cos(a)+150;
_root["unit" + a]._x = Math.sin (a)*(200-Math.sqrt(a)*30)+Math.sin(a)+250;
_root["unit" + a]._rotation = i;
_root["unit" + a]._yscale = i/2;
_root["unit" + a]._xscale = i/2;
if ( a>150 ) _root.stop();
```

recursive_12

This final example is the same as the last, except that we've multiplied the square root value before putting it to use.

```
_root["unit" + a]._y = Math.cos (a)*(200-Math.sqrt(a)*7)+Math.cos(a)+150;
_root["unit" + a]._x = Math.sin (a)*(200-Math.sqrt(a)*3)+Math.sin(a)+250;
_root["unit" + a]._rotation = i;
_root["unit" + a]._yscale = i/2;
_root["unit" + a]._xscale = i/2;
if ( a>700 ) _root.stop();
```

It might be interesting to incorporate an alpha change over time to give an impression of 3-dimensionality in some of these FLAs. The last three FLAs suggested a new avenue of exploration with circular patterns evolving from the trig functions. It might also be interesting to break into an oval or spiral configuration with the introduction of a new counter variable such as:

```
_root["unit" + a]._y = Math.cos(a) * ( 200 - Math.sqrt(a) * newcounter of small increments ) + Math.cos(a) + 275;
```

It would be nice to subtly animate the `unit` clip, bringing the whole animation alive, or perhaps size the unit according the relative position of the mouse.

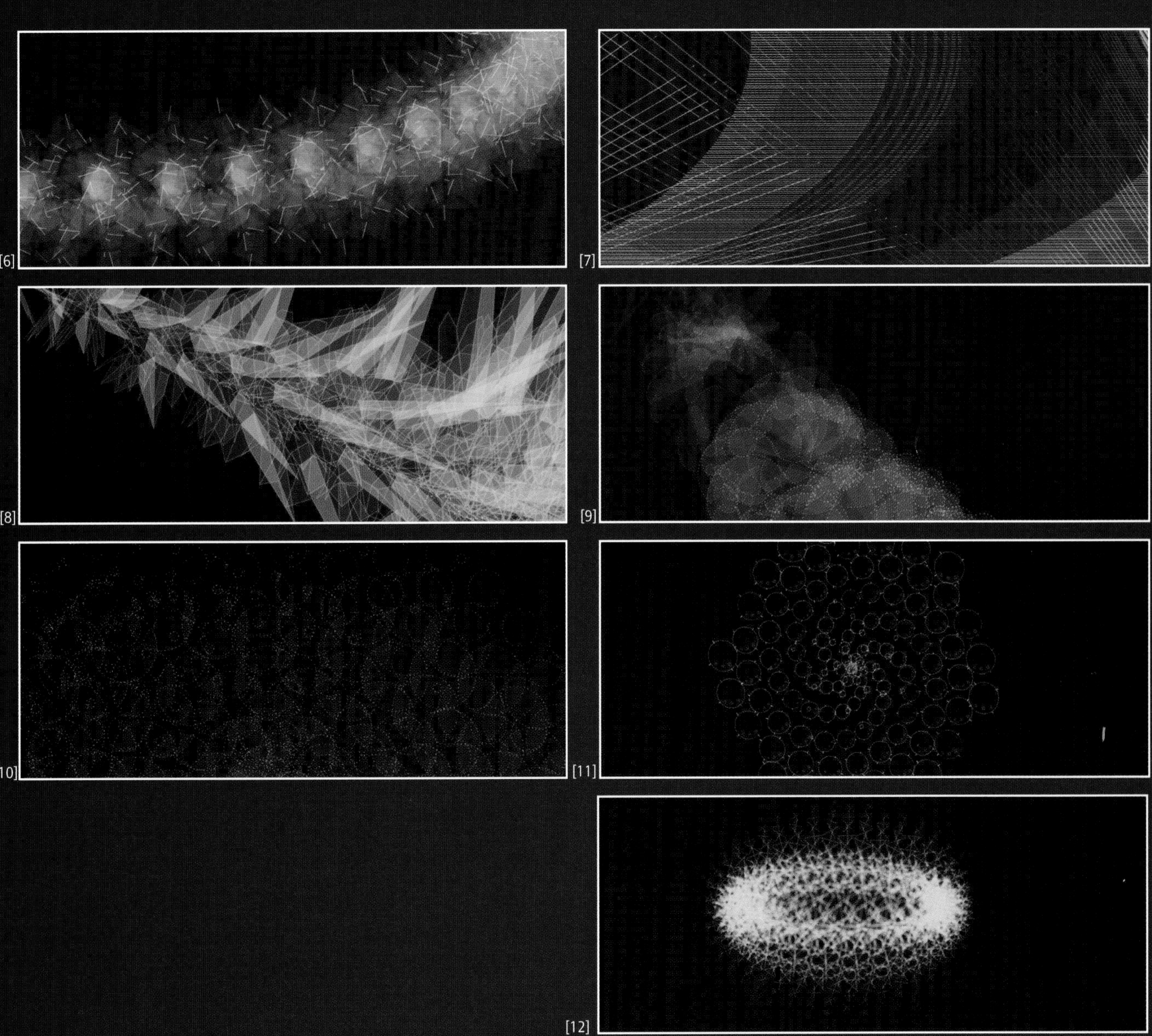

[6] [7] [8] [9] [10] [11] [12]

Swooping

For this experiment the code will sit on the first three frames of the movie on layer 1. On layer 2 the movieclip `line` is placed on frame 1, and it is given an instance name of `line`. Our code in frame 1 will create our initial variables and the code in frame 2 duplicates the movieclip. The code in frame 3 simply consists of the `gotoAndPlay(2)` action that creates a loop that duplicates the required number of clips. The result of our code is that duplicates of the movieclip are placed along a bezier path. A bezier curve is produced mathematically using a minimum of 4 points. Note that the final animation will depend on the processor speed of the computer running it. The code of the base FLA can be found in `swoop_01.fla`.

Here's the code.

Frame 1:

```
// sp
x0 = 0;
y0 = 0;
// dp
x3 = 0;
y3 = 300;
count = 0;

start = getTimer();
speed = 5000;

//bezpoint
x1 = 300
y1 = 30
x2 = 30
y2 = 30
// Bezier trajectory

cx = 3*(x1-x0);
cy = 3*(y1-y0);
bx = (3*(x2-x1))+(cx);
by = (3*(y2-y1))-cy;
ax = x3-x0-cx-bx;
ay = y3-y0-cy-by;
```

Frame 2:

```
elapsed = getTimer()-start;
if (elapsed > speed) {
    _root.stop();

} else {

   count = count+1;
   cube = elapsed/speed;
        square = square*square;
        cube = cube*cube*cube;
   square = cube;

duplicateMovieClip ("line", "line"+count, count);
_root["line"+count]._x = (ax*cube)+(bx*square)+(cx*elapsed/speed)+(x0);
_root["line"+count]._y = (ay*cube)+(by*square)+(cy*elapsed/speed)+(y0);
_root["line"+count]._rotation = count;

count = count+1;

}
```

We also have an `onClipEvent(load)` action attached to the `line` movieclip.

The key variables

x0 = the starting anchor x position for the bezier
y0 = the starting anchor y position for the bezier
x3 = the final anchor x position for the bezier
y3 = the final anchor x position for the bezier
count = the counter
speed = a variable that changes the length and speed of the plot
x1 y1 x2 y2 = the bezier handle coordinates

All the other variables in frame 1 are used to calculate the bezier trajectory and the frame 2 code serves to place our duplicate clips on the bezier curve. So, there's our base FLA and we'll now alter some variables and observe the effect changes. Each experiment will start at the base FLA unless told otherwise.

Iterations

swoop_02

For this FLA we're going to modify three of the variables. We're going to change the starting anchor position of the bezier (`y0`), which will move the starting position down. We'll also change the `x` bezier handle coordinates. If you look through our code you'll see what an impact changing just three variables can have due to the math involved in calculating the bezier curve. For example, `y0` goes toward the bezier trajectory (`cy` and `ay`) and towards the `_x` and `_y` positions of the duplicate movieclips. In the frame 1 code, here are the changes we'll make:

```
y0 = 600;
x1 = 200;
x2 = 0;
```

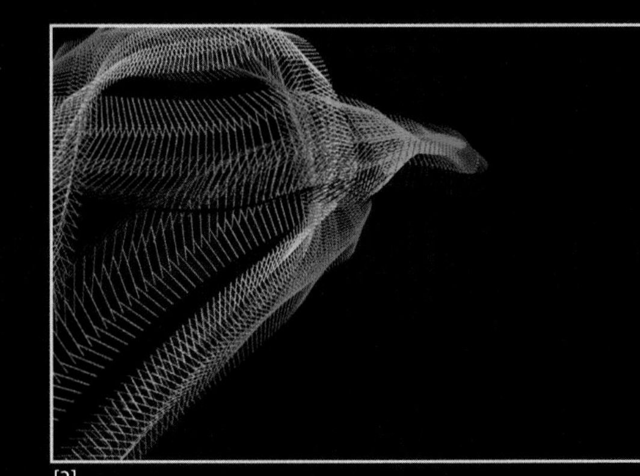
[2]

In this FLA we'll again play with our basic variables in the frame 1 code. This time we're going to modify the final anchor positions for the bezier (**x3** and **y3**) as well as the starting anchor positions. We're also increasing the **speed** variable to change the length and speed of the curve. In frame 2 we're going to add rotation to the **duplicateMovieClip** action. The rotation will be governed by the **count** value. In other words, it will increase by 1 with each clip that is duplicated. Here are the frame 1 modifications:

```
y0 = 150;
x3 = 150;
y3 = 0;
speed = 20000;
x1 = 150;
y1 = 150;
x2 = 300;
y2 = 900;
```

And here's our rotation code to add to frame 2:

```
_root["line"+count]._rotation = count;
```

swoop_03a

This experiment is the same as the last one, except for two modifications. This time **x3** will be set to 600, and we're going to add **_yscale** to frame 2 rather than rotation. As the value of **count** increases the size of the scaling on the y axis increases. Here's a recap in the frame 1 changes for this experiment.

```
y0 = 150;
x3 = 600;
y3 = 0;
speed = 20000;
x1 = 150;
y1 = 150;
x2 = 300;
y2 = 900;
```

Here's the scaling code for frame 2:

```
_root["line"+count]._yscale = count/10;
```

swoop_03b

This time we'll start with **swoop_03a** rather than going back to the base FLA. We'll make three modifications to the frame one variables. We're also going to add the rotation back into frame 2. This time it will have the same value as the scaling. Here are the frame 1 changes:

```
x0 = 300;
y0 = 200;
y3 = 150;
```

Add this to frame 2:

```
_root["line"+count]._rotation = count/10;
```

swoop_03c

This experiment will start with the code in **swoop_03b** and make changes to our scaling and rotation values in frame 2. The scaling value of the clip will be the same as the **count** value (which equates to the number of clips duplicated at that point), and the rotation value will be twice that figure.

```
_root["line"+count]._yscale = count;
_root["line"+count]._rotation = count*2;
```

There are many interesting spatial convolutions to be had from changing these 2 lines and I could go on and on...

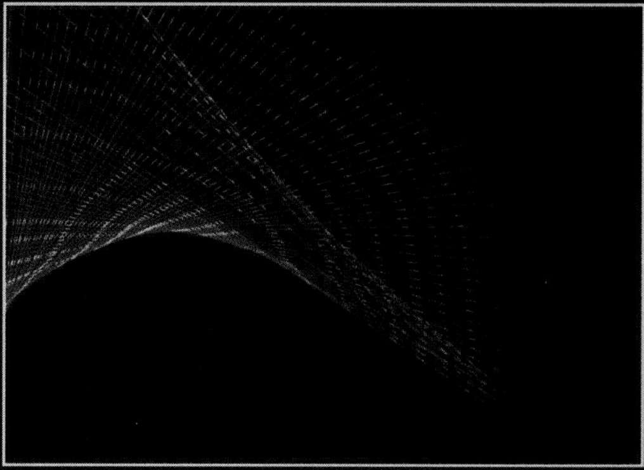

[3]

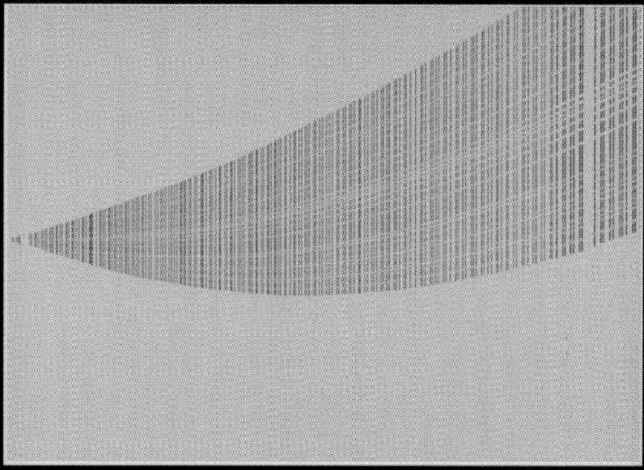

[3a]

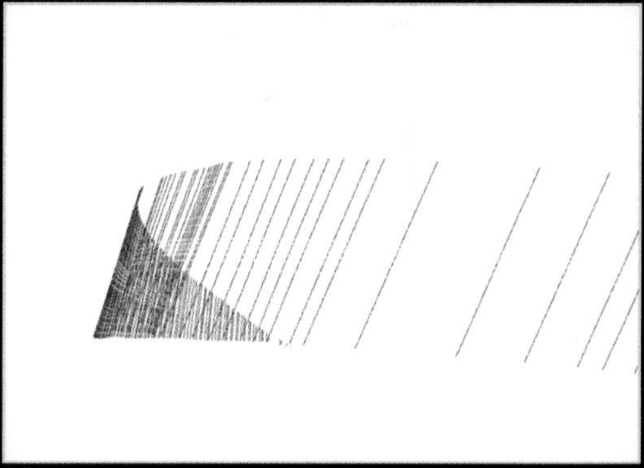

[3b]

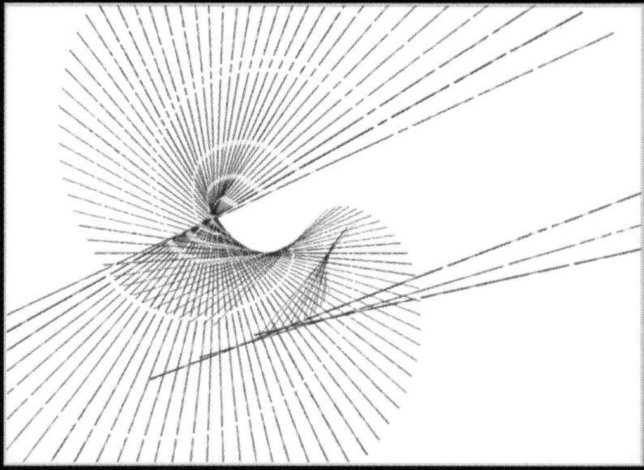

[3c]

swoop_04
We'll now return to the base FLA for the next experiment. We'll make modifications to the frame 1 variables as we did in previous experiments. Our main change here will occur in frame 2 where we're going to add rotation again, but this time it will have a more complex formula based on the bezier handle coordinates. A motion tween has been added to the `line` movieclip for this experiment. Here's the code I've altered in frame 1:

```
y0 = 50;
x3 = 150;
y3 = 0;
speed = 10000;
x1 = 150;
y1 = 150;
x2 = 300;
y2 = 900;
```

Here's our new rotation formula for frame 2:

```
_root["line"+count]._rotation = ((ax*cube)+
  ➥ (bx*square)+(cx*elapsed/speed)+(x0));
```

swoop_05
In this experiment we're once again going to change the base FLA's handle coordinates and start and final anchor positions. Our main changes though will be to the frame 2 `duplicateMovieClip` code. We're going to half the `_x` position of the duplicate clips and set the `_y` position to the value of `count`. Also note that rotation and alpha, again linked to the `count` value, has been added. Our movieclip has had motion tweens added once more. Let's start with the frame 1 modifications:

```
y0 = 150;
x3 = 150;
y3 = 0;
x1 = 150
y1 = 150
x2 = 100
y2 = 300
```

Here's the frame 2 changes:

```
_root["line"+count]._x = ((ax*cube)+
  ➥(bx*square)+(cx*elapsed/speed)+(x0))/2;
_root["line"+count]._y = count;
_root["line"+count]._rotation = count*15;
_root["line"+count]._alpha = 80-(count/5);
```

Finally, we're going to add rotation to the `onClipEvent` handler that we attached to the `line` movieclip as well:

```
onClipEvent ( enterFrame ) {
  _rotation+=1;
}
```

swoop_06
As usual we'll start by altering the frame 1 variables:

```
x3 = 150;
y3 = 150;
speed = 1000;
x1 = 150;
y1 = 150;
x2 = 100;
```

We're going to then add rotation to frame 2, this time using a more complex formula based on the bezier handle coordinates:

```
_root["line"+count]._rotation = ((ax*cube)+
  ➥ (bx*square)+(cx*elapsed/speed)+(x0))*5;
```

As in the last experiment, we're going to add code to the movieclip's `onClipEvent` handler. This again contains rotation, but we're also adding a random scaling based on the mouse position on the x axis. This code makes the movie 'freak out' when the clip is touched with the mouse

```
onClipEvent ( enterFrame ) {
  _rotation+=5;
  if (_root._xmouse>0 && _root._xmouse<300)
    _yscale=Math.random()*100;
}
```

swoop_07
Here's are the frame 1 variables that deviate from the base FLA in this experiment:

```
x0 = 120;
y0 = 50;
y3 = 150;
speed = 2000;
x1 = 250;
y1 = 150;
x2 = 100;
y2 = 1;
```

In frame 2 we're going to add rotation, alpha and scaling:

```
_root["line"+count]._rotation = count*3
_root["line"+count]._alpha = 80-count;
_root["line"+count]._yscale = (cx*elapsed/speed);
```

This time the `onClipEvent` handler will use the mouse's _x position to vary rotation. The code makes the 3D object twist and turn as it's touched:

```
onClipEvent ( enterFrame ) {
  _rotation+=1
  if (_root._xmouse>0 && _root._xmouse<300){
   ➥ _rotation+=_xmouse/50;
  }
}
```

I really liked the way `swoop_07` looked, appearing as a three-dimensional structure turning in space (a flat shape extruded along a bezier!), the twist being affected by the mouse pointer. It would be interesting to develop this further with scaling control and perhaps introduce the color object to subtly change the hues of each of the elements depending on the relative position of the mouse. To give this cocoon/dragonfly organism even more life, it would great to introduce the sound object perhaps playing loops/drones again dependent on the behavior of the organism!

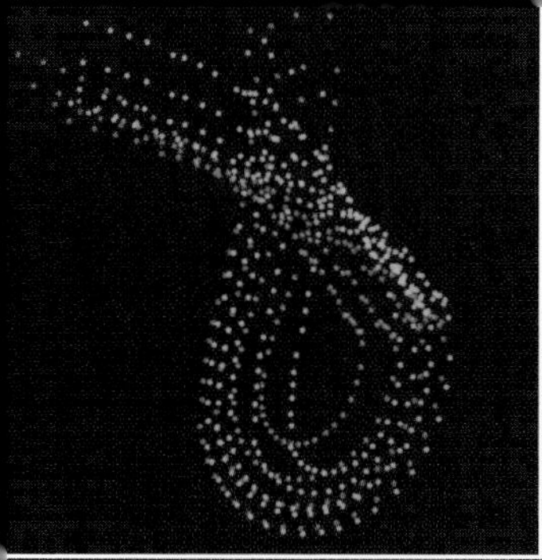

[4]

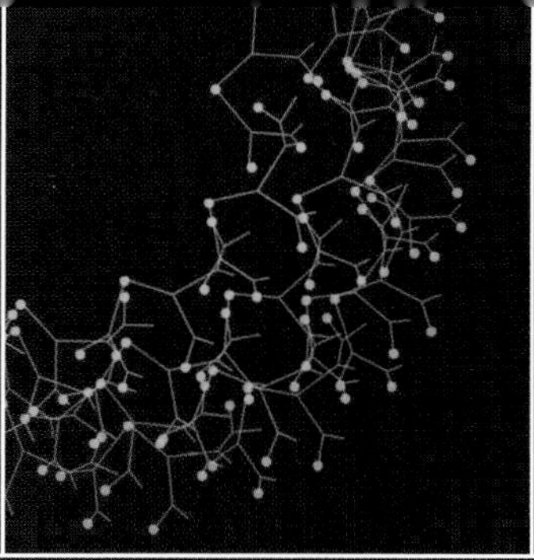

[5]

[6]

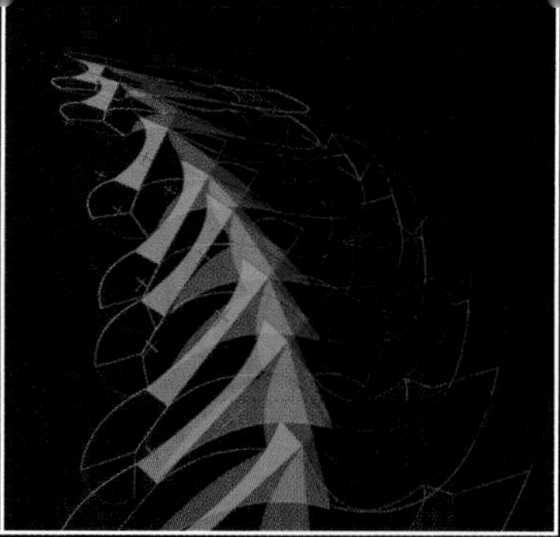

[7]

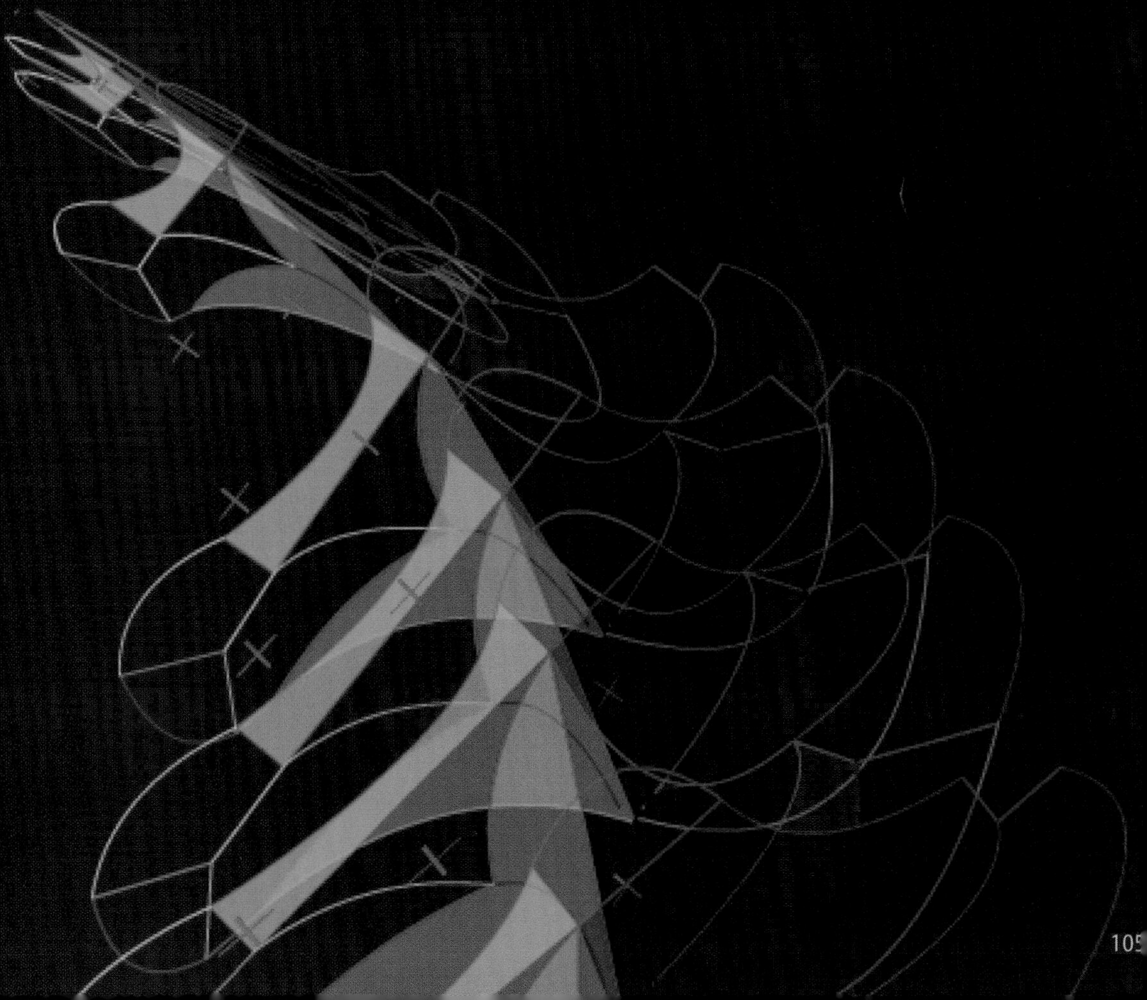

Circling

Our base FLA for this experiment will be **circling_01.fla**. This movie is based around the **line** clip, which is placed off the stage in the **instance** layer of the main movie. The **line** clip has a motion tween over 80 frames and has the instance name **line**. It rotates once over 40 frames shrinking in size, and then returns to its original size rotating once back out in the opposite direction. The code for this experiment is placed over three frames in the main movie's **actions** layer. The first frame contains our variables and a function to degrees to radians:

```
var alphdev = 1;
var kolorcycle = "on";

var curve = Math.floor(Math.random()*100) + 1;
var ydist = Math.floor(Math.random()*10) + 1;

// this function is used to calculate
// a point on a circle

var radius = 1000;
var centerX = 225;
var centerY = 150;
var rotAngleDeg = 0;
var rotAngleRad;

function degreesToRadians(degrees) {
  return (degrees/180) * Math.PI;
}
```

Frame 2 contains our actions to duplicate the **line** movieclip. A counter **x** is also set here:

```
duplicateMovieClip ("line", "line" + x, x);

rotAngleDeg +=5;

rotAngleRad = degreesToRadians(rotAngleDeg);
line._y= centerY - Math.sin(rotAngleRad )*
  ➥ _ymouse/10;
line._x= centerX + Math.cos(rotAngleRad )*
  ➥ _xmouse/10;

if (kolorcycle == "on") {
  var newcol = new color("line");
  newcol.setRGB(x*(16777215/11)) ;
}

line._alpha=x*alphdev;
line._yscale=x/15;
line._xscale=x/15;
line._visible=false

if ( x>70) {
  removeMovieClip ( "line" + (x-70 ));
  x = 1;
}
```

This code basically plots duplications of a movieclip with the instance name **line** on a circular path. However the path is also dependent on the mouse position so the final plot can be oval in the x or y directions. Each newly plotted duplicate is also individually colored using the color object, its alpha and x/y scale set according to a variable. There is a max of 70 duplications on the screen at any one time and the duplications are plotted on the fly creating quite complex animations. On frame 3 we increase the value of **x** by one and create a loop back to frame 2.

```
x++;
gotoAndPlay (2);
```

This code basically plots duplications of a movieclip with the instance name **line** on a circular path. However the path is also dependent on the mouse position so the final plot can be oval in the x or y directions. Each newly plotted duplicate is also individually coloured using the colour object, its alpha and x/y scale set according to a variable. There is a max of 70 duplications on the screen at any one time and the duplications are plotted on the fly creating quite complex animations.

The key variables

alphadev = the variable used to control the **_alpha** values of duplicated clips
kolorcycle = a switch to control whether the color object is set for individual duplicated clips and therefore whether they are individually colored
centerX = the x position of the center of the circular path
centerY = the y position of the center of the circular path
rotAngleDeg = a variable used in the plotting of the circular path at a later stage
rotAngleRad = the rotation increment of the circular path for the next plotted position. It is measured in radians and is calculated from the function defined in frame 1

Let's now experiment with the basic FLA and see what effects we can achieve.

circling_02
In our first variation we're simply going to add rotation to the frame 2 code. This rotation is based on a multiple of our counter variable **x**. The higher the counter value, the higher the rotation value.

```
line._rotation = x*50;
```

circling_03
We'll now modify that rotation for our next experiment. Instead of basing the multiple of **x** on a fixed value we'll base it on the **curve** variable that gives us a random value.

```
line._rotation = curve*x;
```

We'll also add some **onClipEvent** actions to the **line** movieclip. These actions will increment the rotation value and use the mouse position to alter the **_x** and **_y** positions of the clips.

```
onClipEvent(enterFrame){
   _rotation++;
   if (_y<_ymouse) {
      _y=_y+2;
   } else {
      _y=_y-1;
   }

   if (_x<_xmouse) {
      _x=_x+2;
   } else {
      _x=_x-1;
   }
}
```

circling_04
In this example we'll again make positioning affected by the mouse by attaching code to the **line** clip.

```
onClipEvent(enterFrame){
   _rotation++;
   if (_y<_ymouse) {
      _y+=2;
   } else {
      _y-=1;
   }

   if (_x<_xmouse) {
      _x+=2;
   } else {
      _x-=1;
   }
}
```

In frame 2 of the main timeline we're going to modify a few values. The alpha value of the clip will now be reached by multiplying the counter by 10 rather than **alphadev**. The scaling of the clips is being increased by using the value of the counter rather than dividing it by 5. Rotation is added again and is calculated as a multiple of the counter.

```
line._alpha=x*10;
line._yscale=x;
line._xscale=x;
line._rotation = 100*x;
```

circling_05
This experiment changes the color slightly in frame 2 by changing the number that the larger integer is divided by.

```
if (kolorcycle == "on") {
   var newcol = new color("line");
   newcol.setRGB(x*(16777215/30)) ;
}
```

Our scaling and rotation are all set to the value of **x** for this experiment:

```
line._yscale = x;
line._xscale = x;
line._rotation = x;
```

We're also going increase the period that a clip is present by increasing the counter value at which clips are removed:

```
if (x>300) {
   removeMovieClip ("line" + (x-300));
   x = 1;
}
```

Once again we're going to add actions to the duplicated clips. The difference in this example to the last is that the rotation will calculated by mouse movement in the y axis rather than a simple increment.

```
onClipEvent(enterFrame){
   _rotation+=_ymouse/25;
   if (_y<_ymouse) {
      _y=_y+2;
   } else {
      _y=_y-1;
   }

   if (_x<_xmouse) {
      _x=_x+2;
   } else {
      _x=_x-1;
   }
}
```

circling_06
Our deviations from the base file in this experiment start in frame 1 this time. We're going to half the value of **alphdev** and turn off the **kolorcycle** variable.

```
var alphdev = .5;
var kolorcycle = "off";
```

In frame 2 we're changing the scaling factors from **x/15** to **x/10**, making the clips larger. We're going to increase the lifetime of the clips again, this time to 200. Here are the changes:

```
line._yscale=x/10;
line._xscale=x/10;

if (x>200) {
   removeMovieClip ( "line" + ( x-200 ));
   x = 1;
}
```

The actions that we add to the clip this time will revert back to using the standard rotation increment:

```
onClipEvent(enterFrame){
   _rotation++;
   if (_y<_ymouse) {
      _y=_y+2;
   } else {
      _y=_y-1;
   }

   if (_x<_xmouse) {
      _x=_x+2;
   } else {
      _x=_x-1;
   }
}
```

circling_07
This time we'll start where the last example left off rather than going back to the base file. On frame 1 we're going to alter the **alphadev** value again and turn the **kolorcycle** variable back on.

```
var alphdev = .3;
var kolorcycle = "on";
```

In frame 2 we're going to once again change the value that the large integer is divided by to create the new color variable. Finally we'll re-add rotation and set it to the value of the counter.

```
if (kolorcycle == "on") {
    var newcol = new color("line");
    newcol.setRGB(x*(16777215/27));
}

line._rotation = x;
```

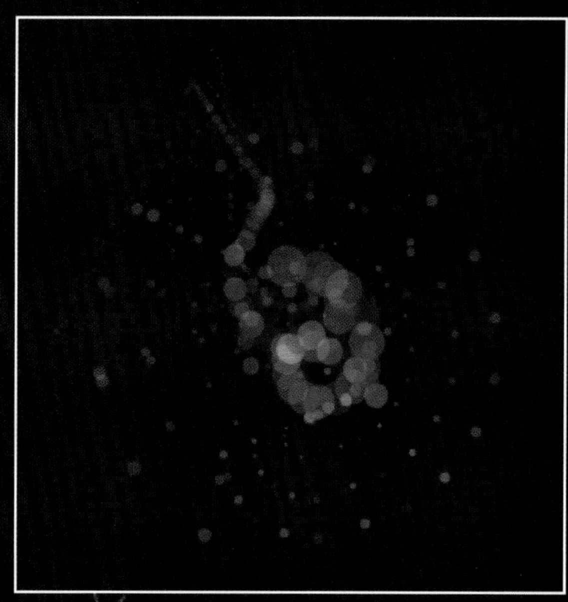

circling_08
We'll now return to the base FLA for our final example and change the **alphadev** value in frame 1:

```
var alphdev = .7;
```

In frame 2 we'll change the divider use to calculate the color again and we'll also add rotation and set that and the scaling using the counter value. Here are the changes:

```
newcol.setRGB(x*(16777215/27)) ;

line._yscale=x/8;
line._xscale=x/8;
line._rotation = x*50;
```

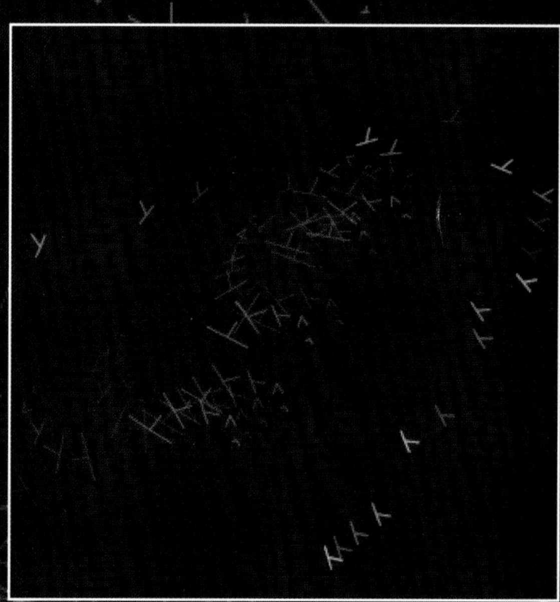

We'll once again add mouse-driven actions to the duplicate clips:

```
onClipEvent(enterFrame){
   _rotation++;
   if (_y<_ymouse) {
      _y=_y+.5;
   } else {
      _y=_y-1;
   }

   if (_x<_xmouse) {
      _x=_x+.5;
   } else {
      _x=_x-1;
   }
}
```

Looking back at this sequence I quite like the way that **circling_05** was working. It might be interesting to add a more dynamic mouse control environment to some of the other experiments in this sequence similar to the way **circling_05** works.

Still

This experiment revolves around a movieclip named `Symbol 4` that is placed just off the stage and given the instance name `line`. If you look at `still_01.fla` you'll see that the code for this experiment all lives on one frame. Here it is:

```
var kolorcycle = "on";
var replikants = 500;
var xpos = 2;
var ypos = 3;
var curve = 1;
var ydist = 1;
var xdist = 1.2;
for (var i = 1; i<=replikants; i++) {
  duplicateMovieClip (line, "line"+i, i);
  _root["line"+i]._x = xpos;
  _root["line"+i]._y = ypos;
  _root["line"+i]._rotation = xpos*curve;
  _root["line"+i]._alpha = i/(replikants/35);

  if (xpos>600) {
    xpos = 1;
  }
  if (ypos>300) {
    ypos = 1;
  }

  if (kolorcycle == "on") {
    var newcol = new color("line");
    newcol.setRGB(xpos*(16777215/50));
  }
  ypos = ypos+ydist;
  xpos = xpos+xdist;
  i++;
}

stop ();
```

Here we're using a simple for loop to duplicate the `line` clip and place instances on the stage. A couple of conditionals check to make sure the next duplication in the loop doesn't appear off of the screen, and another checks to see whether color cycling is switched on or off.

The key variables

`kolorcycle` = a switch to control whether the color object is set for individual duplicated clips and therefore whether they are individually colored
`replikants` = the number of replications to be created
`xpos` = the starting x position for the first duplication
`ypos` = the starting y position for the first duplication
`curve` = a variable used to give a curved appearance to rows of duplication
`xdist` = the incremental x distance between each duplication
`ydist` = the incremental y distance between each duplication

Now let's play with some variations of this base code and see what the results of particular changes are.

We'll start by altering some simple variables such as the number of replications, positioning, curve and distribution. Notice that the value divided by in the `if` loop has been altered, but this will have no effect as we have the color cycle turned off here. Here are the changes you can find in the FLA:

```
var replikants = 1000;
var ypos = 70;
var curve = 10;
var ydist = .2;

if (kolorcycle == "on") {
  var newcol = new color("line");
  newcol.setRGB(xpos*(16777215/50));
}
```

still_03

Starting where we left the last example we'll now turn the color cycle on so that the change we made in the last example will now occur. We'll play with some of the other variables too to examine the impact. We'll make the number of **replikants** smaller than we've used before, we'll make the curve value larger and the **y** distribution much bigger. Here's the code that's been changed in the file:

```
var kolorcycle = "on";
var replikants = 300;
var xpos = 150;
var curve = 50;
var ydist = 50;
```

still_04
We'll now increase the value of the curve by just 1 from its value in `still_03.fla`. This is only a small change, but the configuration of the final replication is completely different. Our only other change will be to alter the divider used to calculate the color. Make the following changes to `5xe_base03.fla`:

```
var curve = 51;
newcol.setRGB(xpos*(16777215/4));
```

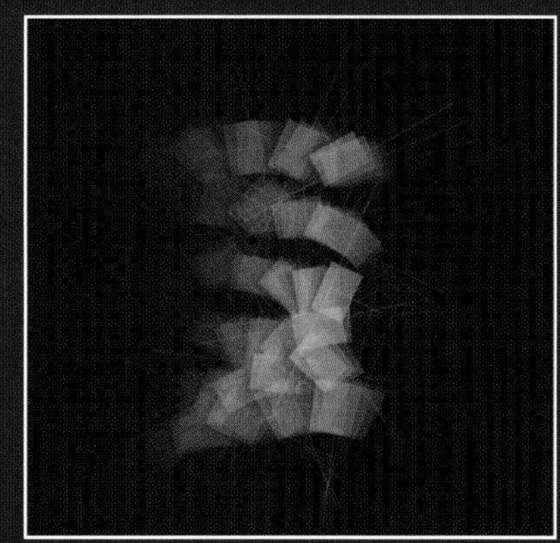

still_05
Continuing from where we left off in `still_04.fla`, we'll turn the color cycle off again. We'll also alter the number of replications, the both the `x` and `y` starting positions and distribution. Here's what's different in the file from the last example:

```
var kolorcycle = "off";
var replikants = 100;
var xpos = 300;
var ypos = 140;
var ydist = .1;
var xdist = .1;
```

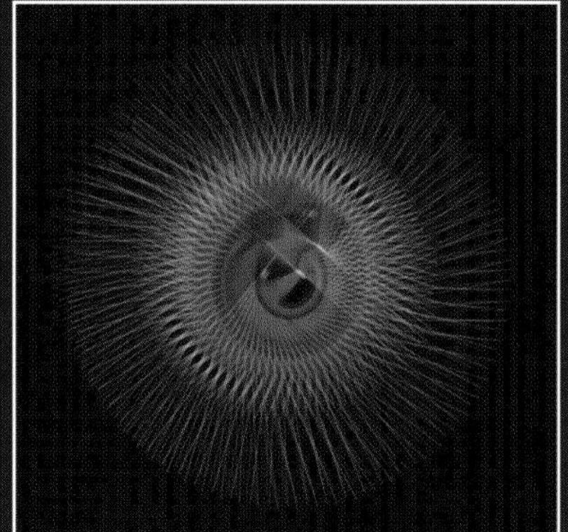

still_06
In the next example we'll once again continue where we left off rather than returning to the base FLA. We'll alter the curve and number of replications, but the main change is the adding of scaling to the `for` loop. This scaling is calculated using the counter value `i`. Here's the code to modify:

```
var replikants = 300;
var curve = 15;

_root["line"+i]._xscale = i/10;
_root["line"+i]._yscale = i/ydist;
```

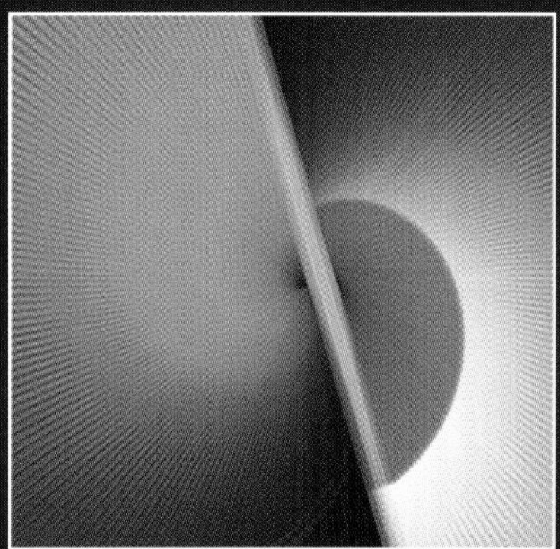

still_07
We'll continue to our next example by modifying the start of `for` loop. We're going to now use sine and cosine values to calculate the `_x` and `_y` positioning. We've removed the scaling and rotation from this example. The loop will now start as follows:

```
for (var i = 1; i<=replikants; i++) {
  duplicateMovieClip (line, "line"+i, i);
  _root["line"+i]._x = Math.sin (i)*(xpos-i)+300
  _root["line"+i]._y = Math.cos (i)*(ypos-i)+150
  _root["line"+i]._alpha = i/(replikants/35);
```

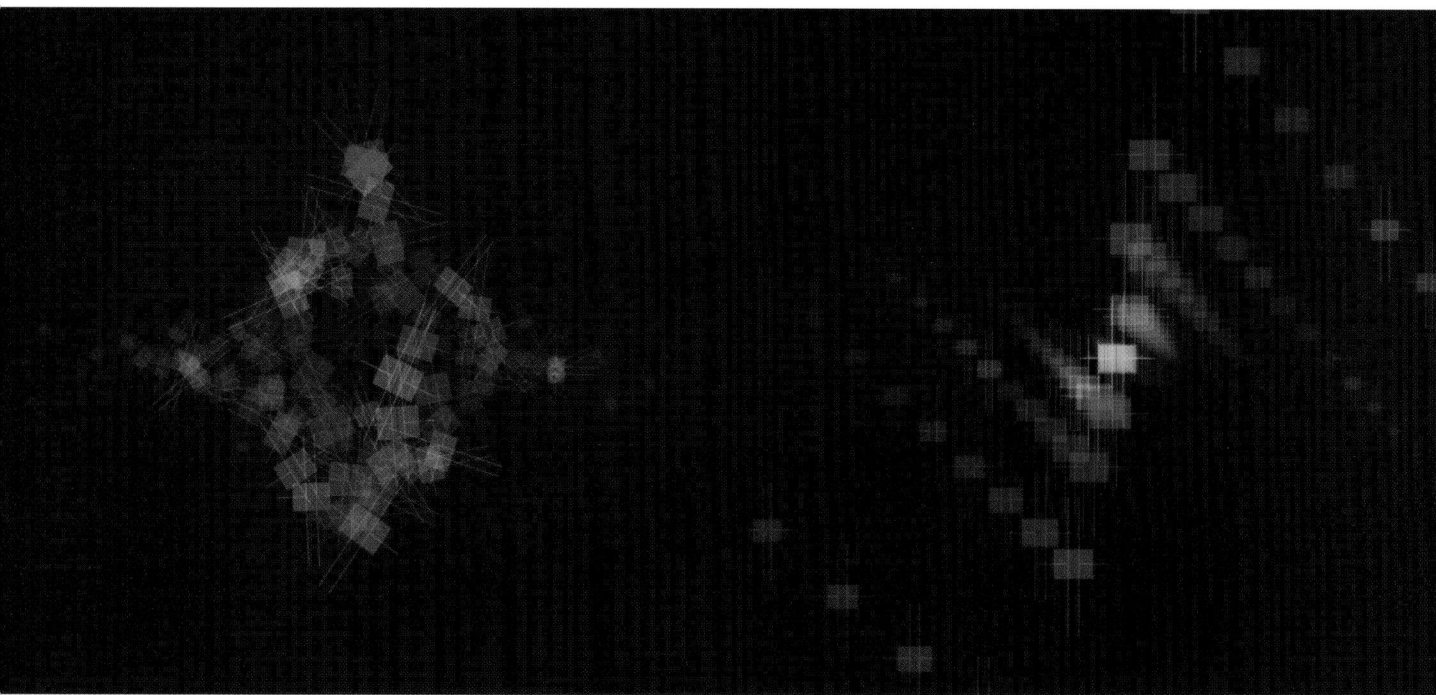

still_08
For this example we're going to take the previous example and build on it. We'll turn the color cycle on once again. We'll also increase the divider used to calculate the color in the `for` loop. The curve value is going to be increased as well. We'll add the rotation and scaling in again and slightly alter the `_y` position math. Here are the modifications:

```
var kolorcycle = "on";

var curve = 99;

for (var i = 1; i<=replikants; i++) {
  duplicateMovieClip (line, "line"+i, i);
  _root["line"+i]._x = Math.sin (i)*
  ➥ (xpos-i)+300;
  _root["line"+i]._y = Math.cos (i)*
  ➥ (ypos-i)+140;
  _root["line"+i]._rotation = ypos*curve;
  _root["line"+i]._alpha = i/(replikants/35);
  _root["line"+i]._xscale = i/10;
  _root["line"+i]._yscale = i/10;


if (kolorcycle == "on") {
  var newcol = new color("line");
  newcol.setRGB(xpos*(16777215/36));
}
```

still_09
For our final example we'll alter the curve value and the divider used to get a color. The main change in this file is that we're using the `tan` value to calculate both the `_x` and `_y` positions rather than `sin` and `cos`. Here are our final changes:

```
var curve = 99;

_root["line"+i]._x = Math.tan (i)*(xpos-i)+300;
_root["line"+i]._y = Math.tan (i)*(ypos-i)+140;

newcol.setRGB(xpos*(16777215/35));
```

With some of these files I would like to have made a slide show moving though each different FLA randomizing various element on each cycle. Later I might add a mask layer above the `line` clip to slowly reveal the configurations as opposed to them suddenly appearing on the screen.

I'm a resident of London, born on 31 January 1973. Having previously worked as a van driver, nanny, ice cream seller, sandwich maker and band manager, in 1997 I answered an ad that said "Do you want to be a web designer?". I now work through my own company Hi-Rise and in collaboration with Anthony Burrill as friendchip. Friendchip's first commercial job was for German electronic band Kraftwerk, and we've gone on to work largely with bands and music companies. Current projects include ongoing work for 13amp.tv, and a new site for Bjork (littleibooks.com). As Hi-Rise I'm working with airside on a multi-player game for 23rdfloor.com.

The longer that you write code, the more you realize that you're amongst the few groups of people that have a use for the algebra they learnt at school. Math is obviously the basis of all computer code, and you can only avoid it for so long.

Creating sound and graphics with code allows you to be surprised by your own work. Computers put things together in ways that no human would. I'm a strong believer in humor in web sites. We are after all in the business of entertainment, and allowing computers to make the choices leads to a lot of humorous situations. At least it makes me laugh.

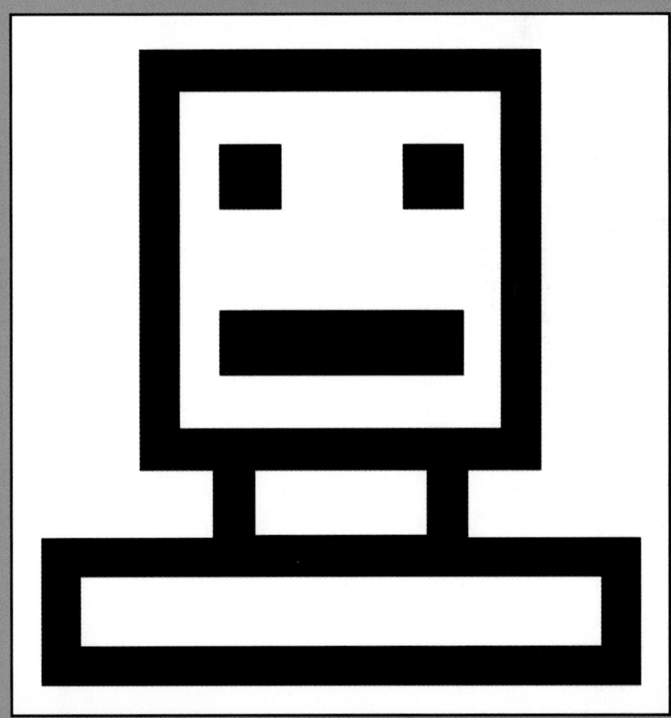

kip parker

friendchip.com

Composeur

This was inspired by a few lines in *Gödel, Escher, Bach*, the Douglas Hoftstadter book loved by geeks everywhere, and also a fine source of interesting mathematical ideas. Whilst discussing computer-generated music, he mentions the thought that a combination of Brownian and random movement produces lines of music closest to those humans write. Brownian motion is movement by steps, as in plus or minus one. This piece proves that whilst that theory may occasionally produce interesting pieces of music, the vast majority is utter drivel.

Take a look in `composeur.fla` to see how this experiment is structured. The movie has just two graphical movieclip symbols and 12 sound symbols in the Library. The movieclips are linked as `one` and `line`, and the sounds are numbered from 12 (low) to 1 (high). The main code is in frame 1 of Layer 2 in the main movie. The code in frame 2 of this layer tells the movie to play and calls the `compose` function. The code in frames 3 to 18 simply consists of the `getSound` statement. The final frame sends the movie back to frame 2, and we'll look at why shortly. Let's take a look at the main code in frame 1 then:

```
range = 300;
pitches = 12;

height = 400;
notes = 16;
tone = range/pitches;
unit = 600/(notes+1);
notesArr = new Array();
//set up movies

for (i=1; i<=notes; i++) {
     _root.attachMovie( "one", "note"+i, i+pitches );
     mv = this["note"+i];
     mv._x = i*unit;
     mv._y = height/2;
     notesArr[i] = mv;
}

for (j=1;j<=pitches;j+=2){
     _root.attachMovie( "line", "line"+j, j );
     line = this["line"+j];
     line._x = 300;
     line._y = (j*tone)+((height-range)/2);
}

function compose(){
    //a starting point
    currPoint = random(pitches)+1;
    for(i=1;i<=notes;i++){
    volume = random(3)+1;
    notesArr[i]._y = (currPoint*tone)+((height-range)/2);
    notesArr[i]._width = volume*10;
    notesArr[i]._height = volume*10;
    notesArr[i].pitch = currPoint;
    notesArr[i].volume = volume;
       if(random(2)==1){
           //random movement
           currPoint = random(12)+1;
       }else{
          if(currPoint == pitches){
             currPoint--;
          }else if(currPoint == 1){
             currPoint++;
          }else{
```

```
                //50% 50% chance
                currPoint++;
            }else{
                currPoint--;
            }
        }
    }
  }
}
```

```
offset = 2;
function getSound(){
    beat = _currentframe - offset;
    aNote = new Sound();
    aNote.attachSound(notesArr[beat].pitch);
    aNote.setVolume(33*notesArr[beat].volume);
    aNote.start();
    notesArr[beat].gotoAndStop(2);
    if(beat == 1){
        notesArr[notes].gotoAndStop(1);
    }else{
        notesArr[beat-1].gotoAndStop(1);
    }
}
```

The key variables

`pitches` = the number of "staves"
`height` = a variable used to help determine the `_y` coordinates of the clips
`notes` = the number of notes
`offset` = the number of frames after which the beats start

Let's now examine how the code works.

The two **`for`** loops at the beginning just set up the movie. It loops through once to layout the number of notes specified by **`notes`**, and then loops through again to layout the **`staves`**. The notes are all stored in an array called **`notesArr`**.

Each time the movie loops through, the **`compose`** function is called. A point at which to start in the range of notes is randomly chosen. Then it loops through for the number of **`notes`**, each time randomly setting a volume that determines the volume of the sound and the width/height of the note. The pitch for the note is then set, which determines the pitch it plays and its position on the stave. Finally, the next note is chosen, using the above theory. It has a random 50/50 chance of either moving randomly to any note in the 12-note range, or moving one up or down.

Earlier I mentioned that frames 3 to 18 contain the **`getSound()`** statement. That's 16 frames – one for each note. **`getSound()`** works out which beat is calling it by looking at the current frame number and subtracting **`offset`**. It then gets the pitch from that clip and creates a new sound object with it in, sets the volume, and then plays the sound. Finally the movieclip is told to got to frame 2, which just turns it to white, and the last clip is told to go back to frame 1 (back to the default state).

Test the effect, which can be found in **`composeur.swf`**. It'll play some decent tunes from time to time.

composeur2

To improve the likelihood of something tuneful, I changed the plus or minus 1 motion to include the possibility of no movement:

```
if (random(2)==1){
      currPoint+=random(3)-1;
}else{
      currPoint--;
}
```

This code replaces:

```
if (random(2)==1){
      currPoint++;
}else{
      currPoint--;
}
```

composeur3

If you like things more spiky you can increase the likelihood of random movement by replacing the original `if(random(2)==1)` condition with:

```
if(random(5)>=1)
```

To go a little further with this experiment it might be worth giving different lengths to each note. This could be achieved by using loops in the sound object.

There are many different ways that the movement of the notes could be graphically displayed. There's no real reason to do it as traditionally as I have.

Another good feature of the sound object is that you can set panning. It might be nice to have the notes bouncing about from ear to ear. Or maybe work out how to do two part harmony.

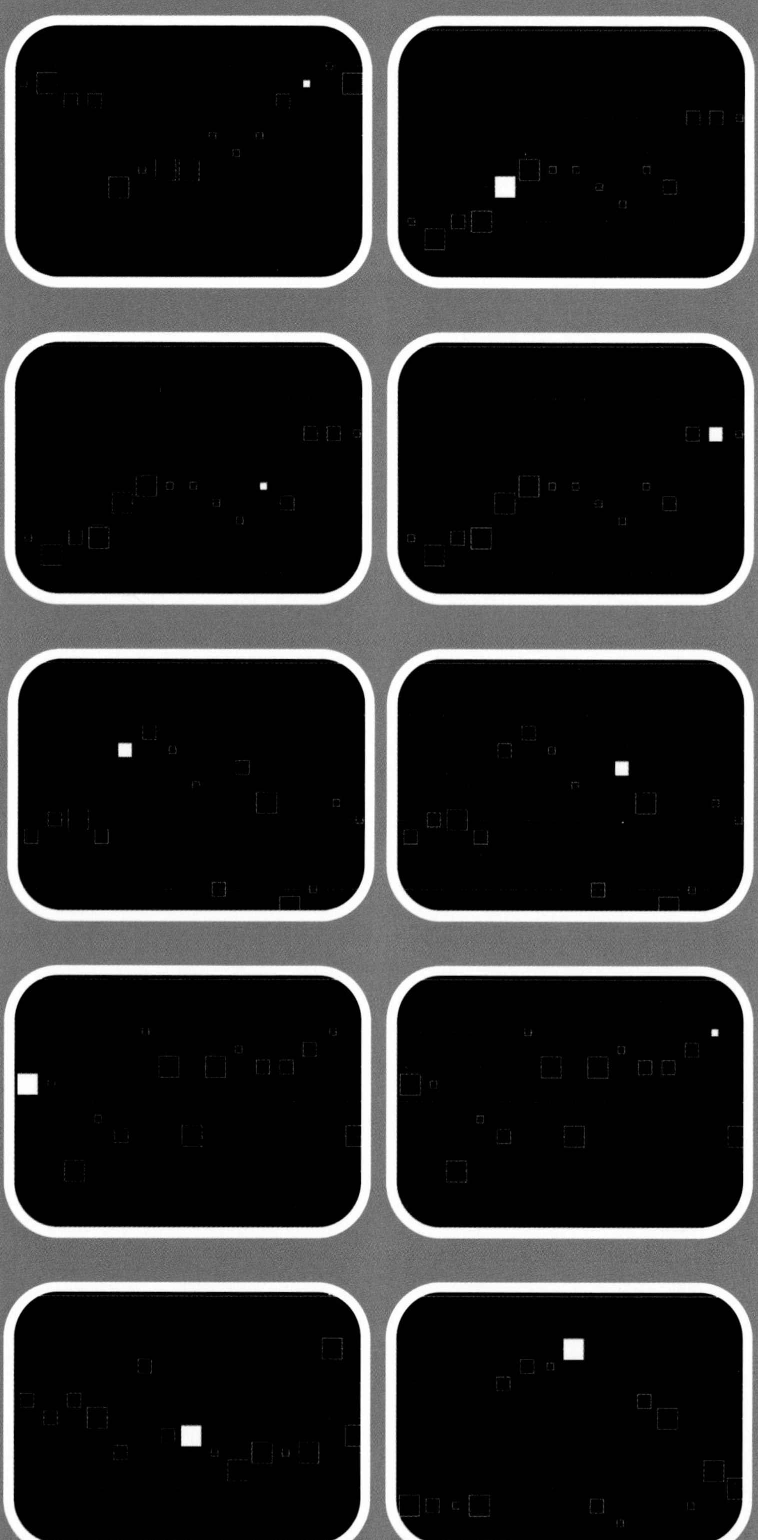

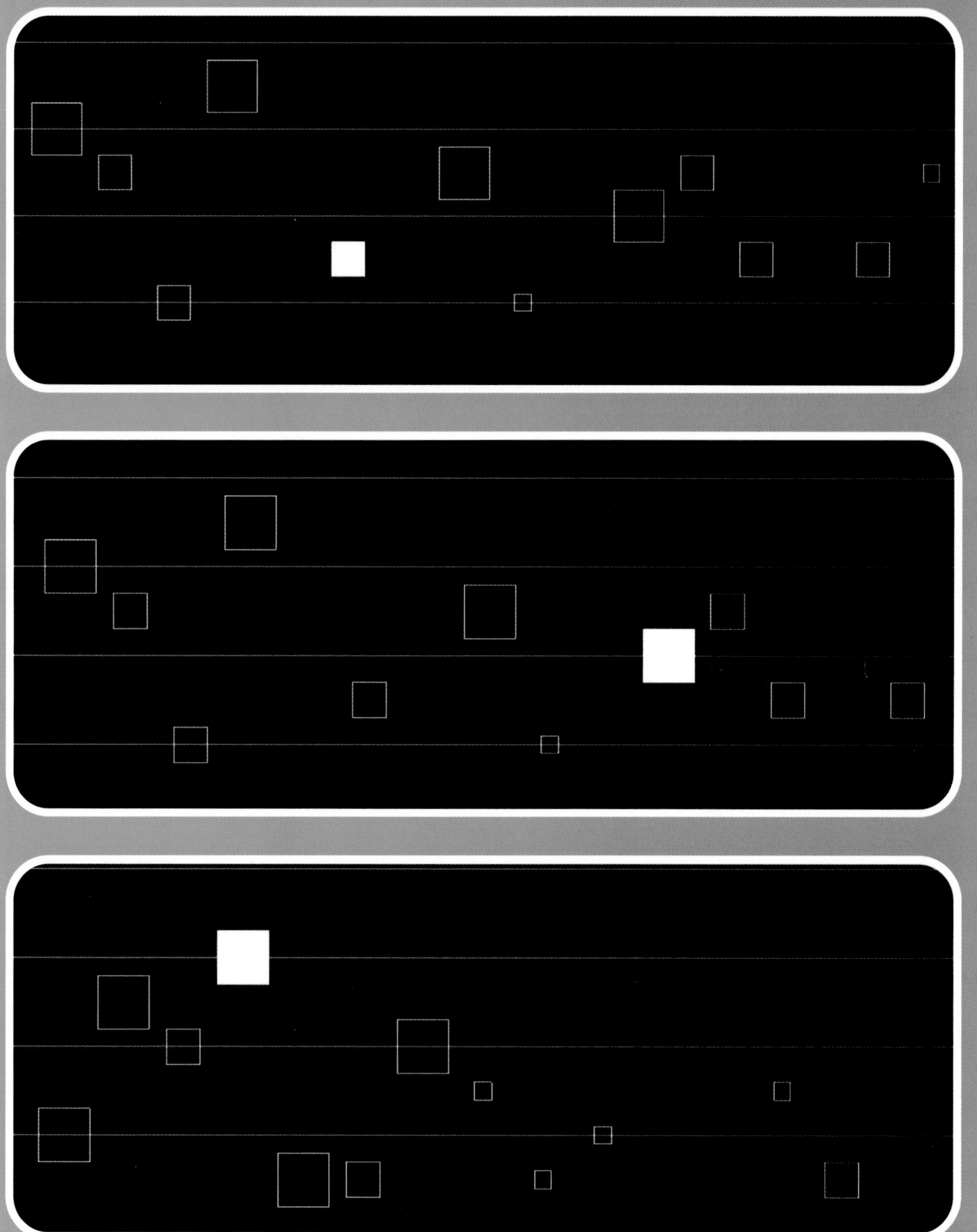

Pause

Inspired, okay stolen, from Bridget Riley's *Movement in Squares*, 1961. The painting was inspired by her desire to record her impressions of when a squall obscured the black-and-white marble pattern of the paving in a piazza.

I wanted to see how well I could copy the piece programmatically. The following code came up with something close to what I was after.

```
height = 30;
width = 30;
across = 600;
down = 400;

min = width/20;
max = width - min;

k = 0;
aimAt = 28;
xPos = 0;

grey = 0;

i = 0;
while(xPos<across){
    width = min+(adjusted(aimAt-i));
    for(j=0; j<down/height; j++){
        k++;
        attachMovie("sq","sq"+k,k);
        clip = this["sq"+k];
        if((k+i)%2==1){
            hex = 0x000000;
        }else{
            hex = 0xffffff;
        }
        colour = new Color(clip);
        colour.setRGB(hex);
        clip._x = xPos + width;
        clip._y = j*height;
        clip._width = width;
        clip._height = height;
    }
    xPos+=width;
    i++;
}


function adjusted(num){
    if(num<0){
        num = num*-1;
    }
    if(num>max){
        num = max;
    }
    return (num);
}
```

Essentially, the code just duplicates an awful lot of the `sq` image movieclip from the library into a grid using `attachMovie`. The clip is given the linkage identifier `sq` and set to export. The code adjusts the width as it moves across each column to create the valley effect. There are two loops that do all the work. The first is a `while` loop, which keeps creating columns until the picture has reached the width set by the variable `across`. It also defines the width for each new column, thereby creating the effect. The second is a simple `for` loop, which creates the squares inside each column. It's also responsible for creating the checked pattern of the squares, which is achieved using a modulus calculation. Checking for `k%2==1` would gives us an alternating pattern, as the equation evaluates as 1,0,1,0 repeatedly. Adding `i` to the equation (`(k+i)%2`) means that the pattern starts at alternating points on each column.

The key variables

`height` = the height of the square to be drawn
`width` = the width of the square to be drawn. If you set either the height or the width too low (<10), your computer might well crash
`across` = horizontal size of the picture
`down` = vertical size of the picture
`min` = the smallest the squares can get
`max` = the largest the squares can get
`k` = the counter that is used to name and set the depth of the duplicates
`aimAt` = which column you wish the effect to happen in. As the counter for the outside loop (`i`) moves closer to `aimAt`, the squares become smaller

The function `adjusted(num)` is used in working out the width. Squares aren't allowed to get wider than `max`, and negative numbers are returned as positive.

Using the above values for the variables gives us something fairly close to Riley's original. There are a couple of variations, which are very simple to try. We'll start with the `grid1.fla` file and build on it with every new variation.

grid2
Let's start by changing the `aimAt` variable a couple of times. With the current square size (width) setting aimAt will create a fold one the far left of the screen:

```
aimAt = 10;
```

grid3
By setting it to 30, the fold will be on the right:

```
aimAt = 30;
```

grid4
You can also use different sizes for the squares. However, when the width and height are changed, `aimAt` needs to change too, as `aimAt` refers to column widths. Change the following variables to see this effect:

```
height = 10;
width = 10;
aimAt = 50;
```

grid5
When the grid gets smaller like in the last example, it can start to look a little boring. I decided to add in a few more folds. You can do this by adding the following line inside the `while` loop just before the `for` loop starts:

```
if(i==aimAt+17){
   aimAt=50;
}
```

The following variables are also changed for this experiment:

```
height = 20;
width = 20;
aimAt = 15;
```

The movie waits until it's 17 columns past `aimAt`, and then gives itself another target further along.

[2] [3] [4] [5]

grid6
It's also possible to put in a number of folds. Let's replace the `if` statement that we just created above with:

```
if(i==aimAt+10){
  aimAt=i+10;
}
```

Every time the movie gets 10 columns past its target, it puts its target 10 columns ahead. We'll also intialize the `aimAt` variable to 10 for this experiment.

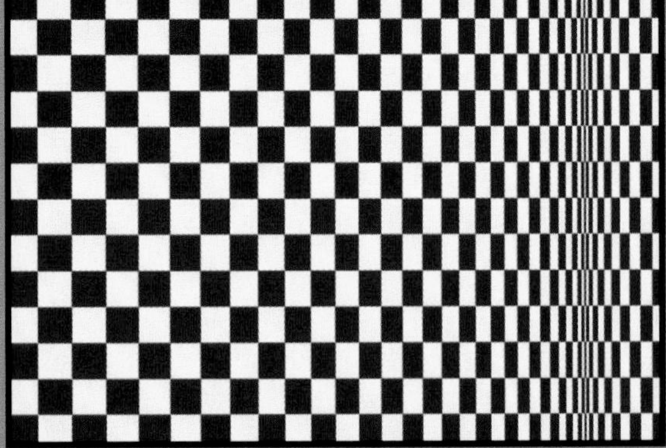

grid7
We'll now go back to our original `grid1.fla` file and change the colors a little. In the code change the color setting lines to:

```
if((k+i)%2==1){
  hex = 0x000066;
} else {
  hex = 0xffffcc;
}
```

This change results in a deep blue and pale yellow effect.

grid8
We used the color object to set colors in the last example. It's also quite easy to shift the color as it moves. Add a new variable inside the `for` loop after where we set the clip properties:

```
dark = parseInt(j*18);
```

Also change the color selection:

```
if((k+i)%2==1){
  hex = dark;
} else {
  hex = 0xffffff;
}
```

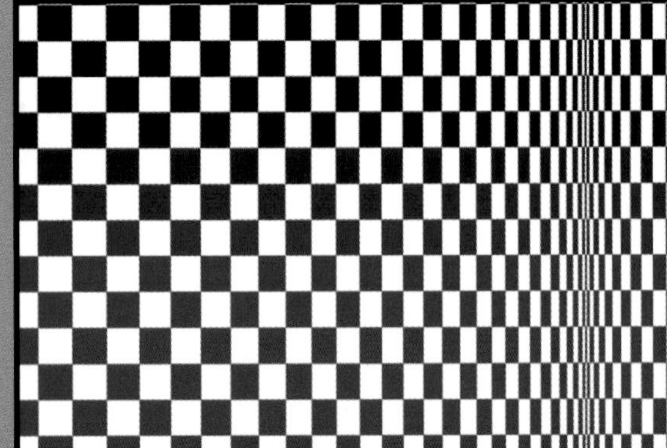

grid9
How about fading out as columns become thinner? Returning to our original base FLA `grid1.fla`, and entering the following code with the rest of the clip properties will do this:

```
clip._alpha = 10 + (width*3);
```

grid10
Finally, the rotation of the clip can also be adjusted to create more complex patterns. Add this line to the base FLA's clip properties to create our final effect:

```
clip._rotation = j*4;
```

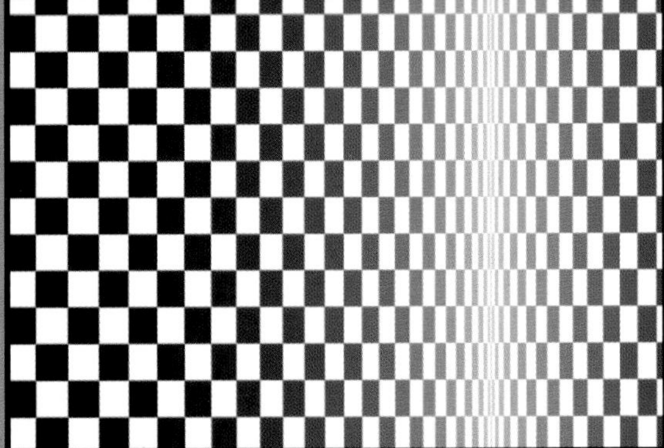

One idea I wanted to try is to have points on both the horizontal and vertical axis that the squares move towards. It would however make the code a fair bit more complex.

It's not too hard to convert the code to show the lines horizontally instead of vertically.

It would be possible to animate this effect so that the line appears as a ripple across the squares. It could be achieved by storing all the squares in an array, and then periodically updating the settings.

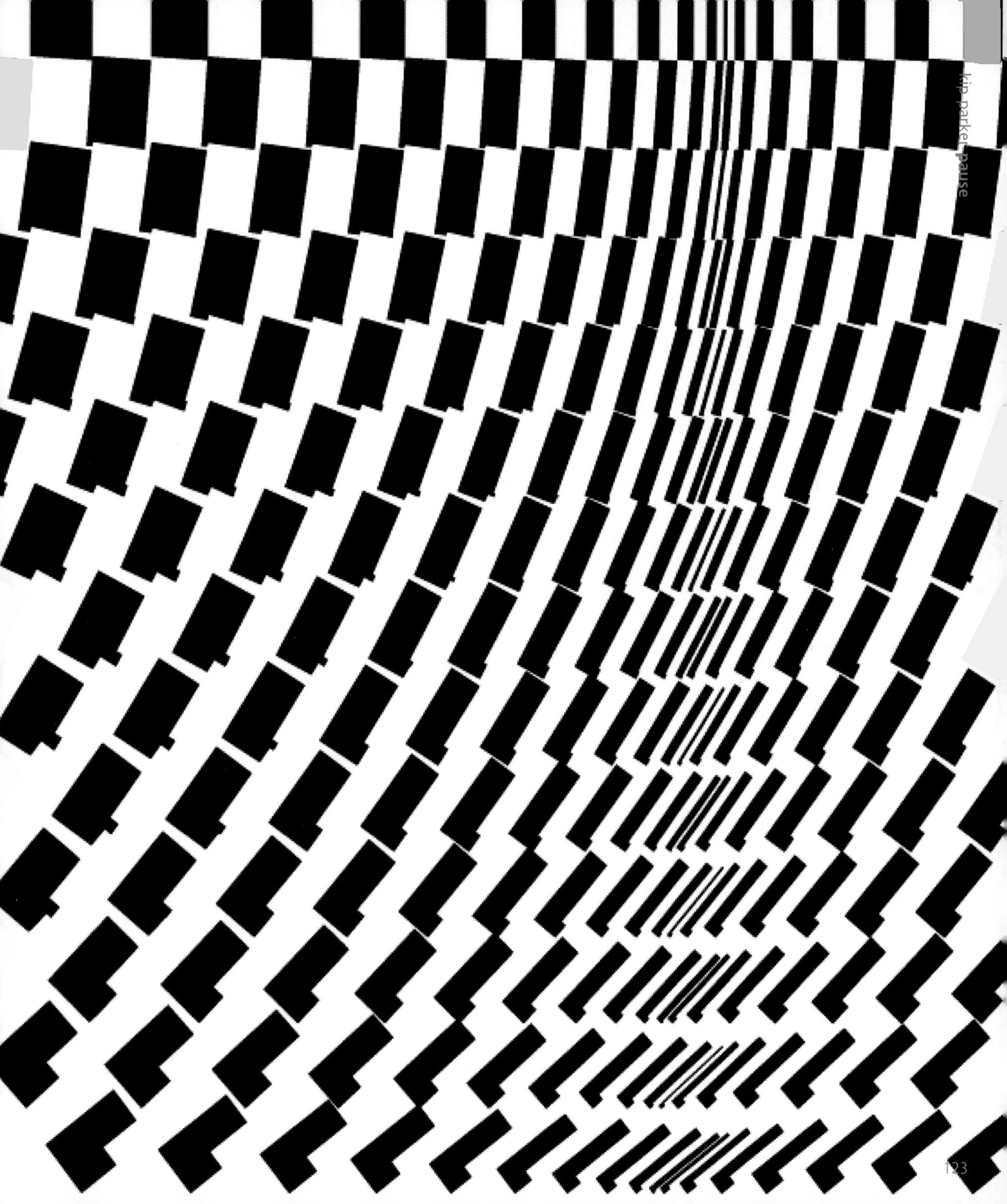

Polygon

Polygon uses an old school favourite, the Pythagoras theorem, to calculate a polygon of any given number of sides. Let's jump straight into the code that affects our single movieclip, which has the linkage identifier `line`.

```
//make the hex array
var RGB = new Array(256);
var k = 0;
var hex = new Array("0", "1", "2", "3", "4", "5", "6", "7", "8", "9", "A", "B", "C", "D", "E", "F");
for (i = 0; i < 16; i++) {
   for (j = 0; j < 16; j++) {
      RGB[k] = hex[i] + hex[j];
      k++;
   }
}

function mixer(r,g,b){
    return(parseInt("0x"+RGB[r]+RGB[g]+RGB[b]));
}

function rad(deg){
    return (Math.PI/180 * deg);
}

counter = 0;

function drawLine(xStart, yStart, xStop, yStop, depth, col) {
   attachMovie("line", "line"+depth, depth);
   ln = this["line"+depth];
   ln._x = xStart;
   ln._y = yStart;
   ln._xscale = xStop-xStart;
   ln._yscale = yStop-yStart;
   aColour = new Color(ln);
   aColour.setRGB(col);
}

counter = 0;
function circulate(r, segments, centreX, centreY){
    pointArr = new Array();
    unit = 360/segments;
    yTop = centreY - r;
    for(i=0; i<=360; i=i+unit){
        x = centreX + Math.sin(rad(i))*r;
        y = yTop + (r-Math.cos(rad(i))*r);
        pointArr[counter] = new Array(x,y);
        if (counter>=1){
            drawLine(pointArr[counter-1][0], pointArr[counter-1][1],
              ➥ pointArr[counter][0], pointArr[counter][1], counter,0xffffff);
            depth++;
        }
        counter++;
    }
counter = 0;
}

circulate(100,5,300,200);

stop();
```

This code uses the standard 45 degree, 100 pixel line to draw the required lines.

The key variables

`segments` = the number of sides
`r` = the radius

The `circulate` function uses the Pythagoras theorem (I found some "math for kids" pages which told me what I needed to know here), to plot all the points of a polygon with the `segments` value as the number of sides and the radius `r`. These x and y points are stored in an array `pointArr`. As soon as there's at least two pairs of coordinates, the function starts making calls to the `drawLine` function to draw the shape.

In the sample file the circulate function is called with the following parameters:

```
circulate(100,5,300,200);
```

This will draw a pentagon with a radius of 100 in the center of the screen. The results can be seen in `polygon1.swf`.

polygon2
The base file works but isn't very interesting. Let's loop the call to circulate to get a spirographesque effect and use the counter `k` to set the radius parameter. Modify the function call so that it has the following loop:

```
for(k=10;k<=400;k+=10){
    circulate(k,5,300,200);
}
```

polygon3
Here, the x axis is moved along:

```
for(k=10;k<=200;k+=10){
    circulate(k,8,100+(k/2),200);
}
```

polygon4
Shifting both axis can give an almost 3D effect:

```
for(k=10;k<=200;k+=5){
    circulate(k,4,100+(k/5),300-(k/3));
}
```

polygon5
Let's now set a shape to repeat across the screen. We'll a add a new variable `interval`, and create a second loop:

```
interval = 150;
for(v = 0;v<400;v+=interval){
    for(h=0;h<600;h+=interval){
        circulate(interval,5,h,v);
    }
}
```

polygon6
Indeed we can make groups of the shapes across the screen with the following code:

```
interval = 150;
for(v = 0;v<400;v+=interval){
    for(h=0;h<600;h+=interval){
        for(k=10;k<150;k+=10){
            circulate(k,5,h,v);
        }
    }
}
```

polygon7
This is my favorite effect and is one of the simplest. Set the loop as follows:

```
for(k=10;k<200;k+=5){
    circulate(k,4,300,200);
}
```

Let's also set the color as:

```
col = mixer(depth,depth,depth);
```

We add this color line before the color object into the `drawline` function.

This little bit of code has everything you need to make far more complex images. Perhaps rotate the shape each time it is drawn, to give a real spirograph effect.

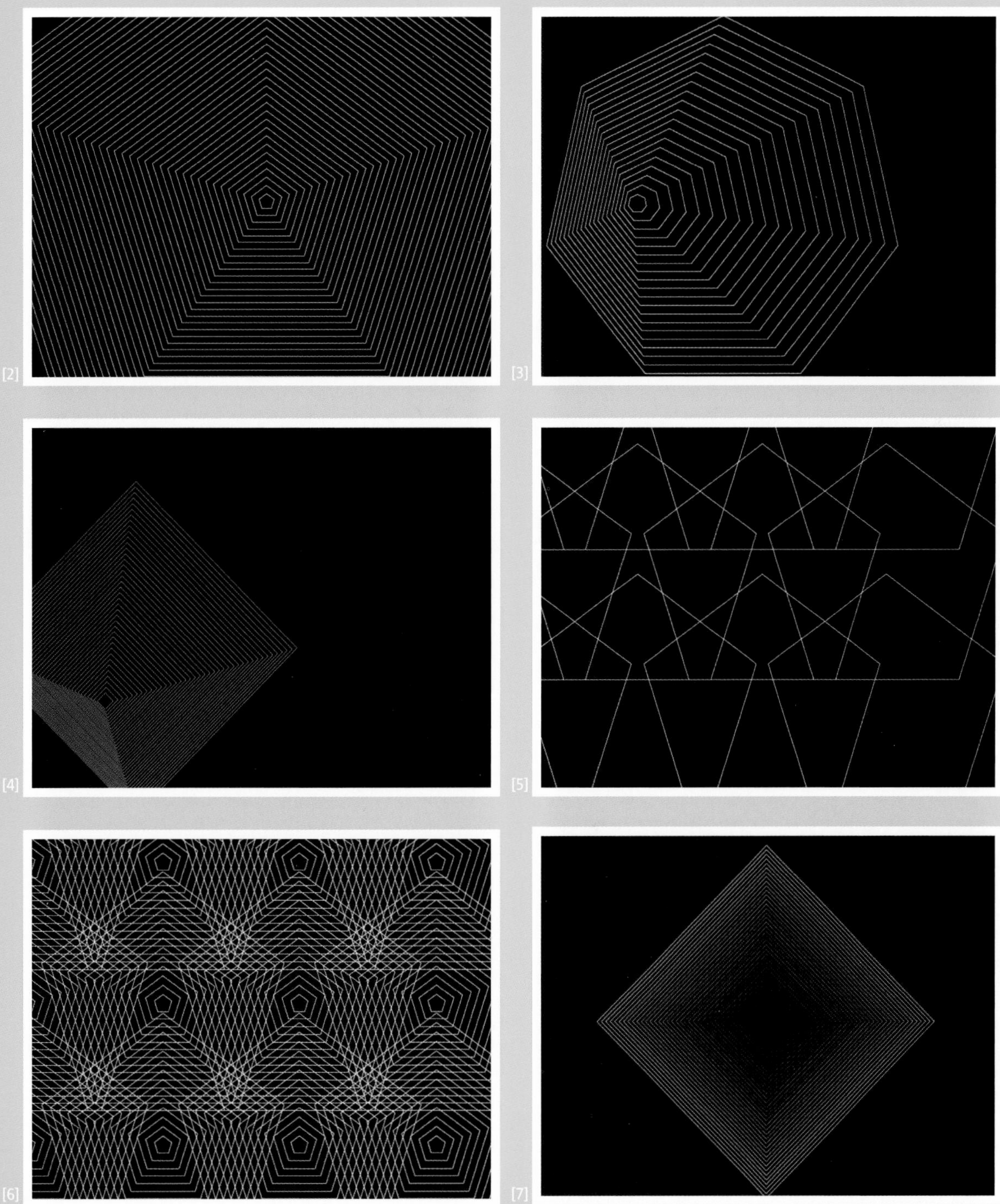

[2] [3] [4] [5] [6] [7]

Sine

The sine wave is one of the most beautiful and simple forms in mathematics, and is also at the foundation of sound theory. If you look at the sample file, `sine1.fla`, you'll see that we only have code on frame 1. We're using the `square` movieclip with its linkage set to export with an identifier name of `sq`. Our results will be a sine curve plotted from the attached clips. Here's the frame 1 code:

```
inc = 12;
//initialise x axis
x = 0;
a = 120;
b = 8;
p = 12;
v = 200;
len = 600/inc;

//width and height of each clip
w = 5;
h = 5;
trans = Math.PI / 180;

for(i=0;i<len;i++){
    attachMovie("sq", "sq"+i, i);
    clip = this["sq"+i];
    // increment independent variable
    x+=inc;
    clip._x= x;
    // y-position of object – calculated with sine wave equation
    clip._y = a * Math.sin ((b * i + p) * trans) + v;
    clip._width = w;
    clip._height = h;
}

stop();
```

The key variables

`a` = amplitude
`b` = period
`p` = phase shift
`v` = value used to display the wave in the center of the movie
`x` = the x position of the clips
`trans` = a constant to translate from degrees to Flash's preferred radians
`w` = the width of each clip
`h` = the height of each clip
`len` = a variable used to stop the duplication of the movies when the right hand edge is reached
`inc` = incremental x distance between each clip

```
counter = 0;
for(v=-100; v<500; v+=30){
    for(i=0; i<len; i++){
     attachMovie("sq", "sq"+counter, counter);
     clip = this["sq"+counter];
     // increment independent variable
      x+=inc;
      clip._x= x;
      // y-position of object – calculated with sine wave equation
      clip._y = a * Math.sin ((b * i + p) * trans) + v;
      clip._width = w;
      clip._height = h;
      counter++;
    }
    x = 0;
}
```

I've used `v`, the vertical adjust property as the loop variable. I've started it off the page at -100, and it goes past the edge of the page to 500 to make sure the whole stage is covered. `inc` is changed to 8 to create a tighter wave.

sine4

Instead of just copying the sine wave everywhere, it can be altered slightly on each iteration. For example, add the following code to the end of the outer loop that we created in the last example (on the line after `x = 0`):

```
a += 10;
```

These initial variables were also changed:

```
a = 10;

inc = 9;
```

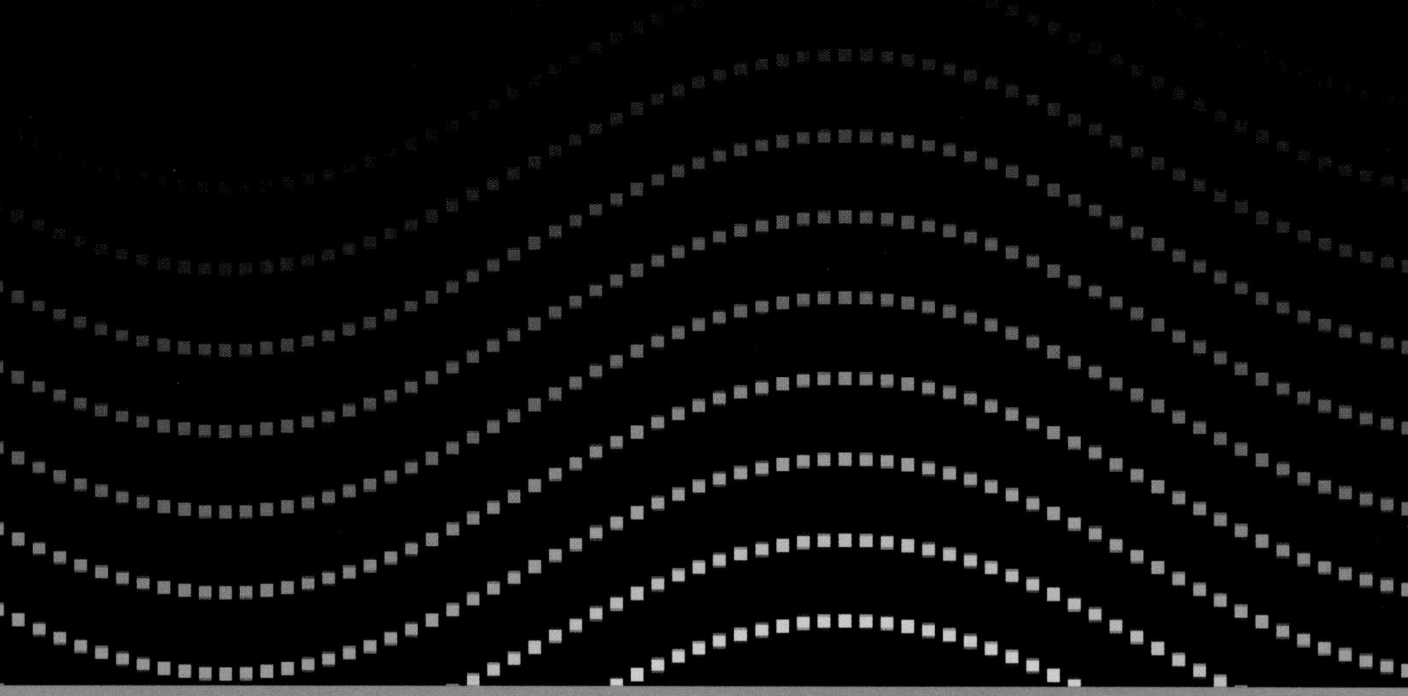

sine5

Let's now use some color transformations on the effect we've just created. Before our initial variables, right at the start of the script, we'll add the following code:

```
var RGB = new Array(256);
var k = 0;
var hex = new Array("0", "1", "2", "3", "4", "5", "6", "7", "8", "9", "A", "B", "C", "D", "E", "F");
for (i = 0; i < 16; i++) {
   for (j = 0; j < 16; j++) {
     RGB[k] = hex[i] + hex[j];
     k++;
   }
}
```

This makes an array called RGB that contains hex values from 1 to 256, meaning that I can convert from an RGB value to a hex value by using the array. This is simplified with the following function:

```
function mixer(r,g,b){
   return(parseInt("0x"+RGB[r]+RGB[g]+RGB[b]));
}
```

This function is placed right at the end of the script, just before the `stop` command.

In this example we're going to use the RGB array to gradually fade from white to darker greys. The grey scale to use is calculated as `256/400*256`, so we should be able to get from 0 to 256 over the course of the movie. I'm going to remove the `a += 10;` line that we added in the last example and replace it with:

```
greyVal = parseInt((256/400)*v);
thisColor = mixer(greyVal,greyVal,greyVal);
```

To complete the effect we add the following lines to set the color of each clip. They are added to the inner loop on the lines below `counter++`.

```
newColor = new Color(clip);
newColor.setRGB(thisColor);
```

One final thing we'll done here is set the initial `a` variable to 40. If you get a bit confused with the code placement here, don't worry. The full code can be found in `sine5.fla`.

sine6

The phase setting in the sine equation sets the stage at which the sine begins to be graphed. So by drawing two sine waves on the same vertical adjustment but with different phase settings, you get two waves weaving in and out of each other. The following code will create two waves in one loop:

```
for(i=0; i<len; i++){
    attachMovie("sq", "sq"+counter, counter);
    attachMovie("sq", "mirror"+(counter+len), (counter+len));
    clip = this["sq"+counter];
    clip2 = this["mirror"+(counter+len)];
    x+=inc;
    clip._x= x;
    clip2._x = x;
    // y-position of object – calculated with sine wave equation
    clip._y = a * Math.sin ((b * i + p1) * trans) + v;
    clip2._y = a * Math.sin ((b * i + p2) * trans) + v;
    clip._width = w;
    clip._height = h;
    clip2._width = w;
    clip2._height = h;
    counter++;
}
```

Place this code into our base FLA (`sine1.fla`). It should replace the original `for` loop that is in that file. In the files initial variables we're going to replace `p` with `p1` and `p2` because we now have two mirrored curves. Let's also change the `inc` and `a` values. Here's the code that we need to alter:

```
inc = 5;
a = 40;
p1 = 1;
p2 = 180;
```

To make something more complex you could introduce the outer loop that we used earlier to this effect.

sine7

For our final effect we'll combine the different techniques we've learnt along the way. The code for this file can be seen in `sine7.fla`. This time instead of just using grays we'll add different colors. You'll also see that we're incrementing the altitude from within the inner loop.

Here's the code:

```
var RGB = new Array(256);
var k = 0;
var hex = new Array("0", "1", "2", "3", "4", "5", "6", "7", "8", "9", "A", "B", "C", "D", "E","F");
for (i = 0; i < 16; i++) {
   for (j = 0; j < 16; j++) {
      RGB[k] = hex[i] + hex[j];
      k++;
   }
}

//distance set along the x axis
inc = 8;
//initialise x axis
x = 0;

b = 6;
p1 = 1;
p2 = 180;
v = 200;
len = 600/inc;

//width and height of each clip
w = 10;
h = 10;
trans = Math.PI / 180;

counter = 0;

for(v=-100; v<500; v+=20){
   a = 10;
   grey1 = parseInt(256-(256/400)*v);
   grey2 = parseInt((256/400)*v);
   c1 = mixer(grey1,0,0);
   c2 = mixer(0,0,grey2);
   for(i=0; i<len; i++){
      attachMovie("sq", "sq"+counter, counter);
      attachMovie("sq", "mirror"+(counter), (1000-counter));
      clip = this["sq"+counter];
      clip2 = this["mirror"+(counter)];
      x+=inc;
      clip._x= x;
      clip2._x = x;
      // y-position of object — calculated with sine wave equation
      clip._y = a * Math.sin ((b * i + p1) * trans) + v;
      clip2._y = a * Math.sin ((b * i + p2) * trans) + v;
      colour1 = new Color(clip);
      colour2 = new Color(clip2);
      colour1.setRGB(c1);
      colour2.setRGB(c2);
      clip._width = w;
      clip._height = h;
      clip2._width = w;
      clip2._height = h;
      counter++;
      a+=5;
   }
   x = 0;
}

function mixer(r,g,b){
   return(parseInt("0x"+RGB[r]+RGB[g]+RGB[b]));
}
```

So, that sine curve isn't as boring as it first appears. Try using some of the techniques you've witnessed here to modify the cosine or tangent curves. The techniques I've shown can be applied to many varied Flash effects.

When I was eighteen, I decided to buy a computer instead of a car. That was back in 1991. I did this also in 1993, 1995, and again this year. To me, this is an absolutely brilliant thing to do - at least until cars can fly.

Even before I owned a computer, in some form or another, I have been borrowing CPU time on other people's computers. I was initially motivated to use computers through the text based adventure games my father would write while I was asleep. It became clear to me that a programmer truly could create something from nothing, and this idea intrigued me.

I completed the ten year program at New Mexico State University and was rewarded a Bachelor of Science in Computer Science for my participation in their experiment. During this time I learned the value of abstracted programming and why I never want to program at a micro level.

My intrigue with the visualization of mathematical processes arises in my eye's inability to discern certain patterns. I enjoy watching the results of computation unfold before me. I see beauty in repeatable patterns and behavior. I take power in seeing a perfect representation of my imagination propagate across networks and lie stored in perfect stasis, for retrieval at any time.

The bulk of these experiments are geometric constructions created with one of two methods: the iterated method, which renders new movieclips one after another in a loop with defined limits, and the recursive method, in which a single instantiation of a movie clip renders itself repeatedly.

Throw in a couple of trigonometric functions and a few gentle geometric shapes, and you have the beginnings of a wondrous universe.

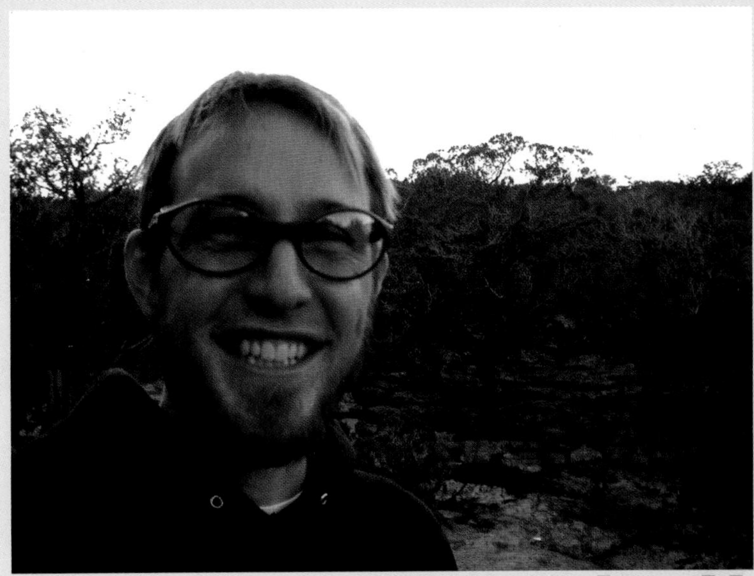

jared tarbell
levitated.net

Iterative inspiration

My first set of experiments uses simple iteration to build up some beautiful pieces of computational art. I have four layers in my movie: `about`, `logic`, `button`, and `background`, but the only one that you really need is `logic`. Each of these layers has two frames to it. The `about` layer just contains some basic info about the file so that when I come back to it in ten years time I'll still know what it was for. The `button` layer contains, as you'd think it would, a button in its second frame. This means that when the movie has finished running, the regenerate button will appear that you can click to start the whole process again. The `background` layer simply contains a square made up of dots to give the image a frame. Lastly, but most importantly, the `logic` layer contains all of the code for our movie, the first frame contains all of the generative script, and the second frame just has a simple `stop` action. Apart from that, there are two other components to my movie, a button that sits on the `button` layer and has the following code on it:

```
on (press) {
   gotoAndPlay(1);
}
```

This just starts the generative process off again once it has finished. The other component is a movieclip called `dapoint`, this is the graphic that we'll be duplicating on the screen to create the images. This clip is exported from the Library with the linkage name `dapoint`. The graphic is made up of five frames, each with exactly the same crescent shape on them, but filled with a different color, allowing us to create unique images by randomly choosing a frame to give a new color for each movieclip duplication. Here's the code that works the magic, it lives on frame 1 of the `logic` layer:

```
depth=0;
jlim=5;
klim=5;
for (j=0; j<jlim; j++) {
   for (k=0; k<klim; k++) {
     for (l=0; l<j+k+1; l++) {
       newmc="mc"+String(depth++);
       this.attachMovie("dapoint",newmc,depth);
       this[newmc]._x=j*420/jlim+210/jlim;
       this[newmc]._y=k*420/klim+210/klim;
       this[newmc]._xscale=100+random(j+k*20);
       this[newmc]._yscale=100+random(j+k*20);
       this[newmc]._rotation=l*360/(jlim+klim);
       this[newmc].gotoAndStop(random(this[newmc]._totalframes)+1);
     }
   }
}
```

The key variables

`depth` = the depth that the current clip will be placed at. We reset the depth to 0 so that when the image is regenerated it will replace the existing one
`jlim` = the number of columns of shapes
`klim` = the number of rows of shapes

Using three nested loops, a single movieclip is attached to the stage a great number of times. The outside two loops (variables `j` and `k`) iterate a fixed number of times as defined by the row and column dimensions. The inside loop (variable `l`) iterates a variable number of times, directly dependent on the current progress through the outside loops. The more times the inside loop iterates, the greater the number of movieclips are placed at that particular row and column. Of course the exact number of attached movieclips, excluding any conditional exceptions, can be computed through `j*k*l`.

With each instantiation, the new object is given unique attributes computed at random and according to the progress of the iteration. This gives us plenty of room for experimentation. We place and rotate each object in the grid space using a multiple of the loop index and a small increment. The small increment is calculated using the limit definitions of each iterative loop for automatic adjustment in loop count changes. Scale is set randomly. At the moment we're using a range that increases proportional to the progress through the loop (groups near the bottom right corner are more jumbled than groups near the top left). As a final, and important step, we set the instantiated movieclip to randomly goto and stop on one of its frames. This allows a palette of unique graphic shapes to be a part of the construction while keeping the code simple. One other thing to note is that I have my stage set to 420x420 pixels, so if you see the numbers 420 or 210 (420/2) appearing frequently in my scripts, then that's why.

Iterations

comp001b
First off, I changed the following lines of code:

```
for (l=0;l<j+k+5;l++)

this[newmc]._xscale=100;
this[newmc]._yscale=100;
this[newmc]._rotation=random(360);
```

I also changed the graphic to a section of a circular pipe. Because of the set scale and random rotation it creates some nice patterns of broken circles.

comp001c
For this iteration I changed the number of duplications again, and also added in a line to set a fixed alpha.

```
for (l=0;l<j+k+1;l++)

this[newmc]._alpha=40;
```

I changed `dapoint` to a simple pale square to get these alpha and color blended images.

comp001d
For this experiment I went a slightly different way by using letters instead of shapes. I increased the amount of duplications considerably to get a good range of letters, so I reduced the number of rows and columns to keep a good generation speed. I set a fixed rotation to get a good spread of letters, and added a new line to give us a random letter each time. I also removed the alpha line that I added last time.

```
jlim=3;
klim=3;

for (l=0;l<18;l++)

this[newmc]._rotation = l*20;
this[newmc].gf = chr(random(26)+92);
```

The big change comes in `dapoint`, this now has only a single frame with a dynamic text box on it set to the variable `gf`.

comp001e
I removed the letter code and went back to my shapes. This time I decided to add a progressive scale to the shapes so that they would grow larger with each successive duplication. To do this, I added a new line at the start to initialize the scale and a new line in the inner `for` loop to update it. Here are the changes that I made:

```
jlim = 7;
klim = 7;
proscale=100;

for (l=0; l<j+k+1; l++)

proscale+=random(15)-7;
this[newmc]._xscale = proscale;
this[newmc]._yscale = proscale;
this[newmc]._rotation=l*360/(jlim+klim);
```

I also changed the graphic back to five frames, but this time with a totally different shape in each frame. It produces some strange random looking patterns.

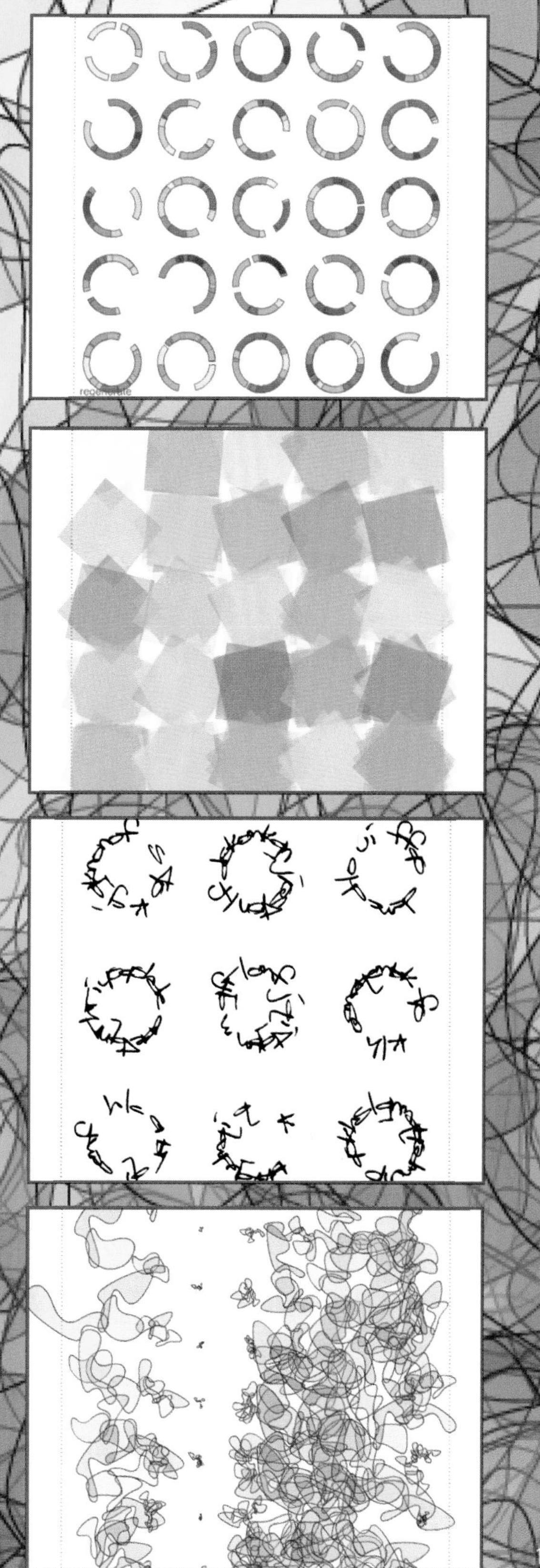

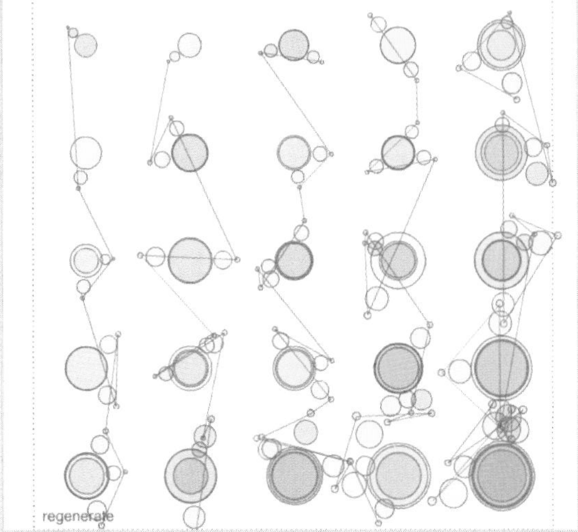

comp001f

Another radical change for this one. I added a second movieclip, this time a 100x100 pixel 45 degree line. This clip is exported as `line` from the Library. I changed `dapoint` to be three successively smaller circles with a different color in each of the five frames. There are exactly 100 pixels between the center of the largest circle and the center of the smallest. The movie works by positioning `dapoint`, remembering its position, and then attaching a line to join it to the next copy of `dapoint`. Here's the code in full:

```
depth=0;
lastpoint = new Object();
jlim=5;
klim=5;
for (j=0; j<jlim; j++) {
   for (k=0; k<klim; k++) {
     for (l=0; l<int((j+k+2)/2); l++) {
       newmc="mc"+String(depth++);
       this.attachMovie("dapoint",newmc,depth+1000);
       this[newmc]._x=j*420/jlim+210/jlim;
       this[newmc]._y=k*420/klim+210/klim;
       scale=10+(j+k)*4+random(20);
       this[newmc]._xscale=scale;
       this[newmc]._yscale=scale;
       this[newmc]._rotation=random(360);
       this[newmc].gotoAndStop(random(this[newmc]._totalframes)+1);
       if ((k>0) || (l>0)) {
         newln="line"+String(depth++);
         this.attachMovie("line",newln,depth);
         this[newln]._x=lastpoint.x;
         this[newln]._y=lastpoint.y;
       }
       lastpoint.x=this[newmc]._x+scale*Math.cos(Math.PI / 180 *
         ➥ this[newmc]._rotation);
       lastpoint.y=this[newmc]._y+scale*Math.sin(Math.PI / 180 *
         ➥ this[newmc]._rotation);
       if ((l>0) || (k>0)) {
         this[newln]._xscale=lastpoint.x-this[newln]._x;
         this[newln]._yscale=lastpoint.y-this[newln]._y;
       }
     }
   }
}
```

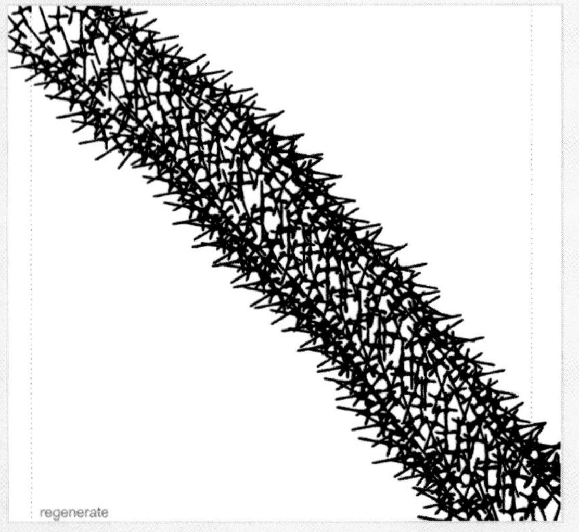

comp001g

Next I went back to the original code, removing the `line` clip and all of its trappings. This time I added some new script that completely hides the grid pattern, instead producing an odd stream of shapes. I changed `dapoint` to a single frame containing a simple cross. I added three new variables at the start to initialize the position of `dapoint`, then added some lines to the inner loop to update these variables and the position and rotation of the shape.

```
xi=5;
yi=5;
si=100;

for (l=0;l<18;l++)

xi+=random(3);
yi+=random(3);
si+=random(9)-4;
this[newmc]._x=xi;
this[newmc]._y=yi;
this[newmc]._xscale=si;
this[newmc]._yscale=si;
this[newmc]._rotation=l*20;
```

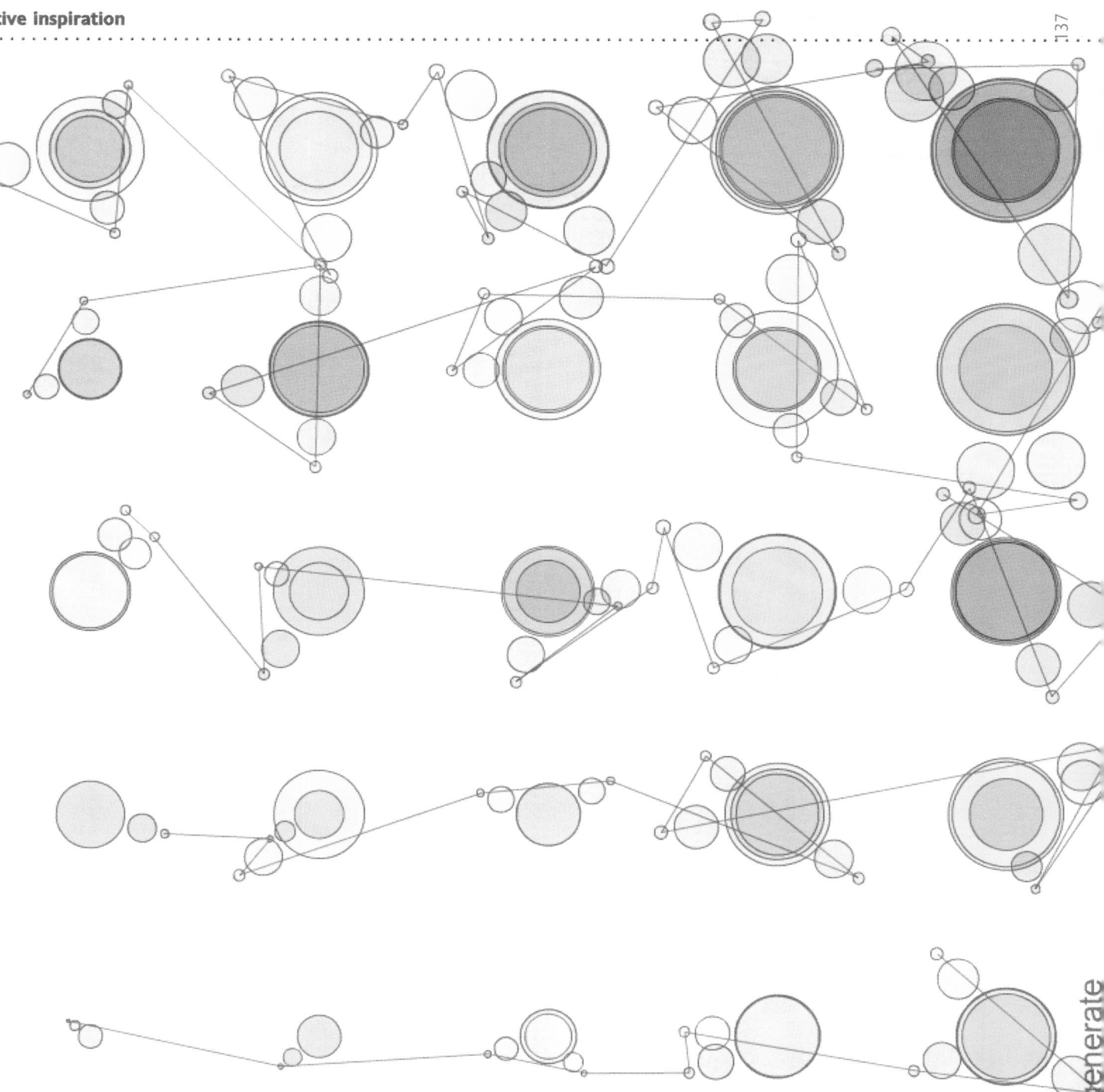

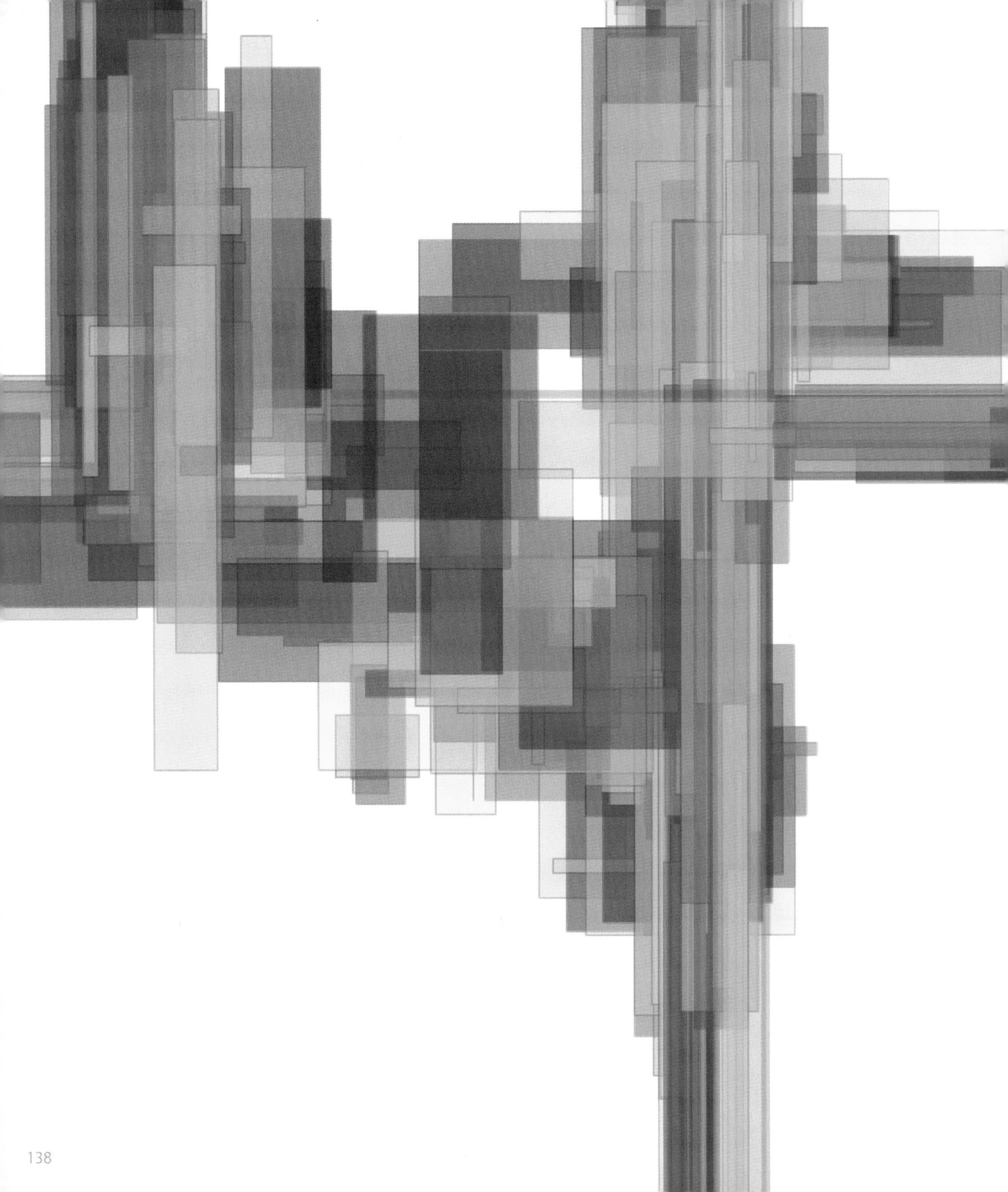

comp001h

I removed the xi, yi, and si lines from the last iteration and replaced it with some new code. This time I added some script to scale and position dapoint next to the previous copy of dapoint. ox and oy are the old x and y positions, and nx and ny are the new ones. I changed dapoint to contain 11 frames of the same 100x100 pixel square with its registration point in the top-left corner, but filled with a different color in each frame. Here are the initial settings:

```
jlim=3;
klim=7;
ox=210;
oy=210;
```

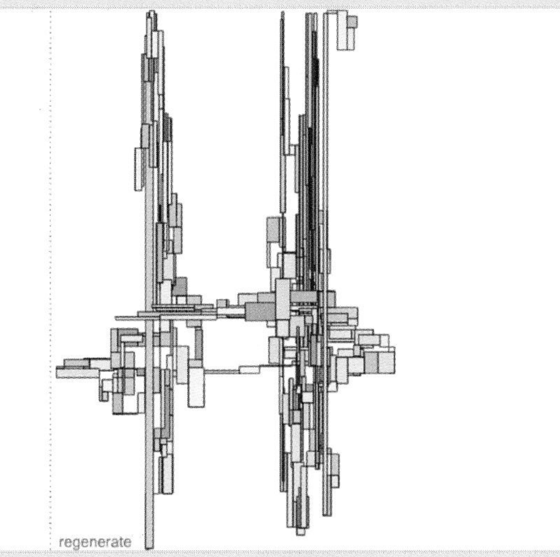

...and here's the inner for loop in full:

```
for (l=0; l<18; l++) {
  newmc="mc"+String(depth++);
  this.attachMovie("dapoint",newmc,depth);
  nx=ox+(j+1)*(random(41)-20)/(k+1);
  ny=oy+(k+1)*(random(41)-20)/(j+1);
  if (nx<0) nx*=-1;
  if (ny<0) ny*=-1;
  if (nx>420) nx=nx%420;
  if (ny>420) ny=ny%420;
  this[newmc]._x=nx;
  this[newmc]._y=ny;
  this[newmc]._xscale=ox-nx;
  this[newmc]._yscale=oy-ny;
  this[newmc]._alpha=100;
  this[newmc].gotoAndStop(random(this[newmc]._totalframes)+1);
  ox=nx;
  oy=ny;
}
```

comp001i

Lastly, I made some a slight change to the code, and changed dapoint to a much larger rectangle so that they overlaps and produce blended colors. The code change I made was just to reduce the alpha:

```
this[newmc]._alpha=50;
```

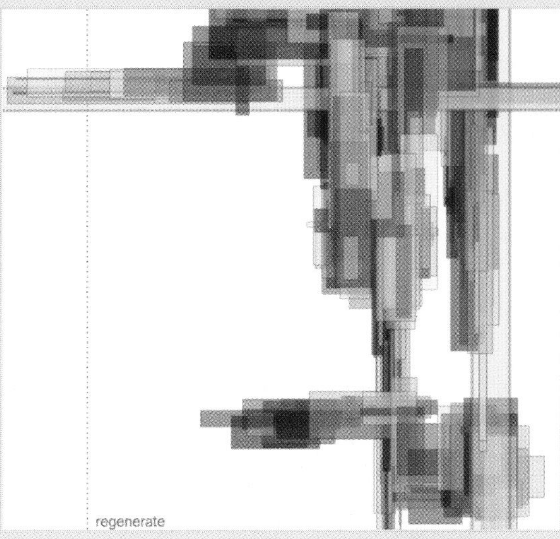

The iterative model for generating graphic structures is quite effective when the specifics are known. Using a series of repeated steps, some truly amazing things can be constructed using simple rules. I believe that this particular set of rules allows for some very beautiful effects because of the commonality between the groupings. Common multiples allow the user to see changes in individual structure, as well as the structures themselves.

My suggestion for immediate gratification is to change the basic graphic object. When doing this, keep in mind the degrees to which the object will be rotated, how variations in scale and color might affect the overall appearance, and how individual objects might look when grouped into multiples. Of course another good change to make is to the number of rows and columns. The placement code has been written in such a way that changing the limits of the grid space will automatically scale and size the objects to fit within it. A change that would be rather tricky to implement, but enjoyable to observe, would be the proportional displacement of each object grouping according to some persistent variable.

Lorenz attractors

Any system expressed in coupled non-linear differential equations is bound to produce some interesting results. There are many such systems, either invented or discovered. One such system is the so-called Lorenz Attractor, the results of which produce beautiful butterfly like results.

For this movie we only have one frame that contains all of the code. The other component is a movieclip called `line` that is exported from the Library with the name `line`. This clip consists of a 300x300 pixel square, with its registration point set a third of the way in from the top-left corner at 100x100 pixels. Here's the code for the first frame of the main movie:

```
var x0 = random(10)/10;
var y0 = random(20);
var z0 = random(10);
var h = 0.01;
var a = 10.0;
var b = 28.0;
var c = 8.0 / 3.0;

for (n=0; n<1000; n++) {
   x1=x0+h*a*(y0-x0);
   y1=y0+h*(x0*(b-z0)-y0);
   z1=z0+h*(x0*y0-c*z0);
   newmc="line"+String(depth++);
   this.attachMovie("line",newmc,depth);
   this[newmc]._x=x0*10+210;
   this[newmc]._y=y0*10+210;
   this[newmc]._xscale=(x1-x0)*10;
   this[newmc]._yscale=(y1-y0)*10;
   x0=x1;
   y0=y1;
   z0=z1;
}
stop();
```

The key variables

`x0`, `y0`, and `z0` = the initial starting point, and subsequently the previous point values
`x1`, `y1`, and `z1` = the new point values
`h`, `a`, `b`, and `c` = the Lorenz constants, best not to change these or you'll no longer have a Lorenz Attractor

It works like this – we take an initial set of values, run them through some equations, and use the results for the next seed of values. Then we repeat this process thousands of times, each time marking the progress of the transformation with the instantiation of a new movieclip, and the end result is the visualization of transformation over time.

Of course doing this with random equations usually results in a point that hovers around for a bit then shoots off the screen towards some infinity (or zero). The trick then, is to find a set of equations that produce a deterministic result, while remaining chaotic in nature. Systems of this class possess basins of attraction.

So here's the formula, as applied to Flash. Start with some initial random values in three-dimensional space (x0, y0, z0). Specify and calculate all constants to be used in the iteration. For our example, we will use Lorenz's constants. Notice that one of the constants is an irrational number (variable c). Changing these may produce some interesting results, but is not recommended.

Next, and as a massive, swooping step, we calculate the first 1000 points of the system and render them to the stage. To do this, we begin by making the first transformation, calculating new values for x, y, and z, and assigning them to temporary variables x1, y1, and z1. Next, we name and create a new movie clip, then finally position and scale the new movieclip to stretch from the last point (x0, y0, z0) to the newly calculated point (x1, y1, z1). In this example, we must multiply the x and y values by 10 to more fully fill the stage. Also, we offset the point so that the entire system is centered on the stage. Finally, we assign the newly calculated value to the seed values for the next iteration. In this process, old values are discarded but not forgotten (they live now as movieclips on the stage).

Iterations

comp002b
For this first iteration I changed the initial starting point, and increased the number of iterations. I also commented out the lines that set the scale of the movieclip. I changed `line` to a small black circle with a dotted outline, this gives an effect where you can easily trace the path of the attractor.

```
var x0 = -12.1;
var y0 = -22;
var z0 = 28.7;

for (n=0;n<1500;n++)
```

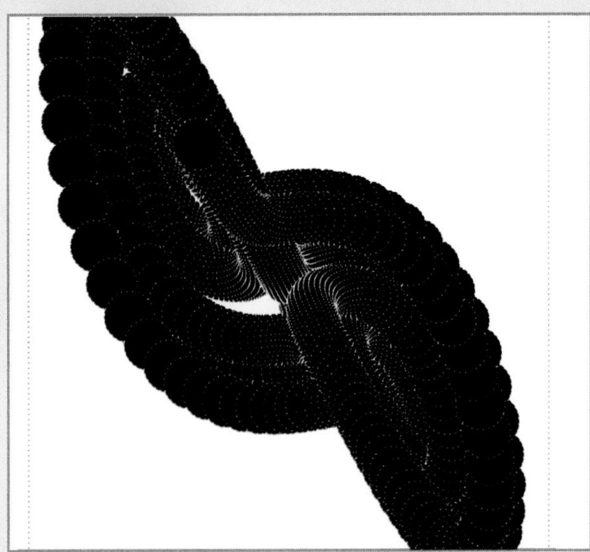

comp002c
This time I changed the start point back to a random value, reduced the number of iterations, and brought back the scale. I changed `line` to a simple outline of a circle, so that you can see an almost wireframe representation.

```
var x0 = (random(50)-25)/2;
var y0 = (random(50)-25)/2;
var z0 = random(25)/2;

for (n=0;n<750;n++)

this[newmc]._xscale=z0*5;
this[newmc]._yscale=z0*5;
```

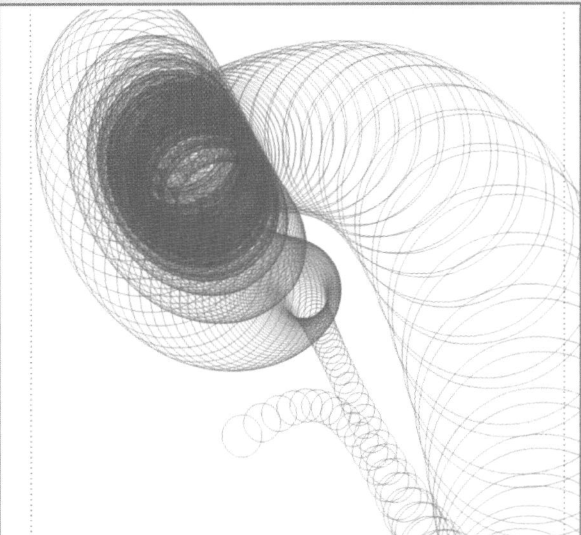

comp002d
I kept exactly the same code in this iteration, but changed the shape of `line` to make a cross filled with white, this produces some amazingly seemingly-3D shapes.

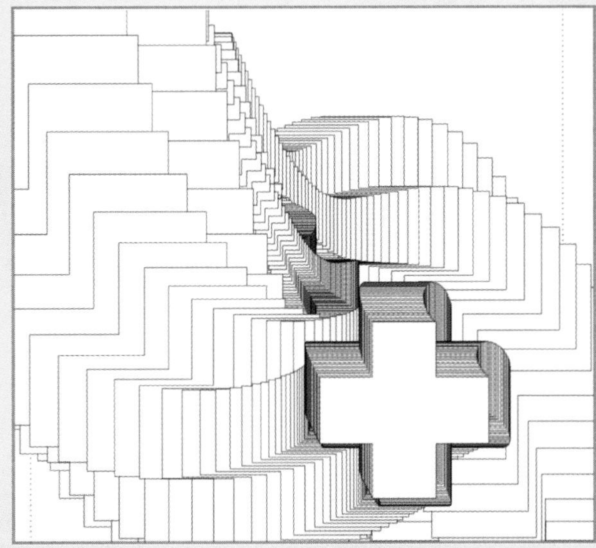

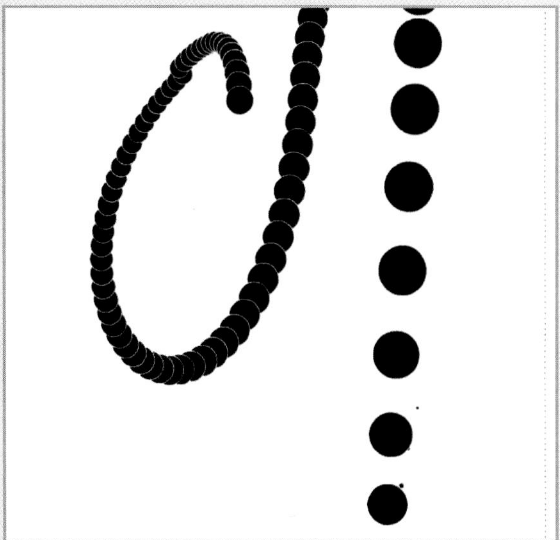
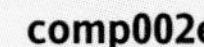

comp002e

I hardly changed the code again for this one, just decreasing the number of iterations, and adding one other line. The main change is to the graphic, where this time I chose to animate it with a simple tween. `line` now contains a small off-center circle that rotate 360 degrees around the center point over 60 frames. The new line goes just after the scale lines, it is used to start each successive duplication of the movieclip at the next frame on so that they appear to follow each other rather than starting from the same point.

```
for (n=0;n<100;n++)

this[newmc].gotoAndPlay(1+(n%60));
```

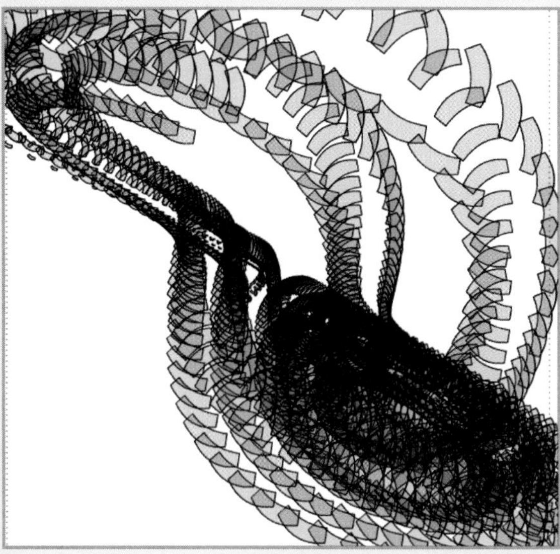

comp002f

I removed the new line from the previous iteration and went back to just changing the existing code. The shape is back to being only one frame, and in this case is a split circle.

```
var x0 = (random(50)-25)/4;
var y0 = (random(50)-25)/4;
var z0 = random(25)/4;

for (n=0;n<500;n++)

this[newmc]._x=x0*12+210;
this[newmc]._y=y0*12+210;
this[newmc]._xscale=z0*3;
this[newmc]._yscale=z0*3;
```

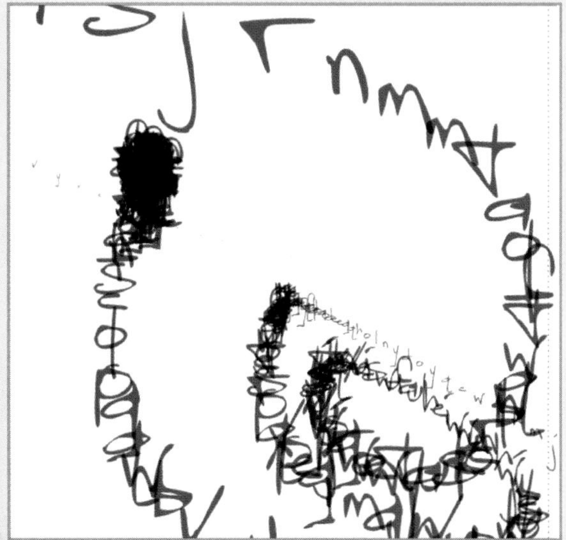

comp002g

Here, as I have done in previous experiments, I changed the graphic to be a random letter. `line` contains a dynamic text box set to the variable `ch`, and a new line is added to the code to generate a random letter each time.

```
this[newmc]._xscale=z0*7;
this[newmc]._yscale=z0*7;
this[newmc].ch=chr(random(26)+96);
```

comp002h
In this iteration I removed the letter code, replacing the text box with a simple circle, and went for something completely different. Instead of just drawing one attractor, why not draw three? I just copied the duplication and positioning code another couple of times, but changed the positioning. I also added a magnitude variable to use as a multiplier. This is initialized at the beginning of the code with this line:

```
var mg = 8;
```

We then use this value to control the scale and position of the attractors, try setting it to a smaller number, say 2, to see the difference. Here are the three duplication and positioning code blocks in full:

```
newmc="line"+String(depth++);
this.attachMovie("line",newmc,depth);
this[newmc]._x=x0*mg+210;
this[newmc]._y=y0*mg+210;
this[newmc]._xscale=(z0+5)*mg;
this[newmc]._yscale=(z0+5)*mg;

newmc="line"+String(depth++);
this.attachMovie("line",newmc,depth);
this[newmc]._x=y0*mg+210;
this[newmc]._y=z0*mg;
this[newmc]._xscale=(x0+5)*mg;
this[newmc]._yscale=(x0+5)*mg;

newmc="line"+String(depth++);
this.attachMovie("line",newmc,depth);
this[newmc]._x=z0*mg;
this[newmc]._y=x0*mg+210;
this[newmc]._xscale=(y0+5)*mg;
this[newmc]._yscale=(y0+5)*mg;
```

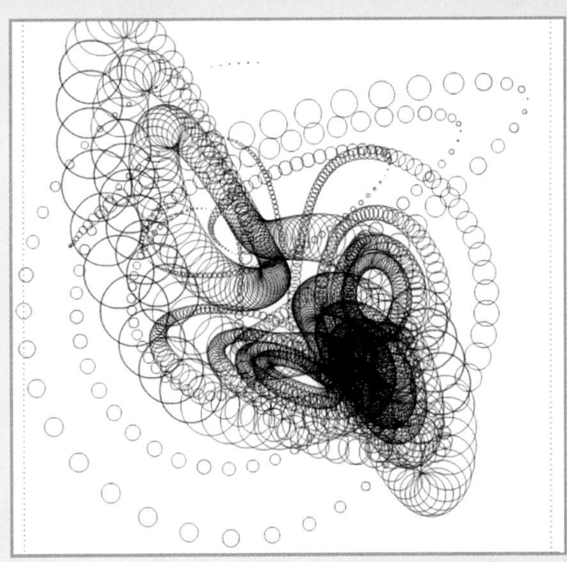

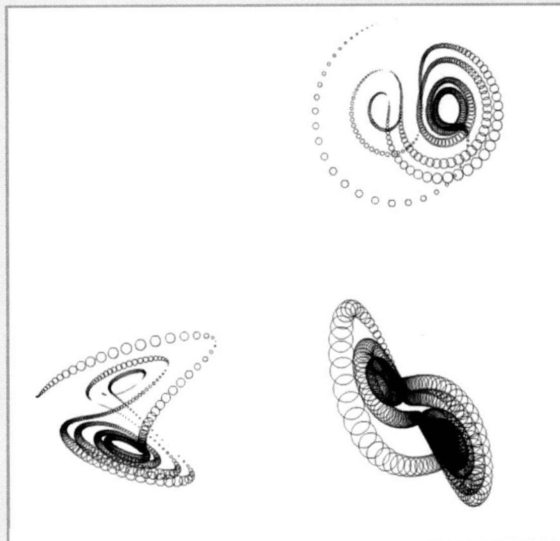

comp002i
For the final iteration I kept the `mg` variable, but only used it to draw one attractor. I removed two of the code blocks and left the last one looking like this:

```
newmc="line"+String(depth++);
this.attachMovie("line",newmc,depth);
this[newmc]._x=z0*mg;
this[newmc]._y=y0*mg+210;
this[newmc]._xscale=50;
this[newmc]._yscale=(x0+5)*mg;
```

I changed `line` to a long, thin rectangle.

You may have noticed that the z value is completely ignored during the creation of the new movie clip. While the current process renders quite beautiful and complex paths, it is actually an inadequate two-dimensional representation of the system. For further exploration, you may choose to use the z value as an attribute effecter. The most obvious use of the z value is as a scaler, so that objects with higher z values appear larger and closer to the user while objects with lower z values appear smaller and further away. It could also be applied to the alpha of a movie clip, or rotation. You might even use the z value as an index into a many framed movie clip, for unusual changes in color, shape, or behavior.

If you are comfortable with this attractor, I would suggest you next attempt to implement the Ikeda attractor, which is a fantastic painterly system.

Recursive inspiration

This is a lightweight computational piece that creates a number of braided, looping ropes. The synchronized twisting and looping is a unique effect achieved through elementary trigonometry and a function of variable flow.

This experiment is slightly more complicated to create than the previous two because there is code on multiple frames. The layer structure of the movie is similar to that of the first experiment with a background, button to regenerate the effect and a `logic` layer that contains the code. The difference here is that the code is on three frames. The movieclip that we're duplicating is also a bit more complicated. The actual graphic is held in a clip called `icon`. This is in turn held in another movieclip called `nug`. `nug` is made up of two layers with five frames in each of them. The top layer holds code, and the bottom layer holds `icon`. `icon` is tweened over the first four frames so that it increases in size, giving the impression of growth when a new clip is duplicated. Now that the movie's set up, let's go back to the main stage and look at the code. Frame 1 looks like this:

```
jlim=3;

for (j=0; j<jlim; j++) {
 newmc="mc"+String(depth++);
 this.attachMovie("nug",newmc,depth);
 this[newmc]._x=j*420/jlim+210/jlim;
 this[newmc]._y=210;
 this[newmc]._xscale=20-Math.abs(5*(j-(jlim-1)/2));
 this[newmc]._yscale=20-Math.abs(5*(j-(jlim-1)/2));

 newmc="mc"+String(depth++);
 this.attachMovie("nug",newmc,depth);
 this[newmc]._x=j*420/jlim+210/jlim;
 this[newmc]._y=210;
 this[newmc]._xscale=-20+Math.abs(5*(j-(jlim-1)/2));
 this[newmc]._yscale=-20+Math.abs(5*(j-(jlim-1)/2));
}
```

Frame 2 looks like this:

```
rot = -30*Math.sin(Math.PI/180*theta);
theta += v;
v += random(3)-1;
if (v<-5) {
   v = -5;
} else if (v>5) {
   v = 5;
}
```

Finally, frame 3 looks like this:

```
gotoAndPlay(_currentframe-1);
```

We use this rather than hard coding a frame number because we'll be adding some more frames to the set-up later on.

Now for the code that's on the `nug` movieclip. This is the code for frame 4:

```
if (depth<80) {
   newnug="nug";
   this.attachMovie("nug",newnug,2);
   this[newnug]._y=-100;
   this[newnug]._xscale=98;
   this[newnug]._yscale=98;
   this[newnug]._rotation=_root.rot;
   this[newnug].depth=depth+1;
}
```

Last of all, frame 5 of `nug` has a `stop` action in it.

The key variables

`jlim` = the number of ropes on the screen
`rot` = controls the coil of the rope
`theta` = an incremental factor used in calculating the rotation
`v` = a random velocity factor used to increase `theta`

The bulk of the computational work is performed within the `nug` movieclip. Each long rope is the result of the instantiation of a single, recursive `nug`. Recursion is the process of movieclips making copies of themselves. The `nug` uses recursion to make itself into a rope.

Recursion is always a tricky business and if you're not careful, it will quickly consume all available memory resources until the computer goes insane. If left unchecked, the `nug` movieclip would replicate itself into eternity, so in this project, our conditional is determined by the variable `depth`, which is increased with each successive `nug`. If the depth is less than 80, it's ok to make another copy, but if not, then we stop it.

Admittedly, the code that we use eventually builds a giant parent-child chain that grows up into absurd levels of hierarchy, which some might say is a bit flaky. My justification is that Flash handles it exceptionally well, and the advantages of nested transformations make it worth the expense.

We position the new movieclip at the end of the current one, and reduce its size by only a bit. Remember that all transformations will have exponential effects due to the nested nature of this assembly. We then use a variable at the root level to determine the change in rotation. This allows the user or a separate function to guide the building process somewhat. The unique twisting and looping effect is achieved by referencing the variable `rot` within the root level. At any given time, `rot` is a sinusoidal function of a randomly accelerating position value. Using a system such as this, many variations of growth can be derived by simply modifying the number magnitudes.

One of the most important steps of the replication is the incrementing of `depth` so that we don't replicate to infinity. Take it out if you really want to understand why (after you save your work of course).

The rest of the project is merely the initial instantiation of a few `nugs` to start the show. This could have really been anything, but for this project, I decided to use an iterative loop create six `nugs`, arranged in pairs, backs against each other, facing in opposite directions. I enjoy watching self-similar braids unfold in multiple scales.

The regeneration button allows the user to repeatedly generate new ropes, which creates in the end a beautiful braided design with fantastic self-similar qualities. At the moment this button will draw a new braid on top of the old one. If you want it to completely replace the old braid, then you need to add the line `depth=0` to the beginning of the code on frame 1 of the root.

comp003b

First of all, I changed the code so that there was only one braid, and it now loops in a different way. I also changed the graphic. All of these code changes are in the first frame of the root:

```
jlim = 1;
depth = 0;

this[newmc]._x=210;
this[newmc]._y=210;
this[newmc]._xscale=20;
this[newmc]._yscale=20;
this[newmc]._rotation=90;

this[newmc]._x=210;
this[newmc]._y=210;
this[newmc]._xscale=-20;
this[newmc]._yscale=20;
this[newmc]._rotation=-90;
```

comp003c

This time I removed the block of code that creates the reflection, and just duplicated the original one at three different angles. Here's the loop for frame one:

```
jlim = 3;

for (j=0; j<jlim; j++) {
   newmc="mc"+String(depth++);
   this.attachMovie("nug",newmc,depth);
   this[newmc]._x=210;
   this[newmc]._y=210;
   this[newmc]._xscale=20;
   this[newmc]._yscale=20;
   this[newmc]._rotation=120*j;
}
```

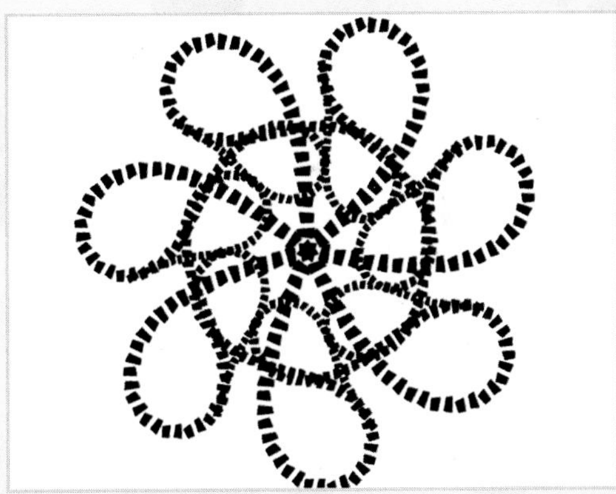

comp003d

For this iteration I increased the number of arms to 7 and changed the graphic slightly to get these spirals that remind me of ancient Greek patterns.

```
jlim = 7;

this[newmc]._rotation=(360/7)*j;
```

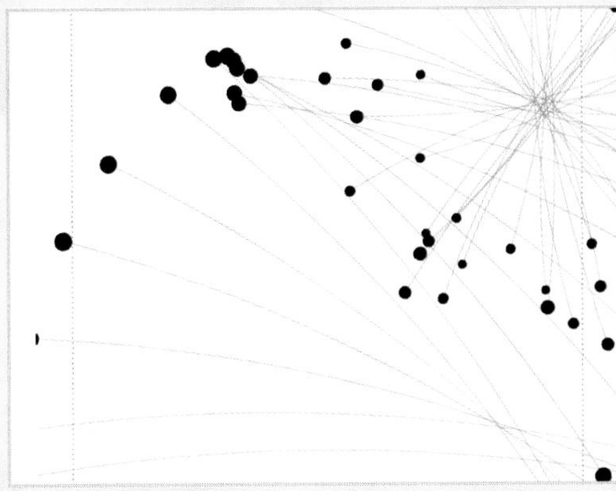

comp003e

I made another couple of small changes to the code here, but the major visual difference comes from the `icon`. It is now a long thin vertical bar with a ball at each end. This produces some wildly different results compared to the previous iterations. Here are the code changes to frame 1:

```
jlim = 1;

this[newmc]._y=420;
this[newmc]._xscale=30;
this[newmc]._yscale=30;
```

Notice that we've changed to a single braid that grows up from the bottom of the screen, we've also removed the rotation line. I changed the second frame too slightly to increase the rotation of the braid:

```
rot=-60*Math.sin(Math.PI / 180 * theta);
```

comp003f
This effect is similar to the last, but I tightened the velocity amongst other things to give an overlapping alpha effect. The shape has been changed to a simple rectangle. These are the changes to frame 1:

```
this[newmc]._y=400;
this[newmc]._xscale=20;
this[newmc]._yscale=20;
```

...and these changes to frame 2:

```
rot=-10*Math.sin(Math.PI / 180 * theta);
v+=random(7)-3;
```

Finally, I changed the scaling on frame 5 of `nug` to 96 so that it scales away a bit quicker.

comp003g
For this iteration I went back to having multiple braids, this time 4 moving away from the center. I also changed icon to eleven frames of the same square, but with a different color in each one. To randomly choose one of these frames, I added the following line to the first frame of `nug`:

```
icon.gotoAndStop(random(icon._totalframes)+1);
```

Make sure that `icon` has an instance name of `icon` within `nug`. I also changed some code back on the main root to give different rotation and scaling. Here's the code for frame 1:

```
jlim = 4;

this[newmc]._y=210;
scl=random(30)+20;
this[newmc]._xscale=scl;
this[newmc]._yscale=scl;
this[newmc]._rotation=90*j+40+random(20);
this[newmc]._alpha=50;
```

I also changed the rotation in frame 2:

```
rot=-50*Math.sin(Math.PI / 180 * theta);
```

comp003h
This time I made some major changes to the structure of the FLA by adding some more frames. There are now 8 frames on each layer of the root, because I've moved around some of the code and added some more. The first frame now contains this:

```
depth=0;
n=0;
v=0;
```

Frame 2 contains the duplication and positioning code that used to be in the first frame:

```
newmc="mc"+String(depth++);
this.attachMovie("nug",newmc,depth);
this[newmc]._x=(n+1)*420/6;
this[newmc]._y=105;
scl=20;
this[newmc]._xscale=scl;
this[newmc]._yscale=scl;
this[newmc]._rotation=180;
```

Frames 3, 4, and 5 are blank to give a slight pause in the drawing of the shape. Frame 6 contains a new loop:

```
n++;
if (n<5) {
   gotoAndPlay(2);
}
```

This loop controls the number of loops will come down the screen. Frame 7 contains the old rotation code for the loops:

```
rot=-30*Math.sin(Math.PI / 180 * theta);
theta+=v;
v+=(random(7)-3)/5;
if (v<-5) {
   v=-5;
} else if (v>5) {
   v=5;
}
```

Finally, frame 8 just contains the same old `gotoAndPlay` action.

There have also been some major changes to `nug`. I created a new movieclip called `petal`. This is a long thin horizontal bar with a ball at each end. This clip sits inside `icon` with the instance name `petal`. `icon` itself is a larger circle with the left-hand ball of `petal` centered in it. The first frame of `nug` contains only this line:

```
if (random(13)) icon.petal._visible=false;
```

This means that there is a 1 in 13 chance a petal appearing. The rest of the code in `nug` is pretty similar, but there are some changes to allow the loops to follow their own paths, here's the code:

```
if (depth<120) {
   newnug="nug";
   this.attachMovie("nug",newnug,1);
   this[newnug]._y=-100;
   // slight reduction in scale
   this[newnug]._xscale=98.7;
   this[newnug]._yscale=98.7;
   // look to mother to determine rotation
   this[newnug]._rotation=_root.rot+random(11)-5;
   // don't forget this!
   this[newnug].depth=depth+1;
}
```

comp003i
This code is similar to the last one, but with a few notable changes. First of all, I inserted another three frames to increase the pause between drawing. Frame 1 is the same, and frame 2 has the following changes:

```
this[newmc]._x=210;
this[newmc]._y=210;
scl=12;
this[newmc]._rotation=180*(n%2);
```

The `if` on frame 9 (was frame 6) has been changed to activate if `n<2`. The code on frames 10 and 11 (were 7 and 8) is the same.

The graphics have changed radically again, `icon` is now a simple cross, but `petal` has become 33 frames of different colored circles with the following code on the first frame:

```
this._alpha=20;
gotoAndStop(random(_totalframes)+1);
stop();
```

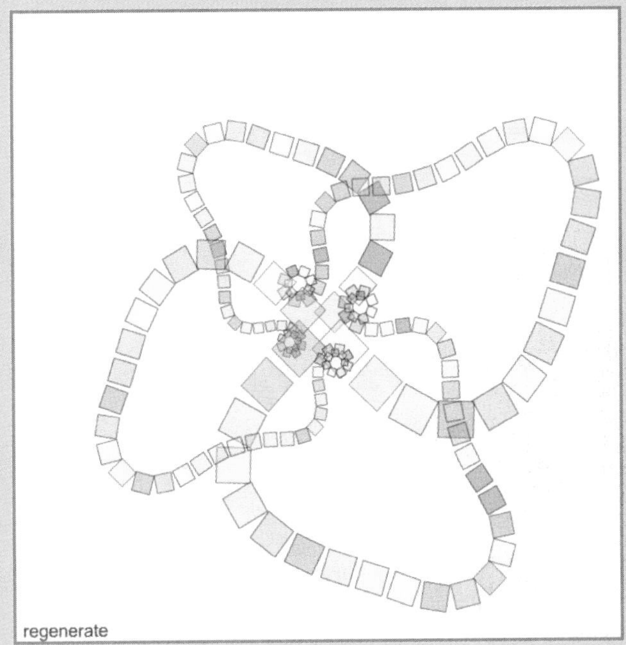

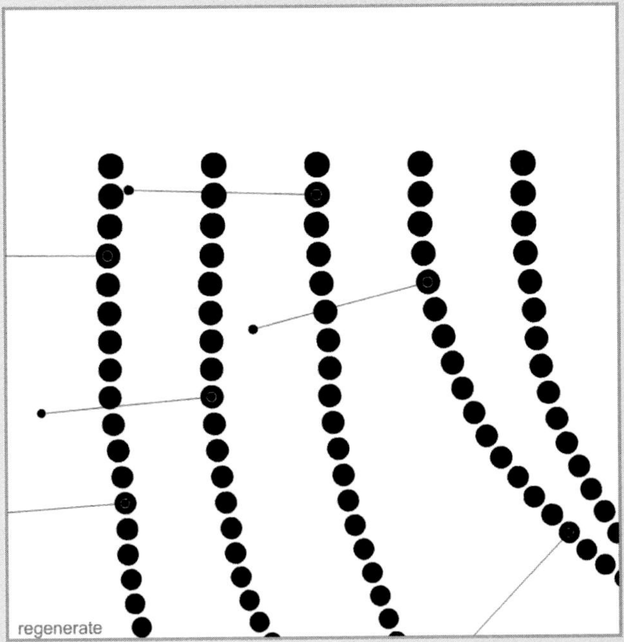

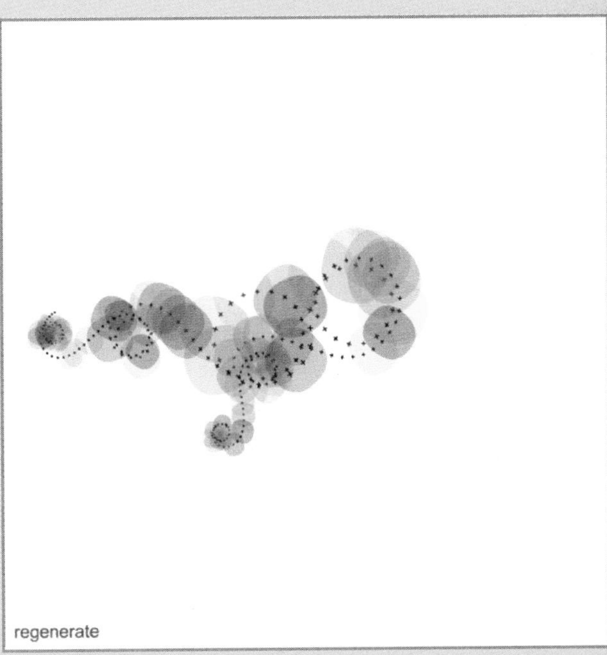

I also changed the code on the first frame of `nug` so that petals appeared 1 in every 3 frames rather than 13.

To really bring the beauty out from this piece, I would suggest making a few quick changes to the braid object's graphic. Try adding thorns, or horizontal lines, or anything large and transparent for some really interesting effects. Another point of modification might be the magnitude of the constants used in the referenced sinusoidal equation. This will cause all kinds of strange growth behavior, as only slight numerical changes will bring about wild effects in recursive constructs. One change to be cautious of is the maximum depth value for each rope. Initially at 80, changing this much larger than 100 will result in some very slow rendering times and memory intensive object structures. Plus, since by default the rope's scale decreases, objects beyond the depth of 80 aren't much bigger than a pixel once they're rendered.

Recursive circles

This is another great example of recursion, a set of concentric circles, each just touching the next one below it. Run `comp004a.swf` to see it in action. I am often more inspired by the end result of a piece than I am to make the piece in the first place, so sometimes I force myself to build something with simple rules that I've used in other projects, while introducing some new bit of randomness. The first few iterations are usually shapes that I expect, while after some time of tinkering, they slowly (sometimes quite suddenly) mutate in constructions I never knew possible. The driving motivation I use in creating pieces such as this, is 'maximum effect with minimum graphic composure'. I view computational art much the same way I do furniture fabric, if I can stare at it day after day and still not recognize the machine that produced the pattern in it, it's a good piece of work.

I think with the subdued color increment and sea creature like spiraling nature, this computational piece is a good example of what I am trying to achieve.

This movie has a similar construction to the previous one, a few frames of code on the root, and a movieclip called `nug` containing some more code and a graphic. There are a couple of differences though, the graphic is placed directly in its own layer in `nug` rather than a separate movieclip, and there is another layer on the main stage called `mothernug`. This layer contains an instance of the `nug` clip in its second and third frames, scaled to fit the screen, and with the instance name `mothernug`. The graphic on `nug` itself is just a dotted outline of a circle. `nug` is exported from the Library with the linkage name `nug`.

The code on the main stage is split into three frames. Here's the code on the first frame:

```
rscale=random(50)+47;
rrot=2*random(7)-3;
```

This initializes some random scale and rotation values. Here's the code on frame 2:

```
mothernug._rotation=random(360);
```

This gives `mothernug` (our instance of `nug` on the main stage) a random rotation. On frame 3 we simply have a `stop` action.

Now for the code inside `nug`. The first frame is currently blank, but we'll be using it soon. The second frame contains this code:

```
if (depth<80) {
 newnug="nuginside";
 this.attachMovie("nug",newnug,1);
 rot=this._rotation+_root.rrot;
 scale=_root.rscale;
 this[newnug]._x=(100-scale)*Math.cos(Math.PI / 180 * rot);
 this[newnug]._y=(100-scale)*Math.sin(Math.PI / 180 * rot);
 this[newnug]._xscale=scale;
 this[newnug]._yscale=scale;
 this[newnug]._rotation=rot;
 this[newnug].depth=depth+1;
}
```

The third frame just has a `stop` action to prevent the code from escaping from the computer and taking over the world. Okay, so it won't really do that, but you know what I mean.

The key variables

`rscale` = a random value used to alter the scale of successive recursions
`rrot` = a random value used to alter the rotation of successive recursions
`depth` = the limit of new recursions, once this limit is reached, the movie stops
`rot` = the rotation value for the current clip
`scale` = the scale value for the current clip

It's basically a simple inward-growing recursive construction. The intersecting strokes of consecutive copies of the same object create subtle spirals inwards towards an unknown point.

A single instance of a recursive movieclip called `nug` sits on the main timeline, it then makes copy of itself and places it somewhere along its perimeter. The copy is scaled and rotated to random values set at the root level. This copy then begins the same growth process by making a copy of itself, within itself, until a maximum of 80 copies has been made. We use a couple of trigonometric functions to place each copy so that its perimeter lies flush with the perimeter of its parent. With a little rotation added, this provides us with the 'spiraling' effect that we see in completed recursions.

Iterations

comp004b

For the first iteration, I decided to try out a trick that I find interesting, replacing the shapes with random letters. This is done by adding the following code to frame 1 of nug:

```
fg=chr(random(26)+97);
```

This selects a random character for us, this is then fed into a dynamic text box, tied to the fg variable, that sits on the stage in place of the graphic in nug. Remember to embed the outlines for the font or you won't see anything. I also changed the depth limit in frame 2 of nug to 10 so that the letters weren't too cluttered to read.

comp004c

For this iteration I removed the letter code that I added last time, and replaced the graphic with a simple translucent square with its registration point in the bottom right corner. The first code change that I made was to the first frame of the root:

```
rscale=random(10)+88;
rrot=random(3)-1;
```

The only other change that I made was to put the depth limit back up to 80.

comp004d

There is very little change to this experiment, but it makes some totally different and really beautiful images. The only change to the code is that I reduced the depth limit to 50. I changed the graphic to a vertical blue bar, a little to the right of the registration point.

comp004e

Again, I kept to the basic idea of the last experiment, only changing the graphic to a text string with the word "further" in it. All of the code is the same.

comp004f

I kept to a similar basic set up once more, changing the scale and rotation code in the first frame on the root and the nug graphic. Here's the code change:

```
rscale=random(5)+94;
rrot=137.5;
```

The graphic is now a set of increasingly smaller circles heading off to the right from the registration point.

[4b]

[4c]

[4d]

[4e]

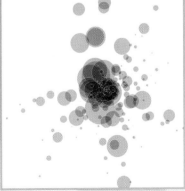

[4f]

comp004g

A bit of a change this time. Now instead of the graphic being directly on the nug clip, it's inside another movieclip called node that is placed onto nug, and given the instance name node. The graphic in node is 32 frames of a filled cross in a different color every frame. There is also a stop action on frame 1. There is also a large change to the other code. I removed all of the code from the root except for a stop action in frame 3. Inside nug, I've added some code to the first frame:

```
node.gotoAndStop(random(node._totalframes)+1);
node._alpha=20;
```

This code selects a random frame – and therefore color – in node, and sets its alpha to 20. I also changed the code in frame 2 to add a for loop to give each nug children. Here's the complete code for frame 2:

```
if (depth<6) {
  children=random(3)+1;
  for (n=0;n<children;n++) {
    newnug="nug"+String(n);
    this.attachMovie("nug",newnug,n+1);
    rot=random(360);
    this[newnug]._x=50*Math.cos(Math.PI / 180 * rot);
    this[newnug]._y=50*Math.sin(Math.PI / 180 * rot);
    scale=50+random(50);
    this[newnug]._xscale=scale;
    this[newnug]._yscale=scale;
    this[newnug]._rotation=rot;
    this[newnug].depth=depth+1;
  }
}
```

comp004h

This iteration is similar to the last. I still have 32 different colored shapes in node, but this time they're almost the opposite of what they were, they're what's left of a square once a cross has been removed from it – just a collection of corners. I changed the code in the first frame of nug to give the shapes an alpha value of 80, making them a bit harder. I also altered the second frame as well, here's what I altered:

```
if (depth<6)

this[newnug]._x=random(100)-50;
this[newnug]._y=random(100)-50;
scale=60+random(40);
```

comp004i

For the final iteration I made a few changes, I set the graphic of node to be a large cross made up of two dotted lines. Because of the size of the cross, I also added a mask to the root to make sure that anything that went off stage would be invisible. I changed frame 1 of nug so that the alpha value for node was 100. The only other changes I made were to the second frame, where I set the depth limit to 5, and removed the rotation line so that the crosses would all have the same orientation.

With a bit of experimentation, the rules underlying this construction method will allow for some very unusual results. For example, try changing the graphic to a simple line, originating from the center. Also try transposing each new child somewhere further from the perimeter. You will be surprised with just how fast and chaotic the construction method actually becomes when using 'non-spherical' shapes.

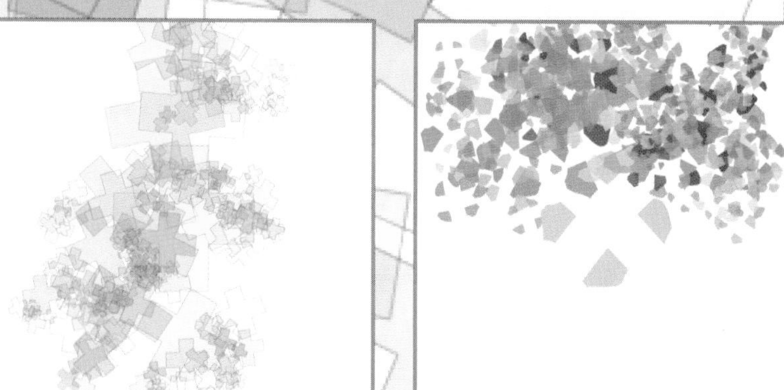

I live in Lynn, Massachusetts with my wife Kazumi. I've been using Flash off and on for about two years now, but far more heavily in the last six months. My personal site, www.bit-101.com launched in August 2001, and I strive to keep up with the experiment-a-day schedule. It features fairly simple graphics, usually relying on math and scripting to build complex forms and movements.

I guess the underlying goal in most of the Flash pieces I come up with is Creation, as in "The Creation", "Let there be light", and so on. When I got my first computer back in 1990, a Commodore Amiga, it came with a 3D modeling program. I still remember being excited about the idea that I was creating my own universe, with its own space, matter, energy, and time. Jump forward a few years to Flash and a processor that's about fifty times faster, and has a hundred fold more memory, and now what do I want to do? I want to create life.

Most of my personal experiments have at least one of these three things in common:

1. They try to model some behavior in as simple a mathematical formula as possible, often delving into basic principles of physics to imitate the real world

2. There is almost always some random element thrown in there

3. There is some user interaction

I'm not so much into making a linear scripted movie, as I am into giving something certain behaviors and sitting back and seeing what *it* decides to do. Or, handing over the reigns to someone else and seeing what they can do with it. I think that echoes the evolution of Flash itself. There are people doing things with it that I believe are far beyond the ideas of the people who created it in the first place. It has really taken on a life of its own.

keith peters

bit-101.com

Dot grid

My first experiment is a simple grid of white dots. By applying a couple of trig formulae to the position of the dots in three dimensions, we can get some pretty complex behaviors so, in keeping with the theme of this book, we'll see how slight changes to the formulae can create all kinds of variations.

OK, first let's create one dot, and then move on to the grid. I have a black background, so the dot is just a 2x2 pixel white circle, no outline, made into a movie clip with the instance name `dot`. That's pretty much it, the rest is just code.

The code attached to `dot` is split into a `load` and an `enterFrame` clip event for initialization and updating:

```
onClipEvent (load) {
    fl = 200;
    xcenter = 270;
    ycenter = 200;
    zcenter = 75;
    y = 100;
    zpos = z+zcenter;
    scale = fl/(fl+zpos);
    xheight = 10;
    zheight = 10;
    xspeed = 10;
    zspeed = 10;
    xangle = x;
    zangle = z;
}

onClipEvent (enterFrame) {
    xwave = Math.sin(xangle*Math.PI/180)*xheight;
    zwave = Math.sin(zangle*Math.PI/180)*zheight;
    ypos = y+xwave+zwave;
    xangle += xspeed;
    zangle += zspeed;
    _x = x*scale+xcenter;
    _y = ypos*scale+ycenter;
    _xscale = _yscale=scale*100;
    xheight = zheight=(400-_root._ymouse)/10;
    xspeed = zspeed=(_root._xmouse-270)/10;
}
```

The other piece of code sits on the first frame of the root, this is the part that creates the grid:

```
num=0;
for(i=-3; i<4; i++){
    for(j=-3; j<4; j++){
      duplicateMovieClip(dot, "dot"+num, num);
      _root["dot"+num].x=i*40;
      _root["dot"+num].z=j*40;
      num++;
    }
}
```

The key variables

`fl` = focal length, how deep the field of vision is
`xcenter` = the horizontal center of the screen
`ycenter` = the vertical center of the screen
`zcenter` = the mid point for the depth of the screen
`y` = the camera position, 0 is ground level
`x` = the horizontal spacing between dots
`z` = the depth spacing between dots
`zpos` = the current depth of the dot
`scale` = the current position of the dot according to the focal length
`xheight` and **`zheight`** = initialize variables for the height positions of the dot wave
`xspeed` and **`zspeed`** = initialize variables for the speed of the dot wave
`xangle` and **`zangle`** = variables for dot spacing on the wave
`xwave` and **`zwave`** = variables for working out the current dot position on the wave
`ypos` = the current dot position on the wave
`i` and **`j`** = loop counters for rows and columns respectively
`num` = the counter to name the duplicate dots

This just creates a series of 49 dots and assigns them **`x`** and **`z`** values in a grid pattern. The code internal to each dot uses the **`x`** and **`z`** coordinates as horizontal position and depth. It then calculates a moving sine wave along the x-axis and another along the z-axis and uses these waves to calculate the **`y`**, or height, of each dot. Then it plots the perspective of each dot and its screen **`_x`** and **`_y`** positions and scale.

Iterations

For all of these iterations I've returned back to the original code to apply changes between experiments rather than accumulating them.

exp1-1

By changing these values in the `load` clip event the wave gets more pronounced, like a rougher sea:

```
xheight=15;
zheight=-15;
```

exp1-2

Using these values you'll get a wave with opposite pulses on the `x` and `z` because `Math.abs` converts all of the negative values to positive ones, and I also reversed the `zspeed`. It gives an effect almost like something breathing.

```
xheight=25;
zspeed=-10;
xangle=Math.abs(x);
```

exp1-3

I tried something different this time, taking control away from the code and giving it to the mouse, making it interactive. First set the other variables back to their original states, and then add these two lines to the bottom of the `enterFrame` clip event code:

```
xheight=zheight=(200-_root._ymouse)/5;
xspeed=zspeed=(_root._xmouse-270)/10;
```

Now just move the mouse around and watch the results.

exp1-4

For this experiment I took the `zpos` and `scale` lines out of the `load` clip event, and then put them back at the top of the `enterFrame` clip event:

```
zpos=z+zcenter;
scale=fl/(fl+zpos);
```

This allows the z-motion and perspective to take place in real-time. Then add this to the bottom of the `enterFrame` code to update the motion:

```
z+=5;
if(z>1000){
    z=-200;
}
```

This will make the grid swim off into the screen, and then when it gets really far away we move it back in front of the screen so that it looks like another grid swimming past us.

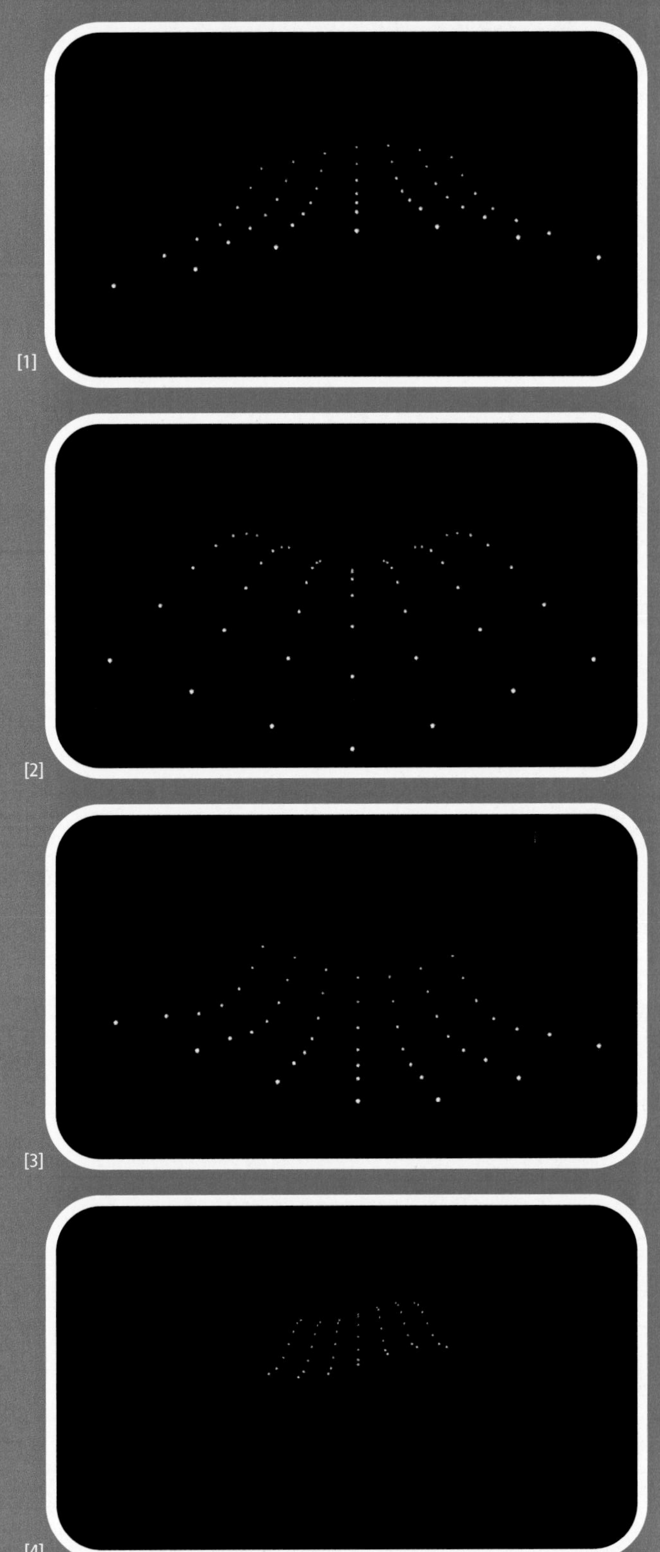

[1]

[2]

[3]

[4]

exp1-5
Here, I went off on a different tangent again, this time rather than applying the wave to the y axis, I've applied it to the x and z instead. This gives a strange shimmering effect like a very calm lake. I also added some code to make the mouse control the speed of the shimmer. Replace the `enterFrame` code with this:

```
xwave=Math.sin(xangle*Math.PI/180)*xheight;
zwave=Math.sin(zangle*Math.PI/180)*zheight;
xpos=x+xwave;
zpos=z+zwave+zcenter;
scale=fl/(fl+zpos);
xangle+=xspeed;
zangle+=zspeed;
_x=xpos*scale+xcenter;
_y=y*scale+ycenter;
_xscale=_yscale=scale*100;
zspeed=(_root._ymouse-200)/5;
xspeed=(_root._xmouse-270)/5;
```

exp1-6
Back to the original code again for this strange effect. First of all change the values of `xheight` and `xspeed` to 2 in the `load` clip event:

```
xheight=2;
xspeed=2;
```

And then alter the `xwave` line in the `enterFrame` code so that it uses the tangent of `xangle` instead of the sine:

```
xwave=Math.tan(xangle*Math.PI/180)*xheight;
```

This effect looks to me like eerily dismembered fingers playing an invisible piano.

exp1-7
Return to the original code, and simply add these lines to the `enterFrame` event:

```
zcenter=zwave*5+100;
zpos=z+zcenter;
scale=fl/(fl+zpos);
```

This updates the scale every frame so that you get a pulsing effect.

exp1-8
Finally, I just changed the above code slightly so that the pulses are affected by the `xwave` rather than the `zwave`:

```
zcenter=xwave*5+100;
```

There are loads of things to play about with in this code. The simplest thing to start with is the speed and height in the `load` clip event. Make `xspeed` high and `zspeed` low and `xheight` low and `zheight` high, and you'll start to get the idea of what's going on. Don't forget to try fractional numbers and negative numbers.

Next go down to the `xangle` and `yangle` variables. These are the initial angles that the wave starts out at, so if you set either one to a constant number, say 0, then the whole row will move as one. By setting them to x and z, as I did at first, each point will be different. Try setting them to different combinations such as these:

```
xangle=x+z;                  xangle=x+z;
zangle=x+z;                  zangle=x-z;
```

Here are some combinations where I've changed all of the above factors:

```
xheight=10;                  xheight=Math.sqrt(z*z+x*x)/2;
zheight=-10;                 zheight=Math.sqrt(z*z+x*x)/5;
xspeed=10;                   xspeed=10;
zspeed=-10;                  zspeed=10;
xangle=x-z;                  xangle=z/2;
zangle=x-z;                  zangle=z/2;
```

You could spend all night on this alone. But let's move on to the `enterFrame` clip event, there's more stuff to play with there...

First, are the sine functions, they can easily be changed to `cos` without much noticeable difference. But give it a try with `tan` like I did in `exp1-6` to see the dramatic difference it makes. To counteract the craziness it's best to lower the speed and height of the axis that you are trying it on.

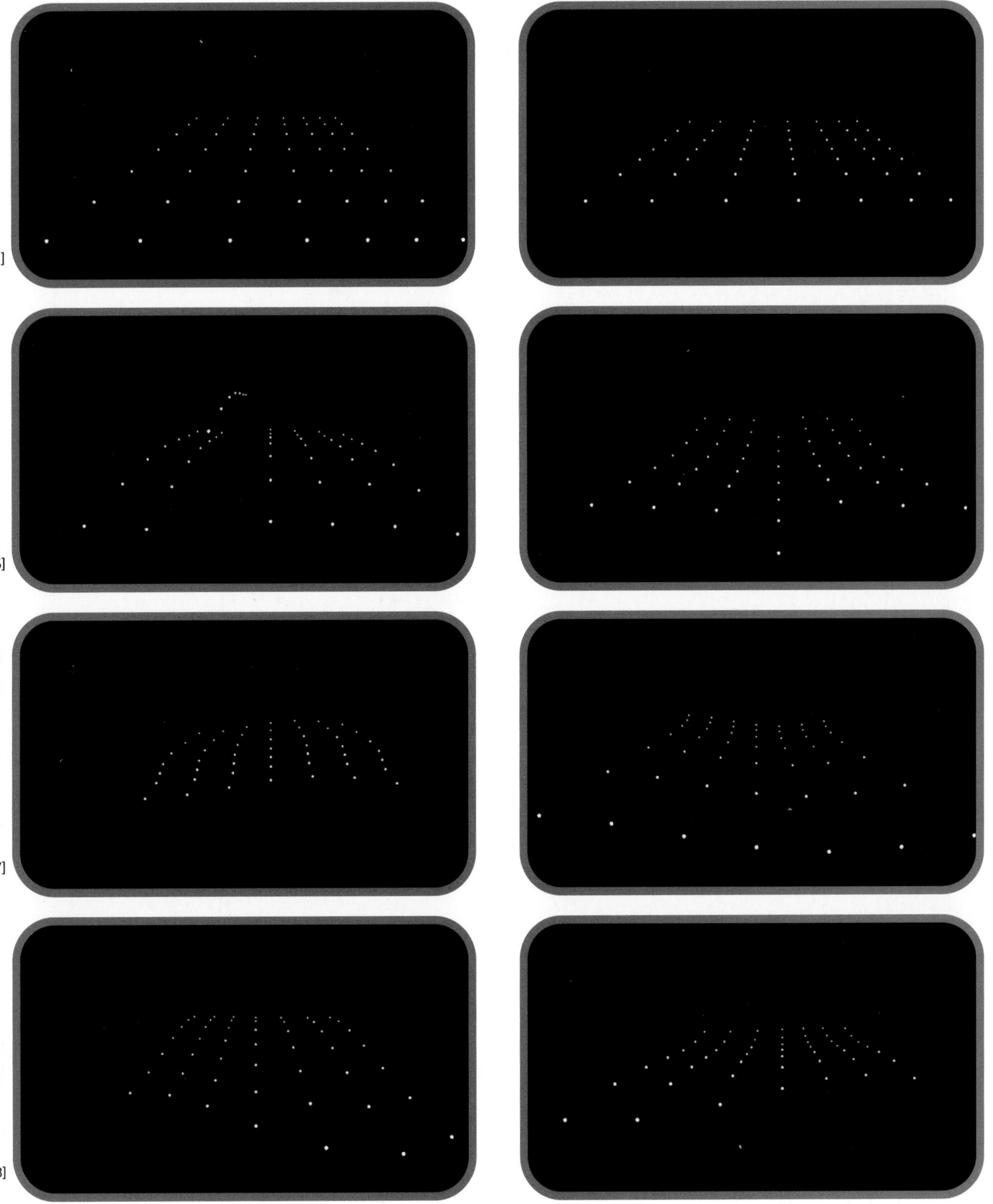

Fractal folia

For my next experiment, I want to delve into some recursion to create a fractal tree. This is where you have a function that calls itself, or in Flash terms you can have a movie clip with a copy of itself inside it. Now if you directly try to drag an object from the Library into itself, Flash is going to complain, so we're going to trick it by using `attachMovie`. It's important to realize that Flash is complaining for a good reason here, so we need to impose a limit on our recursion so that it doesn't try to go to infinity and beyond, and crash.

OK. Start by creating a new movie clip named `target`. Leave it completely blank and go back to the main movie. Now create another new movie clip named `line`, and draw a 100 pixel vertical hairline that has the registration point at its bottom end. Then drag a copy of `target` out of the Library and place it exactly at the top of the line, and give that instance of target the name `t1`. This is where we will be attaching our movie copy. Create a 3-frame `Actions` layer in `line`, and extend the original layer to cover these three frames as well. We need to keep the code inside the clip so that it will still be there when we attach a new copy. Next, go into the Library and give the `line` clip the linkage identifier `line`. Now onto the code...

For now, the only initialization code we will need is how many levels of recursion we will be doing. Six will work pretty well, so in Frame 1 on the `Actions` layer, put:

```
limit=6;
```

Each time we attach a movie in a deeper level, we will be increasing a variable called `level` by one. We'll use that to check if we've surpassed our `limit` or not. If not, we'll attach two copies of `line` to the `target` movie clip, `t1`. Then we will scale and rotate them a bit. Here's the code for Frame 2:

```
if(level<limit){
  t1.attachMovie("line", "line"+1, 1);
  t1.attachMovie("line", "line"+2, 2);
  t1.line1.level=level+1;
  t1.line1._xscale=t1.line1._yscale=50;
  t1.line1._rotation=-45;
  t1.line2.level=level+1;
  t1.line2._xscale=t1.line2._yscale=50;
  t1.line2._rotation=45;
}
```

There is no need to loop just yet, so Frame 3 just gets a `stop` action for now.

Drag an instance of `line` onto the stage, the tree will start growing from the position of the line on the stage so place it near the bottom for that authentically rooted tree feel. Test it to see a nice conventional but basic fractal tree. It's far from realistic, but good to play around with.

Iterations

exp2-2
First, I experimented with changing a few of the scale and rotation variables. I created a more fern-like curve where the branches only grow from one side of the tree by changing these two lines:

```
t1.line1._xscale=t1.line1._yscale=60;
t1.line1._rotation=-20;
```

exp2-3
By changing these values again for both lines you get something more akin to grass, or maybe a weeping willow:

```
t1.line1._xscale=t1.line1._yscale=50;
t1.line1._rotation=20;
t1.line2._xscale=t1.line2._yscale=80;
t1.line2._rotation=30;
```

exp2-4
When you get tired of manually playing with the numbers and have a feel for how the variables affect the tree, you can take it one more step towards realism by creating random numbers for the number of branches and the rotation.

We'll need to determine in advance the maximum and minimum branches that can be formed on each iteration – let's say between 1 and 4, so add this line to frame 1:

```
branch=Math.random()*3+1;
```

Next we need to create a rotation value that will be between -30 and +30. Here is the full code for frame 2:

```
if(level<limit){
  for(i=0;i<branch;i++){
    t1.attachMovie("line", "line"+i, i);
    t1["line"+i].level=level+1;
    scale=50;
    t1["line"+i]._xscale=scale;
    t1["line"+i]._yscale=scale;
    t1["line"+i]._rotation=Math.random()*60-30;
  }
}
```

Now, if you run the movie, you'll have a random tree every time.

Rather than having to re-run the movie every time that you want to generate a new tree, it's easier to make it happen on a mouse-click by attaching this code to the line movieclip that's on the stage:

```
onClipEvent (mouseUp) {
  for (i=0; i<=branch; i++) {
    removeMovieClip (t1["line"+i]);
  }
  gotoAndPlay (1);
}
```

This just cycles back through the clips on the screen and removes them all, then goes back to frame 1 and starts the process again.

exp2-5
At the moment, the trees look a little more like umbelliferous wild chervil, but we can change this by giving them a random scale as well. Change the scale line to see what I mean:

```
scale=Math.random()*10+50;
```

exp2-6
I experimented with the scale and rotation a bit more, and expanded them both to get these crazy trees:

```
scale=Math.random()*30+50;
t1["line"+i]._rotation=Math.random()*180-90;
```

[2] [3] [4] [5] [6]

exp2-7

For this iteration I decided to make a radical change, returning back to the pre-craziness of exp2-5, I added some animation to the tree. First of all I reduced the number of levels in frame 1 to make the animation run a little more smoothly. Set limit to 4. Next change the code in frame 3 to this:

```
angle+=5;
rad=angle*Math.PI/180;
t1._rotation=Math.sin(rad)*60;
```

This will set the rotation of the branches along a sine wave, now we just need to run this every frame to give us a tree that will sway from one side to the other in an electronic wind. To do this we need to add a fourth frame to both layers, and set it up to loop back to frame 3 with this:

```
gotoAndPlay(3);
```

Try substituting rotation for scale to get some dancing trees – see exp2-7a for an example.

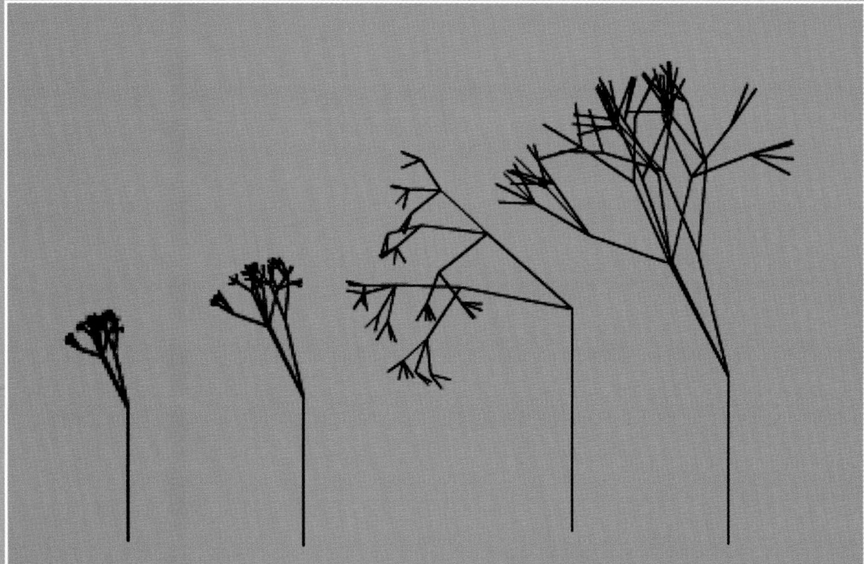

[7]

[7a]

exp2-8
Here I changed the rotation so that it is controlled by the mouse instead of being on a sine curve. The code on frame 3 is now just this:

```
t1._rotation=(_root._xmouse-200)/2;
```

exp2-9
I quite liked the effect of mouse control on the rotation, so I tried applying it to the scale as well by adding this line to frame 3:

```
_xscale=_yscale=(400-_root._ymouse)/2;
```

I love this way this goes totally out of control when you move the mouse to the extremes.

The key values to mess around with to get some cool effects are the `limit`, scaling and rotation. Making the scale and rotation different for `line1` and `line2`, as we did in `exp2-2`, can make some nice lopsided trees. Don't forget to fool around with negative scale factors as well. Another thing to take note of is not to make `limit` too high or you will be waiting forever for your tree to finish growing. Of course there is no need to limit yourself to just a few branches either, but again, don't go too wild or your Flash will crash.

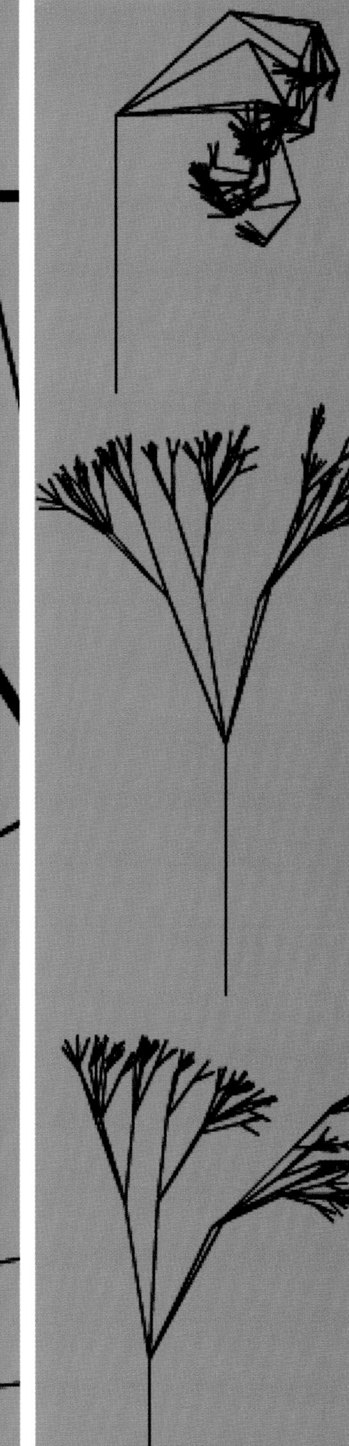
[8]

Wireframe organic

I make a lot of use of the trigonometric functions in Flash, as they are vital to any rotation and 3D functions, and very useful in creating fluid, undulating motion. We'll be making use of them for the latter here to create some weird and wonderful wireframe worm-like structures.

First, make a movieclip with a shape inside it. Any shape will do, but I started with a simple black hairline circle, no fill, 30 pixels in diameter. Try different shapes later for interesting results. Name this instance, `shape` and set its alpha to 10. The next thing to do is to create a blank movieclip called `master`. We'll use this to put all of our code on to duplicate and position the shape. We have the following code attached to `master`:

```
onClipEvent (load) {
    _root.shape._visible = 0;
    xspeed = 1.32;
    yspeed = .56;
    xradius = 100;
    yradius = 100;
}

onClipEvent (enterFrame) {
    i++;
    duplicateMovieClip (_root.shape, "shape"+i, i);
    xangle += xspeed;
    yangle += yspeed;
    xrad = xangle*Math.PI/180;
    yrad = yangle*Math.PI/180;
    _root["shape"+i]._x = Math.sin(xrad)*xradius+270;
    _root["shape"+i]._y = Math.cos(yrad)*yradius+200;
    _root["shape"+i]._rotation = rot++;
    _root["shape"+i]._xscale = Math.sin(xrad)*100;
    _root["shape"+i]._yscale = Math.sin(yrad)*100;
}
```

The key variables

`xspeed` and `yspeed` = the speed that the angles will change
`xradius` and `yradius` = the overall size of the worm's playing field
`xangle` and `yangle` = the current angle that the worm is traveling at
`xrad` and `yrad` = the worm's current angle converted into radians

Basically, the shape moves up and down on a sine wave and back and forth on a cosine wave leaving a trail behind it. The speed values control the wavelength of those two waves, and if you make them the same you should get a circle.

Iterations

The first key values to play with are the `xspeed` and `yspeed` in Frame 1. I find that setting them as decimal figures between 0.5 and 1.5 works well. Higher numbers will give you discrete shapes. Lower numbers will cause the shapes to blend together making a smoother overall form. Very slow speeds will also make the resulting shape much darker, and will of course take longer to draw. Also note that if you use numbers that are exact multiples, such as 0.6 and 1.2, or 0.5 and 1.5, the shapes will double back on each other quickly.

The next things to investigate are the last two lines in the `enterFrame` clip event:

```
_root["shape"+i]._xscale=Math.sin(xrad)*100;
_root["shape"+i]._yscale=Math.sin(yrad)*100;
```

I have `_xscale` using the sin of `xrad` and `_yscale` using the `sin` of `yrad`, but try substituting `cos` for one or both of them, or maybe try using `xrad` for both values. You'll see that this tends to control the "twistiness" of the shape.

Of course there are other things you could investigate, such as making each shape rotate a bit faster or slower or in a different direction. One last idea is to remove old shapes after a certain time, giving it more of a feel of a worm moving along. This can be done very simply by adding these lines to the top of the `enterFrame` clip event:

```
if(i>100){
  i=0;
}
```

Now it'll stick to just 100 circles moving around the screen. Here are a few more things I tried...

exp3-2
First I experimented by increasing the speed of rotation and was pleasantly surprised. I just changed this line to give some beautiful shapes:

```
_root["shape"+i]._rotation=rot+=6;
```

exp3-3
In this iteration I played about with the scale instead. I changed the speed values to this:

```
xspeed=.5;
yspeed=2;
```

...and the last two lines of the `enterFrame` clip event to this:

```
_root["shape"+i]._xscale=Math.tan(xrad)*100;
//_root["shape"+i]._yscale=Math.sin(yrad)*100;
```

Notice that I've just commented out the `_yscale`, giving a strange effect that ends up making a pair of ostrich-like things!

exp3-4
I changed a few more variables here to come up with this wide shape, a bit like a huge crumpled inner tube. Here are the changes to the `load` clip event:

```
xspeed=.83;
yspeed=.52;
xradius=200;
yradius=100;
```

...and here are the changes to the `enterFrame`:

```
_root["shape"+i]._rotation=rot+=2;
_root["shape"+i]._xscale=Math.sin(xrad)*50+80;
_root["shape"+i]._yscale=Math.cos(xrad)*50+80;
```

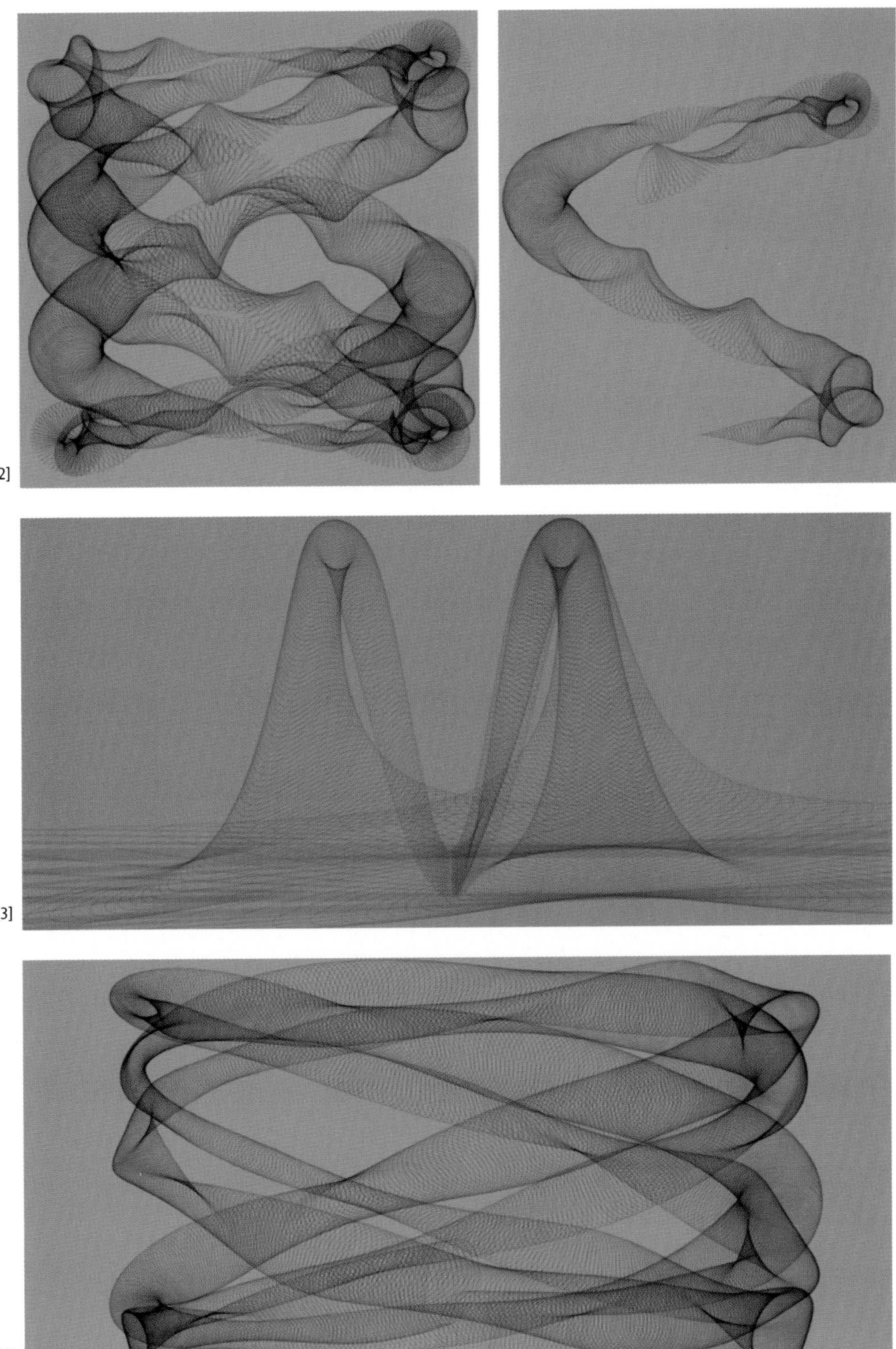

[2]

[3]

[4]

exp3-5
For this iteration I just put the code back in to delete the circles after a while:

```
if(i>50){
   i=0;
}
```

I also changed the `shape` graphic to add another smaller red circle inside the original one. This seems to give it an even more organic appearance.

exp3-6
Here I kept the same shape as the last one, but took out the code that I added to keep the worm 50 circles long. I also sped up the rotation and experimented with a fixed `_xscale`:

```
_root["shape"+i]._rotation=rot+=10;
_root["shape"+i]._xscale=50;
```

This shape leaves a nice trail, and if you leave it long enough it'll pretty much fill its bounding rectangle.

exp3-7
For the final iteration I decided to go a different way. I changed the graphic to a simple black and white radial gradient filled circle. I kept the 10% alpha so that it resembles a pale sphere instead of a ring. The main change though is in the code where I decided to use the `_y` position of the mouse to control the scale of the shape.

Here are the changes to the `load` clip event code:

```
xspeed=.56;
yspeed=1.32;

scale=100;
```

I've created a new variable called `scale` that I'll be using to change the scale of the shape, I initialized it at 100 so that it starts at full size. Here are the changes to the `enterFrame` clip event:

```
if(i>100){
   i=0;
}

//_root["shape"+i]._rotation=rot+=10;
scale+=(_root._ymouse/2-scale)/20;
_root["shape"+i]._xscale=_root["shape"+i]._yscale=scale;
```

Notice here that I've commented out the rotation line because I don't need the shape to rotate as it'll only ever be a circle. I update the new `scale` variable to the position of the mouse, and then do away with `_xscale` and `_yscale` lines and replace them with one line that just set them both to equal `scale`. With a little experimentation and deft mouse-wobbling you can create some really organic shapes.

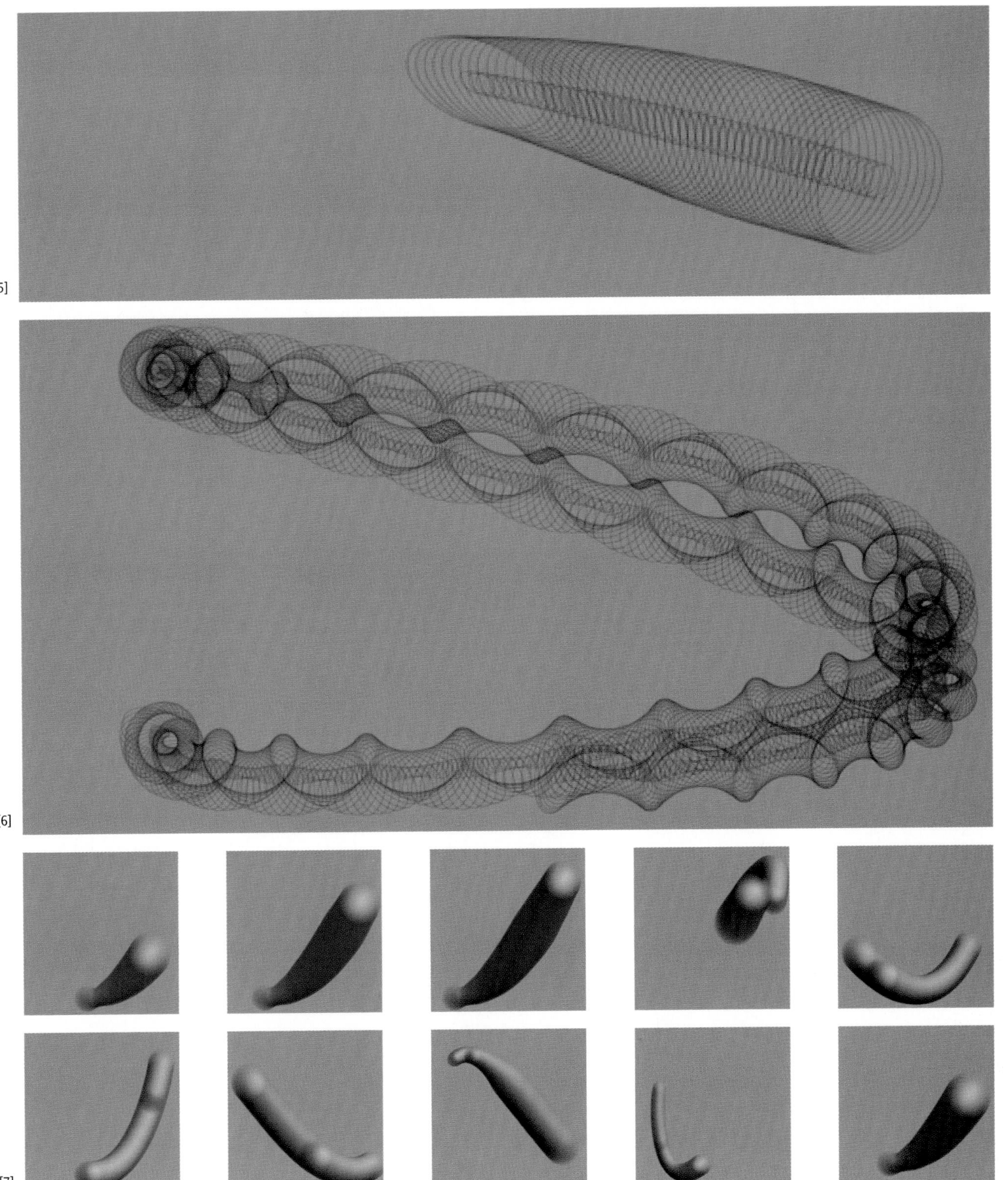

[5]

[6]

[7]

Hungry AI

OK, onto my fourth and final experiment. I always wanted to do some kind of artificial intelligence program and here was my chance. My little creatures have very simple behavioral characteristics. They eat until they're full, and then they go off and rest for a while. When they are hungry again, they head off and look for some more food. I also created the perfect food for them – It gradually depletes as it's eaten, but when it's all gone, more magically appears.

First, the easy part – the food. Make a movieclip with a simple filled shape; I just made mine a circle. It is important that it's centered on the screen so that the creatures can find it and feed from it properly. Put an instance of it on the stage and name it `food`. Since the actions on this are pretty simple, I just put them in a clip event:

```
onClipEvent(enterFrame){
   if(_xscale<10){
      _xscale=_yscale=100;
      _x=Math.random()*500+20;
      _y=Math.random()*360+20;
   }
}
```

Simply translated, when the food is depleted then it goes back to full size and is randomly positioned somewhere else on the screen.

Now for our creature, it's another movieclip of course, and I called mine `skeet`. I made a protozoan with a pointy proboscis, and he's 15 pixels high and 6 wide. You can of course make whatever shape you like, but note that the point of attack, i.e. the mouth, should be at the registration point.

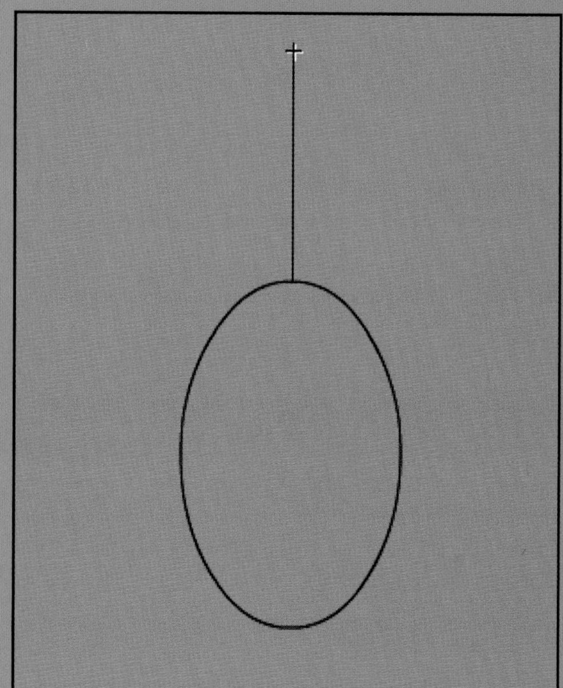

There's a bit more code in this one than my other experiments, but I tried to make it pretty logical and included a lot of explanation in the FLA. As per usual, the code is split into two clip events on the `skeet` clip. Here's the code for the `load` clip event:

```
onClipEvent(load){
   _x=Math.random()*500+20;
   _y=Math.random()*360+20;
   capacity=10;
   speed=10;
}
```

...and here's the code for the `enterFrame` clip event:

```
onClipEvent (enterFrame) {
   if (full) {
      xdist = xrest-_x;
      ydist = yrest-_y;
      ate -= .2;
      if (ate<1) {
         full = false;
      }
   } else {
      xdist = _root.food._x-_x;
      ydist = _root.food._y-_y;
   }

   angle = Math.atan2(ydist, xdist);
   _rotation = angle*180/Math.PI+90;

   if (_root.food.hitTest(_x, _y, 1) && !full) {
      _root.food._xscale -= .5;
      _root.food._yscale -= .5;
      ate++;
      if (ate>capacity) {
         full = true;
         xrest = Math.random()*200-100+_x;
         yrest = Math.random()*200-100+_y;
      }
   } else {
      _x += xdist/10;
      _y += ydist/10;
   }
   _xscale = 40+ate*10;
}
```

Test it to see our little creature in action.

The key variables

`capacity` = the amount that the creature can eat before it's full
`ate` = the current amount of food in the creature
`full` = set to `true` if the creature has eaten its full capacity
`speed` = the speed of the creature (higher number = slower movement)
`xrest` and `yrest` = a random resting spot for the satiated creature
`xdist` and `ydist` = a distance variable, used for both the distance from creature to food, and the distance from creature to rest position
`angle` = used to turn the creature to face either the food or its rest position

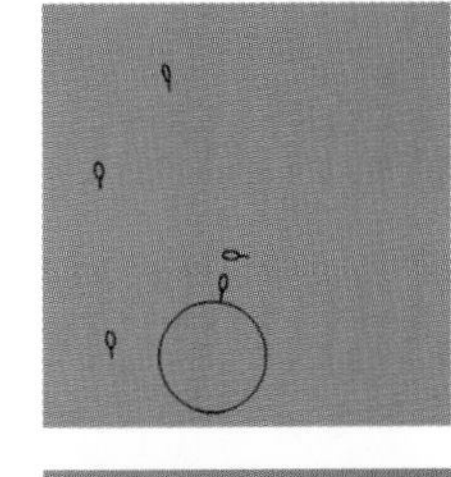

It basically works like this: If the creature's full then it heads to its rest position and works off some of that food until it's hungry again. When it's hungry it turns to face the food and heads towards it. Once it hits the food, it carries on eating until it's full again and then turns and heads off to another random rest position where it repeats the cycle. During this time we scale the creature to give a visual representation of how much it's eaten, and don't forget that we're also scaling the food and constantly checking to see if it's all gone and then replacing and repositioning it.

Iterations

exp4-1
There's a lot of useful material in this file, and a lot of answers to some common questions such as orienting an object to it's direction of motion, easing, and using `hitTest`. Obvious things to experiment with are the initialization variables – how much can he eat, and how fast can he go? The `enterFrame` clip event gives a whole range of things to mess with. Here are a few off-hand:

```
ate-=.2;
```

Change the above variable to make him get hungry faster or slower.

```
_root.food._xscale-=.5;
_root.food._yscale-=.5;
```

These determine how fast the food gets eaten.

```
ate++;
```

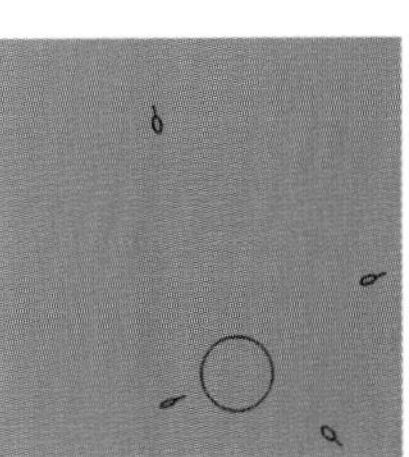

This determines how quickly the creature gets full. You could change it to `ate+=.5`, or `ate+=2` or whatever.

```
xrest=Math.random()*200-100+_x;
yrest=Math.random()*200-100+_y;
```

Mess with these numbers to determine where the creature goes to sleep it off. This is just the starting point, and I think all kinds of more complex behavior could be plugged into these spots.

Now for the tour de force, because of the modularity of our code we can easily have more than one creature on the screen at once. Give the instance of your creature a name (I called mine `skeeter`) and put this on frame 1 of the main timeline:

```
for(i=0;i<10;i++){
   duplicateMovieClip(skeeter, "skeeter"+i, i);
}
```

This will give you ten little protozoan vampires swarming on their food. Gets a little creepy, huh?

exp4-2
First I messed around with their speed and eating habits. These changes make some nice mellow creatures who rest a long way from the food source:

```
speed = 50;

ate-=.1;
xrest=Math.random()*500-250+_x;
yrest=Math.random()*500-250+_y;
```

exp4-3

For this next iteration I pretty much reversed the last one, making some rather voracious little things.

```
speed = 3;

ate-=1;
xrest=Math.random()*100-50+_x;
yrest=Math.random()*100-50+_y;
```

exp4-4

For this iteration I went back to the same code as in `exp4-1`, but changed the code on the `food` to:

```
onClipEvent(enterFrame){
      if(_xscale<10){
         _xscale=_yscale=100;
         _y=400;
      }
      _x+=(_root._xmouse-_x)/10;
      _y+=(_root._ymouse-_y)/10;
}
```

This means that you control the position of the food with the mouse, and the creatures will still attempt to get the food, following it round the screen until they can feed.

exp4-5

Here I added some more code into the `enterFrame` clip event. The new code block goes underneath the current food scaling block, I've shown the old and the new here:

```
//old code to make food get smaller
_root.food._xscale-=.5;
_root.food._yscale-=.5;

//new code to push food
_root.food._x+=xdist/30;
_root.food._y+=ydist/30;
```

Now when the creatures feed they will push the food away from them as they scrabble to get at it.

exp4-6

For the final iteration I kept the creature code from `exp4-5`, but changed the code on the `food` movieclip to this:

```
onClipEvent(enterFrame){
      if(_xscale<10){
         _xscale=_yscale=100;
         _x=Math.random()*500+20;
         _y=400;
         ytarget=Math.random()*300;
      }
      _y+=(ytarget-_y)/10;
}
```

This means that the food will appear from the bottom of the screen at a random position on the x-axis, and head for a random position on the y-axis, whether it makes it or not depends on how hungry your creatures are. Still, it's good to make them work for their prize.

There are loads of things that you can do here, simply changing the graphics is a good start – I kinda liked my minimalist creatures, but make them as realistic as you like, you could even add animation to each stage of their lives – eating, sleeping, and moving. Also mess around with the code to give them different movement patterns, or introduce obstacles to their world that they have to navigate around. The next step might be breeding them, start off with one and just base it on the amount of food they've eaten before they divide into two separate creatures. You could also think about adding a predator to their world, maybe initially just something that chases them that they have to avoid. The possibilities are pretty huge, and their lives are in your hands.

ngry ai

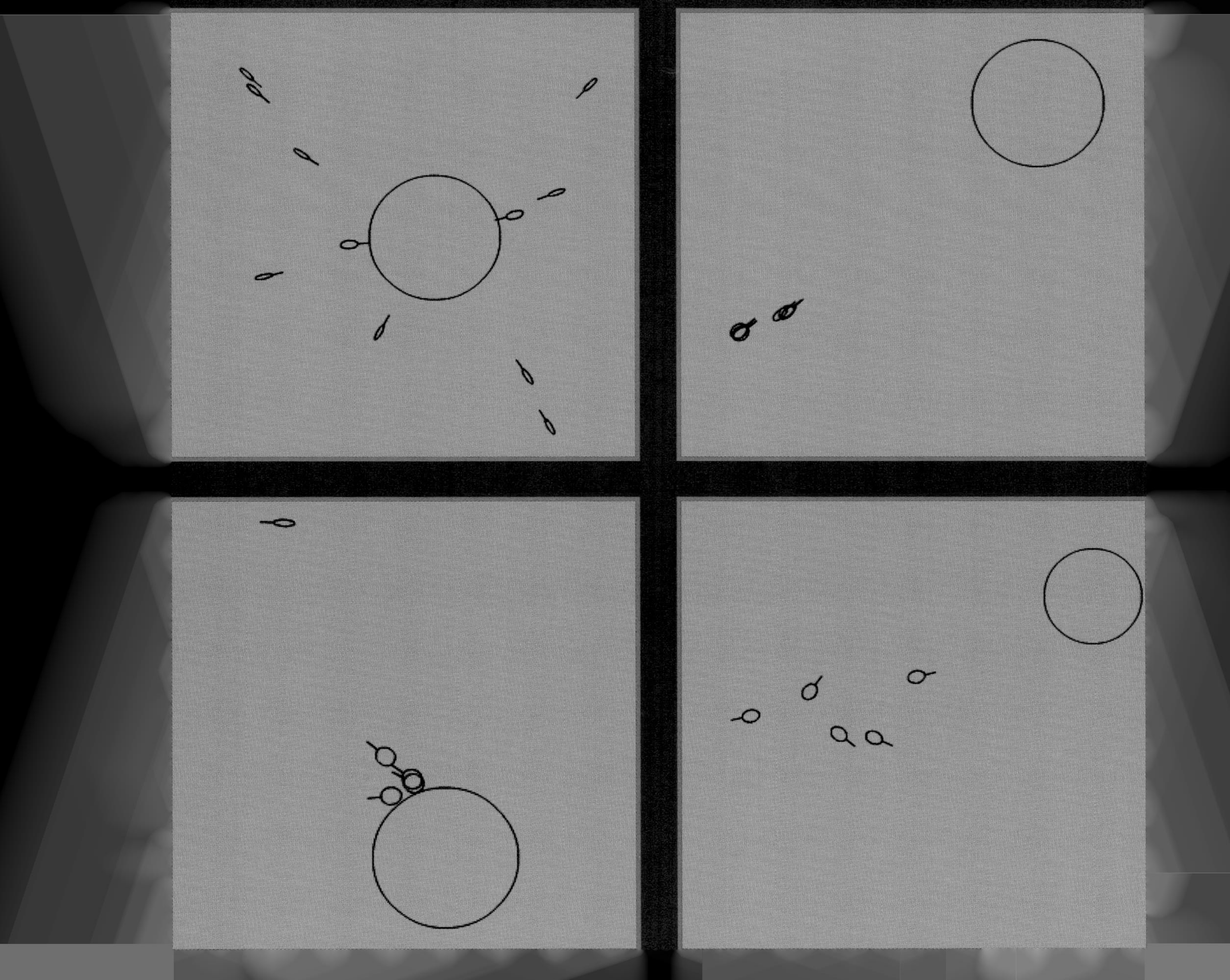

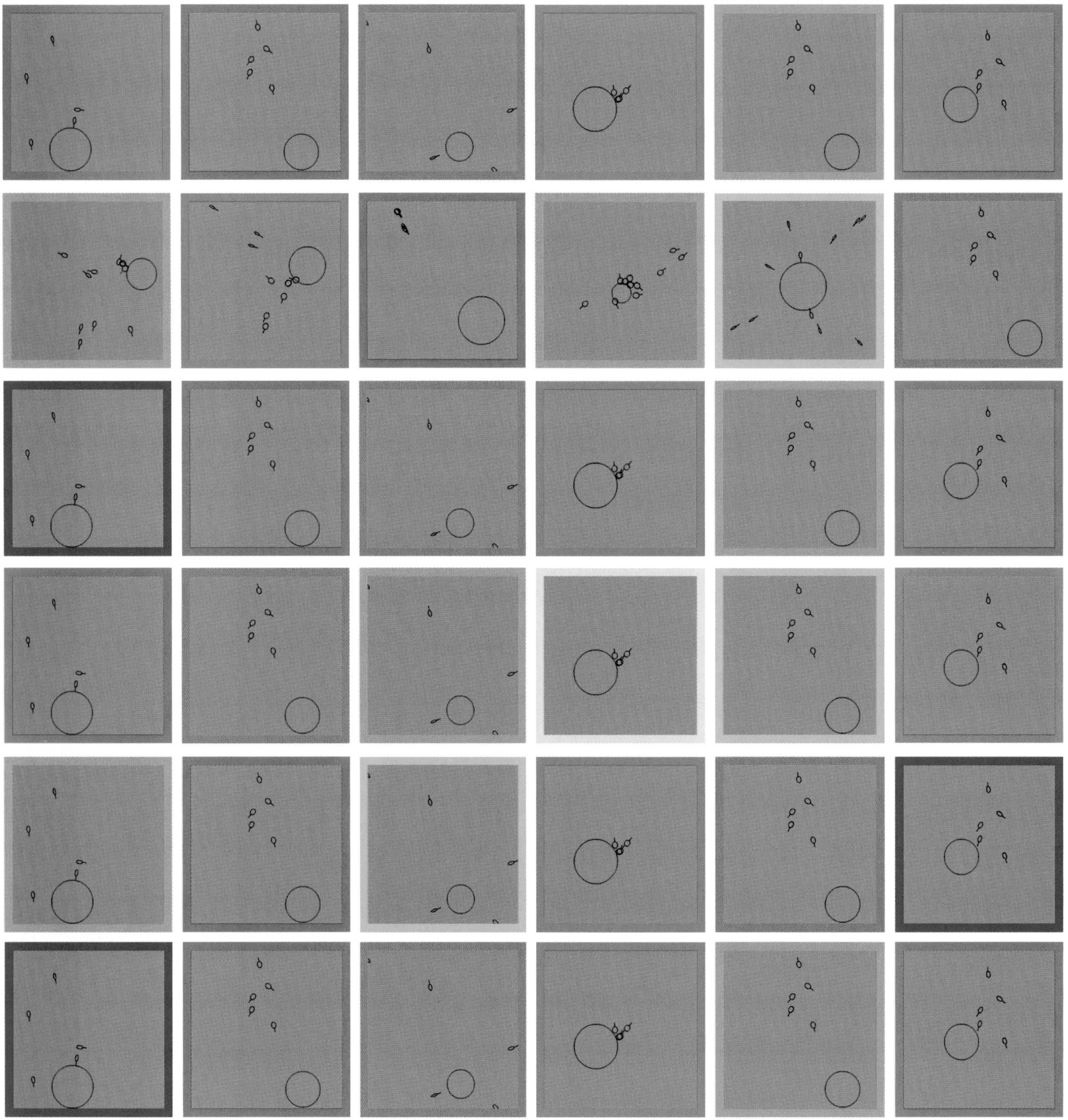

I'm not American and I don't live in London, I just work in the UK as a web developer for cash. My site for this week is pinderkaas.com, and this is my life so far:

Acorn Electron, BBC Micro Model B, Spectrum 48k, ZX Spectrum +, Dragon 16k, Atari ST 520, Amiga 1200, 286, 386SX 25Mhz, 386DX, Pentium 166Mhz, iMac 400, Power Mac G4 450Mhz.

My ambitions were to be a palaeontologist, or a milkman (so I could sit at home, eat fish fingers, and watch *Moonlighting*)

One day I will learn how to tune my guitar.

The first inspirational thing that comes to mind is train journeys. I love sitting, writing, thinking, and watching the country slide by. The next thing that comes to mind is art, and music, and computer games, and comics – especially Cerebus, and Pokemon, and keyboards, guitars, films, video cameras, digital cameras, 16mm film, Pyssla beads, clip art, cheese – the food kind, beetroot, Polaroid cameras, Kinder toys, Sim City, Populous, Chrono Trigger (and probably Chrono Cross if only they'd release it over here), Jackie Chan, Louis Barlow, John McIntyre, Ian MacKaye, Howe Gelb, Pokey the horse, BASIC, Eddie Izzard, Art Adams, Bill Sienkiewicz, the adverts in old Marvel comics, HTML, JavaScript prompt boxes, the Fetch and printy dogs, motorways at night, Nigel Slater, Repton, the Casio SK-1, Paul Auster, the sea air early in the morning, trees, texture, Like a Velvet Glove Cast in Iron, clouds, typewriters, Guiseppe Penone, David Hockney, Norman McLaren, stickers, soft-boiled eggs, fuzzy felt, cat dancing, Robert Pollard and his wet suitcase, elephants, Karl Bez, Franz Kafka, Charles Bukowski, Chilly Gonzales, grasses, and personalized license plates.

Tomorrow it'll probably be rocks.

ken jokol
pinderkaas.com

Growing lines

I like watching things grow and change. At university they had these really unreliable S-VHS cameras, which had the added bonus that they could shoot a frame or so every few minutes. Perfect for filming the passing of time, or so I thought, but as with all cheap analogue video cameras and record button presses, tape tends to rewind itself every now and again. Ignoring this factor, I went ahead and set it up so that it ran overnight. It was set up to look out of my 3rd floor window, pointed at the green opposite. I was hoping to get a sunrise time-lapse reminiscent of those that you see in high-quality nature documentaries. True to the predictability of video and the weary old camera though, it messed up and I got a 3 second clip of night. Oh well...

THE SAME GREEN... A DIFFERENT DAY...

Luckily, when I want to watch something change in Flash, I can. I like to see the seams, and how something is built brick by brick. I'd much rather see a shape drawing in a slow clunky manner than be presented with a polished composition that hides some of the much required production detail. For this purpose I thought I'd build something in Flash that grows bit by bit and turns from a square into an elongated rectangle.

Pre_lines.swf

This was just my proof-of-concept test file, and you'll notice that little happens in it – a shape just grows – but however dull it looks, it forms the basis of these experiments.

The file is a little more complicated than it looks, but only a little. It's actually made up of a long line of 10x10 pixel squares, each colored half blue, and half red (okay, so it' not quite half and half, but who's counting). All of these squares are instances of the movieclip `sq`, which has the following code on it:

```
onClipEvent (enterFrame) {
   _xscale += 10;
}
```

This just makes the square expand horizontally every frame. The movieclip is then duplicated and positioned by this short code on the first frame of the root:

```
for (i=0; i<40; i++) {
   duplicateMovieClip ("sq", "sq"+i, i);
   _root["sq"+i]._y = i * 10;
}
```

This code simply copies the movieclip and places it 10 pixels below the previous one, so that we get the appearance of one continuous shape. For the time being I've left out any code for positioning on the x-axis, so the line will descend from wherever you've placed the original movieclip on the stage, mine's above the stage in the horizontal center of the screen.

Iterations

lines01

First of all, I decided to add some rotation to the root code so that the shape begins to flower.

```
_root["sq"+i]._rotation = i*10;
```

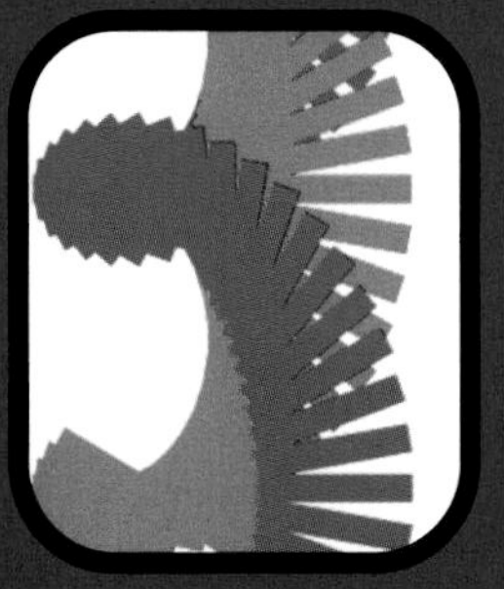

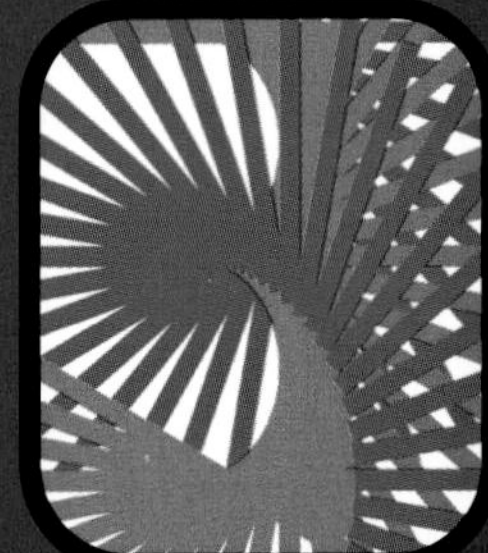

This produces a really interesting pattern, and if you leave it long enough you can see the logic behind making the colors not quite half and half, as the red begins to outgrow the blue. Try moving the square away from the registration point to get different effects.

lines02

Next I experimented with the transparency of the squares by adding this code to the clip event:

```
_alpha -=1;
if (_alpha < 20) {
   _alpha = 20;
}
```

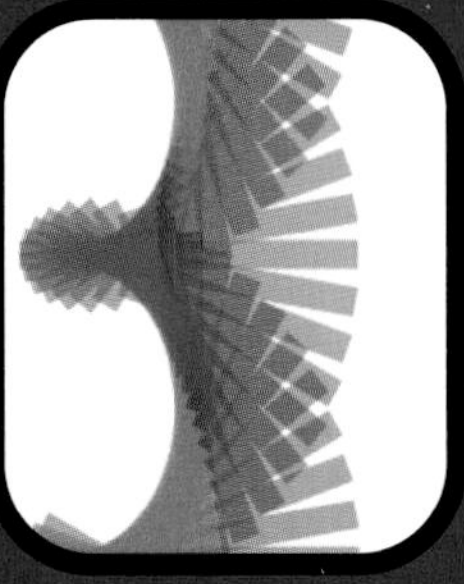

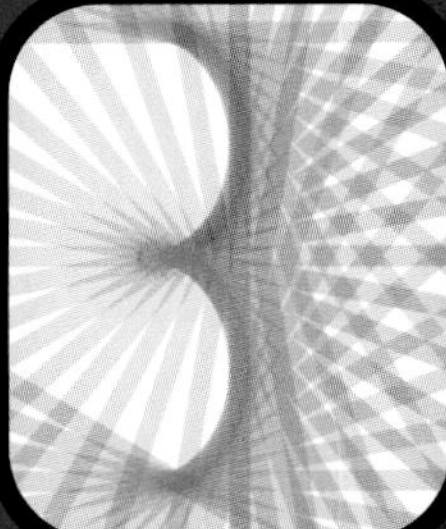

Now the square become more and more transparent as they grow, but I added an `if` statement as a cut off to stop them fading out completely.

lines03
Carrying on with my alpha experiments, I removed the code that I just added to the clip event, and instead put this script in the `for` loop on the root:

```
_root["sq"+i]._alpha = (40-i) * 2.5;
```

This initializes a set alpha for each square so they fade out from top to bottom.

lines04
In this iteration I took out the previous alpha code and reduced the number of squares to produce one smooth arc. I also added to the `y` position of each square to center the arc on the screen. To achieve this, I modified these two lines in the `for` loop:

```
for (i=0; i<19; i++)
_root["sq"+i]._y = i*10+100;
```

Another interesting effect to try here is to add an outline to the square (not set to hairline) so that as the square grows, the outline will get thicker and thicker until it completely covers the original square.

lines05
I decided to go the other way and experiment with larger numbers instead – I wanted 360 movieclips growing on the screen. Normally this wouldn't be the best idea in the world for frame rate reasons, but I had an idea in my head so I went and did it anyway. Resisting the urge to push the frame rate up and reveling as I do in lo-fi and rough aspects of design, I set the SWF quality to low for a little better performance and those beautifully jagged edges. Sometimes limitations are there for a reason. Here's the `for` loop that makes it happen:

```
_quality = "low";
for (i=0; i<360; i++) {
   duplicateMovieClip ("sq", "sq"+i, i);
   _root["sq"+i]._y = i*10;
   _root["sq"+i]._rotation = i;
}
```

If you run this SWF and let it go for a little while, you'll see where the number 360 comes into effect. I also made my square slightly smaller (8x8 pixels), and changed its color and start position. By setting the rotation at a very low amount the resulting curve created by all the duplicated shapes is almost flat, but creates a kind of rough distorted moiré-like pattern as the lines intersect at certain places. If anyone makes anything dirtier from this please let me know. I like dirt.

lines06a–e
Sometimes the simplest equations can give spookily good results. I carried on with the last code, but tried various multipliers for the rotation, so the code is basically:

```
_root["sq"+i]._rotation = i * x;
```

Where `x` is my multiplier amount. Rather than just pick numbers out of thin air, I arrived at them by dividing 360 simple amounts, so if we use the numbers 2 thru 5, we get the results 180, 120, 90, and 72. Try plugging these into the above code to see the difference they make. My personal magic number for rotation is 88, so try that too.

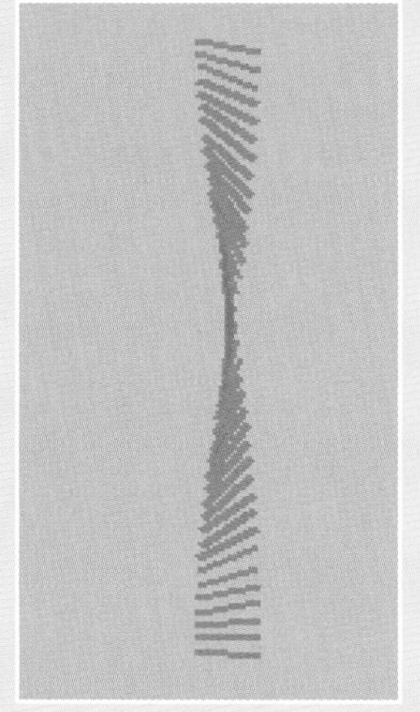

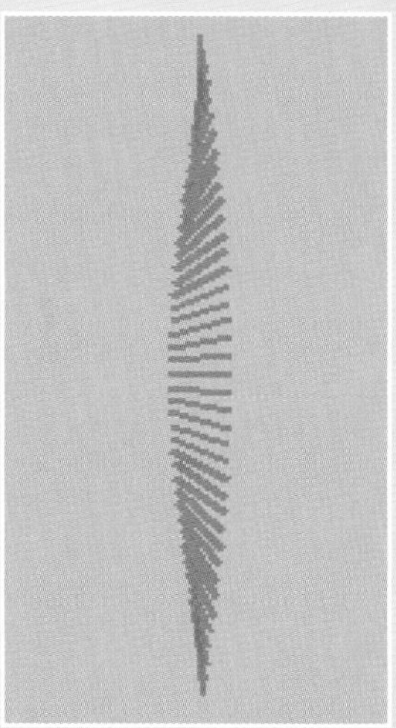

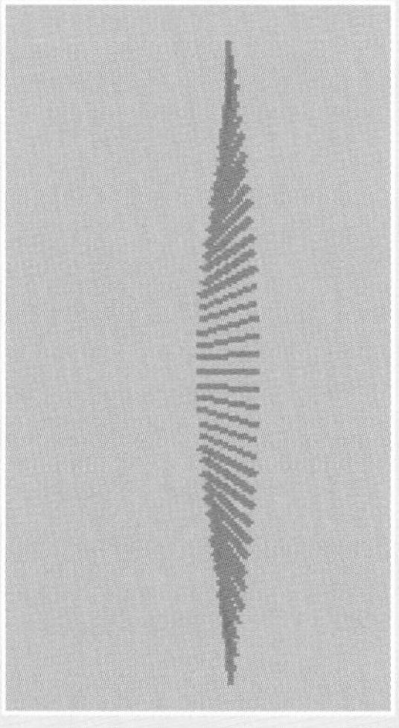

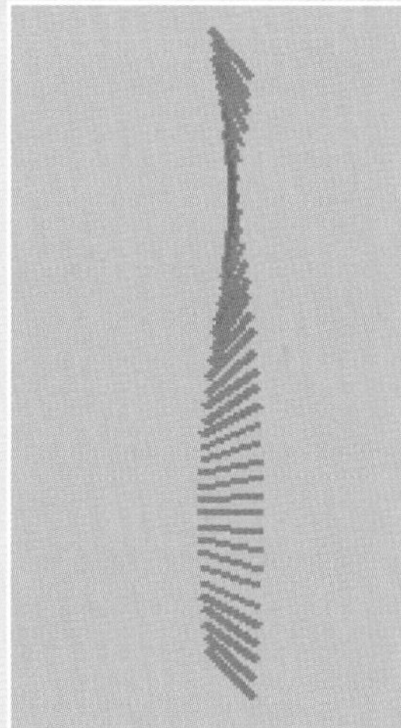

lines07
So far we've seen the square increase in `_xscale` but not `_yscale`, so in this SWF the square does just that, but it increases disproportionately to the `_xscale`. By the way, it's worth mentioning that from now on, the square is set at 50% alpha to add a little more of a visual effect when the shapes overlap. I added this line of code to the clip event:

```
_yscale += 1;
```

I also set up some basic values in the `for` loop; `rotation` is set to `i*10`, and the number of squares is set to 40. The increase begins like an invisible transformation and only becomes apparent when the shapes are at a significant size.

lines08
In this iteration I took out the `_yscale`, and played about with rotation again, but this time I set the rotation in the clip event so the squares are continuously spinning. I also limited the `_xscale` so that they only grow to a set size before stopping and just spinning in waves. The last thing I did was to set the rotation in the root to `i*9`. I arrived at this figure by dividing 360 by the number of squares (40) to get 9. Here's the new clip event code:

```
onClipEvent (enterFrame) {
   _xscale += 10;
   if (_xscale>=100) {
     _xscale = 100;
   }
   _rotation += 10;
}
```

This reminds me of one of those amazing wooden wave machines that they always have in children's science programs. I also achieved some nice effects by reducing the size of the square for thinner lines, or moving the square off-center so that the registration point is on its left hand side.

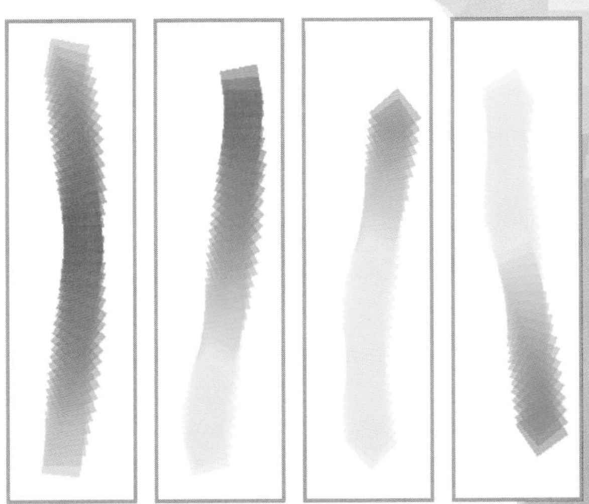

lines09
I now decided to add some color into the mix. First of all I made my square a bit chunkier, about 40x40 pixels, because I want a bit more bulk and blending when the colors overlap. Here's the complete new clip event code:

```
onClipEvent (load) {
   me = new Color(this);
   metr = new Object();
}
onClipEvent (enterFrame) {
   _xscale += 10;
   if (_xscale>=100) {
     _xscale = 100;
   }
   _rotation += 10;
   metr.rb = Math.abs (_rotation);
   metr.gb = Math.abs (_rotation*2);
   metr.bb = Math.abs (_rotation/2);
   me.setTransform(metr);
}
```

This sets the colors depending on rotation so you get a nice wave of color flooding it from top to bottom. Another thing you can try is setting the colors in the `load` clip event so that they stay the same rather than cycling.

lines10
I took this color effect one stage further, so that rather than a static, pre-defined set of colors, the colors now change as the squares grow. Here's the `enterFrame` clip event code:

```
onClipEvent (enterFrame) {
   _xscale += 10;
   _yscale += 1;
   metr.rb = _xscale / 2;
   metr.gb = _yscale;
   metr.bb = _y / 2;
   me.setTransform(metr);
}
```

By making the colors based on different attributes, the color range is a little different and because of the slight changes in `_y`, the colors are banded.

Here are a few other simple, short deviations that I tried from the original SWFs:

distort

For those who love their distortion, I've started you off with `lines11.swf`, which defies a considerable amount of the good taste Flash around. Here's the code for the root:

```
_quality = "low";
for (i=0; i<1000; i++) {
   duplicateMovieClip ("sq", "sq"+i, i);
   _root["sq"+i]._y = i;
   _root["sq"+i]._x = (i*random(5))+100;
}
```

With `lines11a.swf`, I added one line, to create this eventual eye-destroying effect:

```
_root["sq"+i]._rotation = i*10;
```

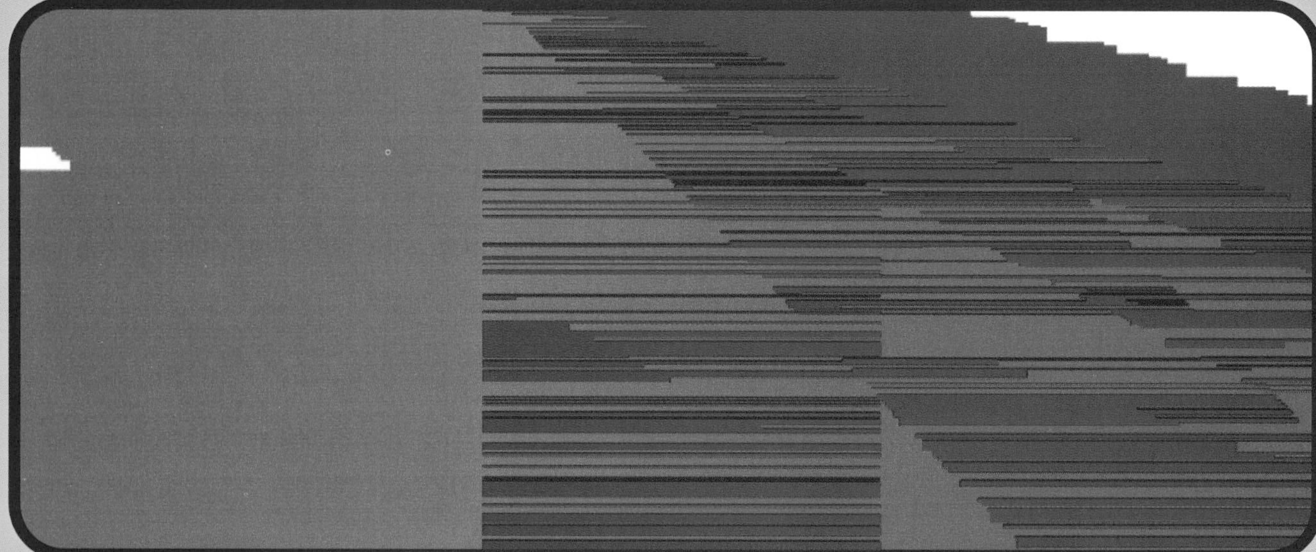

flowers

In lines12.swf, the shape drawn is circular and reminds me of an orange juice carton sunburst (except the colors are all wrong!). Here's the for loop:

```
for (i=0; i<100; i++) {
   duplicateMovieClip ("sq", "sq"+i, i);
   _root["sq"+i]._y = i+150;
   _root["sq"+i]._rotation = (i*10)+100;
}
```

I changed the square into a circle, and played about with the colors, to produce lines12a thru c.

Outlines

For the final couple of experiments I played about with just using outlines, and a bit of randomization code. Check out lines13 and 13a.

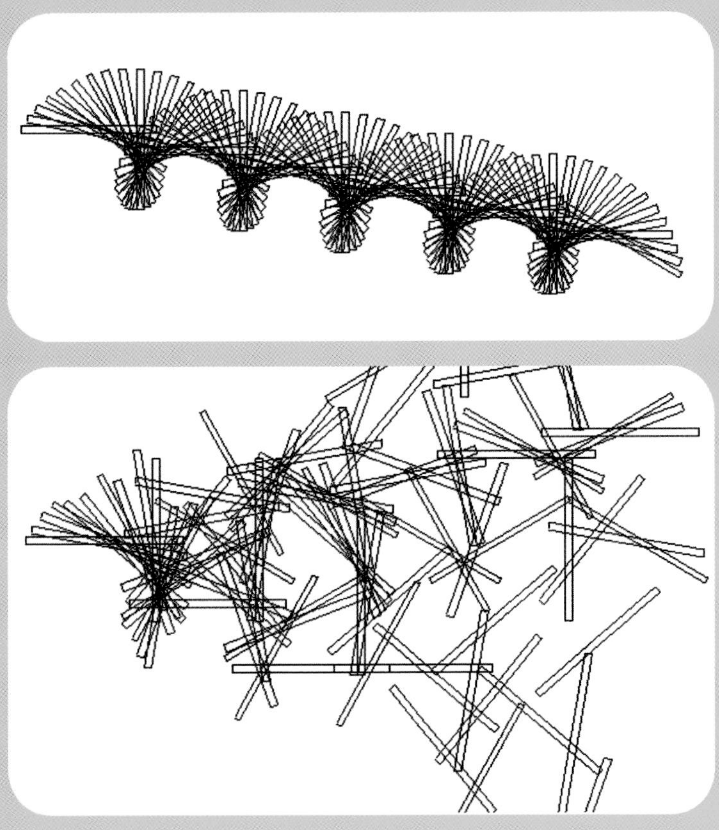

Generative Grid

I'm a little bit of a creative automation freak. My usual intention is to make something in Flash, make a million amendments to it, take screenshots of every permutation and layer, and then edit them in Photoshop. It never actually turns out that way because I get stuck making new SWFs in Flash, but it's a good way to keep me churning out fresh content.

I'm going to dabble a little in generating some simple graphics based on a straightforward grid structure created with a couple of `for` loops. I chose an 8x8 grid to begin with, reminiscent of the oldskool Spectrum days, when I'd painstakingly sit with a ruler and a pile of paper creating my own fonts and typing in all sixty-four 0s and 1s that made up each character (and for what end?).

I'm going to avoid using the Color object this time and try to stick to composition. The concentration here is on generative design, and approaches to manipulating a simple grid structure. Sometimes limitations can force you to look at and approach something in a different way.

Iterations

blocks01
To start off with, I have a simple 50x50 pixel square movieclip, registration point in the top-left corner, on the stage with the instance name `sq`. I then attached the following code to frame 1 of the root:

```
count = 1;
for (i=0; i<8; i++) {
   for (x=0; x<8; x++) {
     duplicateMovieClip ("sq", "sq"+count, count);
     _root["sq"+count]._x = x*50;
     _root["sq"+count]._y = i*50;
     _root["sq"+count]._alpha = i*12;
     count++;
   }
}
```

Here, we simply have a pair of nested `for` loops to create an 8x8 grid. I've then altered the alpha of each row to achieve a gradient effect.

blocks02
In this experiment the alpha gradient is applied using the formula `x*i`, which results in a diagonal slope of color from top left to bottom right:

```
_root["sq"+count]._alpha = x*i;
```

Because each block is a 50 pixel square and the code is positioning them using 50 as a multiplier, then they never overlap or infringe on one another, but great things can happen when they do. Try setting this to a smaller number, say 40, and the squares will overlap and give a little more depth because of the alpha layering.

blocks03
In this SWF, the same rules apply as before, but I introduced a few different shapes to change the general design and to give that square a break. I placed a triangle on frame 2, and a blank frame on frame 3 of the movieclip, with a `stop` action on each frame. The following code is then applied to a clip event on the movieclip to toggle between them and add a little rotation to them:

```
onClipEvent (load) {
   gotoAndPlay (random (3)+1);
   rnd = random (4);
   _rotation = 90 * rnd;
}
```

Try using different shapes, or just moving the shapes around inside the movieclip, you'll get different results depending on whether the registration point is in the top-left of the shape, or in the center.

blocks04
So far our output has pretty much stayed within a rigid grid-like structure, but if we add a few lines of code then our grid becomes unfixed, or appears to be. In this SWF, a simple amount of rotation is added to the clip event and voila – falling tiles:

```
onClipEvent (load) {
   _rotation = random (360);
}
```

blocks05
Now this is where we bend the rules a little. At the moment each square follows a universal pattern of some sort (excluding the randomness that we have used), but by changing the name of the duplicates so that they are easier to reference, we can quickly make a difference. I changed these lines in the `for` loop:

```
duplicateMovieClip ("sq", ""+count, count);
_root[""+count]._x = x*50;
_root[""+count]._y = i*50;
_root[""+count]._alpha = (x*i)+20;
```

The main difference here is when we come to duplicate the shapes. We can cheat Flash with a blank string and then add the `count` variable to it, making the duplicated clips named as just numbers ("1", "2", "3" … "64"). This means that when we come to reference them from the clip event we can simply use `_name` to get it's name and use this in a multitude of ways. The first thing I tried was setting each clip's rotation to `_name`:

```
onClipEvent (load) {
   _rotation = _name;
}
```

I also tried the following couple of tricks with `_name`. First try setting an `enterFrame` clip event to:

```
_rotation += _name/10;
```

This produces some pretty weird uniformity after a while (try speeding this up with a higher frame rate and a lower quality setting). The next thing I tried was:

```
_yscale += _name/20;
```

With this, the blocks grow fastest at the bottom-right, and slowest at the top-left, producing some interesting patterns.

blocks06
Here the shapes grow in `_xscale` and `_yscale` but their direction is reversed when they reach a set size each way. Initially, the pattern is chaotic, but following a little while some waves can be seen:

```
onClipEvent (load) {
   addMe = -_name/20;
}
onClipEvent (enterFrame) {
   if (_xscale<0) {
     addMe = _name/20;
   }
   if (_xscale>100) {
     addMe = -_name/20;
   }
   _yscale += addMe;
   _xscale += addMe;
}
```

[1]
[2]
[3]
[4]
[5]
[6]

blocks07

This SWF produces a cascade of squares dripping from top to bottom. A slight amendment was made to the main `for` loop to change the `_y` position of each square depending on its duplicated number (count):

```
count = 1;
for (i=1; i<9; i++) {
   for (x=1; x<9; x++) {
     duplicateMovieClip ("sq", ""+count, count);
     _root[""+count]._y = i*(count/x);
     _root[""+count]._x = x*40;
     count++;
   }
}
```

I also made a few other small modifications. I changed the loop counters to run from 1 to 9 rather than 0 to 8 so that I didn't get any divide by zero errors, and I reduced the `_x` position slightly to squash them up a bit. The only code that I had on the clip was a line setting the alpha to 20 when it loads.

blocks08

A bit of a radical departure here – I've already mentioned my fascination with 8 bit characters, so I'm stepping it up here to code some basic pixel-style characters. I've upgraded to a 10x10 square grid (shame on you pixel boy!) and my square movieclip is now 40x40 pixels. Here's the new code for the root:

```
count = 0;
for (x=0; x<10; x++) {
   for (i=0; i<10; i++) {
     duplicateMovieClip ("sq", ""+count, count);
     _root[""+count]._x = i*40;
     _root[""+count]._y = (x*40);
     count++;
   }
}
pixel = new Array (12,13,16,17,21,24,25,28,33,34,35,
 ➥ 36,43,46,51,52,53,54,55,56,57,58,61,63,66,68,71,73,
 ➥ 76,78,81,88);
```

Each number in the array refers to a position in the grid, and each single number can be thought of as a pair. So 12 is actually 1 and 2, the first number represents the column and the second the row. These numbers are then picked up in the clip event code:

```
onClipEvent (load) {
   _visible = 0;
   for (a=0; a<_root.pixel.length; a++) {
     if (_name == _root.pixel [a]) {
       _visible = 1;
     }
   }
}
```

This code just initializes every clip as invisible and then turns on the ones that it's told to in the array. To save you a little time I've made a simple drawing application called `blocks_draw.swf` for recording a shape's values for entering into this code.

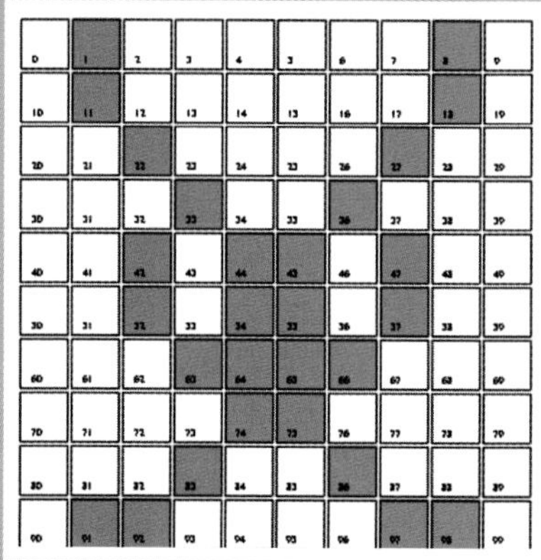

Calculating and typing the code by hand is not exactly the most therapeutic process, but with the cut-and-paste-ability of the drawing app and the ease of increasing the size of the grid, you'll be making cross-stitch patterns in no time. HaHa!

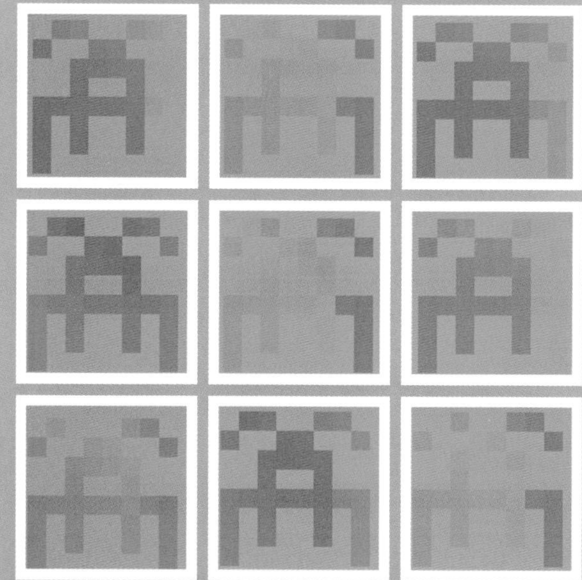

blocks09

Building on the last experiment, I decided to generate a random pattern over half of the canvas, and mirror it in the other half. This is now set instead of the old pixel array in the main code:

```
pixel = new Array();
for (a=0; a<25; a++) {
   pixel[a] = random(50);
   pixel[a+25] = (100-pixel[a])-1;
}
```

Try increasing the number of blocks in a tighter grid to make more abstract patterns.

blocks10

Because each movieclip has an instance name that is simply a number, we can create some patterns using the charAt string command. First of all, I set up a clip event to change the alpha depending on the name:

```
onClipEvent (enterFrame) {
   total = (Number(_name.charAt (0,1)) +
   ➥Number(_name.charAt (1,1))) ;
   _alpha = total * 8;
}
```

I've also added this if statement just inside the second for loop on the root:

```
if (count<10) {
   count = "0"+count;
}
```

This just makes sure that our numbers are all two figures, so 1 will become 01 and so on. The code makes a simple wave as we have seen before, but it shows how much control we have over the object when we can directly reference them by name.

There are numerous places you can take this code now. I started playing with referencing the name with charAt to make interesting patterns. You can also bring in the Color object. Yes, I know I've resisted it throughout, but for generative design color is an essential component. The best rule I find though, is to stick to afew colors and apply these to the objects, that or just go crazy and set each object totally randomly. You can experiment with modularity. The current SWFs that I've made are confined to the main stage and aren't modular. By nesting the grids, patterns can be made by replicating or duplicating these. Make things modular if you want to take something to a different level. Another thing that you can do is just forget about coding and try different shapes, it's simple but effective.

Colorsuck

For this experiment I wanted to play about with the Color object, and also try and make use of `hitTest` because I'm always complaining about how annoying it is to get it to work how I want it to. I came up with the simple idea of having three different colored squares (red, green, and blue) moving around the screen and just sucking color out of each other whenever they touched. I was only experimenting, so this isn't the most perfect OOP code, but it does the job.

There are three simple square movieclips on the stage with the instance names `block1`, `block2`, and `block3`. Here's the code on `block1`:

```
onClipEvent (load) {
  me = new Color(this);
  metr = new Object();
  metr.rb = 255;
  metr.gb = 0;
  metr.bb = 0;
  me.setTransform(metr);
  xspeed = random(10)-random(10);
  yspeed = random(10)-random(10);
}
onClipEvent (enterFrame) {
  if (this.hitTest(_root.block2)) {
    metr.rb -= 5;
    metr.gb += 5;
    me.setTransform(metr);
  }
  if (this.hitTest(_root.block3)) {
    metr.rb -= 5;
    metr.bb += 5;
    me.setTransform(metr);
  }
  if (_x>400) {
    xspeed = random(10);
    xspeed *= -1;
    yspeed = random(10);
  }
  if (_x<0) {
    xspeed = random(10);
    yspeed = random(10);
  }
  if (_y>400) {
    yspeed = random(10);
    yspeed *= -1;
    xspeed = random(10);
  }
  if (_y<0) {
    yspeed = random(10);
    xspeed = random(10);
  }
  _x += xspeed;
  _y += yspeed;
}
```

The code for the other two blocks is pretty similar, the only differences being a different color being set in the initial Color object, different blocks being set for `hitTest`, and different colors being sucked from the blocks. `block1` sucks from 2 and 3, `block2` sucks from 1 and 3, and `block3` sucks from 1 and 2.

The key variables

`xspeed` and `yspeed` = control the speed of each block, these are set to a random value at the beginning of the movie, and are set again whenever the block hits a wall
`me` = the Color object, used to control the color of the block

The main code is really simple, first we define the initial color of the block, with a new color object, and then set an initial random speed and direction. Each block then bounces round the screen (using hard-coded values for the screen dimensions), constantly checking to see if it's in contact with either of the other two blocks. If the block is in contact with another then we minus 5 from its original color, and add 5 to its new color. So let's say for example we are `block1` (red) and we've just come into contact with `block2` (green). `block1` loses 5 red and gains 5 green, and `block2` loses 5 green and gains 5 red. It's easy to understand once you see it in motion. And that's it, colorsuck. One strange thing that I discovered after running this was the correlation that appears between RGB and CMYK, I've never done any color theory before so this all came as quite a surprise to me.

Iterations

colorsuck02
Here I just changed each block so that they were only affected by one other color rather than both, so 1 is affected by 3, 2 is affected by 1, and 3 is affected by 2. This means that rather than changing to new colors, they just swap colors.

colorsuck03
In this iteration I wanted the blocks to leave trails behind them so they'd leave patterns of changing colors. I did this by simply duplicating the movieclip behind itself. I first added this code to the `load` clip event:

```
_visible=0;
count=1;
```

This simply sets the original movieclip to be invisible, and defines a new variable, `count`, that will be used to name the newly attached clips. `count` is set to 1 for the first block, 2000 for the second, and 4000 for the third. This ensures that the new clips will be at different depths. The main change to the code comes in the `enterFrame` clip event where this is added to the end of the code:

```
_root.attachMovie("winky", "box"+count, count);
_root["box"+count]._x = _x;
_root["box"+count]._y = _y;
_root["box"+count].me = new Color(_root["box"+count]);
_root["box"+count].me.setTransform(metr);
count++;
```

Here we attach a new copy of the block clip (which we exported from the Library with the linkage name `winky` – don't ask) and set its position and color to that of the moving block. We attach the clip rather than duplicating it so that it doesn't retain any of the code of the original. It doesn't hurt to set this to low quality for a bit more speed, and try making the squares smaller so you can see more of the lines.

colorsuck04
In this iteration I changed the block into a diagonal line (so that it effectively still took up the same area as the square as far as `hitTest` is concerned, because we're using the bounding box) and added some code to the `enterFrame` clip event to rotate it giving a nice effect when the lines intertwine and the colors flow through the gaps:

```
_root["box"+count]._rotation+=count;
```

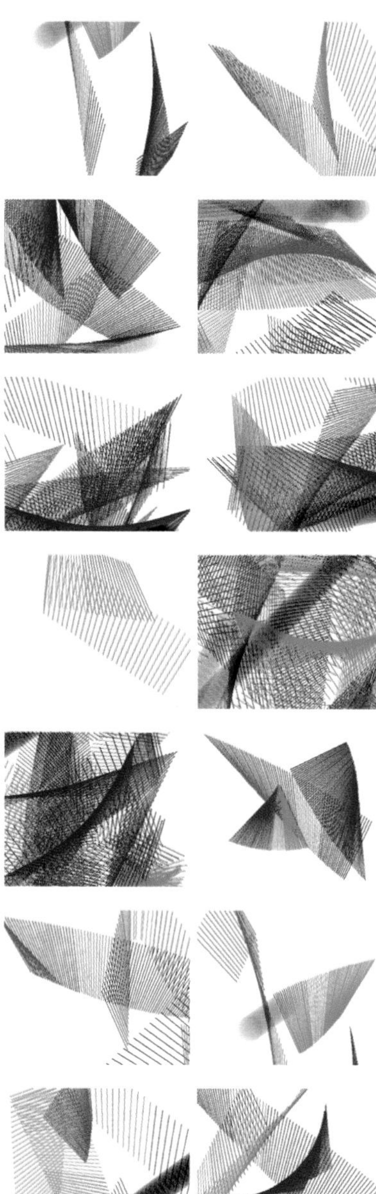

colorsuck05

Now I wanted to try and add alpha to the mix. I began by adding a new circle clip to the stage with similar code to the line clips. The difference is that whenever it hits a line it gains alpha instead of sucking color, here's the code for it, and it's exported from the Library with the name `biff`:

```
onClipEvent (load) {
  count = 10000;
  me = new Color(this);
  metr = new Object();
  metr.rb = 0;
  metr.gb = 0;
  metr.bb = 0;
  metr.ab = -255;
  me.setTransform(metr);
  xspeed = random(10)-random(10);
  yspeed = random(10)-random(10);
}
onClipEvent (enterFrame) {
  if (this.hitTest(_root.block1 || _root.block2 || _root.block3)) {
    metr.ab += 1;
    me.setTransform(metr);
  }
  if (_x>400) {
    xspeed = random(10);
    xspeed *= -1;
    yspeed = random(10);
  }
  if (_x<0) {
    xspeed = random(10);
    yspeed = random(10);
  }
  if (_y>400) {
    yspeed = random(10);
    yspeed *= -1;
    xspeed = random(10);
  }
  if (_y<0) {
    yspeed = random(10);
    xspeed = random(10);
  }
  _x += xspeed;
  _y += yspeed;
  _root.attachMovie("biff", "box"+count, count);
  _root["box"+count]._x = _x;
  _root["box"+count]._y = this._y;
  _root["box"+count].me = new Color(_root["box"+count]);
  _root["box"+count].me.setTransform(metr);
  count++;
}
```

Don't worry if you don't see anything to begin with, the circle starts off invisible and then ghosts in when it hits a line. You could also try altering its speed so that it gets faster as it sucks as well.

colorsuck06

Originally I had intended to use the alpha ball to suck the alpha out of the lines, but I kinda liked the effect it made so I removed the lines altogether and replaced them with three alpha balls. Remember that they start invisible. It reminds me of something like a Rothko painting – you stare at it to see if you can see a difference in the textures, and think you can, but there is nothing there. It's just your mind expecting to see something and visualizing it.

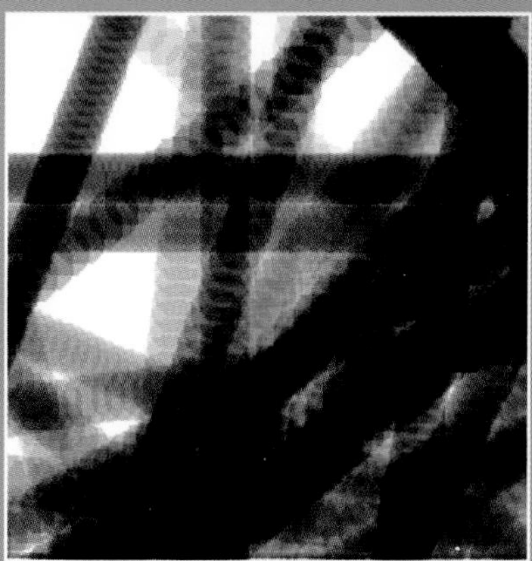

colorsuck07

I played about for a while with different shapes and colors and then decided to try adding sounds as well. I created a set of three simple sounds in SoundEdit and gave them linkage names of `s1`, `s2`, and `s3`. I then added a few lines of code to the `load` clip event:

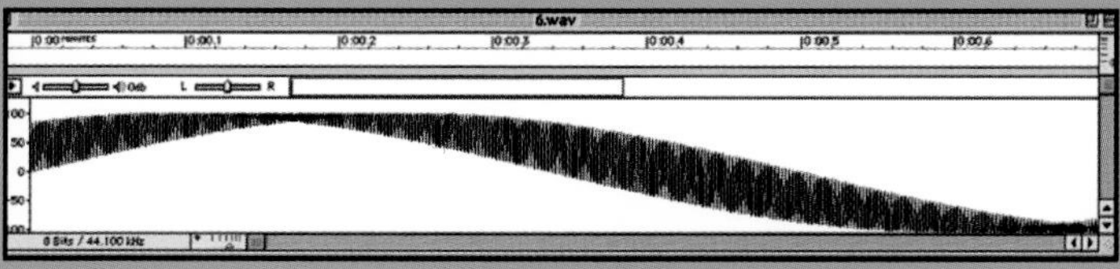

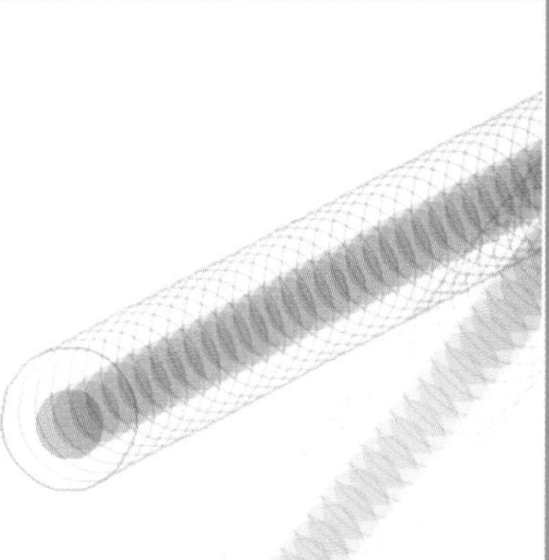

```
sound1 = new Sound(this);
sound1.attachSound("s1");
soundcount=100;
```

This code just creates a new Sound object and attaches the first sound from the Library to it (exported as `s1`). We also define a new variable, `soundcount`, which will control the volume of the sound. Don't forget to change the `sound` number and linkage name for each block, so for `block2` you'll have `sound2.attachSound("s2")` and so on, this goes for the code below too. Now we need to add some code to the `enterFrame` clip event to replace the previous `hitTest` code:

```
if (this.hitTest(_root.block2 || _root.block3)) {
   metr.ab += 1;
   me.setTransform(metr);
   sound1.setVolume(soundcount);
   soundcount–;
   sound1.start();
}
if (soundcount == 0) {
   soundcount = 100;
}
```

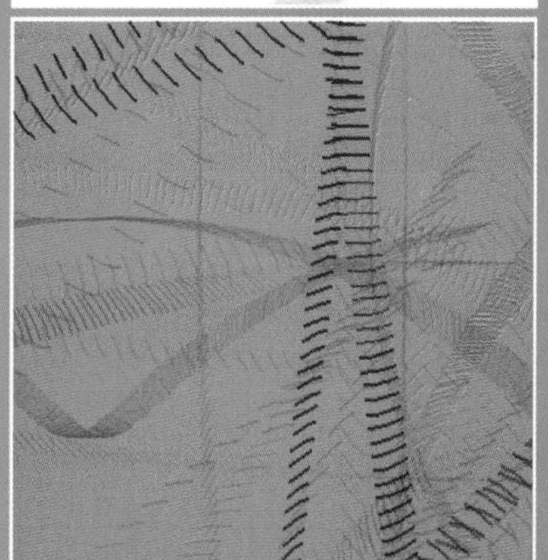

All this does is set the sound volume and start it playing whenever two shapes collide. We also reduce the sound volume so that the sound fades out as it repeats and gives us new and different sound combinations depending on the volume. Lastly, there's a simple if statement to check if the sound has gone all the way down to 0, and reset it to 100 when it does. You may also want to increase the size of the shape so that the sounds appear more often.

colorsuck08

I just started experimenting here with different sounds and different shapes. I reset the colors to RGB for this one and added a bit of rotation.

colorsuck09

Again, this is just a collection of different sounds and shapes, but it produces some beautiful movies.

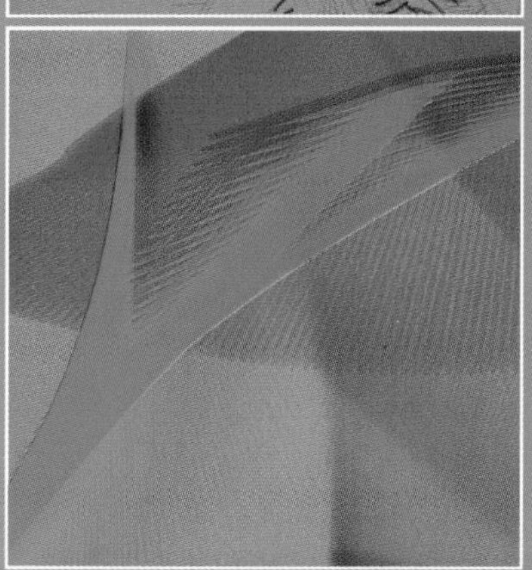

colorsuck10
I now added a few more objects, one for each of my 8 sounds, and set them going. I also changed the color code slightly to give each one a random color:

```
a = random(255);
b = random(255);
c = random(255);
me = new Color(this);
metr = new Object();
metr.rb = a;
metr.gb = b;
metr.bb = c;
metr.ab = -255;
me.setTransform(metr);
```

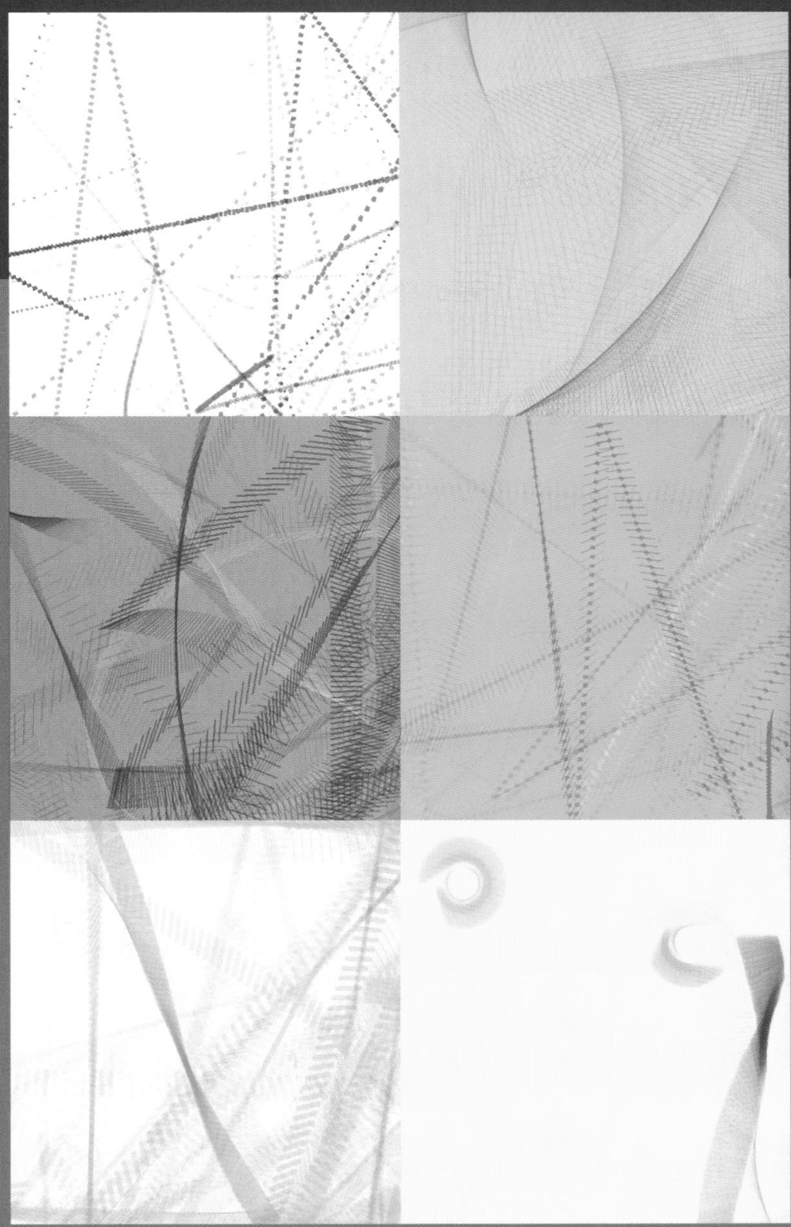

colorsuck11
For this iteration I recorded some new sounds of a slowed down voice speaking numbers on a Mac.

colorsuck12
Again this is just a change in the sounds being played, if you can't work out what they're speaking, it's the three syllables of pinderkaas.

colorsuck13
More sounds again, this time a few notes recorded straight from a guitar. Sometimes it's even quite tuneful.

colorsuck14
For the final iteration I created a set of new sounds and also made a background object with the following code on it:

```
onClipEvent(load){
  a = random(255);
  b = random(255);
  c = random(255);
  me = new Color(this);
  metr = new Object();
  metr.rb = a;
  metr.gb = b;
  metr.bb = c;
  me.setTransform(metr);
}
```

As you can probably tell by now, this just sets the background to a random color when the movie starts. This has got to be my favorite out of all of them, it has beautiful sounds, beautiful colors, and makes beautiful pictures.

I spent hours playing with new shapes and sounds for this, but I won't bore you with them all, go create your own and enjoy.

Squares

This is the ultimate in simplicity; just a static picture inspired by spirographs and old computer magazines. I think though, that this is one of the most absorbing things I've created in a long time just because it's so easy to customize it. I change the graphic a tiny bit – I get a new picture, I change one number in the code – I get a new picture. When I first started playing with this I just sat for hours tweaking things, making tiny changes and loving what came out. I made whole series of differences – adding the Color object here, a bit of animation there, or a liberal sprinkling of invisible roll-overs – but when it came down to choosing which ones I'd put in the book I came right back to the most basic static images just because I love their simplicity. I'll run through a few of the iterations that I liked, but I'd prefer it if you just completely ignored all that I've written and go off and enjoy creating your own.

I'm sure you'll all have seen this first one before, it's just the good old rotating, shrinking square.

```
onClipEvent (load) {
   d = 0;
   for (b=1; b<5; b++) {
     for (a=1; a<5; a++) {
       for (i=0; i<20; i++) {
         d++;
         duplicateMovieClip (_root.square, "square"+d, d);
         _root["square"+d]._x = 50*a;
         _root["square"+d]._y = 50*b;
         _root["square"+d]._rotation += (i*5);
         _root["square"+d]._xscale -= (i*5);
         _root["square"+d]._yscale -= (i*5);
       }
     }
   }
}
```

This code sits on a movieclip called `control` on the main stage. There is also a simple graphic outline of a 100x100 pixel square on the main stage in a movieclip called `square`. This movieclip also has the instance name `square`.

The code is basically just a set of three nested `for` loops, the first to count loops down the screen, the second to count loops across the screen, and the last to actually control the meat of the code – duplicating, positioning, and sizing the individual movieclips.

The key variables

`d` = the overall counter of the number of times the innermost loop loops, and therefore the number of new movieclips that are duplicated onto the screen. It's used to name the new movieclips, but it can also be thrown into other parts of the code to create different effects for each movie clip
`a` and `b` = the two outer loops, they are used as counters for the number of times the inner loop is run across and down the screen. They are used for positioning the movieclips later on
`i` = the counter for the inner loop. The amount of times that the movieclip is duplicated for each position across and down the screen

Iterations

square02

By changing the square for a circle and setting it slightly off center we get a simple spirograph pattern:

```
for (b=1; b<2; b++) {
   for (a=1; a<2; a++) {
     for (i=0; i<100; i++) {
       d++;
       duplicateMovieClip (_root.square, "square"+d, d);
       _root["square"+d]._x = 200*a;
       _root["square"+d]._y = 200*b;
       _root["square"+d]._rotation += (i*5);
       _root["square"+d]._xscale += (5);
       _root["square"+d]._yscale += (5);
     }
   }
}
```

For what it's worth, you could just as easily remove the scaling lines from this one, I only left them in to save retyping them later on.

square03

Here I made the circle smaller (20x20) and set it even further off-center, then changed the inner `for` loop to this, bringing scale back into it:

```
for (i=0; i<200; i++) {
   d++;
   duplicateMovieClip (_root.square, "square"+d, d);
   _root["square"+d]._x = 200*a;
   _root["square"+d]._y = 200*b;
   _root["square"+d]._rotation += (i*45);
   _root["square"+d]._xscale -= (i*2);
   _root["square"+d]._yscale -= (i*2);
}
```

square04

For this experiment I substituted the circle for a gradient-filled ellipse and messed with the scale a bit more to create this slightly ammonite-like shape:

```
_root["square"+d]._rotation += (i*11);
_root["square"+d]._xscale -= (i/2);
_root["square"+d]._yscale -= (i*2);
```

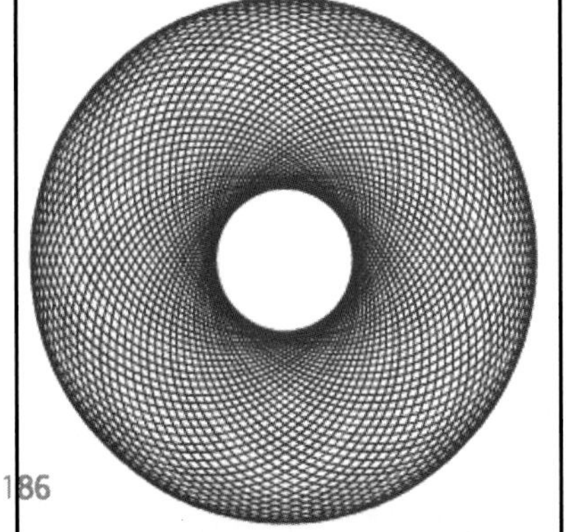

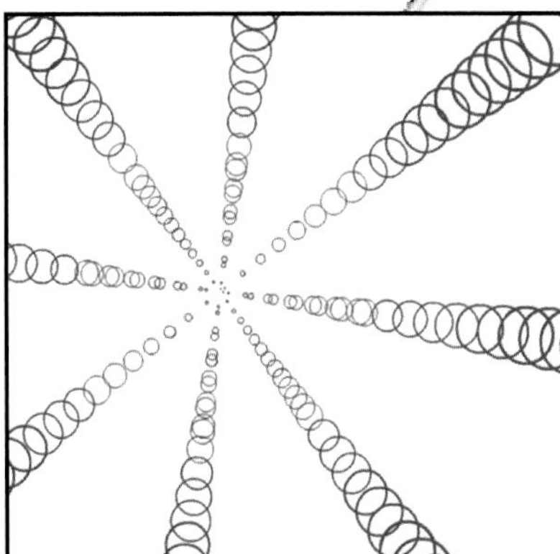

square05
I replaced the ellipse with a simple off-center black/white gradient-filled circle and changed the code slightly to this:

```
for (b=1; b<3; b++) {
  for (a=1; a<3; a++) {
    for (i=0; i<150; i++) {
      d++;
      duplicateMovieClip (_root.square, "square"+d, d);
      _root["square"+d]._x = 150*a;
      _root["square"+d]._y = 150*b;
      _root["square"+d]._rotation+=Math.round(Math.pow(a,b));
      _root["square"+d]._xscale -= (i/a);
      _root["square"+d]._yscale -= (i/b);
    }
  }
}
```

I love the way that the same small piece of code creates four completely different shapes. By moving the circle closer to the center so that it's only a little off to one side then you get a really strange effect almost like a cone being peeled open from the top.

square06
I changed the graphic again, this time to three small black triangles, and altered the code slightly to create this image of chaotic combs.

```
for (b=1; b<6; b++) {
  for (a=1; a<6; a++) {
    for (i=0; i<10; i++) {
      d++;
      duplicateMovieClip (_root.square, "square"+d, d);
      _root["square"+d]._x = 60*a;
      _root["square"+d]._y = 60*b;
      _root["square"+d]._rotation+=Math.round(Math.pow(a,b));
      _root["square"+d]._xscale -= (i*a);
      _root["square"+d]._yscale -= (i*b);
    }
  }
}
```

square07
By simply changing the graphic for a set of three overlapping filled ellipses, I arrived at this piece. It reminds me of 1970s wallpaper, but that could just be me.

square08

For this piece I changed the graphic back to the original simple square, but moved it a little off-center. I also changed the following lines of code to give a strange collection of patterns:

```
_root["square"+d]._rotation +=
  ➥ Math.round(Math.pow(a,b)/d);
_root["square"+d]._xscale -= (d);
_root["square"+d]._yscale -= (d/b);
```

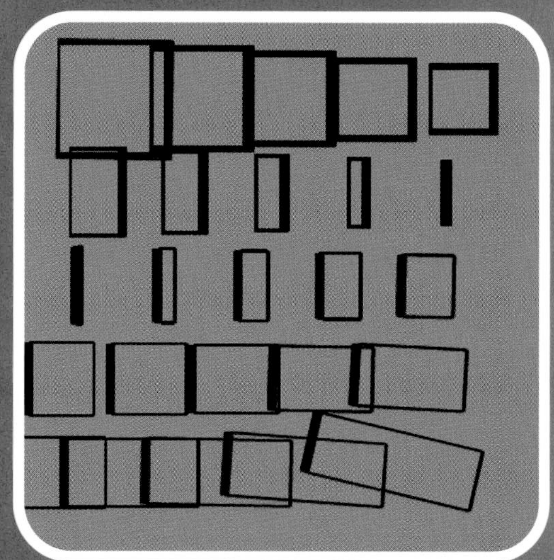

square09

Here I changed one line of code slightly and the squares appear to fall away into chaos as they approach the bottom-right corner:

```
_root["square"+d]._rotation +=
  ➥ Math.round(Math.pow(a,b));
```

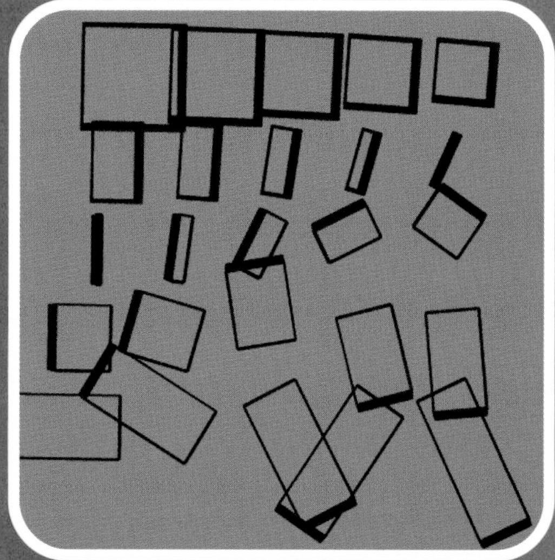

square10

Finally, we get to what I consider the to be one of the nicest of the series. By simply changing a couple of the lines of code again:

```
_root["square"+d]._rotation -=
  ➥ Math.round(Math.pow(a,b)*d);
_root["square"+d]._xscale -= (d/a);
```

We create 25 different shapes all from that one simple piece of ActionScript.

Ty Lettau is a partner at the Fourm Design Studio (fourm.com) in Milwaukee, Wisconsin. He created Fourm with JD Hooge, Craig Kroeger, and Erik Natzke. Ty's personal site (soundofdesign.com) explores and experiments with the possibilities of interactive media. He also teaches design part-time at the Milwaukee Institute of Art and Design. Ty has recently created projects for VectorLounge (vectorlounge.com/04_amsterdam/jam/soundofdesign.html) and Born Magazine (bornmagazine.org/projects/core).

Inspiration is in everything. If you look for it, you'll find it.

ty lettau

soundofdesign.com

Lines

Let's start with our first file, `01.swf`. There's a mask layer over the movie meaning that you'll see a rectangular cutout in the middle with a set of lines spiralling chaotically across it.

This project consists of three movieclips: `MaskClip`, `LineClip`, and `ActionClip`. The `MaskClip` movieclip is just our rectangular cutout mask; it has the instance name `Mask`. The `LineClip` movieclip is the main graphic in the movie. It's just a 100 pixel vertical purple line with the center point at x=50, y=50. This is what we'll be duplicating later. Place `LineClip` on the stage with the center point at x=–10,y=100, and give it the instance name `Line0`. The `ActionClip` movieclip is an empty clip that we're just using as a container to attach the majority of our code to. First of all though, we need to attach some initialization code to the first frame of the root:

```
// ————————
// Movie parameters
// ————————
_highquality = 0;
fscommand ("allowscale", "false");
fscommand ("fullscreen", "true");
// ——————————————————————
// Create a mask on a level higher than the duplicates…
// ——————————————————————
Mask.duplicateMovieClip("Mask",1000);
// ————————
// Stop root playhead
// ————————
stop ();
```

The following code is then attached to the `ActionClip` movie:

```
onClipEvent (enterFrame) {
   if (_root.C<300) {
      // ——————————————————
      // Continually duplicate the "Line" clip.
      // ——————————————————
      _root.C++;
      _root.Line0.duplicateMovieClip("Line"+_root.C,_root.C);
      // ————————————
      // Parameters of duplicates
      // ————————————
      _root["Line"+_root.C]._x = _root.C*2;
      _root["Line"+_root.C]._y = 100;
      _root["Line"+_root.C]._xscale = 100;
      _root["Line"+_root.C]._yscale = random(200);
      _root["Line"+_root.C]._rotation = _root["Line"+(_root.C-1)]._rotation+(random(50)-25);
      _root["Line"+_root.C]._alpha = random(50);
   }
}
```

The key variables

`C` = a counter that simply counts from 0 to 300. It's our only variable here.

We need `C` for several things. First, It allows us to give each duplicate of `Line0` a unique name. As we duplicate `Line0` we're adding the `C` value to the end of its name each time. So when `C is 124`, the duplicated movieclip is named `Line124`. `C` is also used to determine the layer that each duplicate is placed onto.

First of all we set the `_x` position to `_root.C*2`, so as the `C` value counts up, it will move the movieclips across the stage. The `_y` position stays at 100 for each movieclip. The `_xscale` will stay at 100, but the `_yscale` is set to a random value.

We use the same naming convention for the `_rotation` value, but we add `C - 1` to the end of the name. This will give us the second most recent movieclip (that is, the one created two frames ago). So this means that we're adding a random number to the last movieclip's `_rotation`, which makes the movieclips form an uneven spiral. Lastly, we set the `_alpha` to another random number.

The `ActionClip` movie is where we will be making most of the changes, and each change will build on the last one.

Iterations

lines02

```
_root["Line"+_root.C]._rotation = _root["Line"+
    ➥ (_root.C-1)]._rotation+(random(10)-5);
```

All we are doing in this iteration is creating less of a `_rotation` by decreasing the range of the `random` number.

lines03

For this iteration, we 're leaving the `ActionClip` code alone and adding the following to the `Line0` movieclip:

```
onClipEvent (enterFrame) {
    _rotation+=3;
}
```

This will give our lines some motion.

lines04

Now back to the `ActionClip` code:

```
_root["Line"+_root.C]._rotation = _root["Line"+
    ➥ (_root.C- 1)]._rotation+(random(100)-50);
```

We're changing the rotation line again to give a greater random range. The other change that we're making is to the `Line0` clip. Go into it and set the registration point to be at the very top. Now when it's rotated it will behave differently.

lines05

For this iteration, remove all of the code on `Line0` to see what the new rotation settings look like when they're static.

[3]

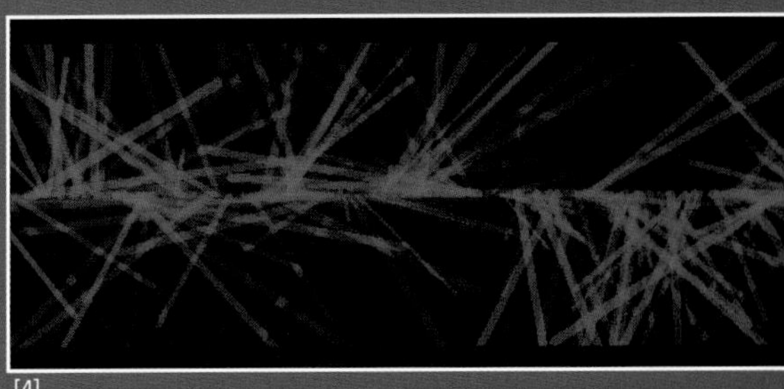

[4]

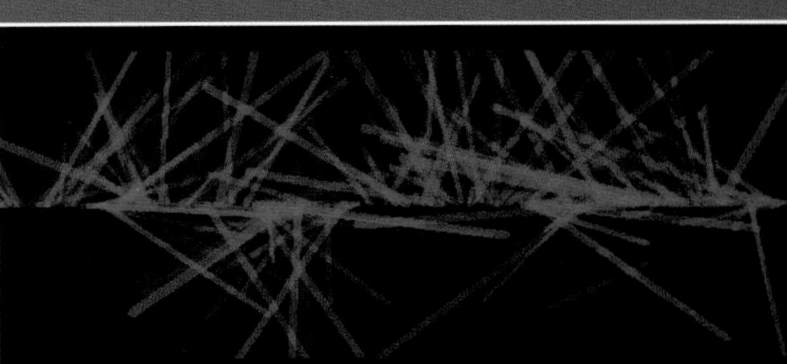

[5]

lines06

By having our `_x` position set to `C*2`, and knowing that our stage is 600 pixels wide, we can tell that a movieclip has reached the edge of the screen when `C = 300`. So when this happens, we can set the next duplicate's `_x` position back to 0 to start it off again from the left. To do this we add in two new variables. We need to temporarily maintain our counter variable, so we replace `C` with a new variable `D`. This is then used in the counter loop. Now `C` will still count, meaning that our naming and level values stay usable, but we have another counter variable that can be reset without compromising our original naming counter. We also have `X`, which will now represent the `_x` position that we used `C` for before. So `D` and `X` count with `C` to start off with, but when they get to 300, `D` and `X` reset to 0 while `C` keeps on counting. Here's the full new code for the `enterFrame` clip event:

```
onClipEvent (enterFrame) {
    if (_root.D<300) {
        _root.C++;
        _root.D++;
        _root.X++;

        _root.Line0.duplicateMovieClip("Line"+
            ➥ _root.C,_root.C);
        _root["Line"+_root.C]._x = _root.X*2;
        _root["Line"+_root.C]._y = 100;
        _root["Line"+_root.C]._xscale = 100;
        _root["Line"+_root.C]._yscale =random(200);
        _root["Line"+_root.C]._rotation =_root["Line"+
            ➥ (_root.C-1)]._rotation+(random(100)-50);
        _root["Line"+_root.C]._alpha = random(50);
    } else {
        _root.D=0;
        _root.X=0;
    }
}
```

So the result is that when the counter hits 300 and the last clip is placed on the right of the stage, the very next clip gets set to 0, or the far left of the stage. All new duplicates then pile on top of the old ones in a new iteration of lines.

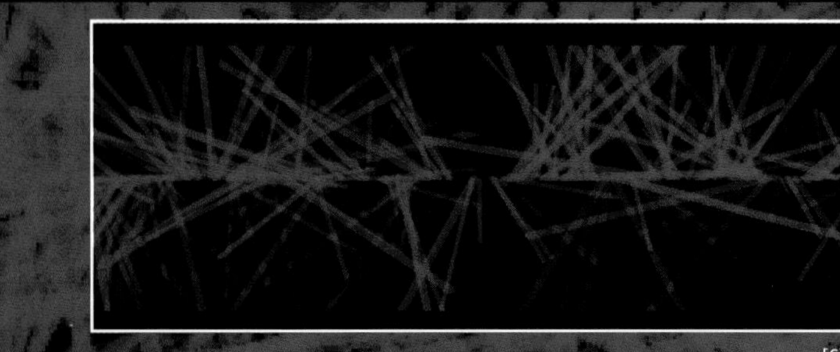

lines07

Click on `LineClip` and make the height 2000 pixels. Now our line will extend to the edge no matter where it is.

lines08

Now let's make a few changes to get something totally different. We're going to go back to our `C` counter, but this time we are going to use it as a way to remove movieclips. In the last iteration, we purposely preserved the `C` value as incremental. This time we are going to reset it after it hits 100. With a few modifications to the parameters such as an `_x` position and `_rotation` relative to the last duplicate, we get something new. Also, we need to move the registration point of `Line0` so that it's in the center. Lastly, we apply two constraints so that if the duplicate goes past 100 to the left, it locks to 100, or if it goes past 500 to the right, it locks to 500. This just keeps everything on the stage. Go back to the `ActionClip` code from `line04.fla` and make the following changes:

```
onClipEvent (enterFrame) {
    if (_root.C<100) {
        _root.C++;

        _root.Line0.duplicateMovieClip("Line"+
            ➥ _root.C,_root.C);
        _root["Line"+_root.C]._x = _root["Line"+
            ➥ (_root.C-1)]._x+(random(120)-60);
        _root["Line"+_root.C]._rotation = _root
            ➥ ["Line"+(_root.C-1)]._rotation+
            ➥ (random(30)-15);
        _root["Line"+_root.C]._alpha = random(50);
        if (_root["Line"+_root.C]._x < 100) {
            _root["Line"+_root.C]._x = 100;
        }
        if (_root["Line"+_root.C]._x > 500) {
            _root["Line"+_root.C]._x = 500;
        }
    } else {
        _root.C=0;
    }
}
```

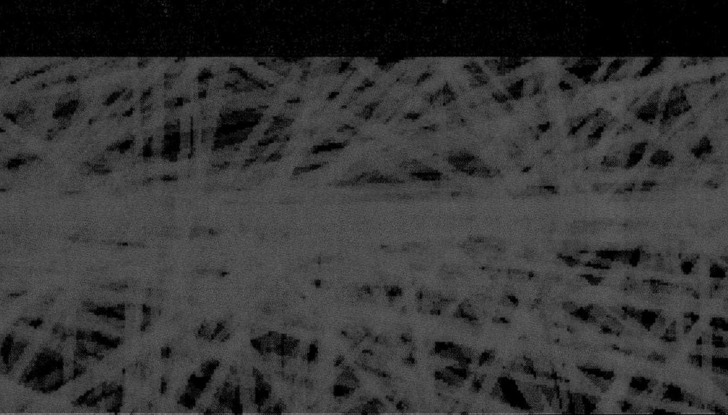

lines09
Let's apply one last feature to the file. We're going to add the function of polarity. First of all, delete the `ActionClip` movieclip. We don't need that anymore.

Rotate `LineClip` by 45 degrees, then convert it into a new movieclip named `LineClip2`. This movieclip should now be inside `LineClip`. Click into `LineClip2` and set the center point of the graphic to x=-100, y=-50 so that as we rotate it, the whole movieclip will seem to orbit. Go into `LineClip` and make a new layer named `Actions`. Make two frames, and on the second frame, write:

```
gotoAndPlay(_currentframe-1);
```

Then on the first frame, write:

```
function radiansToDegrees (radians) {
    return (radians/Math.PI)*180;
}
N1X = _x;
N1Y = _y;
N2X = _root._xmouse;
N2Y = _root._ymouse;
DX = (N2X-N1X);
DY = -(N2Y-N1Y);
A = radiansToDegrees(Math.atan2(DY,DX));
R = Math.floor((A<0?360+A:A)*1000)/1000;
```

`N1X` and `N1Y` mark the point `A`, and `N2X` and `N2Y` mark the point `B`. `DX` and `DY` are the distances on each axis between the two points. We then use these values to arrive at an angle. If we drew a line from the movieclip (`A`) to the cursor (`B`), then this will find the angle perpendicular to that line. Now we need to set the `LineClip2` movieclip to this angle (represented by `R`). Add two clip events to `LineClip2`. First we set the `_alpha` to a random value on load, and then we set the `_rotation` to the `R` value.

```
onClipEvent (load) {
    _alpha = random(50);
}
onClipEvent (enterFrame) {
    _rotation = -_parent.R;
}
```

All we need to do now is replicate `LineClip` several times and position the movieclips where desired. Before we were using the `ActionClip` to tell movieclips what to do. Now we're embedding the code for each movieclip in itself. So each time we physically paste a new copy of `LineClip`, it will behave independently to the others.

lines10
We can click into `LineClip2` now and do anything to the graphic. Let's add two more lines inside to make a more complex pattern. At this point, we can do just about anything and it will result in a large change in the final result. Be crazy.

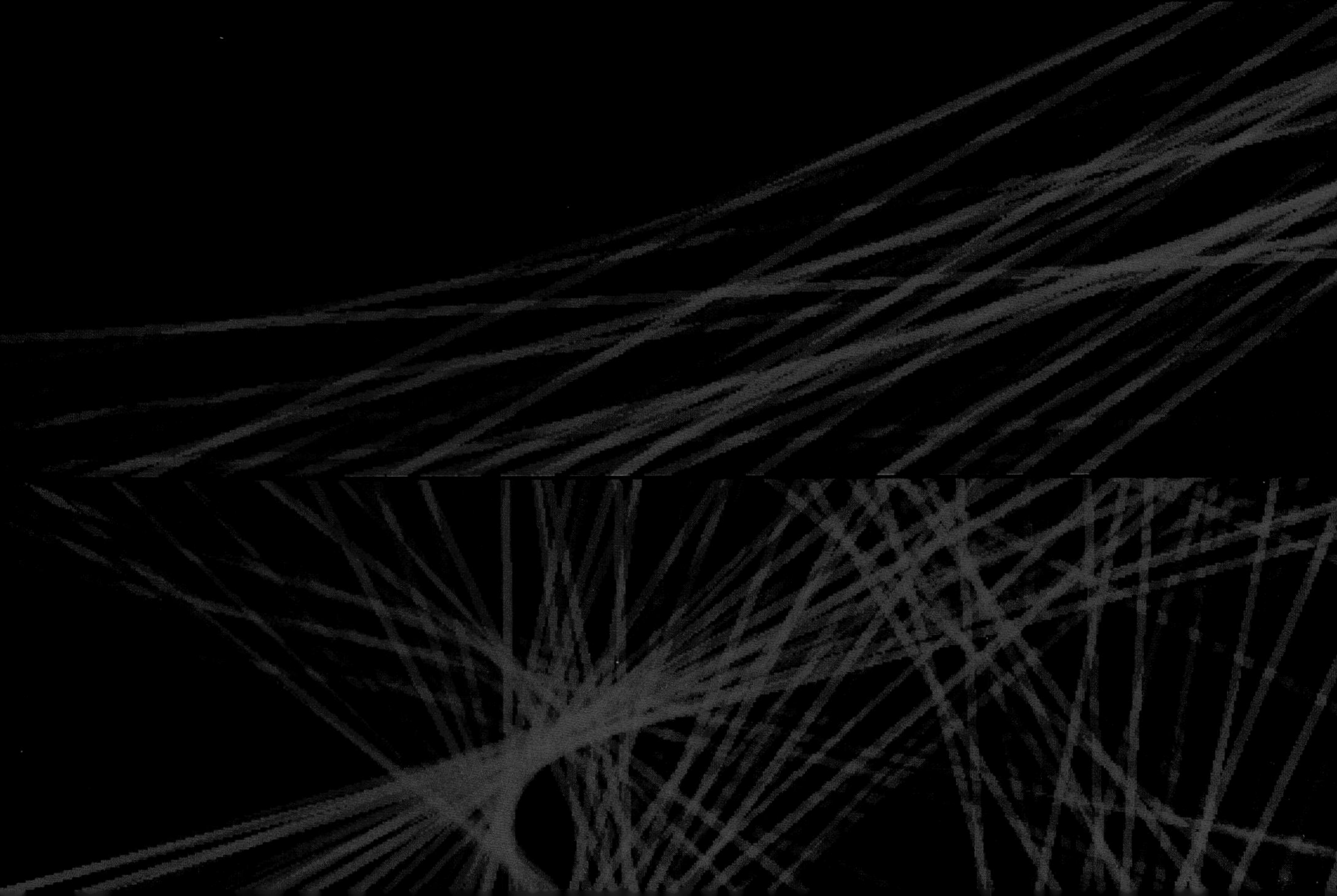

Orbits

The basic set-up for this series of experiments is the same as the last one, but with the addition of a new movieclip: **MoverClip**.

The **LineClip** movieclip consists of the standard 100x100 pixel 45 degree line. Next, select the graphic and make it into a movieclip named **LineClip2**. This will leave us with **LineClip2** nested inside of **LineClip**. We'll use this clip for tweening later on. While still inside **LineClip**, name the original layer **Objects**, and then make a new layer and name it **Actions**. Next, make a keyframe in both layers on frame 30. On the new frame in the **Actions** layer we'll add:

```
removeMovieClip();
stop();
```

This gives the movieclip a lifespan. When it's loaded, it will run for 30 frames and then remove itself. We then make a motion tween between frames 1 and 29 of the **Objects** layer and set the alpha at frame 29 to 0. We then go back to the root level and place **LineClip** on the stage. This is the movie we'll be duplicating later so we'll give it the instance name **Line0**.

The **MoverClip** movieclip is merely a 1x1 pixel blue square centered on the stage. Name the instance **Follow**.

We'll now add some code to frame 1 of the root **Actions** layer:

```
_highquality = 0;
fscommand ("allowscale", "false");
fscommand ("fullscreen", "true");
Mask.duplicateMovieClip("Mask",1000);
stop ();
```

The next step is to attach the following code to the **ActionClip** instance on the stage:

```
onClipEvent (enterFrame) {
    _root.C++;
    _root.Line0.duplicateMovieClip("Line"+_root.C,_root.C);
    _root["Line"+_root.C]._x = _root.Follow._x;
    _root["Line"+_root.C]._y = _root.Follow._y;
    _root["Line"+_root.C]._xscale = _root["Line"+(_root.C-1)]._x-_root.Follow._x;
    _root["Line"+_root.C]._yscale = _root["Line"+(_root.C-1)]._y-_root.Follow._y;
    OX = _root._xmouse;
    OY = _root._ymouse;
    MX = (MX*.96)+(OX-_root.Follow._x)*.13;
    MY = (MY*.96)+(OY-_root.Follow._y)*.13;
    _root.Follow._x += MX;
    _root.Follow._y += MY;
}
```

The key variables

C = a counter
OX = the mouse's **_x** position
OY = the mouse's **_y** position

This is just your basic mouse trail, but with a twist. Check out the SWF to see the effect. Each duplicated line attaches one of its endpoints to the last line, and the other endpoint to a new location. The lines then fade out and are ultimately removed.

The speed in the elasticity engine is controlled by a fixed number, which in this case is 0.13. The 0.96 equates to friction. The result of this code is an elastic string, which responds to the mouse movement. The mouse position is taken by **OX** and **OY** and fed into the **MX** and **MY** equations, which output new **_x** and **_y** positions for the **Follow** movieclip.

Iterations

orbits02

For the first iteration, go into `Line0` and drag both end keyframes from frame 30 to frame 90. Make sure you expand the motion tween as well. All this does is make the life of the movieclip longer, giving a very different visual result.

Let's also change the origin point for the elastic code in our `ActionClip` code. We'll make the origin the direct opposite of where the mouse is:

```
OX = 600-_root._xmouse;
OY = 200-_root._ymouse;
```

orbits03

Here, we'll put the `LineClip` keyframes back to frame 30. We'll also change the same lines of code again. This time let's add a random value to the mouse location. We'll still have very fluid movement, but it won't be as controlled:

```
OX = _root._xmouse+(random(100)-50);
OY = _root._xmouse+(random(100)-50);
```

orbits04

Again, let's put the `LineClip` ending keyframes back to frame 90, to see what a longer string will do with the new random feature.

orbits05

For our final experiment we'll make one more adjustment to the `Line0` movieclip. We'll add keyframes at frame 40 and frame 50 and set the `_alpha` of `LineClip2` at both frames to 0. At frame 89 we'll now bring the alpha back up to 100.

These examples make good use of Flash's scripting and tweening capabilities. Try playing around with more tween, or altering some of the code variables and see what can be achieved. You may want to try altering the visual movieclip to create different effects.

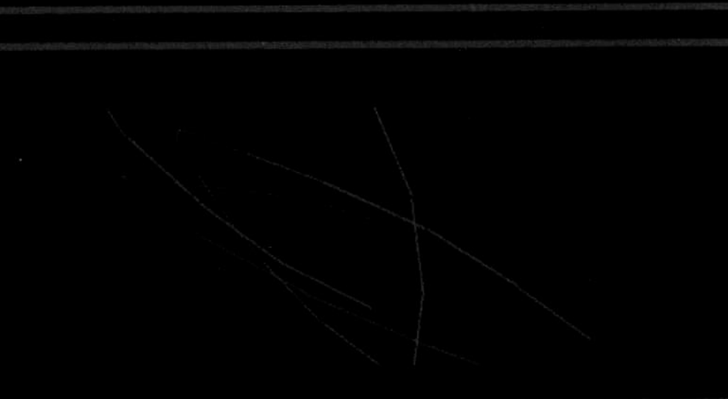

Terra

Our set up for this experiment will be similar to that found in the **Lines** and **Orbits** experiments. **LineClip** is just a vertical green line 100 pixels wide, and centered on the screen. We place this on the stage with the instance name **Line0**. Once again, we've made the graphic into a **LineClip2** symbol nested inside the main **LineClip**.

Here are the basic parameters of our movie, and the function that produces the duplicate clips. They go on frame 1 of the root:

```
_highquality = 0;
fscommand ("allowscale", "false");
fscommand ("fullscreen", "true");
Mask.duplicateMovieClip("Mask",1000);
stop ();
```

Let's now look at the code that we attach to the **ActionClip** movieclip.

```
onClipEvent (enterFrame) {
    if (_root.D < 300) {
        _root.C++;
        _root.D++;
        _root.X++;
        _root.Line0.duplicateMovieClip("Line"+_root.C,_root.C);
        _root["Line"+_root.C]._x = _root.X*2;
        _root["Line"+_root.C]._y = _root["Line"+(_root.C-1)]._y+random(11)-5;
        if (_root["Line"+_root.C]._y < 0) {
            _root["Line"+_root.C]._y = 0;
        }
        if (_root["Line"+_root.C]._y > 200) {
            _root["Line"+_root.C]._y = 200;
        }
    } else {
        _root.D = 0;
        _root.X = 0;
    }
}
```

The key variables

C = the counter used to name clip and define depths
D = the counter used in the loop
X = a counter used to control the **_x** position

This code is very similar to the starting code of the Lines experiment so we won't repeat all the details here. To summarize, the code simply counts, duplicates and positions the **LineClip** instances across the stage. We have three counters in this experiment **C**, **D** and **X**. The **C** counter continuously increases where as the **D** and **X** counter reset when they get to 300. This allows us to use **X** to control the **_x** position. **D** assumes the role of being the counter in the loop and **C**'s purpose is to name the clip and their depths.

Iterations

terra02
On the **ActionClip** movieclip, add these two lines just above the bottom two **if** statements:

```
_root["Line"+(_root.C-1)]._x += (random(50)-25);
_root["Line"+(_root.C-1)]._y += (random(50)-25);
```

Adding these two lines will take each duplicate after it is created, and give it a more random location.

terra03

Now let's change that code again. Remove the two lines we just added and change the `_y` to use the mouse location instead. Also, we're going to change the depth that we set the duplicates to. Rather than using the counter, let's use a random value. This will cause the duplicates to be replaced in a random pattern. For example, if a duplicate is placed at 128, the next time the random value is 128, that last duplicate will disappear to make room for the new one. The result is a disintegrating look:

```
_root.Line0.duplicateMovieClip("Line"+_root.C,random(300));

_root["Line"+_root.C]._y = _root.xmouse;
```

Now we have a ribbon that we can control.

terra04

Go into the `LineClip` movieclip and set the width of the line to 20 in the Info panel, and the center point at x=10, y=0. Now we have a ribbon that is narrower. Moving the mouse fast gives a strange pattern of marks.

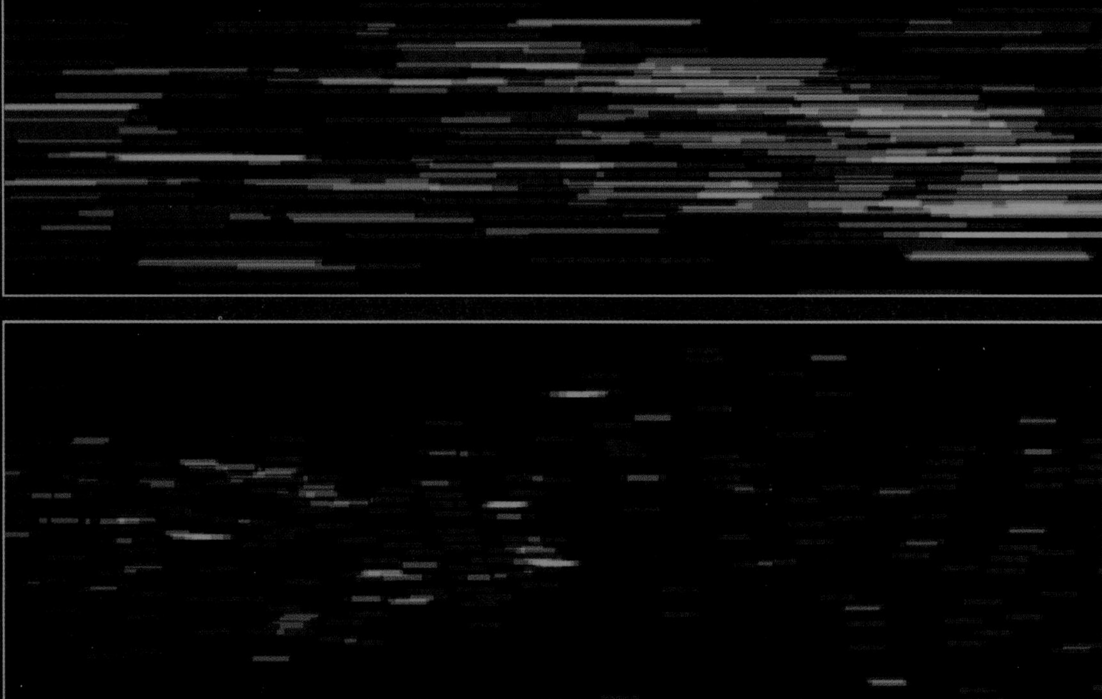

terra05

First, let's change back the depth counter. Then we're going to apply some code that we used in the `Orbits` experiment. We need to go into `LineClip` and make it the 100x100px diagonal line that we used earlier. The four new lines of code we add for this example place and scale the object. Also, the added `if` statement below simply gets rid of the line that is drawn when the duplicates flip back to zero to start over at the left of the stage. Otherwise, we get a long line that goes all the way from right to left. Here's the code in full:

```
onClipEvent (enterFrame) {
    if (_root.D < 300) {
        _root.C++;
        _root.D++;
        _root.X++;
        _root.Line0.duplicateMovieClip("Line"+_root.C,_root.C);
        _root["Line"+_root.C]._x = _root.X*2;
        _root["Line"+_root.C]._y = _root._ymouse;
        _root["Line"+_root.C]._xscale = _root["Line"+(_root.C-1)]._x-_root.X*2;
        _root["Line"+_root.C]._yscale = _root["Line"+(_root.C-1)]._y-_root._ymouse;
        if (_root["Line"+_root.C]._y < 0) {
            _root["Line"+_root.C]._y = 0;
        }
        if (_root["Line"+_root.C]._y > 200) {
            _root["Line"+_root.C]._y = 200;
        }
    } else {
        _root.D = 0;
        _root.X = 0;
    }
    if (_root.D == 1) {
        _root["Line" + _root.C]._visible = 0;
    }
}
```

terra06

This next iteration happened by accident. I changed one value, but forgot to change the other, and the result was very interesting:

```
_root["Line"+_root.C]._y = _root["Line"+(_root.C-1)]._y+random(11)-5;
```

terra07

Let's keep playing with the combinations of this code, and try setting the `_xscale` with a `_y` value:

```
_root["Line"+_root.C]._xscale = _root["Line"+(_root.C-1)]._x-_root._ymouse;
```

terra08

Lastly, let's go into `LineClip` and make a keyframe at frame 30. Set the `_alpha` of this line to 0, and then add a motion tween with a 1 degree CCW rotation so that we have a rotation and alpha fade effect. Now, as the movieclips duplicate, they will form new patterns.

Polarity

The basic set up of the movie will be identical to my other experiments. I won't go into detail with it all because we've done it all before, but here's a quick recap.

The **LineClip** movieclip is just a 10x10 pixel diagonal orange line with its center point at 0,0. This is what we'll be duplicating later, so we'll give it the instance name **Line0**. Once again, we nest the graphic with **LineClip2**. The graphic has its center point within **LineClip** set to 50,50. We offset the center point so that as we rotate, the whole movieclip will seem to orbit. On **LineClip**'s actions layer we add the following in frame 2:

```
gotoAndPlay(_currentframe-1);
```

And in frame 1:

```
function radiansToDegrees (radians) {
     return (radians/Math.PI)*180;
}
N1X = _x;
N1Y = _y;
N2X = _root._xmouse;
N2Y = _root._ymouse;
DX = (N2X-N1X);
DY = -(N2Y-N1Y);
A = radiansToDegrees(Math.atan2(DY,DX));
R = Math.floor((A<0?360+A:A)*1000)/1000;
```

The key variables

N1X = the **_x** value of point A
N1Y = the **_y** value of point A
N2X = the **_x** value of point B
N2Y = the **_y** value of point B
DX = the distance on the x axis between points A and B
DY = the distance on the y axis between points A and B

These variables perform the same angle calculation function as they did back in **lines09.fla**. Now we need to set the **LineClip2** movieclip to this angle (represented by **R**). Attach the following code to **LineClip2**:

```
onClipEvent (load) {
     _alpha = random(50);
}
onClipEvent (enterFrame) {
     _rotation = -_parent.R;
}
```

Now the movieclip will rotate itself based on the mouse location.

Next we add the usual code to the first frame of the root:

```
_highquality = 0;
fscommand ("allowscale", "false");
fscommand ("fullscreen", "true");
Mask.duplicateMovieClip("Mask",1000);
stop ();
```

Now let's add the **ActionClip** code.

```
onClipEvent (enterFrame) {
    if (_root.C<300) {
        _root.C++;
        _root.Line0.duplicateMovieClip("Line"+
           ➡ _root.C, _root.C);
        _root["Line"+_root.C]._x = random(600);
        _root["Line"+_root.C]._y = random(200);
    }
}
```

In this code we're again back to using **C** as our sole counter. It defines the loop length, names our clips, and defines the depths that they sit on.

To start off with, we set the **_x** position and the **_y** position to a random number. We use the proportions of the stage (600x200) as our random range.

polarity02

For the next iteration, let's try altering our line graphic in **LineClip2**. Add a few more lines in this movieclip by copying the line and pasting a new one, placing it wherever you want. Different line patterns will yield different results when you run the SWF. I chose to make a 4x2 grid of the lines with them each 10 pixels apart.

polarity03

For this version, we're going to control the positions of the duplicates a bit more. First, change the line graphic back to a single line, then rotate that line 90° and set its new center point to 20,20.

We need to place **Line0** at a new location on the stage. Set it at 300,100 so that it begins in the center. Let's also change a few lines to the end of our **ActionClip** movie:

```
// ————————————
// Parameters of duplicates
// ————————————
_root["Line"+_root.C]._x = _root["Line"+(_root.C-1)]._x+random(60)-30;
_root["Line"+_root.C]._y = _root["Line"+(_root.C-1)]._y+random(60)-30;
if (_root["Line"+_root.C]._x < 0) {
    _root["Line"+_root.C]._x = 0;
}
if (_root["Line"+_root.C]._x > 600) {
    _root["Line"+_root.C]._x = 600;
}
if (_root["Line"+_root.C]._y < 0) {
    _root["Line"+_root.C]._y = 0;
}
if (_root["Line"+_root.C]._y > 200) {
    _root["Line"+_root.C]._y = 200;
}
```

We change the **_x** and **_y** position to locate where the last duplicate was placed, and then to place the next one within 30px from it on each axis. The four **if** statements are merely constraints to keep the movieclips from being placed off the stage.

polarity04

Go back to the `ActionClip` code. Let's add a bit more structure by reducing the amount that the duplicates can jump from one to the next by changing the following lines:

```
_root["Line"+_root.C]._x = _root["Line"+(_root.C-1)]._x+random(20)-10;
_root["Line"+_root.C]._y = _root["Line"+(_root.C-1)]._y+random(20)-10;
```

polarity05
Let's try something new here: Delete `ActionClip`. The most important thing to do here is to click on `Line0` and remove its instance name. For the next part to work, the movieclip cannot have a name. Go into `LineClip2` and change the line graphic to be at 0,0. Now go back to the root, and manually replicate `LineClip` (which now has no instance name). I chose a grid of 30x5 with the movieclips 10 pixels apart.

This will give us a clear view of how the polarity code actually functions, and will also reveal some very nice patterns.

polarity06
Remember the two clip events we wrote on `LineClip2`? Let's change the second one a little now:

```
onClipEvent (enterFrame) {
     _rotation = -_parent.R;
     _xscale = _parent.DX;
     _yscale = _parent.DY;
}
```

Here we add something that will set the scale based on the distance from the mouse to the movieclip.

polarity07
The last iteration started out as a bit of a mistake, but it created an interesting effect. Sometimes surprises (or happy accidents) can work out. Let's now try to do what I originally intended for the last one. Set the clip event back to it's original value, then go into the line graphic and make it a 20 pixel vertical line, and set the center point to 0,0. Now it will react properly.

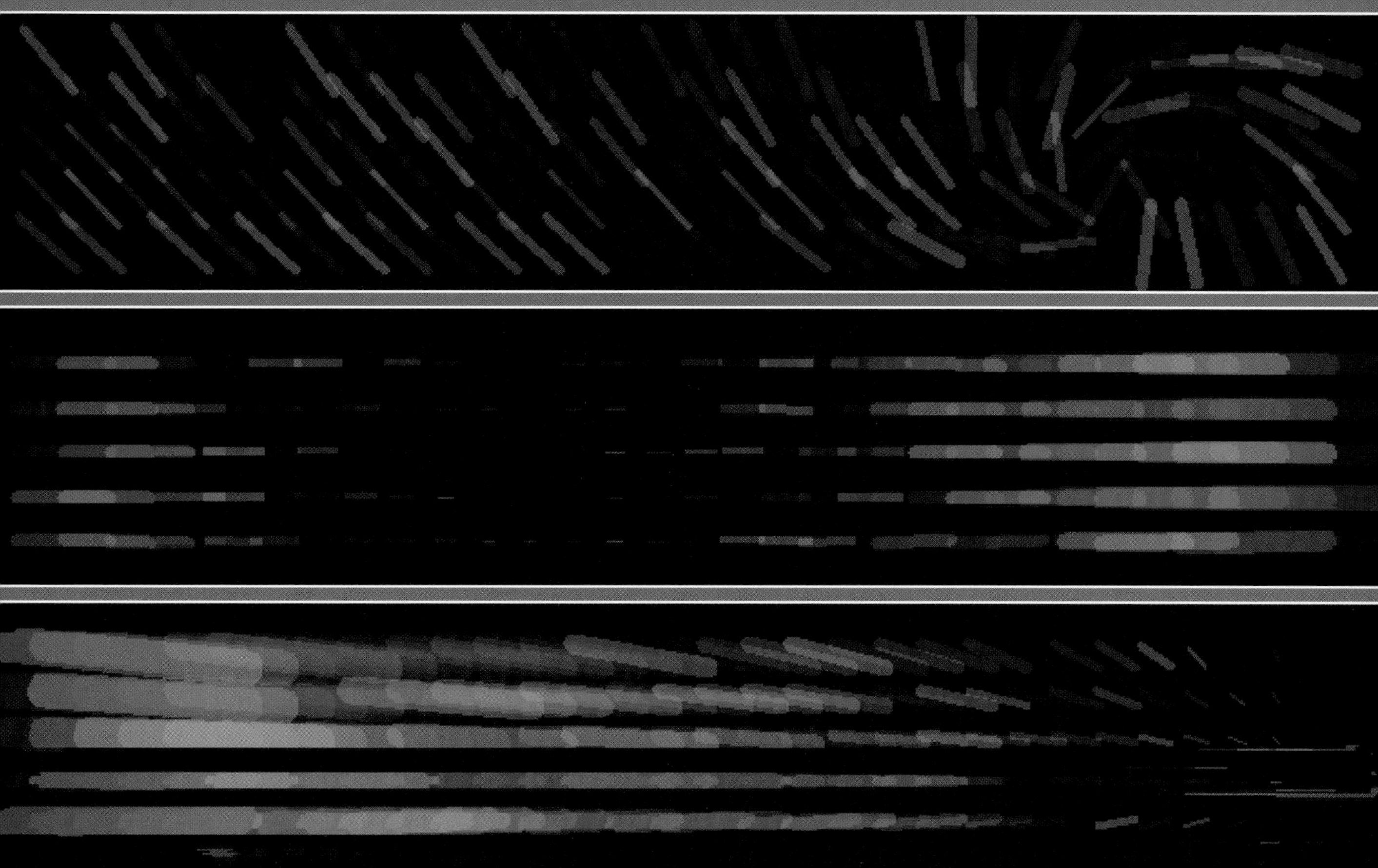

polarity08

This time, go back into `LineClip2` and change the clip event again:

```
onClipEvent (load) {
      _alpha = random(50);
      _xscale = random(1200);
      _yscale = random(1200);
}
```

Now we have a more chaotic pattern again.

polarity09

We'll now change that clip event one last time:

```
onClipEvent (load) {
      _alpha = random(50);
      _parent._rotation = random(360);
      _xscale = random(1200);
      _yscale = random(1200);
}
```

Now our movieclips have the polarity code, but since they start out with random rotations, the pattern fields are gone. As in all the experiments, a slight change in the code can have a drastic impact on the final effect.

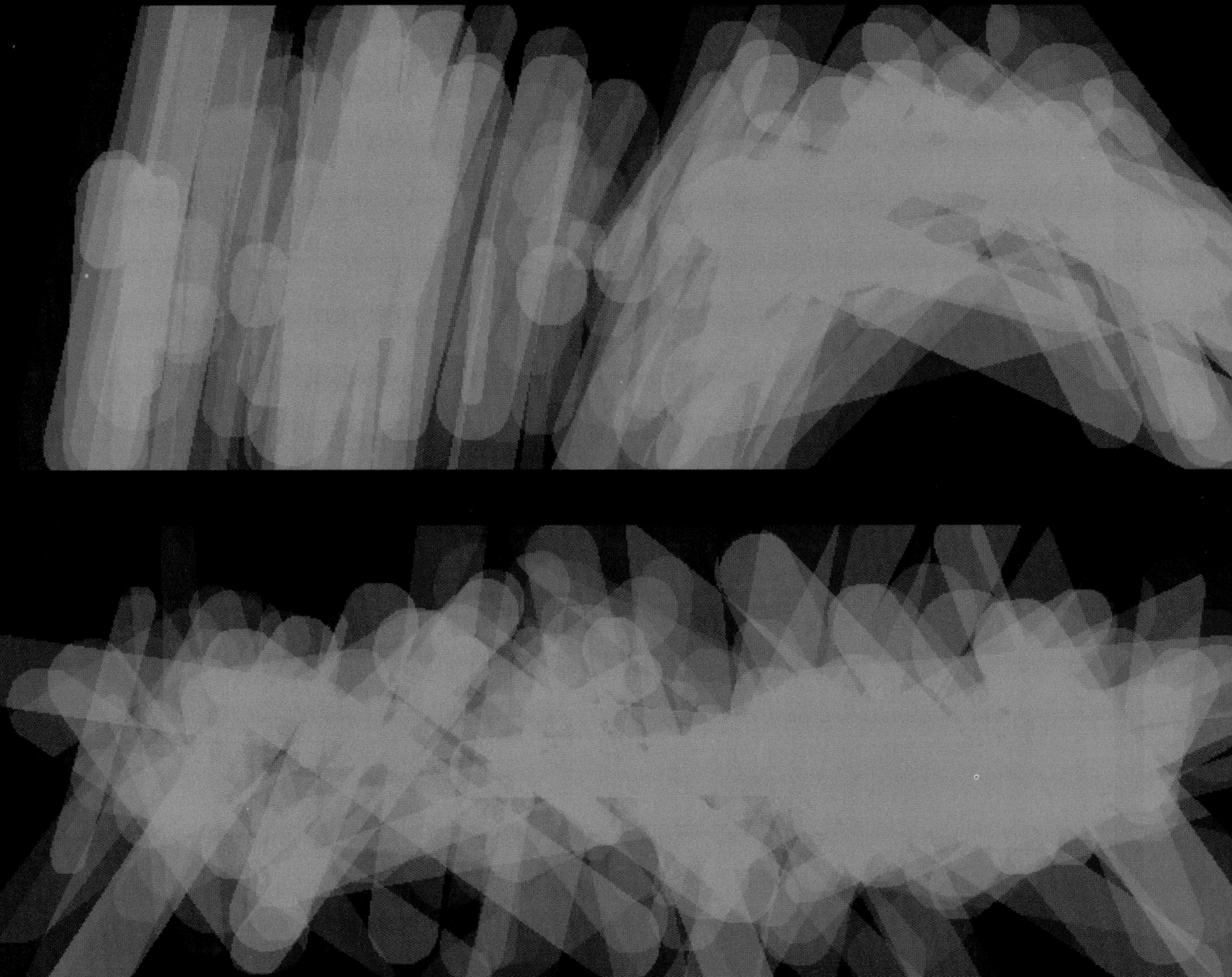

I was born in 1979, and graduated from the department of Computer Science at Moscow State University. During my time there, I researched different methods of texture compression. I'm interested in computer graphics, image processing, 3D visualization, and creating, and playing computer games.

I sometimes think Flash is the best application in the world.

When it came to creating an effect for this book, I started thinking about the amount of 3D and text effects created in Flash and I thought about combining the two. The result was a 3D shape using text as the texture. Taking this a little further and knowing that the best text effects can be manipulated by the user, I set out to create a dynamic application. The result is on display in this chapter, along with a couple of other 3D experiments.

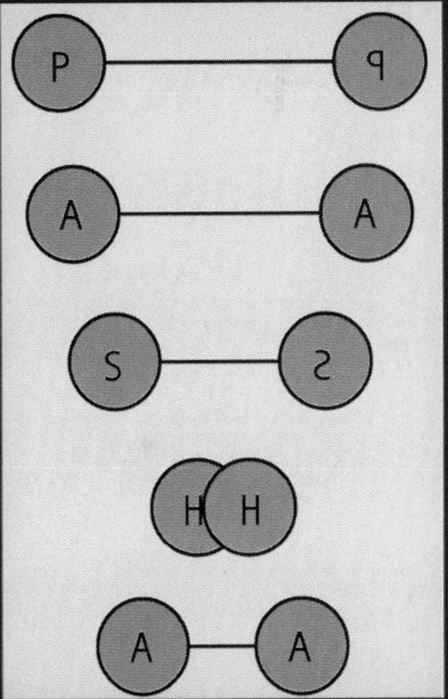

pavel kaluzhny

kaluzhny.nm.ru

Balls

Take a look at the movie **balls_0.fla**. In this experiment we'll see the code that makes up this file and look at the variables that are important to the effect's success.

The main stage contains a movie clip called **Ball**. This clip itself contains the movieclips **B0** and **L0**. **B0** contains the ball shape, while **L0** contains the line shape. These are the only objects in the scene. Let's look at the code that makes our movie work. We'll start with the code that's attached to the **Ball** movieclip:

```
onClipEvent (load) {
   ax = 0;
   ay = 0.4;
   cos2 = Math.cos(ax);
   sin2 = Math.sin(ax);
   cos1 = Math.cos(ay);
   sin1 = Math.sin(ay);
   VPf = 60;
   cx = 320; sx = 10;
   cy = 240; sy = 10;
   _x = 0;
   _y = 0;

   function Rot (p) {
    var y = p.y, z = p.z;
    p.z = cos2 * z - sin2 * p.x;
    p.x = sin2 * z + cos2 * p.x;
    p.y = cos1 * y - sin1 * p.z;
    p.z = sin1 * y + cos1 * p.z;
   }

   bnum = 7;
   for (i=0; i<bnum; i++) {
    if(i)duplicateMovieClip ("B0", "B"+i, i+1000);
    this["B"+i].gotoAndStop (i+1);
    this["B"+i].x = random (17)-8;
    this["B"+i].y = random (17)-8;
    this["B"+i].z = random (17)-8;
    this["B"+i].vx = (random (17)-8)/10;
    this["B"+i].vy = (random (17)-8)/10;
    this["B"+i].vz = (random (17)-8)/10;
   }
   lnum = 12;
   LS = 10;
   pline = [
    [ 1, 1, 1,  1, 1,-1],
    [ 1, 1,-1,  1,-1,-1],
    [ 1,-1,-1,  1,-1, 1],
    [ 1,-1, 1,  1, 1, 1],

    [-1, 1, 1, -1, 1,-1],
    [-1, 1,-1, -1,-1,-1],
    [-1,-1,-1, -1,-1, 1],
    [-1,-1, 1, -1, 1, 1],

    [ 1, 1, 1, -1, 1, 1],
    [ 1, 1,-1, -1, 1,-1],
    [ 1,-1,-1, -1,-1,-1],
    [ 1,-1, 1, -1,-1, 1]
   ];

   for (i=0; i<lnum; i++) {
    if(i)duplicateMovieClip ("L0", "L"+i, i);
    this["L"+i].id = i;
   }
}
```

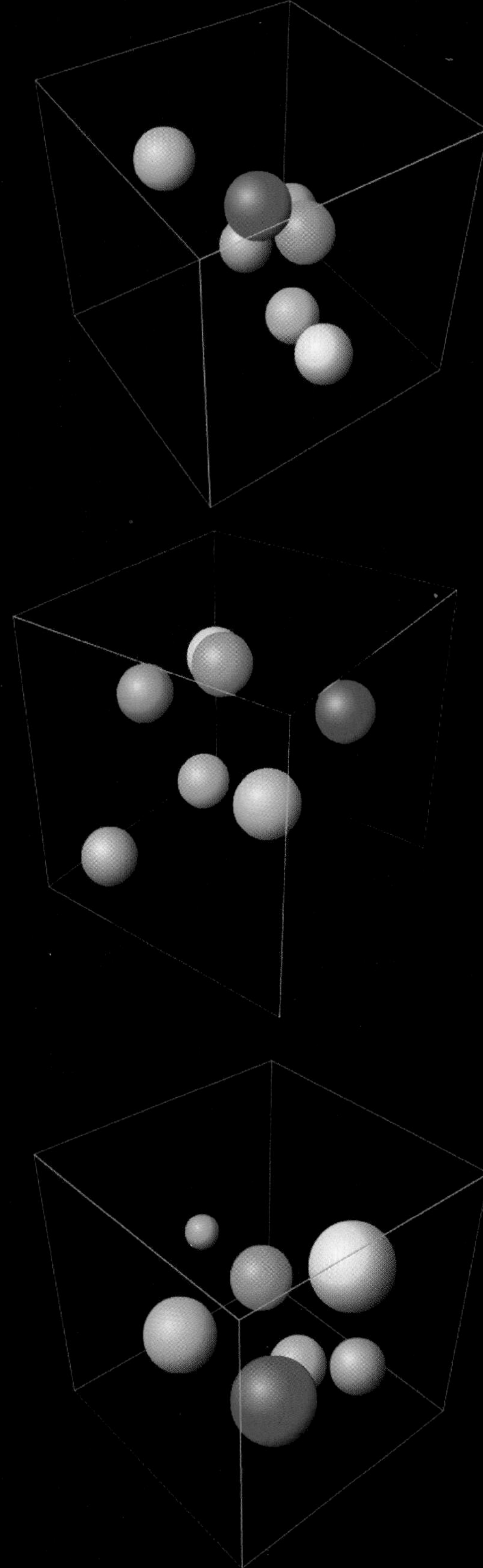

```
onClipEvent (enterFrame) {
  ax += 0.02;
  ay = 0.4 + 0.3 * Math.cos(ax/2.3);
  cos1 = Math.cos(ay);
  sin1 = Math.sin(ay);
  cos2 = Math.cos(ax);
  sin2 = Math.sin(ax);
  for (i=0; i<bnum; i++) {
   this["B"+i].NextStep();
   for ( j=i+1; j<bnum; j++ ) {
    if ( (rr=this["B"+i].len(this["B"+j])) < (rs=this["B"+i].radius+this["B"+j].radius) ) {
     this["B"+i].x = this["B"+j].x+(this["B"+i].x-this["B"+j].x)*(rs/rr);
     this["B"+i].y = this["B"+j].y+(this["B"+i].y-this["B"+j].y)*(rs/rr);
     this["B"+i].z = this["B"+j].z+(this["B"+i].z-this["B"+j].z)*(rs/rr);
     if ( this["B"+i].mass == this["B"+j].mass ) {
      tmp = this["B"+i].vx;
      this["B"+i].vx = this["B"+j].vx;
      this["B"+j].vx = tmp;
      tmp = this["B"+i].vy;
      this["B"+i].vy = this["B"+j].vy;
      this["B"+j].vy = tmp;
      tmp = this["B"+i].vz;
      this["B"+i].vz = this["B"+j].vz;
      this["B"+j].vz = tmp;
     } else {
      tmp = this["B"+i].vx;
      this["B"+i].vx=(this["B"+j].mass*(2*this["B"+j].vx-this["B"+i].vx)+
            ➥ this["B"+i].mass*this["B"+i].vx)/(this["B"+i].mass+this["B"+j].mass);
      this["B"+j].vx = this["B"+i].vx+tmp-this["B"+j].vx;
      tmp = this["B"+i].vy;
      this["B"+i].vy = (this["B"+j].mass*(2*this["B"+j].vy-this["B"+i].vy)+
            ➥ this["B"+i].mass*this["B"+i].vy)/(this["B"+i].mass+this["B"+j].mass);
      this["B"+j].vy = this["B"+i].vy+tmp-this["B"+j].vy;
      tmp = this["B"+i].vx;
      this["B"+i].vz = (this["B"+j].mass*(2*this["B"+j].vz-this["B"+i].vz)+
            ➥ this["B"+i].mass*this["B"+i].vz)/(this["B"+i].mass+this["B"+j].mass);
      this["B"+j].vz = this["B"+i].vz+tmp-this["B"+j].vz;
     }
    }
   }
   this["B"+i].Set3DPos();
  }
  for (i=0; i<lnum; i++) {
   this["L"+i].Set3DPos();
  }
}
```

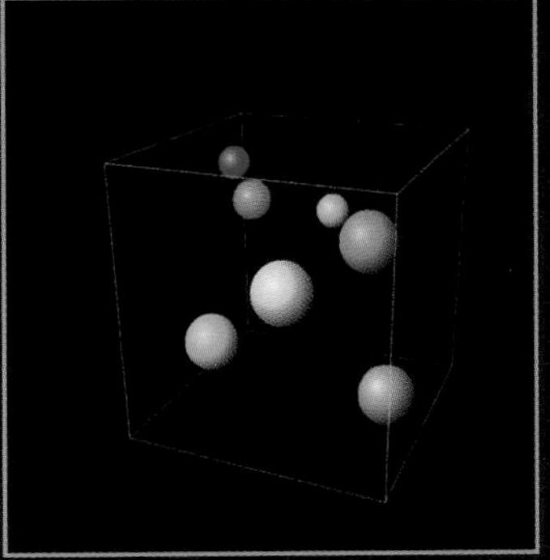
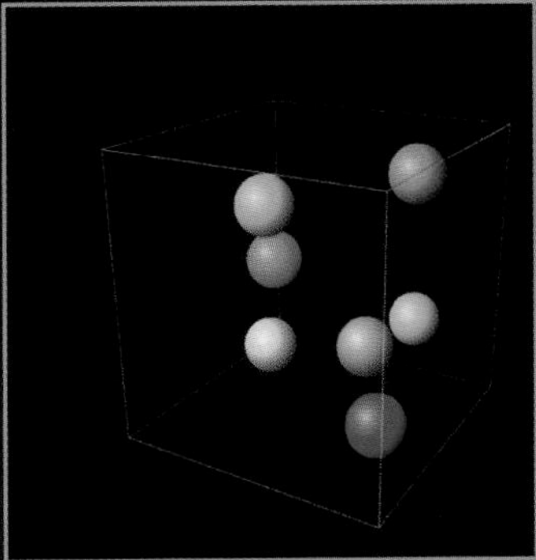
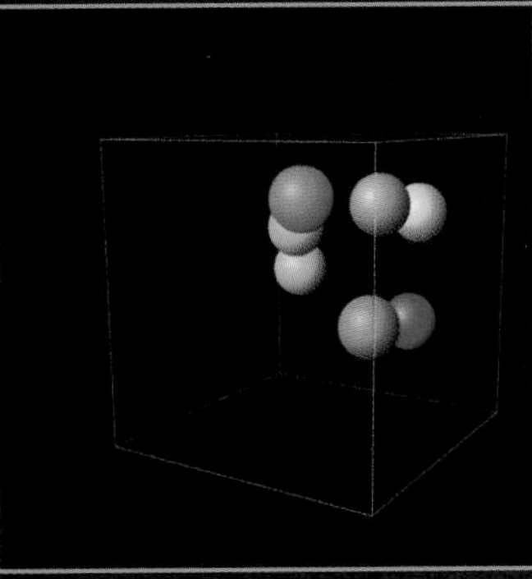

The next block of code is attached to the movieclip `B0`:

```
onClipEvent (load) {
   function len (sibl) {
    return Math.sqrt(
     (x-sibl.x)*(x-sibl.x)+
     (y-sibl.y)*(y-sibl.y)(z-sibl.z)*(z-sibl.z));
   }
   function Set3DPos () {
    pnt.x = x; pnt.y = y; pnt.z = z;
    _parent.Rot(pnt);
    var k = _parent.VPf/(_parent.VPf-pnt.z);
    _x = _parent.cx+_parent.sx*pnt.x*k;
    _y = _parent.cy-_parent.sy*pnt.y*k;
    _xscale = _parent.sx*radius*2*k;
    _yscale = _parent.sy*radius*2*k;
    this.swapDepths(int(pnt.z*1000)+100000);
   }
   function NextStep () {
    x += vx;
    y += vy;
    z += vz;
    if (x<-_parent.LS+radius) {vx=-vx; x=-_parent.LS+radius;}
    if (x>_parent.LS-radius) {vx=-vx; x=_parent.LS-radius;}
    if (y<-_parent.LS+radius) {vy=-vy; y=-_parent.LS+radius;}
    if (y>_parent.LS-radius) {vy=-vy; y=_parent.LS-radius;}
    if (z<-_parent.LS+radius) {vz=-vz; z=-_parent.LS+radius;}
    if (z>_parent.LS-radius) {vz=-vz; z=_parent.LS-radius;}
   }
   radius = 2;
   mass = 1;
   pnt = new Object();
}
```

And finally the code for our line movieclip `L0`:

```
onClipEvent (load) {
   function Set3DPos () {
    pnt1.x = _parent.pline[id][0]*_parent.LS;
    pnt1.y = _parent.pline[id][1]*_parent.LS;
    pnt1.z = _parent.pline[id][2]*_parent.LS;
    pnt2.x = _parent.pline[id][3]*_parent.LS;
    pnt2.y = _parent.pline[id][4]*_parent.LS;
    pnt2.z = _parent.pline[id][5]*_parent.LS;
    _parent.Rot(pnt1);
    _parent.Rot(pnt2);
    _x=_parent.cx+_parent.sx*pnt1.x*_parent.VPf/(_parent.VPf-pnt1.z);
    _y=_parent.cy-_parent.sy*pnt1.y*_parent.VPf/(_parent.VPf-pnt1.z);
    _xscale=_parent.cx+_parent.sx*pnt2.x*_parent.VPf/(_parent.VPf-pnt2.z)-_x;
    _yscale=_parent.cy-_parent.sy*pnt2.y*_parent.VPf/(_parent.VPf-pnt2.z)-_y;
    this.swapDepths(int((pnt1.z+pnt2.z)*3000)+100000);
    gotoAndStop (int((pnt1.z+pnt2.z+20)/4));
   }
   pnt1 = new Object();
   pnt2 = new Object();
}
```

In the code that we attach to the `Ball` movie, the code duplicates the `B0` and `V0` movieclips. The `Ball` movie calculates all the duplicates parameters, such as position, velocity and direction. This experiment models the physics of solid interaction. Each solid ball has a mass and radius. On the collision of two balls, the first ball changes its position and changes its velocity and second ball's velocity. Figure 2 illustrates this step by step.

The key variables and functions

The `_root.Ball` variables and functions

`ax`, `ay` = the two directions of camera rotation around the box (See figure 1)
`sin1`, `cos1` = the sine and cosine of `ay`
`sin2`, `cos2` = the sine and cosine of `ax`
`VPf` = the distance from the camera (View Point) to the center (0, 0, 0)
`cx`, `cy` = the coordinates of image center on the screen.
`sx`, `sy` = the image scale coefficients for x and y
`Rot(p)` = the function to rotate point `p` around `Oy` to an angle defined by `cos2` and `sin2`, and then rotate the point around `Ox` to an angle defined by `cos1` and `sin1`
`bnum` = the number of balls
`lnum` = the number of lines (all the lines are `(A,B)`, `(B,C)`, `(C,D)`, `(D,A)`, `(E,F)`, `(F,G)`, `(G,H)`, `(H,E)`, `(A,E)`, `(B,F)`, `(C,G)` and `(D,E)` – see figure 1 for details).
`LS` = the line scale factor
`pline` = an array of lines coordinates. Each element contains the first and second point of the line

The `_root.Ball.B0` variables and functions

`radius` = the ball radius
`mass` = the ball mass
`pnt` = a temporary object
`Len(sibl)` = the return distance between this ball and `sibl` ball. `Sibl` is a movieclip `BN`, where `N` is number from 0 to `bnum-1`
`Set3DPos()` = the function to change clip parameters (`_x`, `_y`, `_xscale`, `_yscale`) and change the movieclip depth
`NextStep()` = the function to change the 3D location of the ball

Many of the parameters can be changed. For example, if `LS` is set to 15, then the box will be larger. If `vx`, `vy` and/or `vz` are changed in the function `NextStep`, then the balls will fly in space due to the gravitational force. It is possible to create law of gravity between balls, and so on.

In the files `balls_1.swf` to `balls_8.swf`, you'll find iterations of this basic effect. Take a look at what variables I've altered in each file and see what the impacts are on the end result. Obviously you're not limited to the changes I've made. Try changing some variables and see what effect they have.

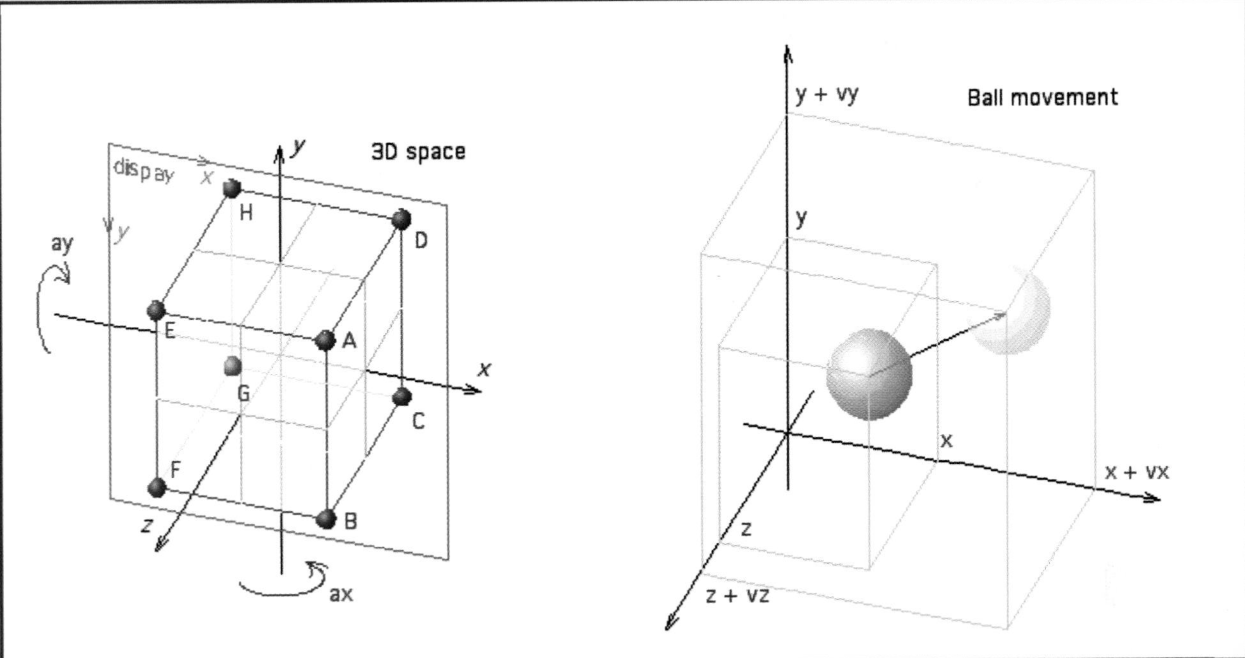

figure 1

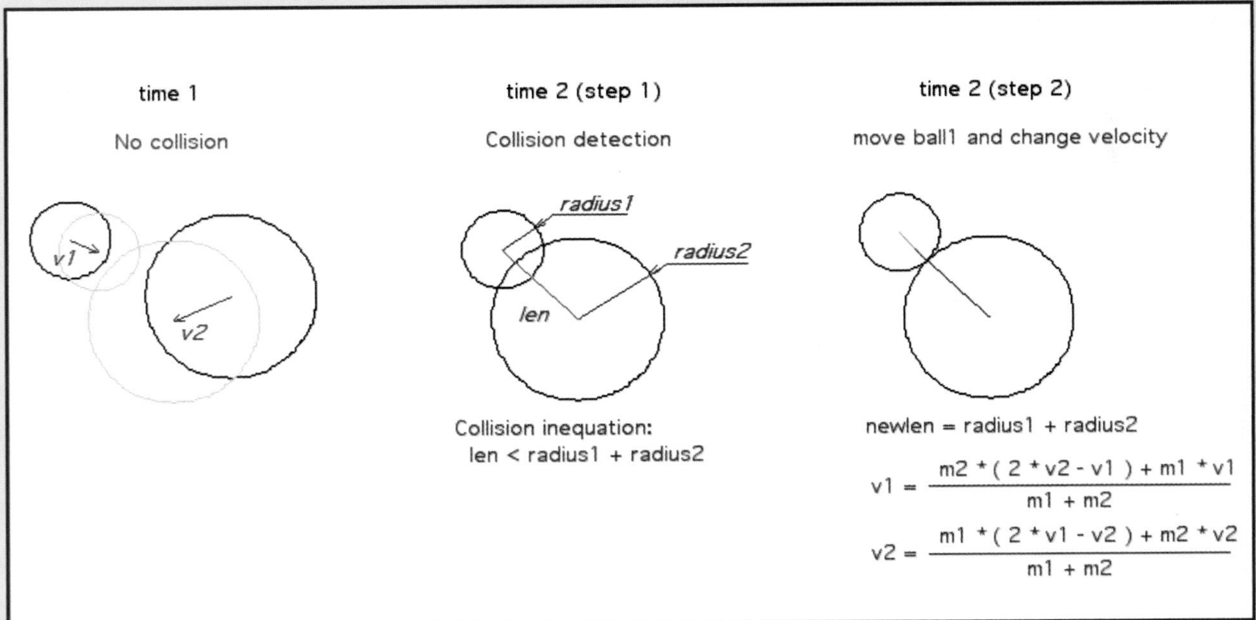

figure 2

Rings

This creates a crazy 3D effect of a sphere moving through a horizontal circle made up of vertical circles. That's not the best description though, so check out `Ring_0.swf` to see what I mean.

The main stage of the movie contains a single movieclip named **Ball**. Within the **Ball** clip live two clips given instance names **RO** and **S**. The movie **R0** itself contains another movieclip called **C**. The **C** clip contains a ring shape that forms the basis of the end visual effect. You can find the code for this file in `Ring_0.fla`.

Frame 1 of Scene 1 contains the following code that is the only code on the main stage itself:

```
for (i=0; i<5; i++) {
   duplicateMovieClip ("Ball", "B"+i, i);
   this["B"+i].timer = -i*10;
}
stop ();
```

The next block of code is attached to the **Ball** clip.

```
onClipEvent (load) {
   rnd1 = 10+random(10);
   rnd2 = 10+random(10);
   rnd3 = 10+random(10);
   rnd4 = 7+random(7);
   rnd5 = 7+random(7);
   VPf = 150;
   centerx = 320;
   centery = 240;
   pnt = new Object();
   pnt0 = new Object();
   pnt1 = new Object();
   pnt2 = new Object();
   _xscale = 100;
   _yscale = 100;
   duplicateMovieClip ("R0", "R1", 1);
   duplicateMovieClip ("R0", "R2", 2);

   function Prf (p) {
    p.x = centerx + p.x * VPf / (VPf - p.z);
    p.y = centery - p.y * VPf / (VPf - p.z);
   }

   function Rot (p, cos1, sin1, cos2, sin2) {
    var x=p.x, y;
    p.x = cos1 * x - sin1 * p.y;
    y   = sin1 * x + cos1 * p.y;
    p.y = cos2 * y - sin2 * p.z;
    p.z = sin2 * y + cos2 * p.z;
   }

   function Set3DPos ( x, y, z, a1, a2 ) {
    pnt.x = x; pnt.y = y; pnt.z = z;
    pnt0.x = 1; pnt0.y = 0; pnt0.z = 0;
    pnt1.x = 0; pnt1.y = 1; pnt1.z = 0;
    pnt2.x = 0; pnt2.y = 0; pnt2.z = 1;
    cos1 = Math.cos(a1);
    sin1 = Math.sin(a1);
    cos2 = Math.cos(a2);
    sin2 = Math.sin(a2);
    rot (pnt0, cos1, sin1, cos2, sin2);
    rot (pnt1, cos1, sin1, cos2, sin2);
    rot (pnt2, cos1, sin1, cos2, sin2);
    pnt0.x += x; pnt0.y += y; pnt0.z += z;
    pnt1.x += x; pnt1.y += y; pnt1.z += z;
    pnt2.x += x; pnt2.y += y; pnt2.z += z;
    Prf (pnt);
    Prf (pnt0);
    Prf (pnt1);
    Prf (pnt2);
```

```
      R0.SetPos(pnt.x, pnt.y,pnt0.x-pnt.x, -pnt0.y+pnt.y,pnt1.x-
       ➥pnt.x, -pnt1.y+pnt.y);
      R1.SetPos(pnt.x, pnt.y,pnt1.x-pnt.x, -pnt1.y+pnt.y,pnt2.x-
       ➥pnt.x, -pnt2.y+pnt.y);
      R2.SetPos(pnt.x, pnt.y,pnt2.x-pnt.x, -pnt2.y+pnt.y,pnt0.x-
       ➥pnt.x, -pnt0.y+pnt.y);
      S.SetPos(pnt.x, pnt.y, VPf/(VPf-z));
      this.swapDepths(int(z*10+5000));
     }
  }

  onClipEvent (enterFrame) {
     timer++;
     Set3DPos(56 * Math.cos(timer / rnd1 + 2), 56 * Math.cos( timer /
      ➥ rnd2 ), 56 * Math.cos(timer / rnd3 + 1), timer / rnd4, timer / rnd5);
  }
```

We also attach code to the `R0` clip that lives with `Ball`:

```
  onClipEvent (load) {
     function SetPos (px, py, a1, b1, a2, b2) {
      k1 = Math.atan2(b2-a1, a2+b1);
      k2 = Math.atan2(b2+a1, a2-b1);
      alpha = 0.5 * ( k1 + k2 );
      phy   = 0.5 * ( k1 - k2 );
      if ( Math.sin(k1) == 0 || Math.sin(k2) == 0 ) {
       sx = 0.5 * ((a2+b1) / Math.cos(k1) + (a2-b1) / Math.cos(k2));
       sy = 0.5 * ((a2+b1) / Math.cos(k1) - (a2-b1) / Math.cos(k2));
      } else {
       sx = 0.5 * ((b2-a1) / Math.sin(k1) + (b2+a1) / Math.sin(k2));
       sy = 0.5 * ((b2-a1) / Math.sin(k1) - (b2+a1) / Math.sin(k2));
      }
      R._rotation = phy * (-180) / Math.PI;
      _xscale = sx * 100;
      _yscale = sy * 100;
      _rotation = alpha * (-180) / Math.PI;
      _x = px;
      _y = py;
     }
     clr = new Color(_target);
  }
```

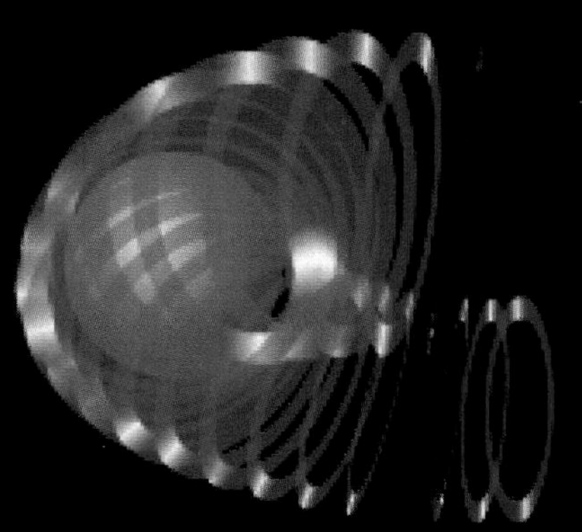

Our final section of code is attached to the `S` movieclip.

```
  onClipEvent (load) {
     function SetPos (px, py, scale) {
      _xscale = scale * 100;
      _yscale = scale * 100;
      _x = px;
      _y = py;
     }
  }
```

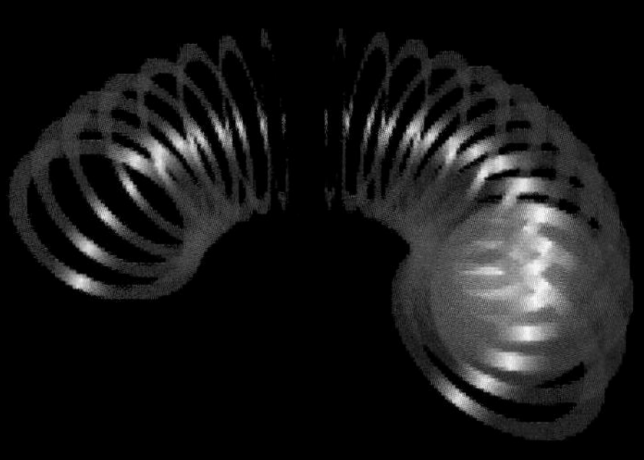

The code starts by creating five duplicates of the `Ball` movieclip. Each ball moves itself separately. The trace of each ball is a Lissajous figure. `Ball` contains three rings, which spins around ball. Figure 1 shows the ring's transformation from movieclip coordinate space to 3D space. We needs 3 points to locate one ring, but only four points are needed to locate three rings as figure 1 on the next page shows. Only 4 points are projected. This is not a precision 3D projection, just a look-a-like faux-3D projection.

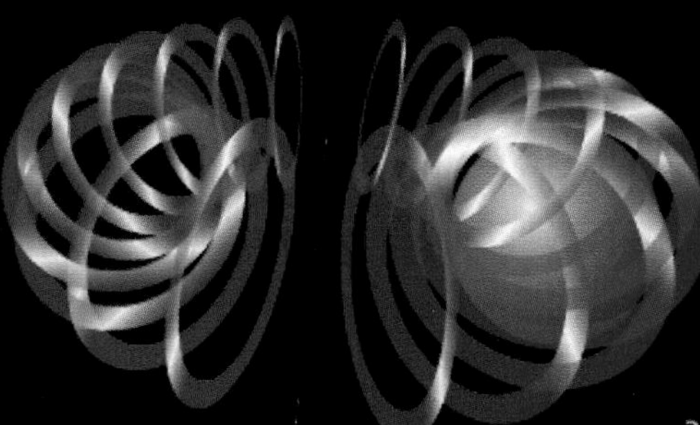

The key variables and functions

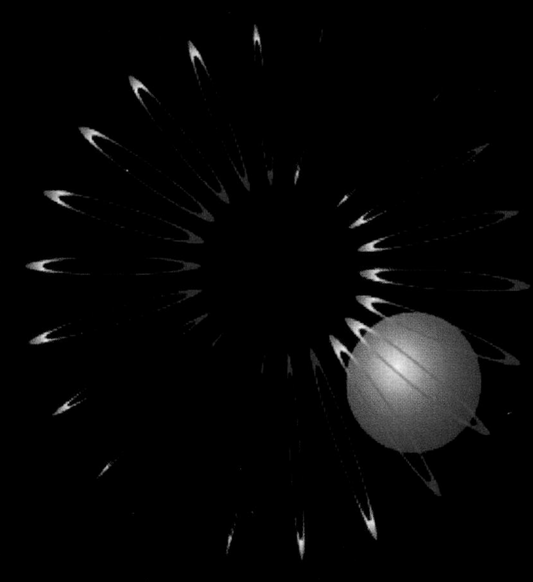

`_root.Ball` variables and functions

`rnd1`, `rnd2`, `rnd3` = the x, y, and z parameters used for the Lissajous figure. `RndN` is the scale factor used on the timer `counter` when it is put into the `cos()` equation
`rnd4`, `rnd5` = the rotation speed of the ball
`VPf` = the distance from the camera (View Point) to the 3D shape
`centerx`, `centerty` = the coordinates of image center on the screen
`pnt`, `pnt0`, `pnt1`, `pnt2` = temporary 3D points (object `this` x, y and z properties)
`PrF(p)` = a function which projects a point `p(x, y, z)` to the plane `Oxy` from `ViewPoint(0,0, VPf)`, and then returns the result to itself as `p(x, y)`
`Rot(p, cos1, sin1, cos2, sin2)` = a function to rotate the point `p` around `Ox` to an angle defined by `cos1` and `sin1`, and then rotate point around `Oz` to an angle defined by `cos2` and `sin2`
`Set3DPos(x, y, z, a1, a2)` = a function that moves the movieclips `R0`, `R1`, `R2` and `S`
`x`, `y`, `z` = the ball center coordinates
`a1`, `a2` = the ball rotation

`_root.Ball.R0` variables and functions

`SetPos(px, py, a1, b1, a2, b2)` = a function to change clip parameters (`_rotation`, `_xscale`, `_yscale`, `_x`, `_y`):
  `py` = screen coordinates of a ring (shape center – point a) (see figure 1)
  `(px+a1, py+b1)` = the screen coordinates of a ring (point b) (see figure 1)
  `(px+a2, py+b2)` = the screen coordinates of a ring (point c) (see figure 1)
  `k1`, `k2`, `alpha`, `phy`, `sx`, `sy` = temporary variables in function body

Figure 1

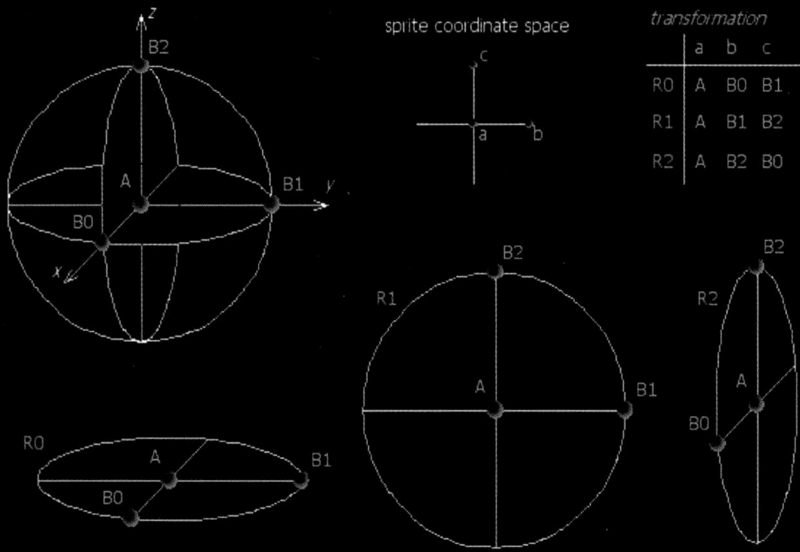

	a	b	c
R0	A	B0	B1
R1	A	B1	B2
R2	A	B2	B0

This is a nice little vehicle for some great effects. By playing with the variables we can take this effect and move it to another level. A good example of this can be seen in the `Ring_4.fla` file. Take a look at this and the other iterations and you'll see how the basic model we've got above can easily be developed into something quite stunning.

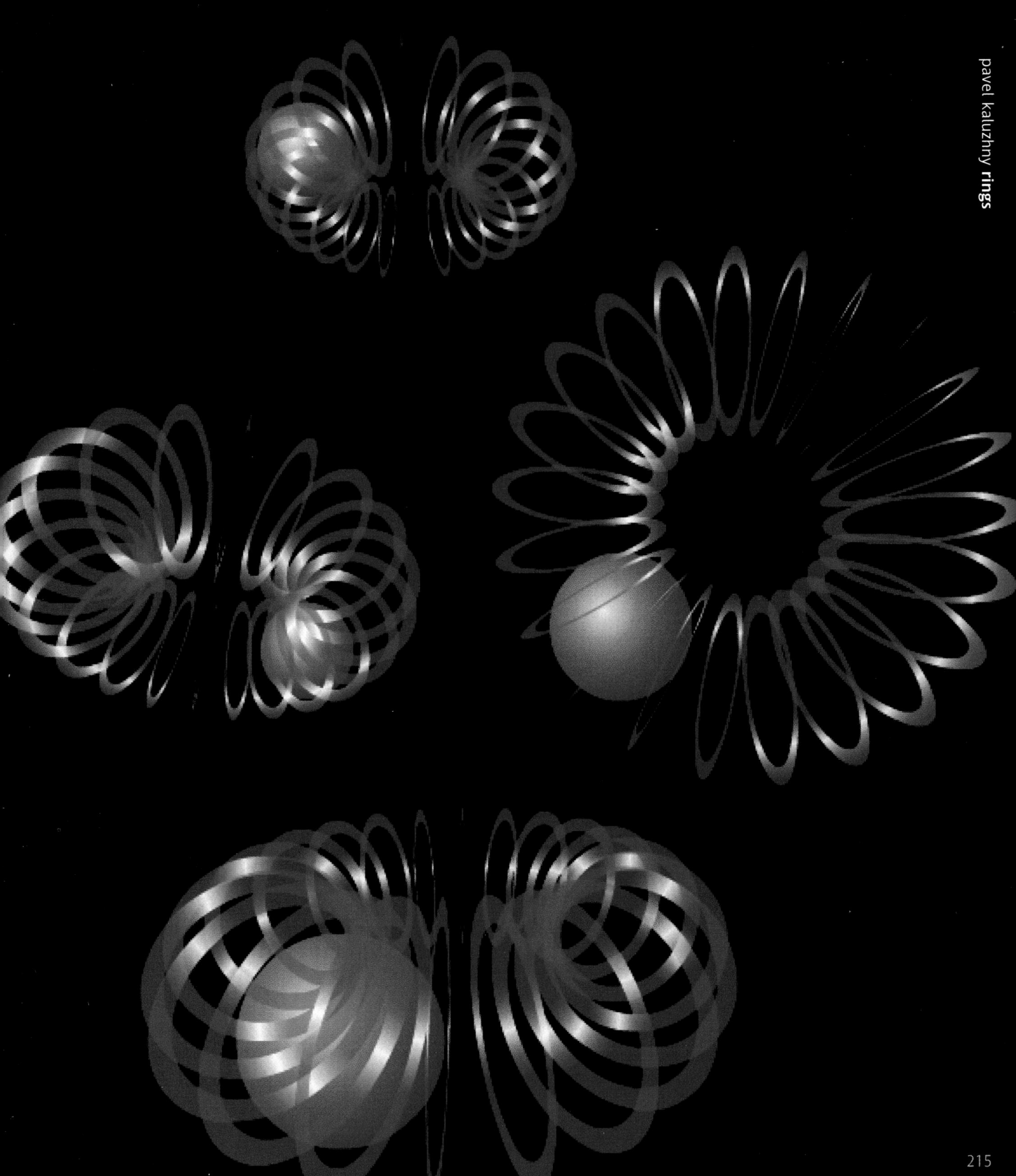

3D Text

This effect will create the illusion of 3D text, which you map over a surface or animate. The results of the code listed can be seen in the file `txt_I_0.fla`. Let's look at what that file consists of.

The main stage contains a movieclip called `3D text` with an instance name `Text3D`. `Text3D` contains a movieclip called `3DChar` (instance name `char`), which itself contains a movieclip called `char` (instance name `c`). `c` contains one dynamic text field associated with variable also called `c`.

Let's see the code that creates this great effect. We'll start with the code that sits in frame 1 of Scene1:

```
inputText += "You may type  any" + "\n";
inputText += "text. This is" + "\n";
inputText += "3D-shape of text" + "\n";
inputText += "and other symbols." + "\n";
inputText += "cool text effect" + "\n";
```

There is also some code on frame 2:

```
Text3D.SetText(inputText);
stop ();
```

That's all the code for the main timeline, so we'll now add the code that we attach to our various clips.

This code is attached to the `Text3D` instance:

```
onClipEvent (load) {
 VPf = 260;
 centerx = 160;
 centery = 120;
 pnt = new Object();
 pnt1 = new Object();
 pnt2 = new Object();
 Char._visible = 0;
 _xscale = 200;
 _yscale = 200;

 function FsF (u, v, p) {
  p.x = (u - 8)*10;
  p.y = (4-v)*7+Math.cos(Math.sqrt((u-8)*(u-8)+(3-v)*(3-v))/2+timer/4)*18;
  p.z = (v-4)*10;
 }
 function Prf (p) {
  p.x = centerx + p.x * VPf / (VPf - p.z);
  p.y = centery - p.y * VPf / (VPf - p.z);
 }


 function SetText ( str ) {
  for ( i=0; this["C"+i]._visible != undefined; i++ ) {
   removeMovieClip ("C"+i);
  }
  x = 0;
  y = 0;
  num = 0;
  for ( i=0; i<str.length; i++ ) {
   ch = substring(str, i+1, 1);
   if ( ord(ch) > 0x20 ) {
     duplicateMovieClip ("Char", "C"+num, num);
     this["C"+num].u = x;
     this["C"+num].v = y;
     this["C"+num].C.c = ch;
     this["C"+num]._visible = 0;
     num++;
     x++;
   } else if ( ch == " " ) {
     x++;
   }
```

```
      if ( ord(ch) < 0x20 ) {
        y+=1.5;
        x = 0;
      }
     }
   }

   function UpdateView () {
    for ( i=0; this["C"+i]._visible != undefined; i++ ) {
      this["C"+i]._visible = 1;
      FsF(this["C"+i].u, this["C"+i].v, pnt);
      FsF(this["C"+i].u, this["C"+i].v+1, pnt1);
      FsF(this["C"+i].u+1, this["C"+i].v, pnt2);
      c = (int(128+(pnt.y + pnt.z*0.7)*3) & 0xFF);
      c = (c << 16) | (c << 8) | 0xFF;
      this["C"+i].clr.setRGB(c);
      PrF(pnt);
      PrF(pnt1);
      PrF(pnt2);
      this["C"+i].SetPos(pnt.x,pnt.y,pnt1.x-pnt.x,-pnt1.y+pnt.y,
          ➥ pnt2.x-pnt.x, -pnt2.y+pnt.y)
    }
   }

 }
 onClipEvent (enterFrame) {
   timer++;
   UpdateView();
 }
```

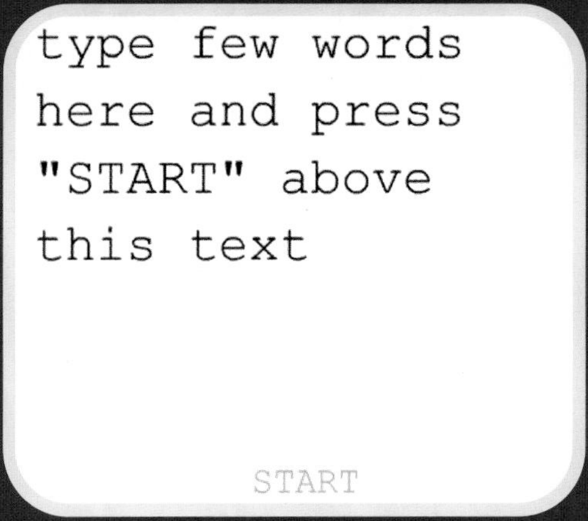

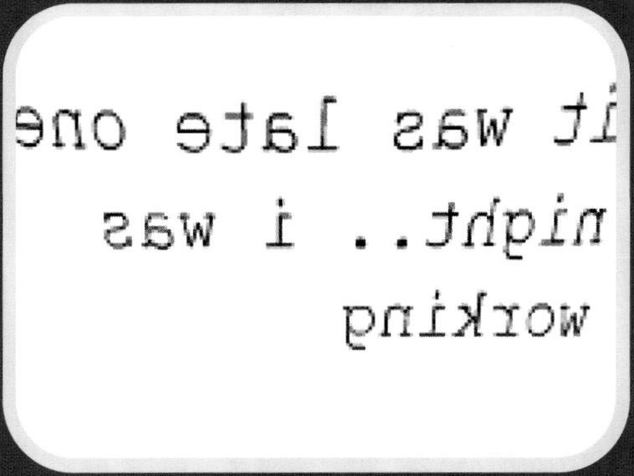

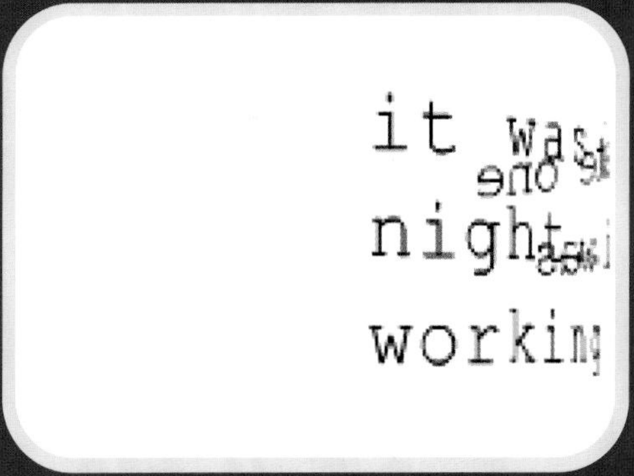

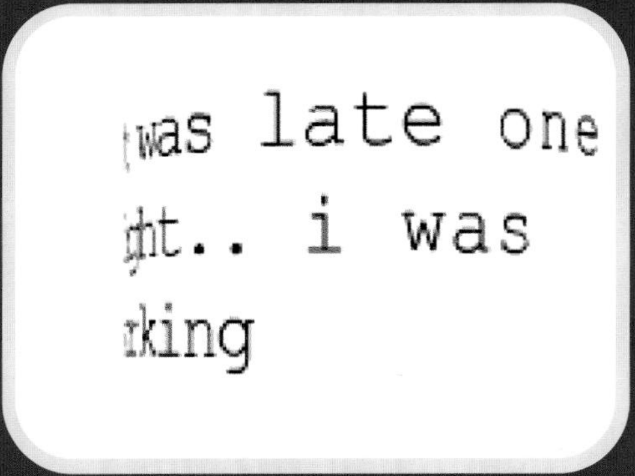

This code sits inside a movieclip called `3Dchar` that we gave the instance name `Char`:

```
 onClipEvent (load) {
   function SetPos (px, py, a1, b1, a2, b2) {
    k1 = Math.atan2(b2-a1, a2+b1);
    k2 = Math.atan2(b2+a1, a2-b1);
    alpha = 0.5 * ( k1 + k2 );
    phy   = 0.5 * ( k1 - k2 );
    if ( Math.sin(k1) == 0 || Math.sin(k2) == 0 ) {
     sx = 0.5*((a2+b1) / Math.cos(k1) + (a2-b1) / Math.cos(k2));
     sy = 0.5*((a2+b1) / Math.cos(k1) - (a2-b1) / Math.cos(k2));
    } else {
     sx = 0.5*((b2-a1) / Math.sin(k1) + (b2+a1) / Math.sin(k2));
     sy = 0.5*((b2-a1) / Math.sin(k1) - (b2+a1) / Math.sin(k2));
    }
    C._rotation = phy * (-180) / Math.PI;
    _xscale = sx * 100 / 24;
    _yscale = sy * 100 / 24;
    _rotation = alpha * (-180) / Math.PI;
    _x = px;
    _y = py;
   }
   clr = new Color(_target);
 }
```

The code just divides the input text into the single symbols. Each symbol has text field space coordinates and 3D space coordinates (see figure 1). `Text3D` updates parameters on the enter frame. Each symbol transforms itself, as can be seen at the bottom of figure 1.

figure 1

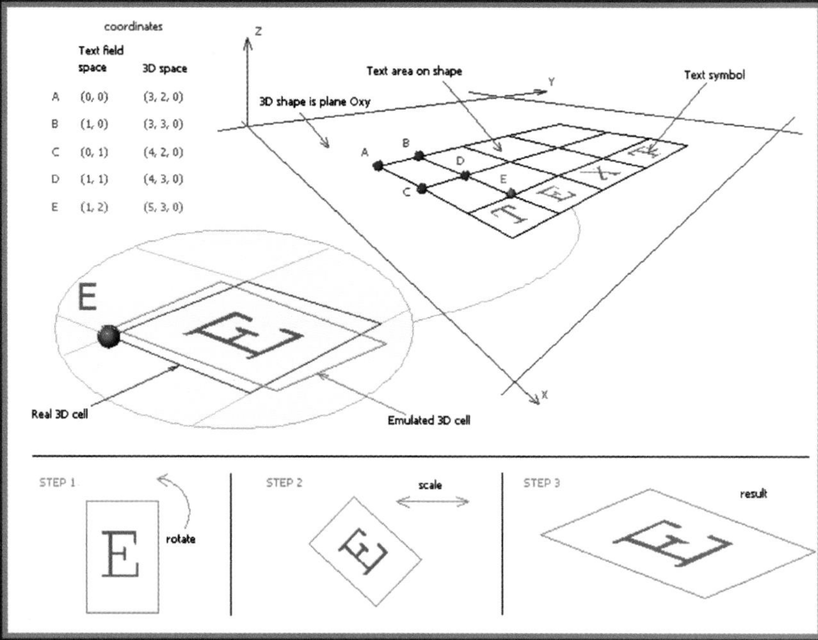

The key variables and functions

`_root` variables

`InputText` = the main text for effect, available for changing

`_root.Text3D` variables and functions

`VPf` = the distance from the camera (View Point) to the 3D-shape
`centerx`, `centerty` = the coordinates of the image center on the screen
`pnt`, `pnt1`, `pnt2` = temporary 3D points (object `this` x, y and z properties)
`FsF(u, v, p)` = a function to determine the 3D shape. The function takes `(u, v)` coordinates of text field space and return point `p` in 3D space. Figure1 shows points coordinates in Text field space and coordinates in 3D space
`PrF(p)` = a function that projects point `p(x, y, z)` to the plane `Oxy` from View Point `(0,0, VPf)`, and returns result to itself: `p(x, y)`
`SetText (str)` = a function that creates or updates symbols. At first it remove all old objects, and it then duplicates new movieclips from `Char`. Variables `x` and `y` are `u` and `v` coordinates in text field space
`UpdateView()` = a function that draws the image. It changes each symbol's parameters

`_root.Text3D.Char` variables and functions

`clr` = a color or symbol
`SetPos(px, py, a1, b1, a2, b2)` = a function to change clip parameters (`_rotation`, `_xscale`, `_yscale`, `_x`, `_y`)
`px`, `py` = the screen coordinates of a symbol (left top corner)
`(px+a1, py+b1)` = the screen coordinates of a symbol (right top corner)
`(px+a2, py+b2)` = the screen coordinates of a symbol (left bottom corner)
`k1`, `k2`, `alpha`, `phy`, `sx`, `sy` = temporary variables in the function's body

Take a look at the other files to see how diverse the output can be just be changing a few variables here and there.

We can expand on this initial FLA by making simple code changes. Take a look at my sample files for inspiration. You can even create a SWF where you enter what text you'd like to transform into the SWF and the movie displays it on a 3D wave for you (**`txt_IV_0.swf`**).

Где пьется, там

Где пьют, там и льют

Где раки зимуют

Где родился, там и пригодился

Где рука, там и голова

Где сердце лежит, туда и око бежит

Где слова привета, там улыбка для ответа

Где слова редки, там они вески

Где слуги в шелках, там баре в долгах

Где совет, там и свет

Где суд - там и неправда водится

Где сядешь - там и слезешь

Где тонко - там и рвется

Где тонко, там и рвется

Где тонко, тут и рвется, а где худо, ту

Где ум, там и толк

Где хозяи ходит, там земля хлеб родит

Герой - с дырой

Гладко было на бумаге, да забыли про о

Гладко было на бумаге, да забыли про ов

Глаза боятся (страшатся), а руки делают

Глаза бояться, а руки делают

Глаза завидущи, а руки загребущи

Глаза по ложке, а не видят ни крошки

Глаза страшат, а руки делают

Глазам стыдно, а душа радуется

Глас народа - глас Божий

Глубокая вода не мутиться

й киснет, а умный всё промыслит

ит, а умный рассудит

бедни н

After graduating from design school in 2000, I started the Fourm Design Studio with 3 close friends. Since then, I have been dedicated to educating and inspiring audiences through interactive experiences. I am constantly learning, probing and absorbing information and insight to bring into my own work. Above all, I enjoy solving problems, whether working with a client or on a side project. In my spare time, I have been working on several time-consuming projects such as infourm.com, gridplane.com, miniml.com, and have recently been collaborating on installations for a conceptual art gallery in Milwaukee.

I am inspired by what is living, breathing, and inherently based upon solid structure. In the past year, I have focused primarily on creating intuitive interfaces. My main concentration has been navigation. Things that have inspired me lately are math, music, the science of numbers and patterns, the possibilities of ActionScript, and of course my friends and peers in the industry who are pushing boundaries. More and more I find myself turning off the television, going outside, listening to music, taking photographs, reading books, paying more attention to the mundane, and soaking up the tangible world.

jd hooge

gridplane.com

Terraforming

This set of four movies contain all of the controls that you'll need to alter the values in them in real-time. That isn't to say that you can't go in and fiddle with the code, I'll give you some suggestions for that later, but there should be enough there to keep you busy for a while.

There are three layers on the main timeline: `code`, `objects`, and `grid`. The `code` layer contains the majority of the code for the movie, but there will also be some in a couple of other movieclips. The `objects` layer contains the interface elements of the movie, all of the sliders, buttons, and labels, it also contains a movieclip with function calls in it that will update and draw the graphics every frame. The `grid` layer contains a movieclip with a grid in it, it's wrapped in a movieclip so that we can control the alpha of it with a slider allowing us to fade it in and out.

I'll explain the main areas of code here and look at what they do, but please check the FLA for the layout of the controls, and the construction details of the buttons and movieclips.

Here's the code for frame 1 of the root timeline:

```
// ==============  initialize a few things
fscommand ("allowscale", "false");
fscommand ("fullscreen", "true");
_quality = "LOW";
pressed = 1;
label = 0;
timer = 10;
bar1.drag._x=15
bar2.drag._x=50
// ==============  attach points and lines
for (i=1; i<10; i++) {
   attachMovie("pointclip", "point"+i, i*1000);
   this["point"+i]._x = 200;
   this["point"+i]._y = 0;
}
for (i=1; i<9; i++) {
   attachMovie("lineclip", "line"+i, i+50);
}
// ==============  draw and connect lines
function drawLine () {
   for (i=1; i<9; i++) {
     this["line"+i]._x = this["point"+i]._x;
     this["line"+i]._y = this["point"+i]._y;
     this["line"+i]._xscale = this["point"+(i+1)]._x-this["point"+i]._x;
     this["line"+i]._yscale = this["point"+(i+1)]._y-this["point"+i]._y;
   }
}
// ==============  trace the original lines
function traceLines () {
   if (j<control3) {
     j++;
   } else {
     j = 0;
   }
   // attach new lines
   for (i=1; i<9; i++) {
     this.attachMovie("traceclip", "L"+i+"_"+j, j+(i*100));
   }
   // set the position, scale, and alpha of new lines
   for (i=1; i<10; i++) {
     this["L"+i+"_"+j]._x = this["line"+i]._x;
     this["L"+i+"_"+j]._y = this["line"+i]._y;
     this["L"+i+"_"+j]._xscale = this["line"+i]._xscale;
     this["L"+i+"_"+j]._yscale = this["line"+i]._yscale;
     this["L"+i+"_"+j]._alpha = 50;
     // set color of new lines
     new Color(this["L"+(i-1)+"_"+j]).setRGB(R << 16 | G << 8 | B);
     R=90, G=190, B=70+(i*20);
   }
}
// ===============  set up the controls
function controls () {
   control1 = bar1.drag._x/100;
   control2 = bar2.drag._x/100;
   control3 = bar3.drag._x;
   control4 = bar4.drag._x;
}
```

The next important piece of code is on frame 1 of the `clip_Point` movieclip:

```
display = _name.substring(5);
function move () {
   // set accel and elast equal to their sliders
   accel = _root.bar1.drag._x/100;
   elast = _root.bar2.drag._x/100;
   if (i<timer && Math.abs(_y-yn)>3) {
     i++;
   } else {
     // When i catches up with timer,
     // set new destinations for all points
     if (_root.pressed) {
      yn = 140;
     } else {
      yn = (random(5)+1)*60;
     }
     xn = -50+(Number(display)*50);
     i = 0;
     timer = random(20)+10;
   }
   // position _x
   _x -= x=(x+(_x-xn)*accel)*elast;
   // position _y
   _y -= y=(y+(_y-yn)*accel)*elast;
   // toggle labels
   if (_root.label) {
     label._visible = 1;
   } else {
     label._visible = 0;
   }
}
```

The final piece of code that we'll look at is attached to the `Run_Functions` movieclip that sits on the main stage. It looks like this:

```
onClipEvent (enterFrame) {
   for (c=1; c<10; c++) {
     if (Math.abs(_parent["Point"+c]._xmouse)>20 || Math.abs(_parent["Point"+c]._ymouse)>10) {
      _parent["Point"+c].move();
     } else {
     }
   }
   _parent.drawLine();
   _parent.traceLines();
   _parent.controls();
}
```

The rest of the code is just button and slider code, so I won't go into that here, take a look in the FLA to see what it does.

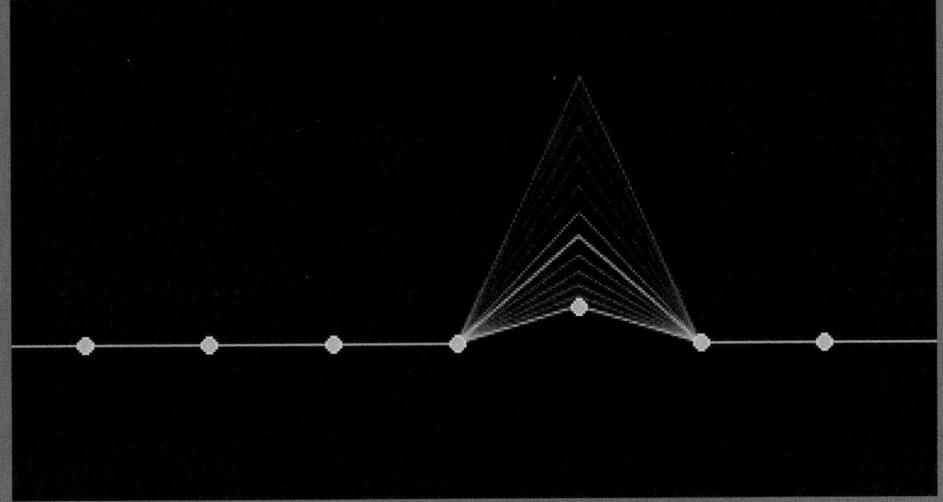

The key variables, functions, and components

clip_Point = the anchor point for the lines
clip_Line = the line that connects the points
clip_Trace = the line that create the trails
pressed = a toggle for the auto-run button, 1 means it's off, 0 means it's on
label = a toggle for the point labels, 1 means they're there, 0 means they're not
timer = the time it takes for a point to change direction, updated as a random number later on
bar1 = the acceleration slider
bar2 = the elasticity slider
bar3 = the number of trails slider
bar4 = the grid alpha slider
pointclip = the linkage name of **clip_Point** in the Library
lineclip = the linkage name of **clip_Line** in the Library
drawLine = a function to scale and position the new lines
traceLines = a function to attach new movieclips to trace the original lines
control1 to control4 = variables containing the values of the **bar** clips of the same number
traceclip = the linkage name of **clip_Trace** in the Library

display = a dynamic text box inside **clip_Point** to display the number of the point – if the name of the clip is **point3**, then it counts along 5 (remember it starts from 0) and returns the number 3
move = a function to update the position of the current point
accel = the value of the acceleration slider
elast = the value of the elasticity slider
yn = the **y** destination of the point, if auto-run is not on then it's automatically set to the center, otherwise it's a random value
xn = the x destination of the point, each point has a fixed x position

So, here is how it works – first we create several points (attached from the Library) and place them in a row. We then create several lines (also attached from the Library) and use them to connect the points. Then whenever a point is moved up or down the lines to either side move with it to keep it connected to the next point, and we create another line at the same spot that sits where it is, fades out, and then removes itself. The creation and removal of these lines is what gives us our trailing effect. You can either drag the point around yourself, or set it to uto-run meaning that the points will automatically keep moving to random positions, leaving you free to play about with the various sliders.

The primary script (on frame 1 of the main timeline) does the following:

Attaches all the points and lines
Connects the points with the lines
Moves and scales all lines
Traces the original lines
Colors the tracer lines
Sets up the controls

The secondary script (on frame 1 of **clip_Point**) does the following:

Moves the points based on random calculations
Toggles the labels on/off

I have given default values for the controls that create a very fluid motion. However, there are many different aspects that you could change to get different types of motion. For instance, if you turn the **accel** way down and the elast way up, you will start to get images resembling terraforming. If you turn up the amount of lines created, you will increase this effect. Things you could do manually are replacing the **clip_Trace** movieclip with a shape of some sort, or adding rotation to that clip. Also try changing the RGB values in the primary script, or removing the graphic of the point and the line to just leave the traced lines moving around the screen. Another thing to try is setting the **x** position to a similar random value to the **y** so that the lines can travel all round the screen.

Trailing lines

This experiment is similar to the last one, but with some distinct differences, run **exp_2.swf** to see what I mean. This time rather than having all of the points along one horizontal line, there is an axis in the center of the screen, and one point on each arm of the axis. I've also changed some of the sliders: there is no auto-run toggle for this experiment – it's always on, and there is an additional slider that controls the timer variable so you can set how often the points move. The set up on the main stage is similar, except I've added a new layer containing a background movieclip. This clip simply fades the background in when the movie begins.

As before, I'll attach all of the main code here, and then give an explanation of what each section does, and how it all works together.

Here's the code for the first frame of the root timeline:

```
// ==============  initialize a few things
fscommand ("allowscale", "false");
fscommand ("fullscreen", "true");
_quality = "LOW";
label = 0;
bar1.drag._x = 10;
bar2.drag._x = 77;
bar3.drag._x = 15;
bar4.drag._x = 15;
bar5.drag._x = 35;
// ==============  attach points and lines
for (i=1; i<5; i++) {
 attachMovie("pointclip", "point"+i, i+600);
 this["point"+i]._x = 200;
 this["point"+i]._y = 0;
 attachMovie("lineclip", "line"+i, i+50);
}
// ==============  draw and connect lines
function drawLine () {
 for (i=1; i<5; i++) {
  this["line"+i]._x = this["point"+i]._x;
  this["line"+i]._y = this["point"+i]._y;
  this["line"+i]._xscale = this["point"+(i+1)]._x-this["point"+i]._x;
  this["line"+i]._yscale = this["point"+(i+1)]._y-this["point"+i]._y;
 }
 line4._x = point4._x;
 line4._y = point4._y;
 line4._xscale = point1._x-Point4._x;
 line4._yscale = point1._y-Point4._y;
}
// ==============  trace the original lines
function traceLines () {
 if (j<control4) {
  j++;
 } else {
  j = 0;
 }
 // attach new lines
 for (i=1; i<5; i++) {
  this.attachMovie("traceclip", "L"+i+"_"+j, j+(i*100));
 }
 // set the position, scale, and alpha of new lines
 for (i=1; i<6; i++) {
  this["L"+i+"_"+j]._x = this["line"+i]._x;
  this["L"+i+"_"+j]._y = this["line"+i]._y;
  this["L"+i+"_"+j]._xscale = this["line"+i]._xscale;
  this["L"+i+"_"+j]._yscale = this["line"+i]._yscale;
  this["L"+i+"_"+j]._alpha = 50;
  // set color of new lines
  new Color(this["L"+(i-1)+"_"+j]).setRGB(R << 16 | G << 8 | B);
  R=90, G=190, B=70+(i*20);
 }
```

```
// ===============  set up the controls
function controls () {
 control1 = bar1.drag._x/100;
 control2 = bar2.drag._x/100;
 control3 = int(bar3.drag._x);
 control4 = int(bar4.drag._x);
 control5 = int(bar5.drag._x);

// ===============  run timer based on random
 timer = random(20)+control3;
}
```

Here's the code for the first frame of the `clip_Point` movieclip:

```
// ================ Displays the name
display = _name.substring(5);
// ================ Function that controls the movement
function move () {
 // set accel equal to the accel slider
 accel = _root.bar1.drag._x/100;
 // set elast equal to the elast slider
 elast = _root.bar2.drag._x/100;
 if (i<_root.timer) {
  i++;
 } else {
  // When i catches up with timer,
  // set new destinations for all 4 points
  if (display == 1) {
   // point 1
   yn = (random(8)+1)*20;
   xn = _root.xaxis._x;
  } else if (display == 2) {
   // point 2
   yn = _root.yaxis._y;
   xn = (random(8)+12)*20;
  } else if (display == 3) {
   // point 3
   yn = (random(8)+12)*20;
   xn = _root.xaxis._x;
  } else if (display == 4) {
   // point 4
   yn = _root.yaxis._y;
   xn = (random(8)+1)*20;
  }
  i = 0;
 }
 // ———————————————————
 // position _x
 _x -= x=(x+(_x-xn)*accel)*elast;
 // position _y
 _y -= y=(y+(_y-yn)*accel)*elast;
 // ———————————————————
 // toggle labels
 if (_root.label) {
  label._visible = 1;
  // on
 } else {
  label._visible = 0;
  // off
 }
}
```

And finally, here's the code on the Run_Functions clip on the main stage:

```
onClipEvent (enterFrame) {
 for (c=1; c<10; c++) {
  if (Math.abs(_parent["Point"+c]._xmouse)>20 || Math.abs(_parent["Point"+c]._ymouse)>10) {
  _parent["Point"+c].move();
   } else {
  }
 }
 _parent.drawLine();
 _parent.traceLines();
 _parent.controls();
}
```

The key variables, functions, and components

clip_Point = the anchor point for the lines
clip_Line = the line that connects the points
clip_Trace = the line that create the trails
label = a toggle for the point labels, 1 means they're there, 0 means they're not
bar1 = the acceleration slider
bar2 = the elasticity slider
bar3 = the timer slider
bar4 = the number of trails slider
bar5 = the grid alpha slider
pointclip = the linkage name of clip_Point in the Library
lineclip = the linkage name of clip_Line in the Library
drawLine = a function to scale and position the new lines
traceLines = a function to attach new movieclips to trace the original lines
traceclip = the linkage name of clip_Trace in the Library
control1 to control5 = variables containing the values of the bar clips of the same number
timer = the time it takes for a point to change direction

display = a dynamic text box inside clip_Point to display the number of the point – if the name of the clip is point3, then it counts along 5 (remember it starts from 0) and returns the number 3
move = a function to update the position of the current point
accel = the value of the acceleration slider
elast = the value of the elasticity slider
yn = the y destination of the point, set to a random value along the axis
xn = the x destination of the point, set to a random value along the axis

It works like this: first we create 4 points (attached from the Library, 2 are placed on the x-axis, and 2 on the y-axis). We then create 4 lines (also attached from the Library) and connect the points with the lines. Then we move the points along the x- and y-axis every frame. After that, all we do is create another line in the same spot of the original every time the frame loops. These lines don't move, so they create a trail behind the main moving line (they also fade out and remove themselves).

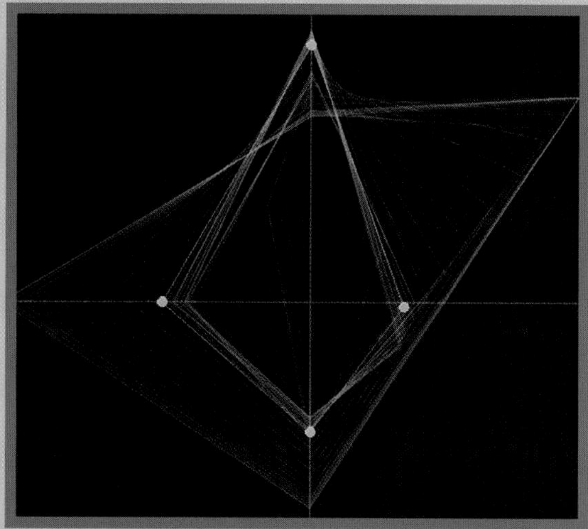

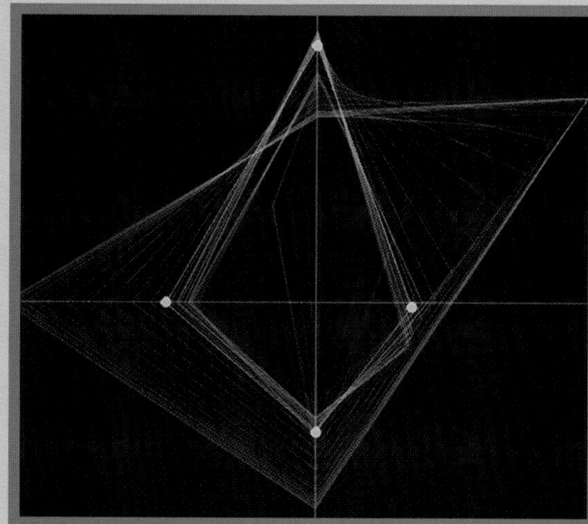

The primary script (on frame 1 of the main timeline) does the following:

Attaches all the points and lines
Connects the points with the lines
Moves and scales all lines
Traces the original lines
Colorizes the tracer lines
Sets up the controls

The secondary script (on frame 1 of `clip_Point`) does the following:

Moves the points based on random calculations
Toggles the labels on/off

As before, I have given default values for the controls to create a fluid motion. However, there are many different aspects that you could change to get different types of motion. I would suggest that you mess around with the controls for a good amount of time because there are many possible variations. Things you could do manually are replacing the `clip_Trace` movieclip with a shape of some sort, or adding a tween to it to bend the line or rotate it, even just replacing the hairline with a thick normal line and putting its alpha down a bit will give you some good results.

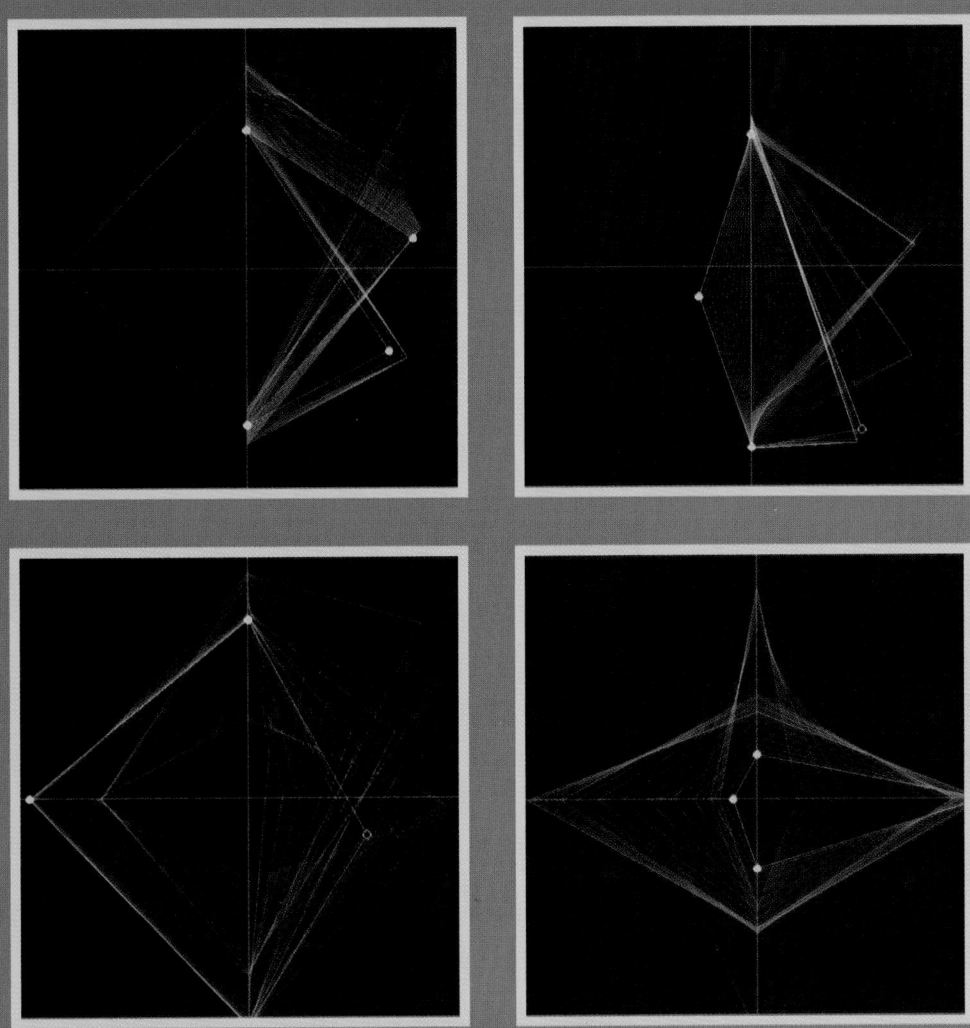

Elastic waves

This is a completely new effect, but it's based on some similar principles to the early experiments. This time rather than setting up trails of fading lines behind the originals, we're setting the points up in a line of vertical pairs, and joining each point in a pair together with a line. The points can then move along the y-axis depending on some bounds put upon them by the user with some new sliders on the left-hand side of the screen. If this experiment is set to auto-run then the expanding and contracting pairs will produce waveforms that can then be controlled with the sliders. The waves will move back and forth along the screen, bouncing back off each side and causing splashes of repercussions in the next wave.

The basic layer set-up is the same as before, but on the `objects` layer there are some new sliders on the left-hand side clustered around a bar. The left-most sliders control the base point of the wave – that is, the line that they oscillate around and will return to when they become still. To see the effect of this line, try turning auto-run off and then moving the sliders. The sliders on the right-hand side of the bar control the peak destination of the wave, the points can go above or below this depending on the acceleration, but this will be the average.

The main code for this is in the same three places as the other experiments, so I'll list it here as I did before. To start with, here's the code from the first frame of the main timeline:

```
// ==============  initialize a few things
fscommand ("allowscale", "false");
fscommand ("fullscreen", "true");
_quality = "LOW";
num = 39;
half = 19;
over = 0;
pressed = 1;
bar1.drag._x = 15;
bar2.drag._x = 90;
toggle = true;
// ==============  attach points and lines
for (i=1; i<half+1; i++) {
  attachMovie("pointclip", "p"+i, i*1000);
  this["p"+i]._x = 200;
  this["p"+i]._y = 120;
}
for (i=half+1; i<num; i++) {
  attachMovie("pointclip", "p"+i, i*1000);
  this["p"+i]._x = 200;
  this["p"+i]._y = 180;
}
for (i=1; i<20; i++) {
  attachMovie("lineclip", "line"+i, i+50);
}
// ==============  draw and connect lines
function drawLine () {
  for (i=1; i<num; i++) {
    this["line"+i]._x = this["p"+i]._x;
    this["line"+i]._y = this["p"+i]._y;
    this["line"+i]._xscale = this["p"+(i+half)]._x-this["p"+i]._x;
    this["line"+i]._yscale = this["p"+(i+half)]._y-this["p"+i]._y;
    // set color of lines
    new Color(this["line"+i]).setRGB(R << 16 | G << 8 | B);
    R=90, G=190, B=140+(i*5);
  }
}// ===============  calculate wave pattern
function sequence () {
  if (counter<0) {
    plus = 1;
    minus = half;
    counter = plus;
  }
  if (plus<half) {
    minus = half;
    plus++;
    go = true;
```

```
    } else {
      minus--;
      go = false;
    }
    if (go) {
      counter = plus;
    } else {
      counter = minus;
    }
  }
  // ==============  set up the controls
  function controls () {
    control1 = bar1.drag._x/100;
    control2 = bar2.drag._x/100;
    control3 = bar3.drag._x;

    dest_1 = dest1._y;
    dest_2 = dest2._y;
    static_1 = static1._y;
    static_2 = static2._y;
    grid._alpha = control3;
    if (toggle) {
      over = counter;
    }
  }
```

Here's the code that's on the first frame of `clip_Point`:

```
  // Display the name
  display = _name.substring(1);

  function move () {
    // set accel and elast equal to their sliders
    accel = _root.bar1.drag._x/100;
    elast = _root.bar2.drag._x/100;

    // set destinations and heights for all points
    if (display<20) {
      if (_root.over == display) {
        yn = _root.dest_1;
      } else {
        yn = _root.static_1;
      }
    } else {
      if (_root.over == display-19) {
        yn = _root.dest_2;
      } else {
        yn = _root.static_2;
      }
    }
    if (display<20) {
      xn = 50+(Number(display)*20);
    } else {
      xn = 50+(Number(display-(_parent.half))*20);
    }
    // ------------------
    // position _x
    _x -= (_x-xn)*.5;
    // position _y
    _y -= y=(y+(_y-yn)*accel)*elast;
  }
```

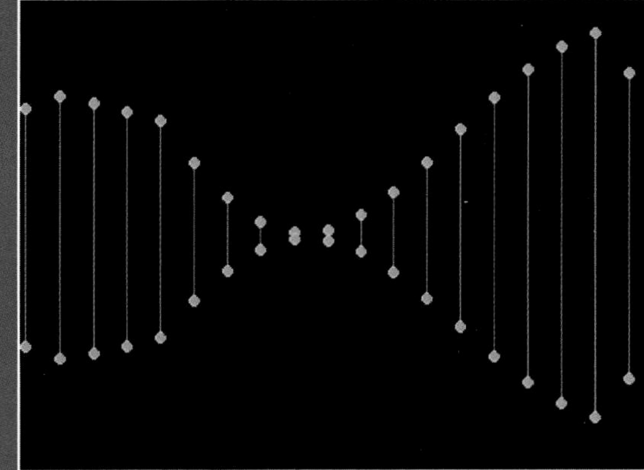

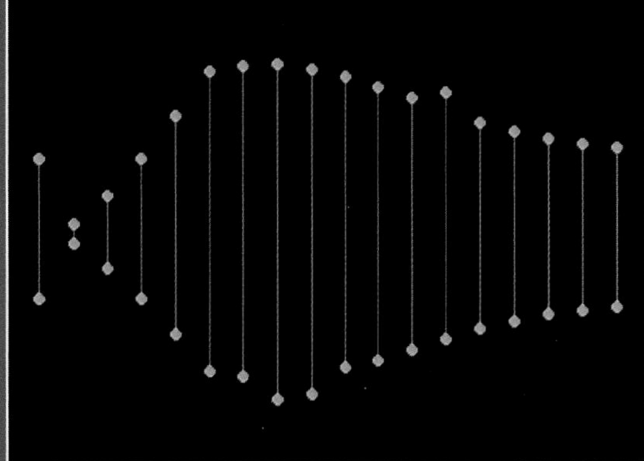

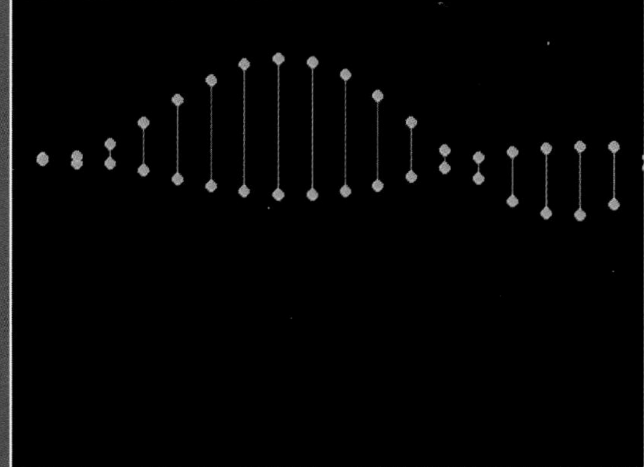

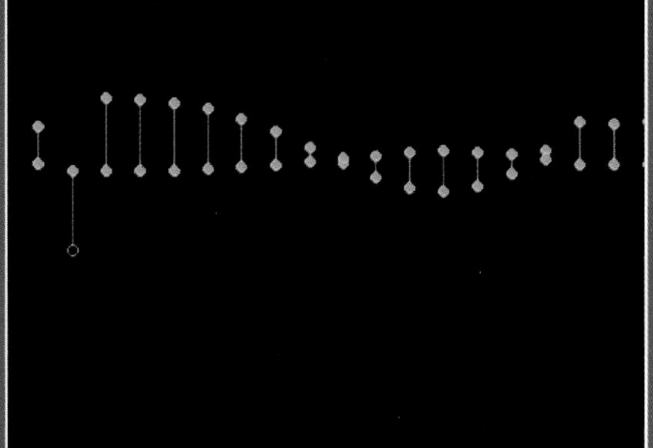

And lastly, here's the code on the Run_Functions clip on the main stage:

```
onClipEvent (enterFrame) {
  for (c=1; c<_parent.num; c++) {
    if (Math.abs(_parent["p"+c]._xmouse)>20 or Math.abs(_parent["p"+c]._ymouse)>5 ) {
      _parent["p"+c].move();
    }
  }
  _parent.drawLine();
  _parent.controls();
  _parent.sequence();
}
```

The key variables, functions, and components

num = the total number of points
half = half of the total number of points, therefore the number of points on each row
bar1 = the acceleration slider
bar2 = the elasticity slider
bar3 = the grid alpha slider
toggle = the auto-run toggle
pointclip = the linkage name of clip_Point in the Library
lineclip = the linkage name of clip_Line in the Library
drawline = a function to scale and position the lines
sequence = a function to calculate the wave pattern
control1 to control3 = variables containing the values of the bar clips of the same number
dest_1 = the value of the top destination arrow position
dest_2 = the value of the bottom destination arrow position
static_1 = the value of the top static arrow position
static_2 = the value of the bottom static arrow position
display = the number of the current point
move = a function to update the position of the current point
accel = the value of the acceleration slider
elast = the value of the elasticity slider
yn = the y destination of the point
xn = the x destination of the point, this is currently a fixed position

Here's how it works: We create 2 rows of points (attached from the Library). After that we create a row of lines (also attached from the Library), connect the points with the lines, and then move the points along the y-axis. We control the static position of the points as well as the position that they will bounce up or down to. We also run a calculation that counts up to 20 and then back down, over and over again. We tell the points where to bounce based on this sequence to get the wave pattern effect.

The primary script (on frame 1 of the main timeline) does the following:

Attaches all the points and lines
Connects the points with the lines
Moves, colorizes, and scales the lines
Calculates the wave pattern number sequence
Sets up the controls

The secondary script (on frame 1 of clip_Point) does the following:

Moves the points based on the controls
Toggles the labels on/off

Once more, I have given default values for the controls to give a good wave pattern. As per usual, the easiest way to make a quick difference is to alter the graphics. There are also many code changes that you can make, ranging from simple color changes to mad alterations to scale, position, and bounce.

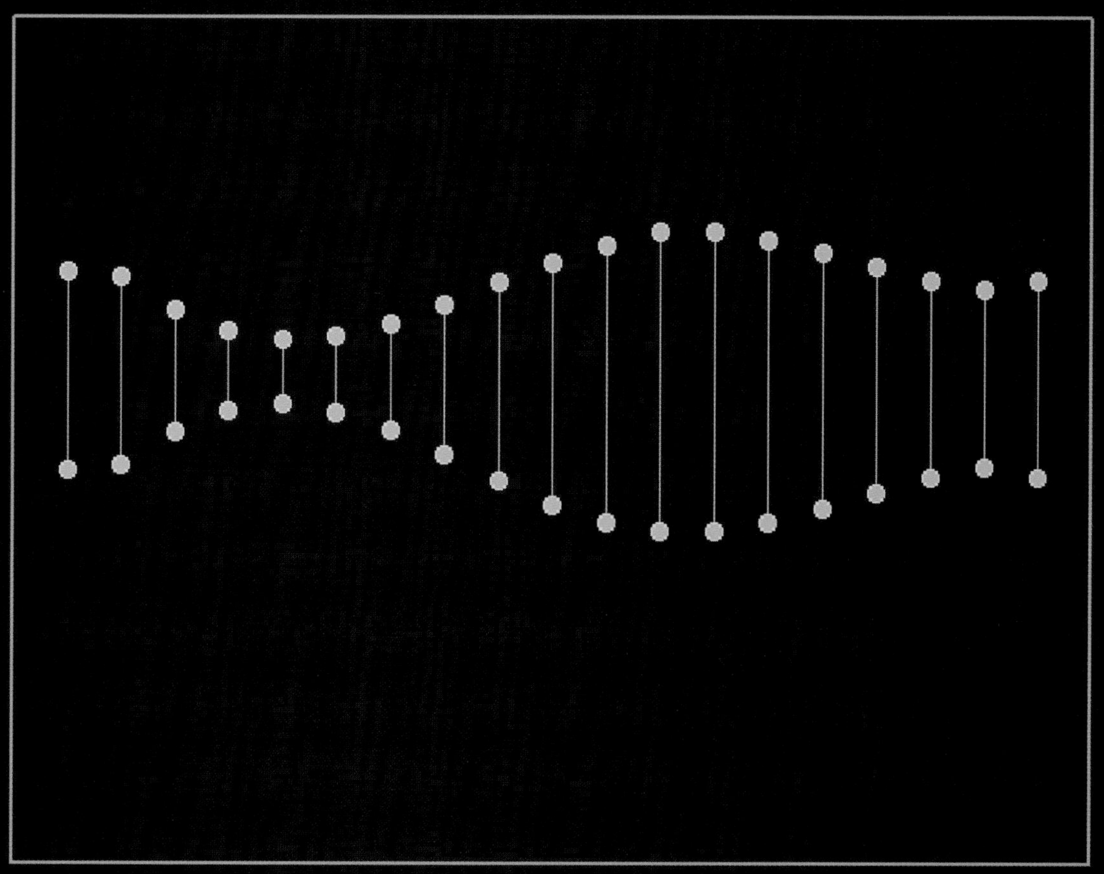
AUTO RUN ON/OFF
ACCEL
ELASTIC
GRID

Phantom shapes

Again, this experiment takes some of the elements from the earlier movies in this series and combines them to create something completely new. We're still using the same point and line combination, but this time we're rotating it round in a circle, and duplicating a low-alpha shape after it. This shape runs through a quick tween then fades out and removes itself. Because the line is spinning quite quickly, we get a really nice morphing effect where the shapes overlap each other giving a strange amorphous blob. The controls that the user has allow the alteration of the radius of the circle that the line spins in, the number of shapes in the trail, and whether or not the line and circle are displayed.

The layer set-up is slightly different to the other experiments, there are four layers here called **`Code`**, **`Main Clip`**, **`Controls`**, and **`Diameter`**. **`Main Clip`** contains an instance of **`clip_Main`** in the center of the stage with the instance name **`main`**. **`Controls`** contains the sliders and other interface components. **`Diameter`** contains a copy of **`clip_Circle`** in the center of the stage with the instance name **`circle`**. The main code is on the first frame of the main movie, the first frame of **`clip_Main`**, and attached to the instance of **`clip_Main`** on the stage. There is also some code to control the various buttons and sliders, you can find this code in **`exp_4.fla`**.

Here's the primary script that sits on frame 1 of the main timeline:

```
_quality = "LOW";
fscommand ("fullscreen", "true");
fscommand ("allowscale", "false");
// Set default value for control1;
bar1.drag._x = 60;
// Set default value for skeleton;
skeleton = false;
// function controls;
function controls () {
  control1 = int(bar1.drag._x*1.5);
  control2 = bar2.drag._x;
  main.radius = control1;
  circle._xscale = circle._yscale=control1;
  main.axis._xscale = main.axis._yscale=control1;
  // Toggle skeleton elements on/off;
  if (_root.skeleton) {
    _root.circle._visible = 0;
    _root.main.axis._visible = 0;
    _root.main.point1._visible = 0;
    _root.main.point2._visible = 0;
    _root.main.line._visible = 0;
  } else {
    _root.circle._visible = 1;
    _root.main.axis._visible = 1;
    _root.main.point1._visible = 1;
    _root.main.point2._visible = 1;
    _root.main.line._visible = 1;
  }
}
```

Here's the code that sits on the first frame of `clip_Main`:

```
// ==============  Set default value for degree;
degrees = 0;
// ==============  Attach line and points
attachMovie("lineclip", "line", 1000);
attachMovie("pointclip", "point1", 2000);
attachMovie("pointclip", "point2", 3000);
// ==============  function setAngle;
function setAngle () {
  Angle = degrees*(Math.PI/180);
  degrees = degrees+4;
}
// ==============  function drawPoints;
function drawPoints () {
  Xpos = Radius*Math.cos(Angle);
  Ypos = Radius*Math.sin(Angle);
  // draw
  Point1._x = Xpos+centerPoint._x;
  Point1._y = Ypos+centerPoint._y;
}
// ==============  function drawLine;
function drawLine () {
  line._x = point1._x;
  line._y = point1._y;
  line._xscale = point2._x-point1._x;
  line._yscale = point2._y-point1._y;
}
// ==============  function drawShapes;
function drawShapes () {
  if (j<_root.control2) {
    j++;
  } else {
    j = 0;
  }
  // Attach the shapes;
  for (i=1; i<2; i++) {
    this.attachMovie("shapeclip", "L"+i+"_"+j, j+(i+2));
    // Set the color of the shapes
    new Color(this["L"+i+"_"+j]).setRGB(R << 16 | G << 8 | B);
    R=70, G=150, B=100+j;
  }
  // Set the position, scale, and alpha of the shapes;
  for (i=1; i<2; i++) {
    this["L"+i+"_"+j]._x = line._x;
    this["L"+i+"_"+j]._y = line._y;
    this["L"+i+"_"+j]._xscale = line._xscale;
    this["L"+i+"_"+j]._yscale = line._yscale;
    this["L"+i+"_"+j]._alpha = 50;
  }
}
```

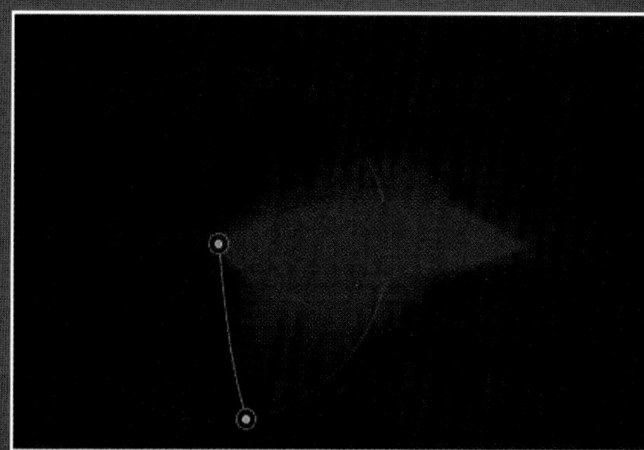

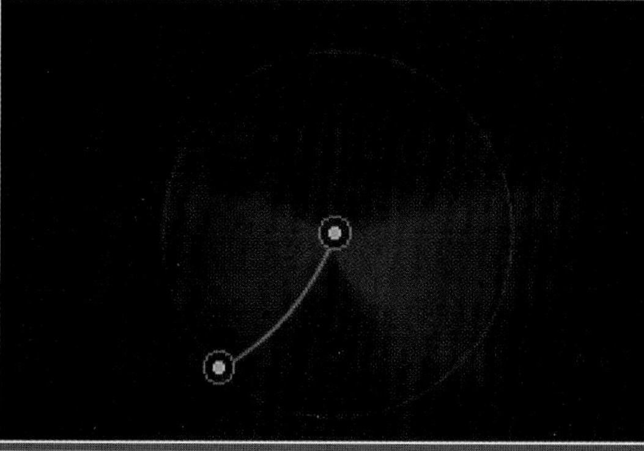

And finally, here's the code that's attached to the instance of `clip_Main` on the stage:

```
onClipEvent (enterFrame) {
  _root.controls();
  setAngle();
  drawPoints();
  drawLine();
  drawShapes();
}
```

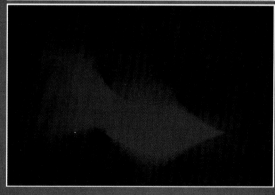

The key variables, functions, and components

bar1 = the radius slider
bar2 = the number of shapes slider
skeleton = the toggle for displaying the line and circle
controls = function to set-up the interface controls
control1 = the value of **bar1**
control2 = the value of **bar2**
radius = the radius of the circle, used for scaling the **diameter** clip on the stage

degrees = the initial rotation of the line
lineclip = the linkage name of **clip_Line** from the Library
pointclip = the linkage name of **clip_Point** from the Library
shapeclip = the linkage name of **clip_Shape** from the Library
setAngle = a function to convert the **degrees** value into radians, and then update it
drawPoints = a function to position the two points (center and outer) on the stage
drawLine = a function to position and scale the line connecting the points
drawShapes = a function to attach a new shape to the stage and set its color, position, scale, and alpha

It works like this – we create two points (attached from the Library), and then create a line (also attached from the Library) and connect the points with it. Then we run a calculation that moves one point around a specified radius. We create the shapes by attaching a new clip each time the frame loops. These shapes are positioned in the same spot as the line and do not move, so they create a great fading trail behind the line.

The primary script (on frame 1 of the main timeline) sets up the controls.

The secondary script (on frame 1 of **clip_Main**) does the following:

Attaches the 2 points and I line (**clip_Point**, **clip_Line**)
Positions and scales the points and lines
Attaches the shapes (**clip_Shape**)
Sets the color, position, scale, and alpha of the shapes

I would suggest that you first of all try changing the **clip_Shape** movieclip. You could create different shapes or simply change the tween that already exists there. Also, changing the color of that clip or the color of the background can make significant differences.

My name is Manuel Tan but almost everybody calls me Manny. I currently work for a design shop called The Fin Company here in New York. In my spare time I update my sites www.uncontrol.com, and www.66mph.com. Both deal with programmatic movement in Flash. Uncontrol is the place for me to experiment with motion and behaviors through code, while 66mph is where I do my more arty farty stuff. I've been published in a few books like New Masters of Flash 2002 annual, 72 DPI, and Young Guns NYC III as well as exhibiting works at OFFF in Barcelona and ADC in New York. I was recently involved in the Biennial at Tirana and was exhibited locally at the Deitch Gallery in Soho, NY. When I'm not doing Flash stuff I build Bandai models, mountain bike, and grow my herbal plants on my windowsill.

I find that the best way to understand something is to try and recreate it to the best of my abilities. Sometimes I am able to recreate it perfectly for what I want it to do, while other times I fall flat on my face. My computer is filled with hundreds of iterations of experiments that don't work but it's no big deal, I just move on and try to make something else work. Eventually, after a few cigarettes, a few more cups of coffee, and a fresh perspective, I'll come back and try to solve it again – primarily just because I don't like leaving things unfinished and undone. The good thing is that I have enough screwed up work lying around to last me for a long while. I try and get into the mindset of code, understanding why it works and especially why it doesn't work.

manuel tan

uncontrol.com

Color blend

Open up `experiment_a.swf` and have a play with it. The buttons at the top change the shape of the lines, and the slider bars control the spread of the lines. The movie consists of three main component types, the `master_mc`, which sits on the stage and contains all of the code, the `line` movieclip that we use to duplicate, which sits in the Library with the linkage name `line_link`, and lastly the interface elements.

As I said, all of the main code (apart from the interface code) is contained the `master_mc` clip on the main stage. I'll give it in full here, and then walk through its creation and function straight afterwards:

```
onClipEvent (load) {
   // ———————————————————
   // FOR loop variables
   // ———————————————————
   z_objects = 6;
   y_objects = 6;
   x_objects = 6;
   counter = 1;

   // ———————————————————
   // creates objects and assigns color to each object
   // ———————————————————
   for (z=1; z<=z_objects; z++) {
      for (y=1; y<=y_objects; y++) {
        for (x=1; x<=x_objects; x++) {
          // ———————————————————
          // creates objects and assigns color to each object
          // ———————————————————
          _parent.attachMovie("line_link", "line_"+counter, counter);
          wing_color_spot_01 = new Color(_parent["line_"+counter]);
          new_color_spot_01 =
           {
            rb:(x*51) - 51,
            gb:(y*51) - 51,
            bb:(z*51) - 51,
            aa:25
           };
          wing_color_spot_01.setTransform(new_color_spot_01);

          // ———————————————————
          counter++;

        }
      }
   }
   // ———————————————————
   // initialize sinusodial variables
   // ———————————————————
   slider_speed = 5;
   slider_radius = 100;
   slider_offset = 200;
   slider_increment = 1;

}
```

```
onClipEvent (enterFrame) {
  // ————————————————————
  // grabs data from slider bars
  // ————————————————————
  data_y = _parent.nav_vertical.nav_vertical_square_bottom._y;
  data_x = _parent.nav_horizontal.nav_horizontal_square_right._x;
  slider_radius = data_x;

  // ————————————————————
  // start of position script
  // ————————————————————
  counter = 1;
  for (z=1; z<=z_objects; z++) {
     for (y=1; y<=y_objects; y++) {
       for (x=1; x<=x_objects; x++) {
         // ————————————————————
         // changes line style
         // ————————————————————
         _parent["line_"+counter].gotoAndStop(_parent.color_status);

         // ————————————————————
         // computes sinisodial variables
         // ————————————————————
         slider_increment_offset = (z/x*y*10);
         slider_sin = Math.sin((slider_increment+slider_increment_offset)
 ➥ /Math.PI/slider_speed)*slider_radius + slider_offset;

         // ————————————————————
         // plots points from variables including offsets
         // ————————————————————
         _parent["line_"+counter]._x = (y*2) + (z*12) + slider_sin-50;
         _parent["line_"+counter]._y = (x*(data_y/3)) - data_y + 200;

         // ————————————————————
         counter++;
       }
     }
  }
  slider_increment++;
}
```

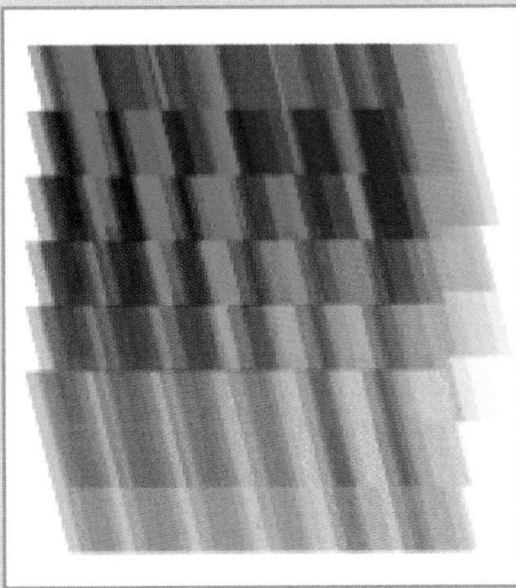

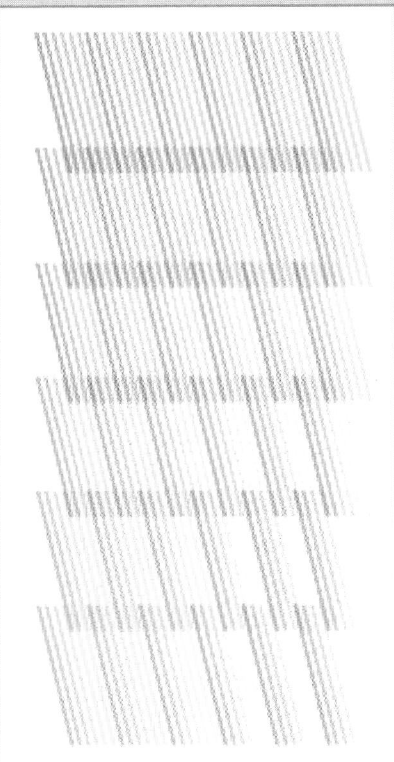

I commented as many areas of the code as I could to better explain some of the parts, so be sure to check through it if you get confused. One of the first things I saw with the script was an easy way of generating the hexadecimal color chart. There are 3 primary colors values used to create the range of colors (Red, Green, Blue), and there are 6 main increments of each primary color (00, 33, 66, 99, CC, FF). The embedded `for` loops allow me to cycle through all of the RGB values. So each one loops 6 times giving a total of 256 iterations. I decided to pull these three loop counter values out of the loop, so if I use the `for` loops again for a different number of iterations, I only have to change it in one place. You can find these variables at the top named `z_objects`, `y_objects`, and `x_objects` to coincide with the counter variable for each loop (`z`, y, and `x`). Before I begin adding color to an object, I need to first create an object to add it to. I didn't want to use the `duplicateMovieClip` action because I feel it clutters the stage unnecessarily. Instead I opted for the `attachMovie` method. I used a simple counter, called `counter`, to create the names and level of each new clip. The last thing I did, which wasn't necessary but it was aesthetically pleasing, was to change the spacing of the color value lines to make it easier to read. Here's the end result:

```
// ——————————————————
// FOR loop variables
// ——————————————————
z_objects = 6;
y_objects = 6;
x_objects = 6;
counter = 1;

// ——————————————————
// creates objects and assigns color to each object
// ——————————————————
for (z=1; z<=z_objects; z++) {
  for (y=1; y<=y_objects; y++) {
    for (x=1; x<=x_objects; x++) {
      // ——————————————————
      // creates objects and assigns color to each object
      // ——————————————————
      _parent.attachMovie("line_link", "line_"+counter, counter);
      wing_color_spot_01 = new Color(_parent["line_"+counter]);
      new_color_spot_01 =
       {
         rb:(x*51) - 51,
         gb:(y*51) - 51,
         bb:(z*51) - 51,
         aa:25
       };
      wing_color_spot_01.setTransform(new_color_spot_01);

      // ——————————————————
      counter++;

    }
  }
}
```

This is all just for preparation. Now I have to actually make it move in the `enterFrame` clip event. I think it would have been great to have just placed these objects on a simple grid pattern, and I would have done so if it weren't for my desire to make it move. One of the first things I wanted to do was to make it move back and forth. A smooth and realistic way to do this was to use sinusoidal movement, which simply means the oscillating object will accelerate and decelerate from one point to another using the sine and cosine functions. I started by reusing the same loop structure from the earlier to cycle through all the objects. I replaced the scripts inside the `for` loops with:

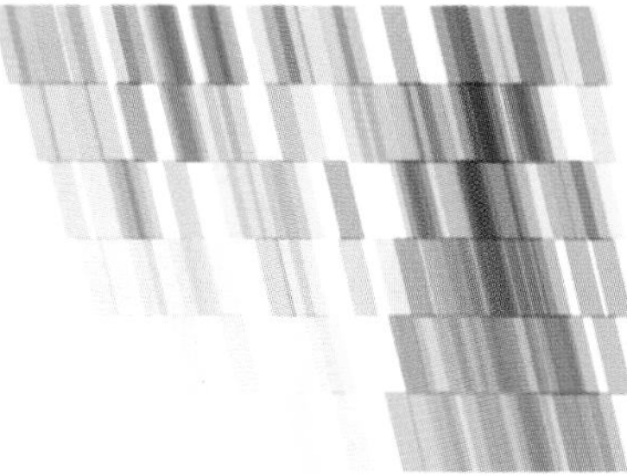

```
_parent["line_"+counter]._x = (x*10);
_parent["line_"+counter]._y = (y*5) + (z*40);
```

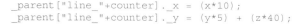

The numbers multiplied with the variables are completely arbitrary. I used them to spread out all the objects so I could see them. The next thing is to add the sinusoids (I love using that word; it reminds me of a toy I played with when I was a kid). Think of the sinusoids as moving along the perimeter of a circle at a constant speed. If you completely disregard the y-axis, the object will move similar to a pole from a carousel at eye level. There are many ways of writing this equation. I prefer this one because it's simple:

```
slider_sin = Math.sin(slider_increment/Math.PI/
➥ slider_speed)* slider_radius + slider_offset;
slider_increment++;
```

To use this, I needed to initialize a bunch of variables like speed, radius, and offset. I added these variables to the `load` clip event earlier. If you don't understand this, that's okay. To re-use the carousel analogy, all that this refers to is how fast you are spinning around, how close you are to the center of the carousel, and where the carousel is placed. You can get a better idea of what these variables do if you change these numbers around. The last variable, called `slider_increment`, probably doesn't look too familiar, it's a counter script that generates all the values for the oscillating movement. I attached this to the x-axis and came up with this:

```
_parent["line_"+counter]._x = slider_sin;
```

When I tested this, all the objects moved at the same time and that was pretty boring, so we need to offset/separate them. The easiest and most logical way to separate them was to have each object along a row start at different times. To go back to our earlier analogy, at the moment our carousel effectively has only one pole. All we want to do now then is disperse poles for a more even carousel. To do this with our code, we replace the `slider_increment` value with something else that is unique to each character. I decided to integrate the x, y, and z values into an equation:

```
slider_increment_offset = (z/x*y*10);
slider_sin = Math.sin((slider_increment + slider_increment_offset)/
➥ Math.PI/slider_speed)*slider_radius + slider_offset;
```

That code looks pretty complex and to be honest, I don't really know exactly how it translates into the current moving thingy. This is where I throw my math book out the door and opt to create something that looks good through trial and error. My only prerequisite was to use all three values. I used the same trial and error to create these final scripts between the `for` loops:

```
_parent["line_"+counter]._x = (y*2) + (z*12) + slider_sin - 50;
_parent["line_"+counter]._y = (x*(data_y/3)) - data_y + 200;
```

While I was building this I also wanted to make it interactive so I created two slider bars that gave me values. These values are dumped into 2 variables called `data_x` and `data_y` to represent the horizontal and vertical axes. `data_x` is used to change the radius of the 'carousel' while `data_y` is used to evenly spread out the objects along the horizontal focal point.

The last bit of code changes the style of the object. I just made 4 simple styles and placed them on 4 frames in the `line` movieclip. The code below just targets a specific frame in there:

```
_parent["line_"+counter].gotoAndStop(_parent.color_status);
```

That's it for the first experiment, give the carousel a whirl and see what you think. Try adding some new shapes to the `line` clip and seeing what effects you can make, but to be honest, I wouldn't try drawing a full carousel horse, things would probably get a little messy.

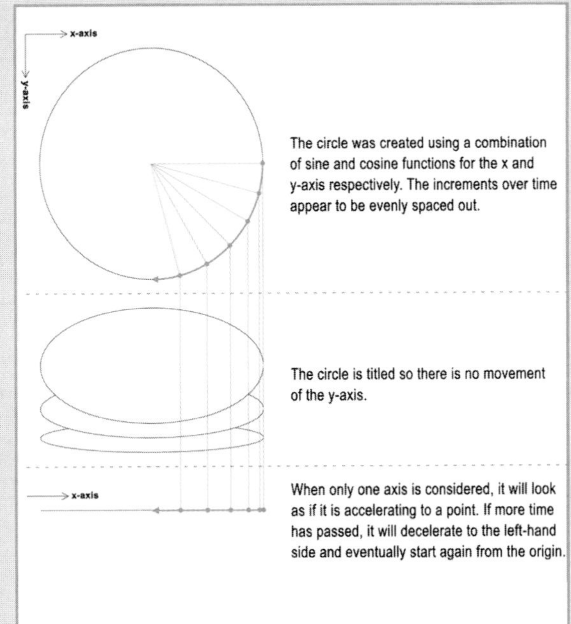

The circle was created using a combination of sine and cosine functions for the x and y-axis respectively. The increments over time appear to be evenly spaced out.

The circle is titled so there is no movement of the y-axis.

When only one axis is considered, it will look as if it is accelerating to a point. If more time has passed, it will decelerate to the left-hand side and eventually start again from the origin.

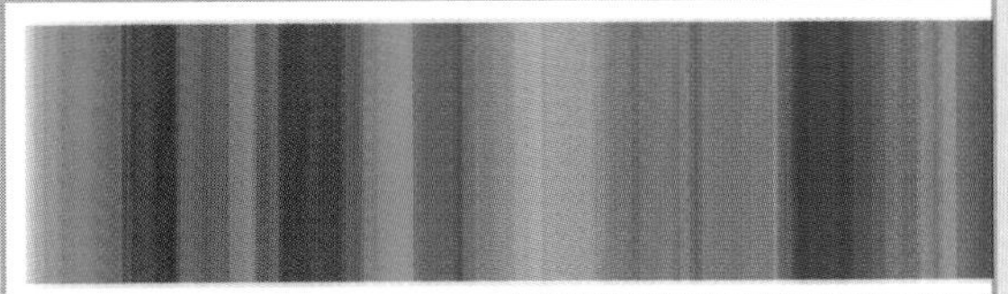

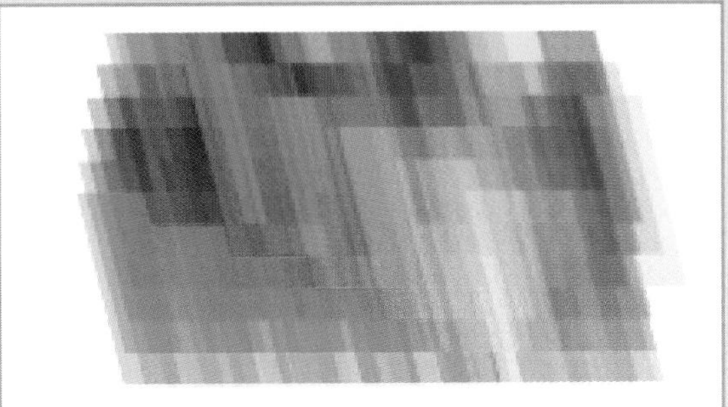

Spinner

Take a look at `experiment_b.swf`. The top-left buttons and the sliders perform a similar function as they did in the previous experiment, but there are two new sets of buttons. The middle set control the position of the shapes, and the top-right set control the scale of the shapes, giving them perspective. The shapes have changed too, now instead of a series of different colored lines, there are three layers of squares with a grid of nine squares in each layer. The layers appear to move around each other depending on the position of a focal clip that's moving around a circle in the center of the screen. The best way to understand it is just to watch it; you'll see what I mean. The code, as per the last experiment, is all on the `master_mc` movieclip on the main stage, bar the script on the buttons and sliders. Here is the main code in its entirety:

```
onClipEvent (load) {
  // ———————————————————
  // initialization of all the variables for the nav
  // ———————————————————
  _parent.nav_position["position_1_"+4].gotoAndStop(2);
  _parent.nav_position["position_2_"+4].gotoAndStop(2);
  _parent.nav_position["position_3_"+4].gotoAndStop(2);
  _parent.nav_scale["position_1_"+3].gotoAndStop(2);
  _parent.nav_scale["position_2_"+3].gotoAndStop(2);
  _parent.nav_scale["position_3_"+3].gotoAndStop(2);
  _parent.color_status = 1;
  _parent.x_offset = -2;
  _parent.y_offset = -2;
  _parent.z_offset = -2;
  _parent.xscale_offset = 30;
  _parent.yscale_offset = 30;
  _parent.zscale_offset = 100;
  _parent.scale_increment = 10;

  // ———————————————————
  // FOR loop variables
  // ———————————————————
  z_objects = 3;
  y_objects = 3;
  x_objects = 3;
  counter = 1;

  // ———————————————————
  // creates objects and assigns color to each object
  // ———————————————————
  for (z=1; z<=z_objects; z++) {
   for (y=1; y<=y_objects; y++) {
    for (x=1; x<=x_objects; x++) {
      // ———————————————————
      // creates objects and assigns color to each object
      // ———————————————————
      _parent.attachMovie("square_link", "square_"+counter, counter);
      wing_color_spot_01 = new Color(_parent["square_"+counter]);
      new_color_spot_01 =
       {
         rb:255 - (x*102-51),
         gb:255 - (y*102-51),
         bb:255 - (z*102-51),
         aa:50
       };
      wing_color_spot_01.setTransform(new_color_spot_01);

      // ———————————————————
      counter++;
    }
   }
  }
```

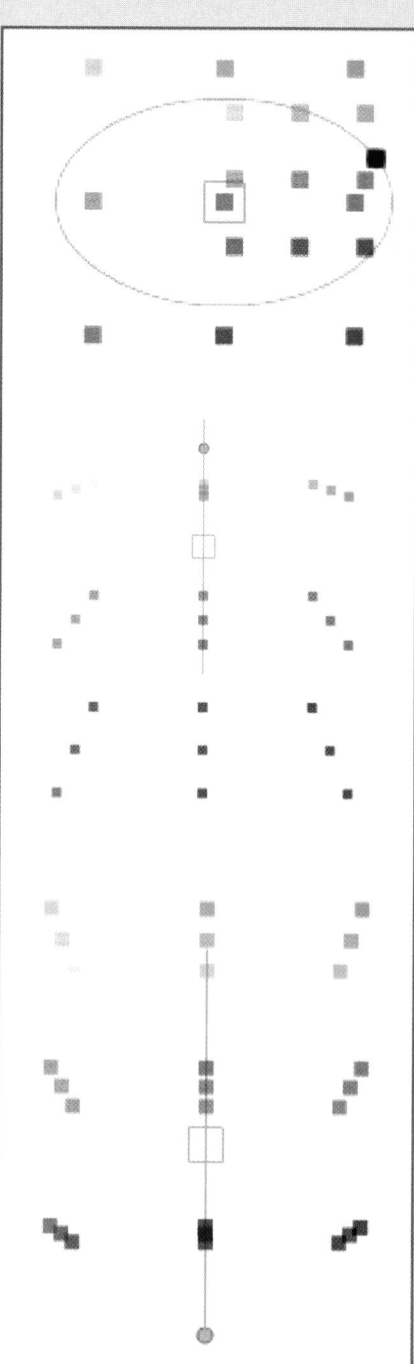

```
    // ——————————————————————
    // initialize sinusodial variables
    // ——————————————————————
    slider_speed = 2;
    slider_increment = 1;
    slider_offset = 200;

}
onClipEvent (enterFrame) {
    // ——————————————————————
    // data from nav sliders
    // ——————————————————————
    data_x = _parent.nav_horizontal.nav_horizontal_square_right._x;
    data_y = _parent.nav_vertical.nav_vertical_square_bottom._y;

    // ——————————————————————
    // scales grey circle
    // ——————————————————————
    _parent.circle._xscale = data_x;
    _parent.circle._yscale = data_y;

    // ——————————————————————
    // moves master_point_00 around circle using data from nav sliders
    // ——————————————————————
    _parent.master_point_00._x = Math.cos(slider_increment/Math.PI/
  ➥ slider_speed)*data_x + slider_offset;
    _parent.master_point_00._y = Math.sin(slider_increment/Math.PI/
  ➥ slider_speed) * data_y + slider_offset;
    slider_increment++;

    // ——————————————————————
    // start of position script
    // ——————————————————————
    counter = 1;
    for (z=1; z<=z_objects; z++) {
     for (y=1; y<=y_objects; y++) {
      for (x=1; x<=x_objects; x++) {
        // ——————————————————————
        // changes line style
        // ——————————————————————
        _parent["square_"+counter].gotoAndStop (_parent.color_status);

        // ——————————————————————
        // takes given data and parses it through 3d engine function
        // ——————————————————————
        _parent.convert_array_to_3d
                (
                        "square_"+counter,
                        (x+_parent.x_offset)*_parent.xscale_offset,
                        (y+_parent.y_offset)*_parent.yscale_offset,
                        (z+_parent.z_offset)*_parent.zscale_offset
                );

        // ——————————————————————
        counter++;
      }
     }
    }
}
```

I created a simple one-point perspective 3D engine function a while back and I had an idea that this code would work pretty well with it. The function is called `convert_array_to_3d`, and what it does is take the x, y and z coordinates of a 3d point and convert them onto a Cartesian plane.

The 3D engine function requires four variables to position an object: the name of the object, its x-position, its y-position, and its z-position in that order. If you look in the `enterFrame` clip event between the `for` loops, I put each variable on its own line, making it easier for me to read. For this script to work, you also need to know where two specific points are: the absolute coordinates (0,0,0), and the focal point in the horizon. These are taken care of by two objects found on the main stage called `masterpoint_0` and `masterpoint_00` respectively. From my experience, the script tends to get' screwy when you use extreme numbers along the z-axis. For example if you want to set a point 1000 pixels into the distance or -1000, it will flip up and over the event horizon (at least I think that's what it's called; I saw too many sci-fi films to remember properly) and land on some weird spot. I specifically built this script to handle smaller numbers. I arbitrarily decided that the maximum distance around the absolute point would be between -200 and 200 on all axes.

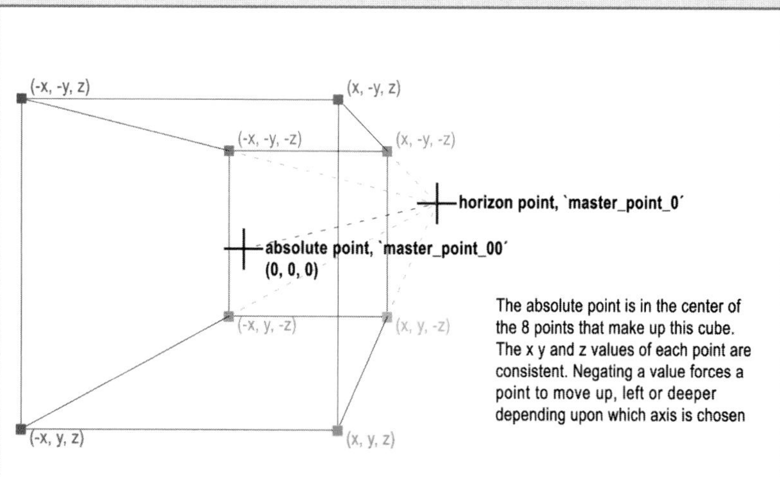
(-x, -y, z)
(x, -y, z)
(-x, -y, -z)
(x, -y, -z)
horizon point, `master_point_0´
absolute point, `master_point_00´
(0, 0, 0)
(-x, y, -z)
(x, y, -z)
(-x, y, z)
(x, y, z)
The absolute point is in the center of the 8 points that make up this cube. The x y and z values of each point are consistent. Negating a value forces a point to move up, left or deeper depending upon which axis is chosen

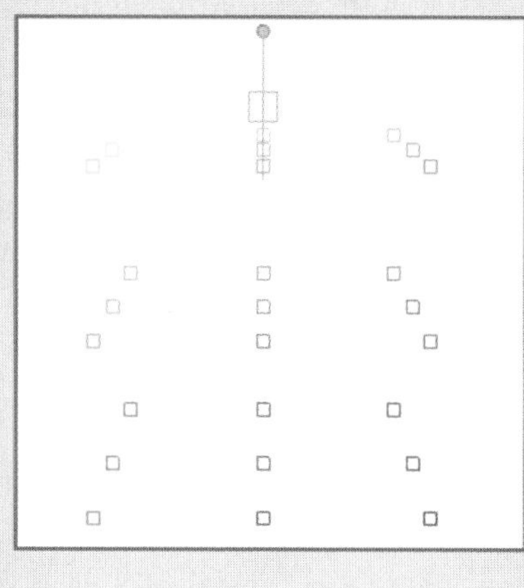

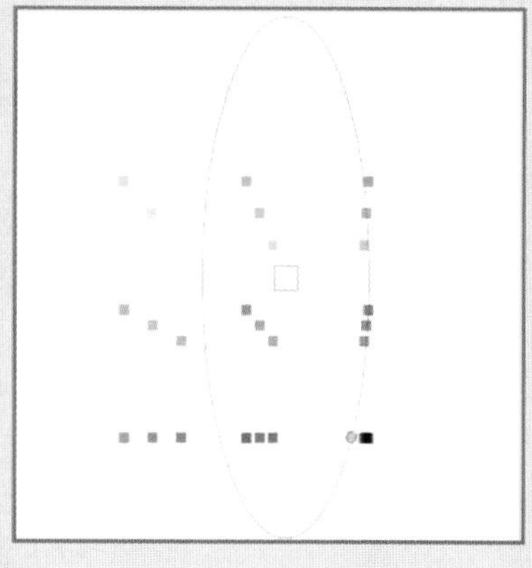

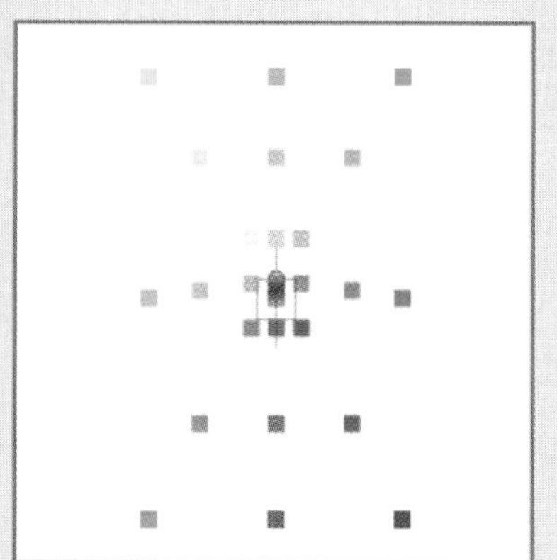

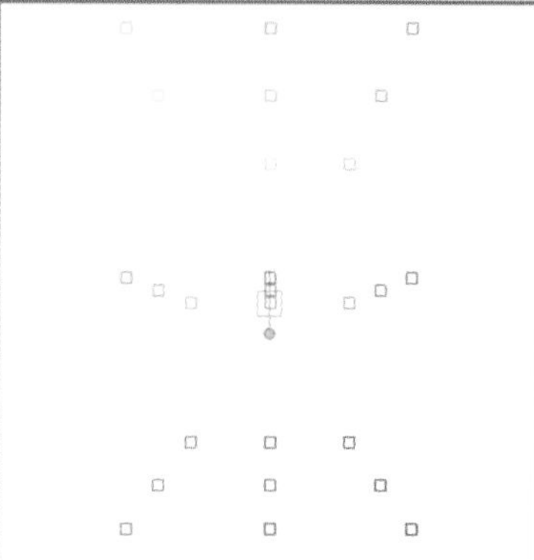

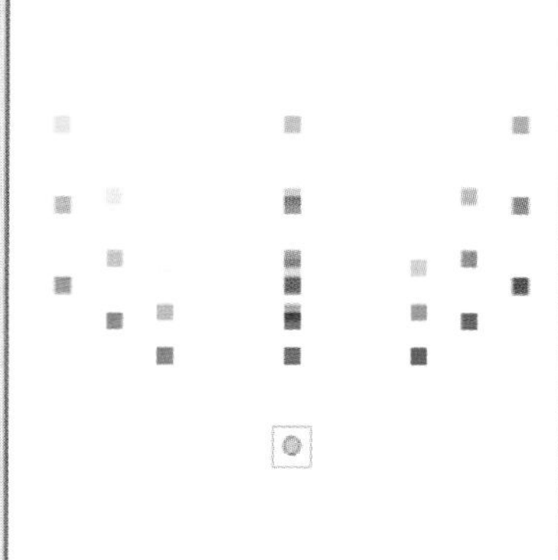

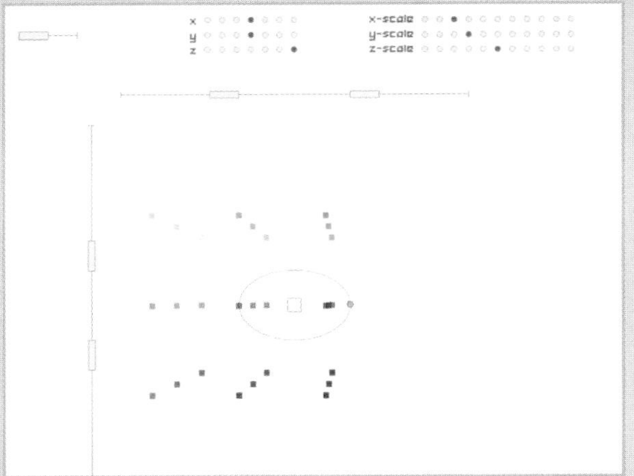

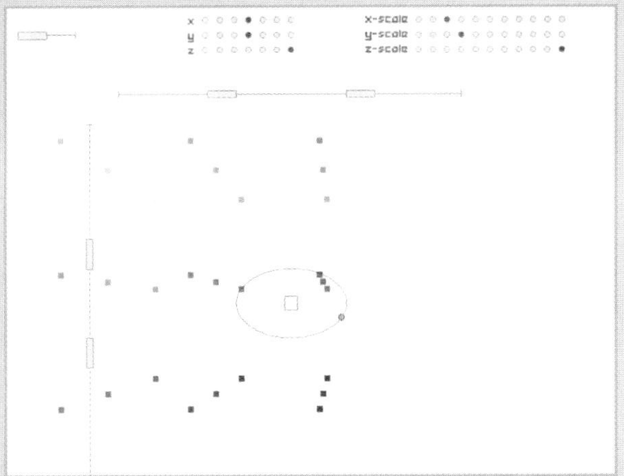

As explained earlier, the `for` loops in the `load` clip event are there to create the objects needed, as well as defining a specific color. The `for` loops in the `enterFrame` clip event are there to cycle through all of the given points – the inner loop establishes the horizontal coordinates; the middle loop controls the vertical movement, and the outer loop controls the depth. There are two sets of variable that create the cube. The first set deal with the translation, or positioning, of the objects as a whole, and these are labeled as `x_offset`, `y_offset`, and `z_offset`. Adding them to the `x`, `y`, and `z` variables repositions them. The second set deal with scaling as a whole, they're labeled `xscale_offset`, `yscale_offset`, and `zscale_offset`. Multiplying them by the `x`, `y`, and `z` variables scales them. Here's an example that changes the position and scaling along the z-axis:

```
(z+_parent.z_offset)*_parent.zscale_offset
```

You'll notice that the `z_offset` is executed first and then the `zscale_offset`. There is a precise and mathematical explanation to it but all that information was lost in my head after I moved on to college and discovered beer. Instead, I kept messing around, mixing and matching simple Math functions until I got it to work. Notice in the very beginning of the `load` clip event where a bunch of variables are initialized. The top half initialize the radial button navigation, while the bottom half initialize the actual variables needed to make this work. That's basically all there is for the position and scaling of the objects as a whole, now lets get in to making them oscillate.

The only thing I move to make it oscillate is the focal point or `masterpoint_00` position. Using the example from the first experiment, we have:

```
_parent.master_point_00._x = Math.sin(slider_increment/Math.PI/slider_speed)*slider_radius + slider_offset;
slider_increment++;
```

You should know what each variable does already from the previous example. This script will only oscillate on the x-axis. We want to make it move along a circle using both x- and y-axis, so we add this:

```
_parent.master_point_00._x = Math.sin(slider_increment/Math.PI/slider_speed)*slider_radius + slider_offset;
_parent.master_point_00._y = Math.cos(slider_increment/Math.PI/slider_speed)*slider_radius + slider_offset;
slider_increment++;
```

The trick to making an object move around in a circle is to have one axis that uses the sine function while the other axis uses the cosine function. I don't think there's too much of a penalty deciding which axis goes with which trigonometry function, so you should go with what you feel comfortable with. The only value that changes is the radius of the circular orbit. The trick is that both the x- and y-axis' radii can be different, so we swap `slider_radius` from the two lines and replace it with a unique variable. I duplicated the same navigation bars from the previous example to provide us with data for this experiment. Here's the final code:

```
_parent.master_point_00._x = Math.cos(slider_increment/Math.PI/slider_speed) * data_x + slider_offset;
_parent.master_point_00._y = Math.sin(slider_increment/Math.PI/slider_speed) * data_y + slider_offset;
slider_increment++;
```

The last thing is to create a circular path for `master_point_00` to follow. I just made a simple circular outline and I scaled that circle based on the radii data:

```
_parent.circle._xscale = data_x;
_parent.circle._yscale = data_y;
```

There are a few more little pieces left but since I explained them already in the first experiment, I won't do so again now here.

Fluid dynamic

This experiment is similar to the last one, but rather than having a grid of squares, I've got a wave of squares. Check out `experiment_c.fla` to see the effect. The other major change that I've got is that instead of the focus spinning around a circle, it's now controllable by the user, try dragging the focus around the screen and seeing the difference it makes. Another new addition is a line clip that's used to join the squares to give even more of an impression of a wave. You can also remove the squares altogether, and just have a wave made up of lines. As per usual, the majority of the code is on `master_mc` on the main stage, but there is also some code on the main timeline as well.

Here's the code that's attached to `master_mc`:

```
onClipEvent (load) {
   counter = 1;
   // ————————————————————
   // removes objects and blue lines
   // ————————————————————
   for (z=1; z<=10; z++) {
      for (y=1; y<=10; y++) {
         for (x=1; x<=10; x++) {
            removeMovieClip ( _parent["square_"+ x + "_" + y + "_" + z]);
            _parent.removeline ("line_"+line_depth);

            // ————————————————————
            counter++;
            line_depth++;
         }
      }
   }
   // ————————————————————
   // creates objects and assigns color to each object
   // ————————————————————
   for (z=1; z<=_parent.z_objects; z++) {
      for (y=1; y<=_parent.y_objects; y++) {
         for (x=1; x<=_parent.x_objects; x++) {
            // ————————————————————
            // creates objects and assigns color to each object
            // ————————————————————
            _parent.attachMovie("square_link", "square_"+ x + "_" + y + "_" + z, counter);
            wing_color_spot_01 = new Color(_parent["square_"+ x + "_" + y + "_" + z]);
            new_color_spot_01 =
               {
                  rb:255 - (x*102),
                  gb:255 - (y*102),
                  bb:255 - (z*102),
                  aa:50
               };
            wing_color_spot_01.setTransform(new_color_spot_01);

            // ————————————————————
            counter++;
         }
      }
   }
   // ————————————————————
   // initialze sinisoid variables
   // ————————————————————
   slider_speed = 4;
   slider_radius = 15;
   slider_increment = 1;

}
onClipEvent (enterFrame) {
   // ————————————————————
   // initialze counter variables
   // ————————————————————
   counter = 1;
   line_depth = 100;
   // ————————————————————
   // start of position script
   // ————————————————————
   for (z=1; z<=_parent.z_objects; z++) {
      for (y=1; y<=_parent.y_objects; y++) {
         for (x=1; x<=_parent.x_objects; x++) {
```

```
        // ————————————————————
        // changes line style
        // ————————————————————
        _parent["square_"+ x + "_" + y + "_" + z].gotoAndStop (_parent.color_status)


        // ————————————————————
        // creates data
        // ————————————————————
        slider_offset_y = (y*10) - 25;
        slider_offset_z = (z*100);
        slider_radius = 15*((_parent.y_objects - y + 1)*.25);
        slider_increment_offset = z*20;
        slider_cos = Math.cos((slider_increment+slider_increment_offset)/Math.PI/slider_speed)*
         ➥ slider_radius + slider_offset_y;
        slider_sin = Math.sin((slider_increment+slider_increment_offset)/Math.PI/slider_speed)*
         ➥ slider_radius + slider_offset_z;
        // ————————————————————
        // takes given data and parses it through 3d engine function
        // ————————————————————
        _parent.convert_array_to_3d
          (
            "square_"+ x + "_" + y + "_" + z,
            (x*10) - 10,
            slider_cos,
            slider_sin
          );
        // ————————————————————
        // creates and removes blue lines
        // ————————————————————
        if (z != 1) {
            if (_parent.line_status == 1) {
                   _parent.line_blue_link("square_"+ x +"_"+y + "_" + z,"square_" + x + "_" + y +
                     ➥ "_" + Number(z-1), "line_"+line_depth, line_depth);
            } else {
                   _parent.removeline ("line_"+line_depth);
            }
        }
        // ————————————————————
        counter++;
        line_depth++;
        // ————————————————————
      }
    }
  }
  slider_increment++;
  // ————————————————————
  // draws grey line
  // ————————————————————
  _parent.line_grey_link ("master_point_0", "master_point_00", "line_"+line_depth, line_depth);
}
```

Here's the code that's on the first frame of the main timeline:

```
_quality = "LOW";
z_objects = 4;
y_objects = 4;
x_objects = 1;
// ————————————————————
for (x=1; x<=5; x++) {
  this["circle_1_"+x].gotoAndStop(1);
}
for (x=1; x<=5; x++) {
  this["circle_2_"+x].gotoAndStop(1);
}
for (x=1; x<=5; x++) {
  this["circle_3_"+x].gotoAndStop(1);
}
// ————————————————————
for (x=1; x<=x_objects; x++) {
  this["circle_1_"+x].gotoAndStop(2);
}
for (x=1; x<=y_objects; x++) {
  this["circle_2_"+x].gotoAndStop(2);
}
for (x=1; x<=z_objects; x++) {
  this["circle_3_"+x].gotoAndStop(2);
}
```

And finally, here's the code that's on the third frame of the main timeline:

```
color_status = 1;
line_status = 1;
x_offset = -2;
y_offset = -2;
z_offset = -2;
xscale_offset = 30;
yscale_offset = 30;
zscale_offset = 100;
scale_increment = 10;
// ------------------------------------------------------------
function convert_array_to_3d (point_name, xx, yy, zz) {
  // -----------------------
  // master points
  // -----------------------
  x = 0;
  y = 1;
  z = 2;
  focul_point_x = master_point_00._x;
  focul_point_y = master_point_00._y;
  pivot_point_x = master_point_0._x;
  pivot_point_y = master_point_0._y;
  // -----------------------
  // 3d plotting function
  // -----------------------
  this[point_name]._x = (pivot_point_x-
➥focul_point_x)*(zz/1000+1)+xx*(zz/1000+1)+focul_point_x;
  this[point_name]._y = (pivot_point_y-
➥focul_point_y)*(zz/1000+1)+yy*(zz/1000+1)+focul_point_y;
}
// ------------------------------------------------------------
function line_blue_link (start_point, end_point, line_name, line_depth) {
  attachMovie("line_blue_link", "line_"+line_name, line_depth);
  this["line_"+line_name]._x = this[start_point]._x;
  this["line_"+line_name]._y = this[start_point]._y;
  this["line_"+line_name]._xscale = this[end_point]._x-this[start_point]._x;
  this["line_"+line_name]._yscale = this[end_point]._y-this[start_point]._y;
  this["line_"+line_name]._alpha = 50;
}
function line_grey_link (start_point, end_point, line_name, line_depth) {
  attachMovie("line_grey_link", "line_"+line_name, line_depth);
  this["line_"+line_name]._x = this[start_point]._x;
  this["line_"+line_name]._y = this[start_point]._y;
  this["line_"+line_name]._xscale = this[end_point]._x-this[start_point]._x;
  this["line_"+line_name]._yscale = this[end_point]._y-this[start_point]._y;
  this["line_"+line_name]._alpha = 50;
}
function removeline (line_name) {
  removeMovieClip ( "line_"+line_name );
}
// ------------------------------------------------------------
stop ();
```

A while ago I saw a math/physics website that taught you all about fluid dynamics, about how objects move underwater. There was even an interactive model written in Java of how particles moved in the water. The interesting thing was that the particles moved in a circular motion like an orbit. They showed a series of particles equally spaced out vertically and horizontally. Rows of particles moved at the same rate but at a different increment. Columns of particles had varying radii. The top row had large radii while the bottom row barely moved. From our previous scripts we can interpolate this with sinusoidal motion. We can control the radius, speed, and increment of circles across a given area. It would have been easy to stick with two dimensions and replicate the movement, but I'm a glutton for punishment. I wanted to move it in a 3-dimensional environment specifically along the y- and z-axis. On top of that, I wanted to connect the points together with a line.

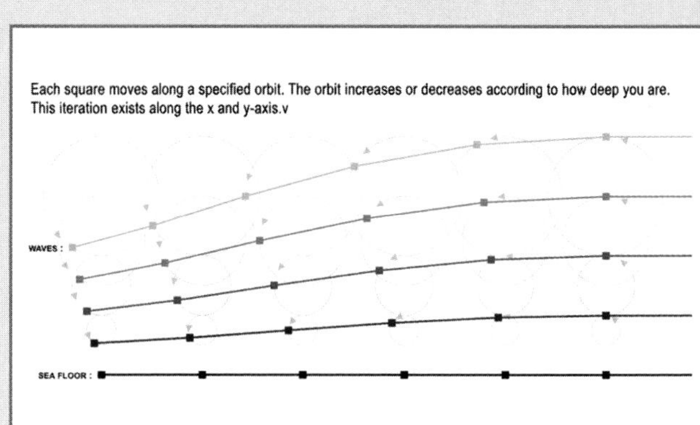
Each square moves along a specified orbit. The orbit increases or decreases according to how deep you are.
This iteration exists along the x and y-axis.v
WAVES :
SEA FLOOR :

Okay so where the hell do we start? First I extrapolated as much data as I could from the previous experiment. I placed the `for` loops on the `load` clip event to build and color the points. I then placed another set of `for` loops in the `enterFrame` clip event to work with the `convert_array_to_3d` function. The main difference so far is that before, I used the counter to name all the objects, but since this time I needed to target specific points, I instead used the x, y, and z variables as a naming convention. Another thing I did was add the base sinusoidal motion into the loop from the previous example as shown here:

```
slider_cos = Math.cos(slider_increment/Math.PI/
 ➥ slider_speed)*slider_radius + slider_offset;
slider_sin = Math.sin(slider_increment/Math.PI/
 ➥ slider_speed)*slider_radius + slider_offset;

_parent.convert_array_to_3d
  (
    "square_"+ x + "_" + y + "_" + z,
    (x*10) - 10,
    slider_cos,
    slider_sin
  );
```

Subtracting 10 allows me to start it at the `x=0` point along our 3D space. `slider_cos` deals with the y movement while `slider_sin` deals with the z movement. Let's look at the `increment_offset` first. Since `increment_offset` deals with particles along the z-axis, we use the `z` variable to change values. We also need to change the radius of each particle orbit so it grows bigger as it goes higher. That can be done with the `y` variable. To save time, I also changed the `slider_offset` to make the movement along the y- and z-axes more dramatic:

```
slider_offset_y = (y*10) - 25;
slider_offset_z = (z*100);
slider_radius = 15*((_parent.y_objects-y+ 1)*.25);
slider_increment_offset = z*20;
slider_cos = Math.cos((slider_increment+
➥ slider_increment_offset)/Math.PI/
➥ slider_speed)*slider_radius + slider_offset_y;
slider_sin = Math.sin((slider_increment+
➥ slider_increment_offset)/Math.PI/
➥ slider_speed)*slider_radius + slider_offset_z;

_parent.convert_array_to_3d
  (
    "square_"+ x + "_" + y + "_" + z,
    (x*10) - 10,
    slider_cos,
    slider_sin
  );
```

Everything looks good so far, except for `slider_radius`, which looks pretty monstrous. That equation was done with some bodgering (this is a term I learned from Junkyard Wars, it means fitting a square peg in a round hole using the maximum amount of force). I'm not going to try to explain it, I'm just glad it works.

So we have the points, now we just need to connect them with lines. I created another function called `line_blue_link` that draws a simple blue line between two points. All you need is a starting object, an ending object, the line name and the line depth. It almost looks like an `attachMovie` method but bigger. Since I'm just connecting the z coordinates, I offset the z index by one to connect it to the previous line:

```
if (z != 1) {
  _parent.line_blue_link ("square_"+ x+ "_"+ y+
➥ "_"+z,"square_"+x+"_"+y+"_"+ Number(z-1),
➥ "line_"+line_depth, line_depth);
}
```

Since there are no values when the z index is 0, I just put a quick Boolean condition in to stop it before `z` goes past 1.

One big thing I wanted to do was dynamically change the number of points and lines created. The best way to do this was through the `x_objects`, `y_objects`, and `z_objects` variables. The problem with this was that I had to constantly load the actions in the `load` clip event. I opted to go with a Flash 4 style clip setup. Frame 1 initializes the variables, frame 2 is blank so we can change these same variables and frame 3 runs the script. When you change the variables, it reorders all the `for` loops and recreates the appropriate amount of objects. The only problem is that sometimes you have an excess of objects on the screen. The best way to get around this is to remove all of the other objects on the screen before you create them.

The last things are the style changes of the points, and style changes of the lines. You already know where to change the style of the points. For the lines, it's the same as wiping it out and starting from scratch again. Here's the final `line` script:

```
if (z != 1) {
  if (_parent.line_status == 1) {
    _parent.line_blue_link ("square_"+x+"_"+ y+
➥ "_"+z, "square_" +x+ "_"+ y +"_"+ Number(z-1),
➥ "line_" + line_depth, line_depth);
  } else {
    _parent.removeline ("line_"+line_depth);
  }
}
```

There are a couple of things left to do, but they're pretty simple, so I'll leave you to figure them out. If you want to change things, start by fiddling with the graphics, and then head into the code and get dirty.

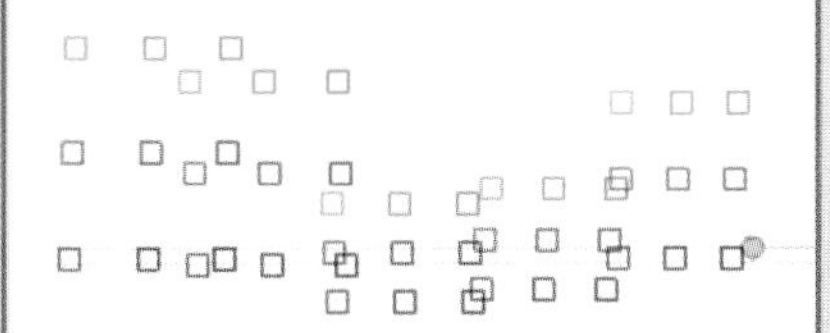

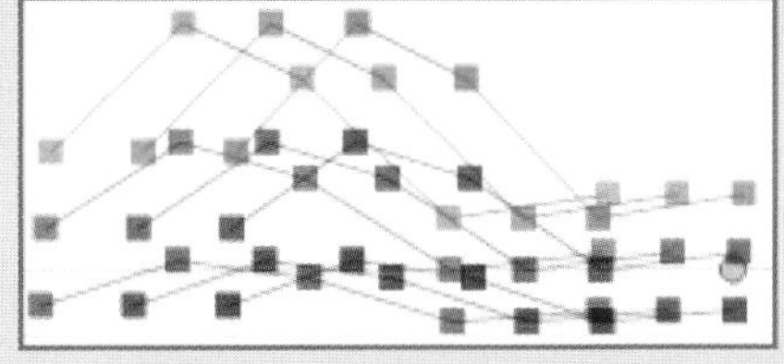

Vortex vase

Staying with the 3D engine, I modified it again to create this new, and fairly cool, effect. We've now got a spinning 3D vortex that we can alter in a number of ways. Take a look at `experiment_d.fla` and see what you think. You can move the sliders either side of the vortex up and down as well as from side to side to alter the size of it. The central slider is the midpoint, and the vortex will flare out at either side of it. The only buttons that you haven't encountered before are the `offset` buttons. These control the distance between the first and last points that make up the spout, clicking on the far right button will give a perfect, closed vortex, and the further left you go, the more open the vortex will be. Try it out to see the difference it makes. The majority of the code is on the `master_mc` clip on the main stage, but there's also some on the first frame of the root timeline.

Here's the code on `master_mc`:

```
onClipEvent (load) {
   // ------------------------
   // FOR loop variables
   // ------------------------
   z_objects = 5;
   y_objects = 8;
   x_objects = 1;
   counter = 1;


   // ------------------------
   // creates objects and assigns color to each object
   // ------------------------
   for (z=1; z<=z_objects; z++) {
     for (y=1; y<=y_objects; y++) {
       for (x=1; x<=x_objects; x++) {
         // ------------------------
         // creates objects and assigns color to each object
         // ------------------------
         _parent.attachMovie("square_link", "square_"+ x + "_" + y + "_" + z, counter);
         wing_color_spot_01 = new Color(_parent["square_"+ x + "_" + y + "_" + z]);
         new_color_spot_01 =
           {
                 rb:255 - (x*102),
                 gb:255 - (y*102),
                 bb:255 - (z*102),
                 aa:50
           };
         wing_color_spot_01.setTransform(new_color_spot_01);

         // ------------------------
         counter++;
       }
     }
   }

   // ------------------------
   // initialze sinisoid variables
   // ------------------------
   slider_speed = 5;
   slider_offset = 0;
   slider_increment = 1;
   _parent.rotate_offset = 1;

}
onClipEvent (enterFrame) {
   // ------------------------
   // initialze counter variables
   // ------------------------
   counter = 1;
   line_depth = 100;

   // ------------------------
   // start of position script
   // ------------------------
   for (z=1; z<=z_objects; z++) {
     for (y=1; y<=y_objects; y++) {
       for (x=1; x<=x_objects; x++) {
         // ------------------------
```

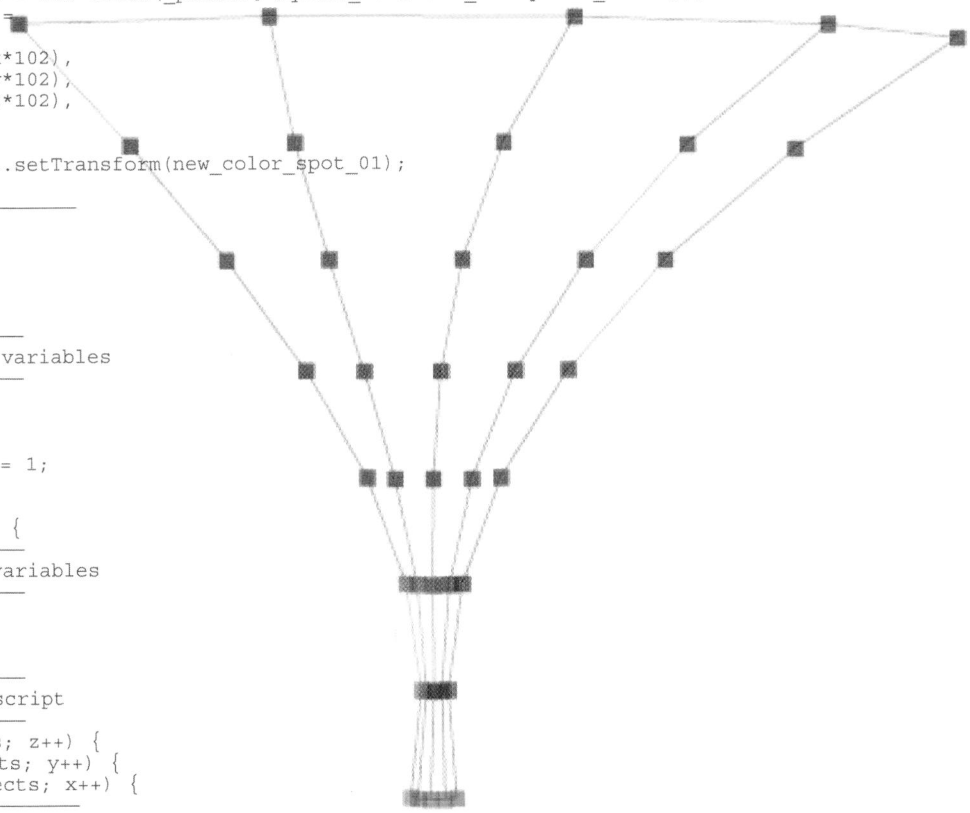

```
        // changes line style
        // ——————————————————————
        _parent["square_"+ x + "_" + y + "_" + z].gotoAndStop (_parent.color_status);


        // ——————————————————————
        // creates data
        // ——————————————————————
        // parabola variables
        xx = y - (100-_parent.vertical_bar.dragger._y)*.05;
        aa = (_parent.vertical_bar.dragger_square_right._x-15)*.075;
        bb = 4;
        cc = 5;

        // sinisoid variables
        slider_radius = (aa*Math.pow(xx, 2))  +  (bb*(xx))  +  (cc);
        slider_increment_offset = counter*_parent.rotate_offset;
        slider_cos = Math.cos((slider_increment+slider_increment_offset)/Math.PI/slider_speed)*
➥ slider_radius+slider_offset;
        slider_sin = Math.sin((slider_increment+slider_increment_offset)/Math.PI/slider_speed)*
➥ slider_radius+slider_offset;

        // ——————————————————————
        // takes given data and parses it through 3d engine function
        // ——————————————————————
        _parent.convert_array_to_3d
          (
               "square_"+ x + "_" + y + "_" + z,
               slider_sin,
               (y*-25)+112.5,
               slider_cos
          );

        // ——————————————————————
        // creates and removes blue lines
        // ——————————————————————
        if (y != 1) {
               if (_parent.line_status == 1) {
                       _parent.drawline ("square_"+ x + "_" + y + "_" + z, "square_"+ x + "_" +
➥ Number (y-1) + "_" + z, "line_"+line_depth, line_depth);        line_depth++;
               } else {
                       _parent.removeline ("line_"+line_depth);      line_depth++;
               }
        }
        // ——————————————————————
        counter++;
        line_depth++;
        // ——————————————————————
      }
    }
  }
  slider_increment++;
  // ——————————————————————
  // draws or removes line to connect all top and bottom points
  // ——————————————————————
  if (_parent.line_status == 1) {
    _parent.drawline ("square_1_1_1", "square_1_1_2", "line_"+line_depth, line_depth++);
    _parent.drawline ("square_1_1_2", "square_1_1_3", "line_"+line_depth, line_depth++);
    _parent.drawline ("square_1_1_3", "square_1_1_4", "line_"+line_depth, line_depth++);
    _parent.drawline ("square_1_1_4", "square_1_1_5", "line_"+line_depth, line_depth++);

    _parent.drawline ("square_1_8_1", "square_1_8_2", "line_"+line_depth, line_depth++);
    _parent.drawline ("square_1_8_2", "square_1_8_3", "line_"+line_depth, line_depth++);
    _parent.drawline ("square_1_8_3", "square_1_8_4", "line_"+line_depth, line_depth++);
    _parent.drawline ("square_1_8_4", "square_1_8_5", "line_"+line_depth, line_depth++);
  } else {
    _parent.removeline ("line_"+line_depth++);
    _parent.removeline ("line_"+line_depth++);
    _parent.removeline ("line_"+line_depth++);
    _parent.removeline ("line_"+line_depth++);
    _parent.removeline ("line_"+line_depth++);
```

```
    _parent.removeline ("line_"+line_depth++);
    _parent.removeline ("line_"+line_depth++);
    _parent.removeline ("line_"+line_depth++);
    _parent.removeline ("line_"+line_depth++);
    _parent.removeline ("line_"+line_depth++);

  }

}
```

And here's the code from the first frame of the root timeline:

```
_quality = "LOW";
// ————————————————————————————————————————
color_status = 1;
line_status = 1;
x_offset = -2;
y_offset = -2;
z_offset = -2;
xscale_offset = 30;
yscale_offset = 30;
zscale_offset = 100;
scale_increment = 10;
// ————————————————————————————————————————
function convert_array_to_3d (point_name, xx, yy, zz) {

  // ——————————————
  // master points
  // ——————————————
  x = 0;
  y = 1;
  z = 2;
  focul_point_x = master_point_00._x;
  focul_point_y = master_point_00._y;
  pivot_point_x = master_point_0._x;
  pivot_point_y = master_point_0._y;

  // ——————————————
  // 3d plotting function
  // ——————————————
  this[point_name]._x =(pivot_point_x-focul_point_x)*(zz/1000+1) + xx*(zz/1000+1)+focul_point_x;
  this[point_name]._y = (pivot_point_y-focul_point_y)*(zz/1000+1) + yy*(zz/1000+1)+focul_point_y;
}
// ————————————————————————————————————————
function drawline (start_point, end_point, line_name, line_depth) {
  attachMovie("line_link", "line_"+line_name, line_depth);
  this["line_"+line_name]._x = this[start_point]._x;
  this["line_"+line_name]._y = this[start_point]._y;
  this["line_"+line_name]._xscale = this[end_point]._x-this[start_point]._x;
  this["line_"+line_name]._yscale = this[end_point]._y-this[start_point]._y;
  this["line_"+line_name]._alpha = 50;
}
function removeline (line_name) {
  removeMovieClip ( "line_"+line_name );
}
// ————————————————————————————————————————
stop ();
```

Halfway through building the third experiment, I wanted to see how a particle moved around the y-axis in 3d space. The framework had already been created in the previous experiments; all I had to do was create a new form. I didn't have a clue as to what I was making, I just kept on changing and adding things until it resembled what you see here. Halfway through building this last experiment, I decided to use parabolic motion, which is an equation my high school teachers drilled into my skull in math class. This made all the difference in making this, my fourth experiment. Before I describe it though, we have to examine the steps it took to get there.

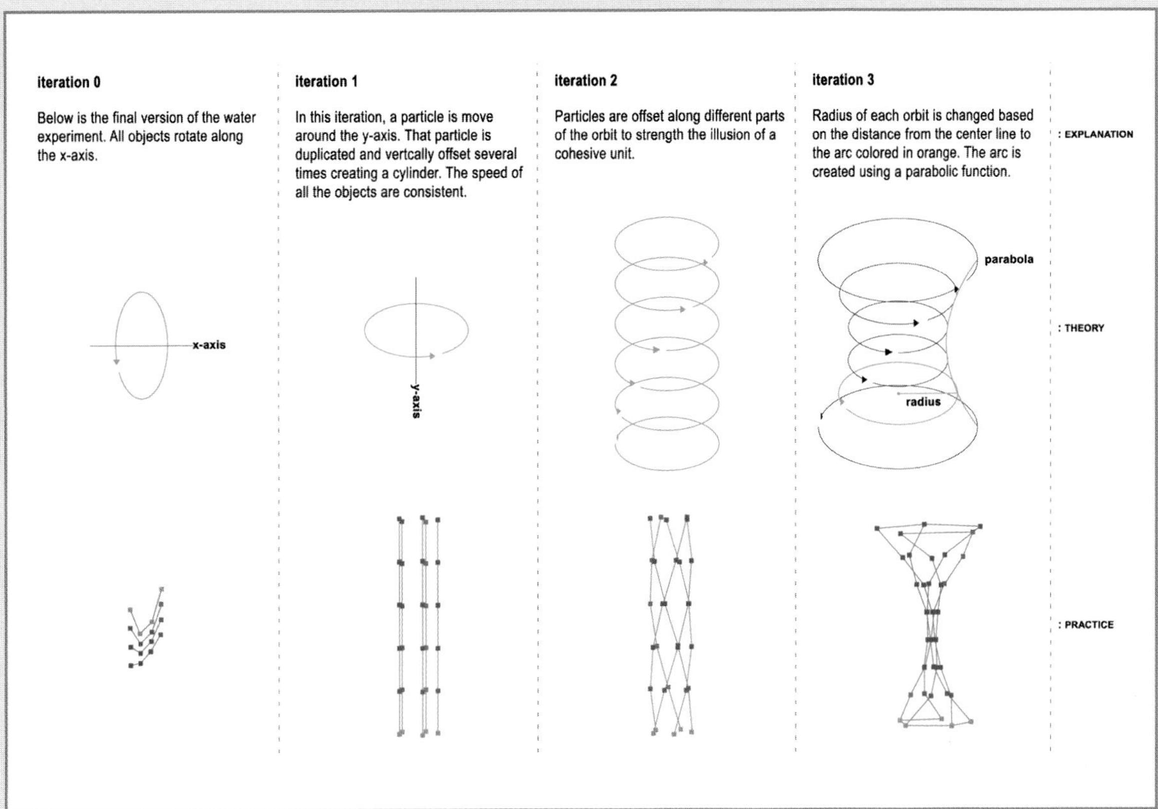

iteration 0
Below is the final version of the water experiment. All objects rotate along the x-axis.
iteration 1
In this iteration, a particle is move around the y-axis. That particle is duplicated and vertcally offset several times creating a cylinder. The speed of all the objects are consistent.
iteration 2
Particles are offset along different parts of the orbit to strength the illusion of a cohesive unit.
iteration 3
Radius of each orbit is changed based on the distance from the center line to the arc colored in orange. The arc is created using a parabolic function.
: EXPLANATION
x-axis
y-axis
parabola
radius
: THEORY
: PRACTICE

Using the previous experiment as a boilerplate, I placed the `x_`, `y_`, and `z_object` variables, as well as our new creating and coloring `for` loop, into the `load` clip event. I simplified the script in the `enterFrame` clip event from the third experiment, and this time I switched around the order in the `convert_array_to_3d` function so that it would rotate and spin around the y-axis:

```
slider_increment_offset = counter*_parent.rotate_offset;
slider_cos = Math.cos((slider_increment+slider_increment_offset)/Math.PI/
 ➥ slider_speed)*slider_radius+slider_offset;
slider_sin = Math.sin((slider_increment+slider_increment_offset)/Math.PI/
 ➥ slider_speed)*slider_radius+slider_offset;


_parent.convert_array_to_3d
   (
    "square_"+ x + "_" + y + "_" + z,
    slider_sin,
    (y*10) - 10,,
    slider_cos
   );
```

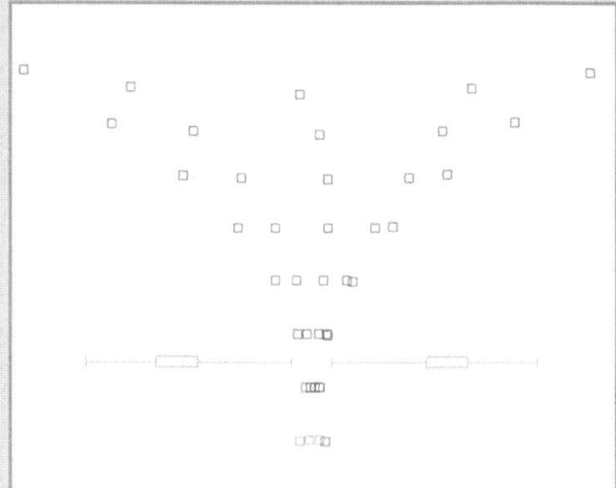

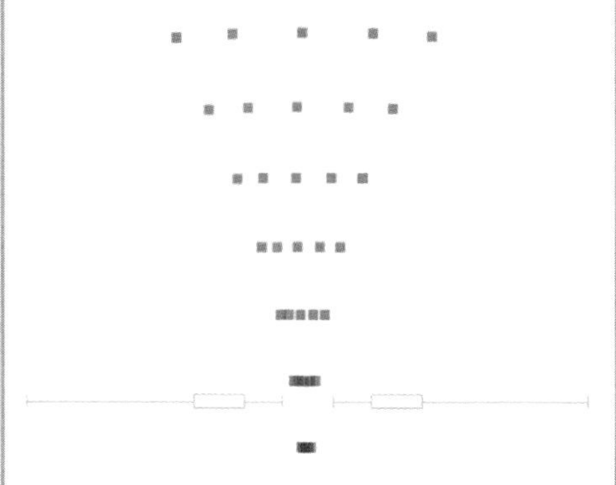

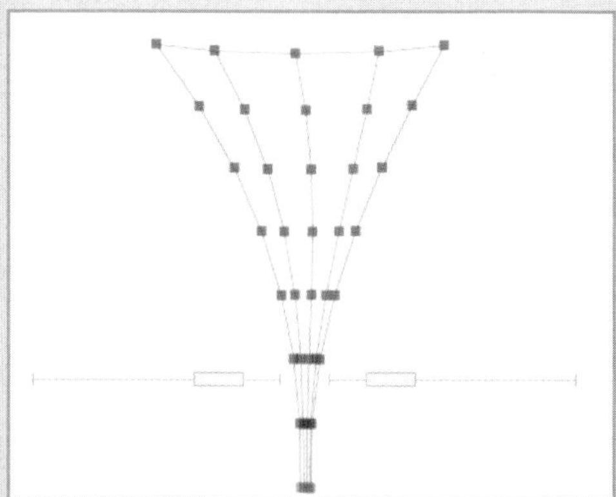

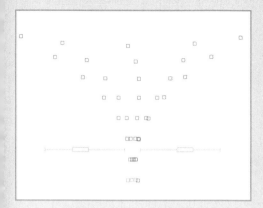

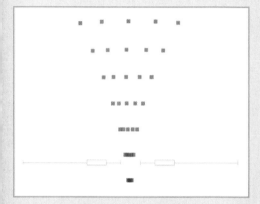

As in the third experiment, I increased y just so it's easier to use. I also added our slider increment because I wanted to offset the points again. The only difference is that I used a variable called rotate_offset, which is a variable pulled from the top right set of buttons. So, what we have now is something that looks like a rotating cylinder. What we want to do next, is dynamically change the radius of each orbit by using another script. The variable that is being changed is slider_offset, and the script uses the parabolic function. If you remember high school math class you should remember this polynomial equation:

```
y=ax^2 + bx + c
```

Variables x and y plot the points, while a, b, and c are constants. To spin it around, we need to reverse the values of x and y:

```
x=ay2 + bx + c
```

Now we just take this equation and convert it into ActionScript:

```
xx = y - (100-_parent.vertical_bar.dragger._y)*.05;
aa = 3;
bb = 4;
cc = 5;

slider_radius = (aa*Math.pow(xx, 2)) + (bb*(xx)) + (cc);
```

This looks pretty straightforward with the exception of the xx variable. A parabolic line assumes that the values of meta-x and meta-y are still variables, so it solves for all points along a Cartesian plane creating a smooth, curved line. For this script to work, we need to create the points along one axis in order to create the values of the second. So if you know that meta-y is equal to 10 you can easily figure out the value of meta-x and the position of that on the plane. xx creates those initial variables for us, whilst slider_radius gives us its corresponding value. xx is made more complex with the addition of the y and _parent.vertical_bar.dragger._y variables used to properly space out the meta-y values. The thing that I had a hard time understanding was that the values used for the parabola do not represent the plotted points for our 3d function, and nor are they coordinate points for positioning movieclips. They are used primarily as a step in a process that takes data and converts it, similar to that of an unspecified function. I used the 'meta-' term in the hopes of clarifying the differences between this and our already existing x and y values.

That's pretty much the bulk of the script. There are other functions here like drawline and removeline that are used to connect or to remove lines, but they have been explained in the earlier experiments.

There are plenty of other parts of this and all the other experiments that I didn't explain – like how data is being pushed from the slider bars to the function, how to set up all of the symbols and Library elements, and going line by line through some of the predefined functions and explaining them. This is because all I really wanted to do was show you the key features of each experiment. Explaining every little thing seems redundant and only insults your intelligence. That and I just didn't feel like writing about it. That's about it, I hope you got something out of these experiments and explanations, and I hope they inspire you in making your own.

Michael Brandon Williams is a senior at Spring Woods High School in Houston, Texas, with many years of mathematics and computer science study in his c.v. His mathematics focus has been single and multivariable calculus, real analysis, linear algebra, ordinary differential equations, elementary combinatorics, and number theory. His computer science experience is based on programming design, object-oriented programming, and problem solving. His goal is to pursue a Ph.D. in Mathematics. In his spare time, he helps run the math forum at Were-Here (www.were-here.com) under the name of ahab, and works for Eyeland Studios (www.eyeland.com) as a games programmer.

Flipping through any math book, from analytic geometry to calculus, you can usually find a section dealing with mathematics in three dimensions. In geometry you see shapes such as spheres and cylinders, and define geometric objects such as vectors. In calculus you discuss the calculus of surfaces: their rates of change in various directions and the volume underneath. The pictures in these books grab everyone's attention no matter how complex the mathematics become. The continuous, wireframe surfaces are sensational sights, sometimes mimicking the very terrain we see in the countryside. These amazing eye candies are what I wanted to create in Flash. I wanted to develop a program so that I could simply change one equation, the function of the surface itself, and create that beautiful wireframe representation of a surface that I had seen in countless textbooks. I also wanted to be able to change the range of x- and y-values graphed and the angle at which I viewed the graph. I would then use that program to discover the different possibilities of three-dimensional graphs and see what kind of incredible forms would arise. This is that program.

brandon williams

www20.brinkster.com/ahab/index.htm

Plotter

This is a slightly different experiment, but it's the logical conclusion to this book. It's a full function graph plotter in Flash, just type in the function and away you go. Check out base.swf to see some ready-made functions, just select the one that you want and hit the plot button. For experiment we're just going to build the bare bones of the plotter that you can delve into and get you hands dirty with. The code for this is longer than that for other experiments, but don't let that put you off, it's well worth it. Rather than having a separate section for the key variables and functions, I've instead heavily commented the code so you should be able to easily follow through it and get a good idea of what's going on. I've given a more thorough explanation of the workings of it after the code listing.

just the effect

We start with a simple movieclip called line. This is the standard diagonal line drawn between the corners of an imaginary 100x100 pixel square. The line runs at a 45-degree angle running from the registration point at its top left point, down to the bottom right. The movieclip is exported from the Library with the linkage name `line`.

Now onto the main stage, the only things that I have here are two layers, the first called `actions`, and the second called `plotting`. The `actions` layer will contain the majority of the code to make all of the calculations and so on, and the `plotting` layer will just contain the data for the physical dimensions – grid size, scale, rotation, and position – of the graph. Each of these layers has only a single frame. Without further ado, here's the code for the actions layer:

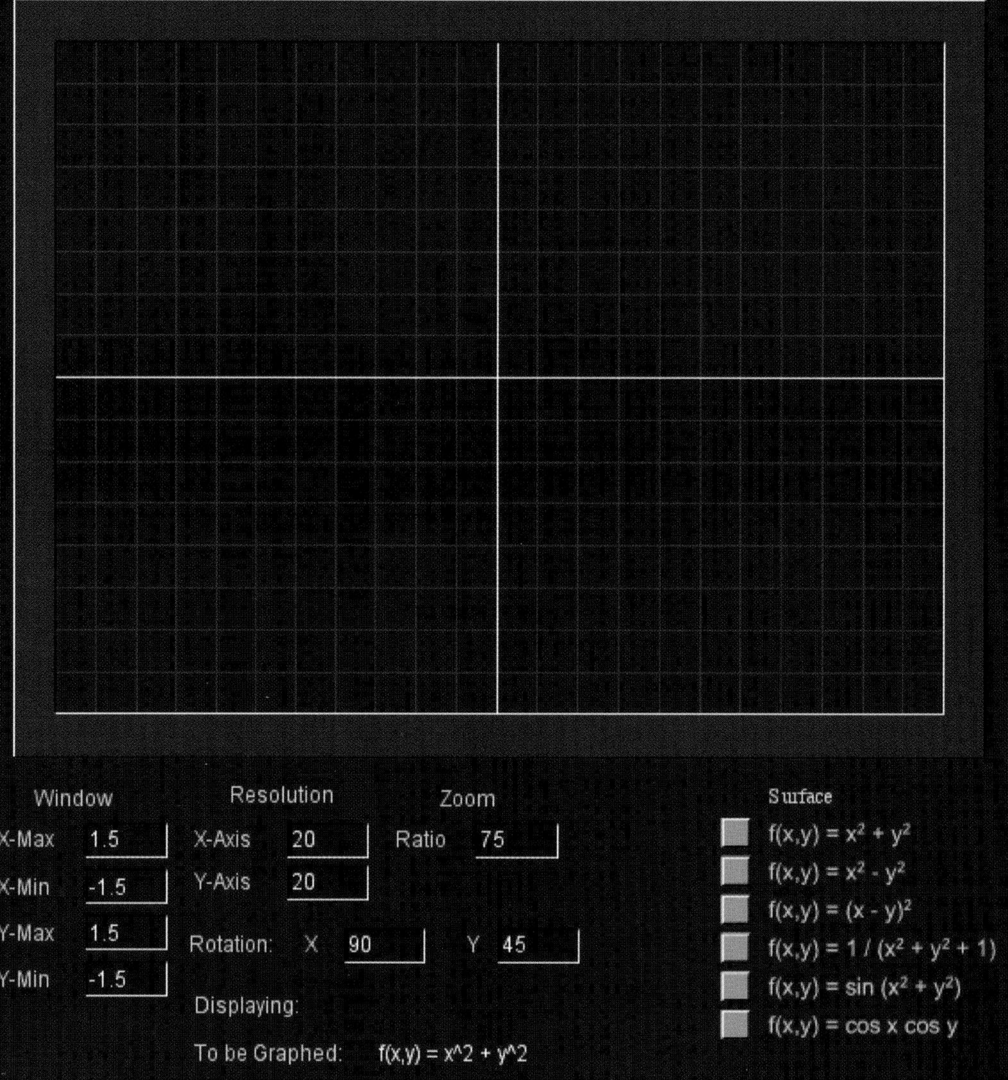

```
// math constant -- used for translating between degrees and radians
Math.trans = Math.PI / 180;


// creates a two dimensional array
Array.prototype.init_two_dim = function (x, y)
{
   for (var j = 0; j < x; j++)
   {
    this[j] = new Array (y);
   }
}


// graph object -- draws a new graph
// PARAMETERS
// x_max, x_min, y_max, y_min - dimensions of the window for the graph
// num_points_x, num_points_y - number of points to be plotted along the x- and y-axis
// zoom - a ratio of how much to zoom in ... adjusting this makes graphs easier to view
// rotate_x, rotate_y - orientation of graph
// center_x, center_y - the origin as it should appear on Flash's Stage
function graph (x_max, x_min, y_max, y_min, num_points_x, num_points_y, zoom, rotate_x, rotate_y, origin_x, origin_y)
{
   // rectangular region that surface will be drawn over (domain) -
   // D = {(x, y) | x_min < x < x_max, y_min < y < y_max}
   this.x_max = x_max;
   this.x_min = x_min;
   this.y_max = y_max;
   this.y_min = y_min;

   // number of points to be placed along the x- and y-axis
   this.num_points_x = num_points_x;
   this.num_points_y = num_points_y;

   // zoom ratio
   this.zoom = zoom;

   // orientation of graph on the x- and y-axis
   this.rotate_x = rotate_x;
   this.rotate_y = rotate_y;

   // increments to go along the x- and y-axis
   this.increment_x = (this.x_max - this.x_min) / this.num_points_x;
   this.increment_y = (this.y_max - this.y_min) / this.num_points_y;

   // position of the origin
   this.origin_x = origin_x;
   this.origin_y = origin_y;

   // sine and cosine of rotation angles
   this.sin_x = Math.sin (this.rotate_x * Math.trans);
   this.cos_x = Math.cos (this.rotate_x * Math.trans);
   this.sin_y = Math.sin (this.rotate_y * Math.trans);
   this.cos_y = Math.cos (this.rotate_y * Math.trans);
}


// multivariable function that depend on both "x" and "y" -
// mess with the return value to render different surfaces
// NOTE: when using trigonometric functions, multiply the expression within the parentheses by
// "Math.trans" to change degrees into radians
graph.prototype.function_xy = function (x, y)
{
   return (4 * Math.sin ((x * y - x*x + y*y) * Math.trans));
}


// stretches "mc" to connect point (x1, y1) and (x2, y2) -
// "mc" should be the full path to the movie clip
graph.prototype.draw_line = function (mc, x1, y1, x2, y2)
```

```
   mc._x = x1;
   mc._y = y1;
   mc._xscale = x2 - x1;
   mc._yscale = y2 - y1;
}


// plots a 3d surface z = f(x, y)
graph.prototype.plot = function ()
{
   // take away all the movie clips from last time
   this.remove_old ();

   // get the position of the points on the surface
   this.calculate_points ();

   // connect all the points with lines -- to create the grid
   this.draw_grid ();
}


// removes all the duplicated movie clips from the stage
graph.prototype.remove_old = function ()
{
   for (var j in _root)
   {
    if (_root[j] != _root.controls)
    {
     _root[j].removeMovieClip ();
    }
   }
}


// connects all the points with lines to create the grid
graph.prototype.draw_grid = function ()
{
   // used to keep the depths sorted out
   var depth = 0;

   // the position of the two points a line will connect
   var x1, y1, x2, y2;


   // loop through and connect all the lines going vertical
   for (var j = 1; j < this.num_points_x+1; j++)
   {
    for (var k = 0; k <= this.num_points_y; k++)
    {
     // attach the line to the _root
     _root.attachMovie ("line", "line" + depth, depth);

     // find the two points the line is to connect
     x1 = this.points[j][k].perspective_x;
     y1 = this.points[j][k].perspective_y;
     x2 = this.points[j-1][k].perspective_x;
     y2 = this.points[j-1][k].perspective_y;

     // connect the two points with the line
     this.draw_line (_root["line" + depth], x1, y1, x2, y2);

     // keep everything at a separate depth
     depth++;
    }
   }

   // loop through and connect all the lines going horizontal
   for (var j = 0; j <= this.num_points_x; j++)
   {
    for (var k = 1; k <= this.num_points_y; k++)
    {
```

```
      // attach the line to the _root
      _root.attachMovie ("line", "line" + depth, depth);

      // find the two points the line is to connect
      x1 = this.points[j][k].perspective_x;
      y1 = this.points[j][k].perspective_y;
      x2 = this.points[j][k-1].perspective_x;
      y2 = this.points[j][k-1].perspective_y;

      // connect the two points with the line
      this.draw_line (_root["line" + depth], x1, y1, x2, y2);

      // keep everything at a separate depth
      depth++;
     }
    }
}


// calculates the position of the points to be rendered
graph.prototype.calculate_points = function ()
{
    // two dimensional array of objects that hold the position of every point
    this.points = new Array ();

    // loop through the x-values
    for (var j = 0; j <= this.num_points_x+1; j++)
    {
     // add another dimension to the array
     this.points[j] = new Array ();

     // loop through the y-values
     for (var k = 0; k <= this.num_points_y; k++)
     {
      // create a new object in the array's element to keep track of the ordered triplet (x,y,z)
      this.points[j][k] = new Object ();

      // calculate the ordered triplet
      this.points[j][k].x = this.index_to_coord ("x", j);
      this.points[j][k].y = this.index_to_coord ("y", k);
      this.points[j][k].z = this.function_xy (this.points[j][k].x, this.points[j][k].y);

      // change the point from Flash's coordinate system to a real math rectangular system
      this.exchange_point (j, k);

      // rotate the point around the x- and y-axis
      this.rotate_point (j, k);

      // zoom into graph
      this.scale_point (j, k);

      // add perspective to point
      this.perspective_point (j, k);

      // translate point to the origin
      this.translate_point (j, k);
     }
    }
}


// changes index values (j, k) of an array to coordinates (x, y) on the graph
graph.prototype.index_to_coord = function (determine, index)
{
    return (index * this["increment_" + determine] + this[determine + "_min"]);
}


// changes the window of the graph
graph.prototype.change_window = function (x_max, x_min, y_max, y_min, z_max, z_min)
{
```

```
    // update the window dimensions
    this.x_max = Number (x_max);
    this.x_min = Number (x_min);
    this.y_max = Number (y_max);
    this.y_min = Number (y_min);

    // update the increments along the x- and y-axis
    this.increment_x = (this.x_max - this.x_min) / this.num_points_x;
    this.increment_y = (this.y_max - this.y_min) / this.num_points_y;
}


// changes the number of points to be plotted along the x- and y-axis
graph.prototype.change_num_points = function (num_points_x, num_points_y)
{
    // update the number of points to be placed along the x- and y-axis
    this.num_points_x = Number (num_points_x);
    this.num_points_y = Number (num_points_y);

    // update the increments along the x- and y-axis
    this.increment_x = (this.x_max - this.x_min) / this.num_points_x;
    this.increment_y = (this.y_max - this.y_min) / this.num_points_y;
}


// changes the function to be graphed
graph.prototype.change_equation = function (equation)
{
    // update equation
    this.equation = equation;
}


// changes the zoom ratio
graph.prototype.change_zoom = function (zoom)
{
    this.zoom = Number (zoom);
}


// changes the rotation angles
graph.prototype.change_rotation = function (rotate_x, rotate_y)
{
    this.rotate_x = Number (rotate_x);
    this.rotate_y = Number (rotate_y);

    // update the sine and cosine of the rotation angles
    this.calculate_sine_cosine ();
}


// changes a point from Flash's coordinate system to a real math rectangular system
graph.prototype.exchange_point = function (a, b)
{
    // the ordered triplet of the point
    var x, y, z;

    // get the ordered triplet
    x = this.points[a][b].x;
    y = this.points[a][b].y;
    z = this.points[a][b].z;

    // change from Flash's system to rectangular
    this.points[a][b].x = y;
    this.points[a][b].y = z;
    this.points[a][b].z = x;
}


// rotates a point (passed as an Object) by "a" and "b" on the x- and y-axes
graph.prototype.rotate_point = function (a, b)
{
    // ordered triplet to be rotated
    var x, y, z;
```

```
   // temporary rotated coordinates
   var rx1, ry1, rz1, rx2, ry2, rz2;

   // get ordered triplet
   x = this.points[a][b].x;
   y = this.points[a][b].y;
   z = this.points[a][b].z;

   // rotate point on y-axis
   rx1 = x * this.cos_y - z * this.sin_y;
   ry1 = y;
   rz1 = z * this.cos_y + x * this.sin_y;

   // rotate point on x-axis
   rx2 = rx1;
   ry2 = ry1 * this.cos_x - rz1 * this.sin_x;
   rz2 = rz1 * this.cos_x + ry1 * this.sin_x;

   // update the values in the position array
   this.points[a][b].x = rx2;
   this.points[a][b].y = ry2;
   this.points[a][b].z = rz2;
}


// scales the graph -- appears to "zoom"
graph.prototype.scale_point = function (a, b)
{
   this.points[a][b].x *= this.zoom;
   this.points[a][b].y *= this.zoom;
   this.points[a][b].z *= this.zoom;
}

// changes an ordered triplet to an ordered pair
graph.prototype.perspective_point = function (a, b)
{
   // used for perspective -- distance from the viewer's eye to the screen
   var D = 500;

   // perspective ratio -- used for changing an ordered triplet to an ordered pair
   var perspective_ratio;

   // if point is in front of view calculate position of screen
   if (this.point[a][b].z > -D)
   {
    // calculate the perspective ratio
    perspective_ratio = D / (this.points[a][b].z + D);

    // calculate the position of the point on the screen
    this.points[a][b].perspective_x = perspective_ratio * this.points[a][b].x;
    this.points[a][b].perspective_y = perspective_ratio * this.points[a][b].y;
   }
   else
   {
    // point is behind user so it should not be drawn
    this.points[a][b].perspective_x = null;
    this.points[a][b].perspective_y = null;
   }
}

// translates the point to make the origin where the user specifies
graph.prototype.translate_point = function (a, b)
{
   this.points[a][b].perspective_x = this.origin_x + this.points[a][b].perspective_x;
   this.points[a][b].perspective_y = this.origin_y - this.points[a][b].perspective_y;
}

// calculates the sine and cosine of the rotation angles
graph.prototype.calculate_sine_cosine = function ()
{
   this.sin_x = Math.sin (this.rotate_x * Math.trans);
   this.cos_x = Math.cos (this.rotate_x * Math.trans);
   this.sin_y = Math.sin (this.rotate_y * Math.trans);
   this.cos_y = Math.cos (this.rotate_y * Math.trans);
```

The plotting layer is far simpler, and it only contains the following code:

```
// set up a new graph -- initial settings: parabaloid, 10x10 square region, 5x zoom, and no rotation
my_graph = new graph (10, -10, 10, -10, 20, 20, 15, -45, 20, 275, 200);

my_graph.plot ();
```

Explanation

To understand the script you must first understand multivariable functions. The level of theory covered in this short explanation is elementary to say the least; it is material that could have been covered in a middle school Algebra class.

In Algebra, a function of x took every x in its domain and assigned to it a y value. When you plotted many x and y ordered pairs you eventually saw a graph forming; anything from a parabola to a sine curve. For a function of x and y, also called a multivariable function, you assign a z value for every combination of x and y in the function's domain. Once you have the x, y, z ordered triplet you plot the point by moving x units along the x-axis, y units along the y-axis, and z units along the z-axis. After plotting more and more of these ordered triplets, a three-dimensional graph takes shape.

I thought that this could be programmed quite easily in Flash. First, I would define what range of x and y values that I wanted to graph. Then, I would simply loop through all of the different combinations of x and y values in that range and assign them a z value by plugging **`x`** and **`y`** into a multivariable function. However, a slight problem arose: how would I keep track of all these numbers? I opted for a two dimensional array. The indices of the array would be the number of points graphed along the x- and y-axis, then for every element in the two dimensional array I would have an object with variables for the **`x`**, **`y`**, and **`z`** position of the point, as well as the position of the point when perspective is added.

After I calculated the ordered triplet of the points I still wasn't entirely done, as I had a few coordinate transformations that I wanted to put the points through. I translated, rotated, and scaled the points before I finally calculated them with perspective. The translation simply shifts the graph to the center of the screen, since Flash's origin is at the top-left of it. The rotation allows me to view the graph from different angles, and the scale allows me to zoom in and out of the graph so that I can have more precision.

When the points were initially calculated, transformed, and then projected onto the computer screen for perspective, I was ready to render the graph. Because I wanted the surface to be a wireframe object, I created a 100-pixel long line at a forty-five degree angle for connecting two points. I then looped through the graph's range of x values and connecting all the lines that run horizontally, and through the range of y values to connect all the lines that run vertically. Once the lines were drawn, the rendering was complete and I beheld a wondrous three-dimensional graph in Flash.

Here's a run-down of some of the important functions and the part they play in the movie:

Because there had to be a lot of interaction between the graph and the user (changing window dimensions, resolution, zoom, orientation), I created a "graph" object that I would attach functions to, which would be invoked elsewhere in the movie and script. The "graph" object holds all the important variables: the ranges of x and y values to be graphed, the number of points to be graphed along the x- and y-axis, the rotation of the graph, the sine and cosine of the rotation angles, as well as other values. These variables would then be used in the functions that I was going to attach to the object.

The first function I attached was one for connecting two points with a line, called **`draw_line`**. The function is passed the path to the movie clip that will be stretched to connect two points as well as the **`x-`** and **`y-`**positions of the two points.

The next function is the multivariable function that we talked about earlier, **`function_xy`**. This requires an input of **`x`** and **`y`** and then returns the value of the mathematical function. It is this return value that you will want to mess around with to create different surfaces.

The next series of functions take care of the task of when the user wants to change one of the rendering parameters, like the number of points to be plotted along the x- and y-axis. These functions take care of when the user wants to change the dimensions of the viewing window, the number of points to be plotted along the x- and y-axis, the zoom amount, and the rotation angles of the graph. They are **`change_window`**, **`change_num_points`**, **`change_zoom`**, and **`change_rotation`**.

When calling the function that updates the rotation angles another function is called to find the sine and cosine of the angle, it's called **`calculate_sine_cosine`**.

The next series of functions do all of the coordinate transformations. One takes care of the rotation, one for zooming, one for translating, and one last one for changing an ordered triplet into an ordered pair. However, these functions do not operate on all of the points but instead on only one; the specific point to be transformed is passed to each function by the means of two variables, **`a`** and **`b`**. These variables are the indices of where the point can be found in the position array. The functions are: **`rotate_point`**, **`scale_point`**, **`perspective_point`**, and **`translate_point`**.

A problem that I ran into at one point was that the rotation of the graph was a little awkward. After racking my brains for a few hours I figured that it was because I have set up Flash's 3D coordinate system differently from how it is in mathematics. In Flash, I have the x- and y-axis as usual and the z-axis coming out at you. In math, the x-axis comes towards you, the y-axis goes off to the sides, and the z-axis goes up and down. Therefore, I simply wrote a function to change the points to the math coordinate system. This function is called **`exchange_point`**.

The next function is the big one: it calculates the position of all of the points to be connected with lines. It loops through the number of points along the x- and y-axis so that it can index the array that keeps track of the position of the points. But, if you remember, to use the multivariable function we were to give the function two values: x and y. Those values were positions of points in the xy-plane, and when they were plugged into the multivariable function you got a z-position. You cannot, however, plug in indices of an array and get the z-position. Therefore, you must change the index values to actual x- and y-positions. After the indices are changed to coordinates you calculate the z-positions, and finally go through all the coordinate transformations. These two functions are called **`calculate_points`**, and **`index_to_coord`**.

The last function in the rendering process is the one that connects the points with lines, **`draw_grid`**. The function handles this in two parts. First it connects all of the lines running vertical, and then the lines going horizontal.

Finally, you only have a few functions left that just tie up some loose ends. One function clears all the lines off the stage, called **`remove_old`**, and the other is the one that's called when you want to plot a new surface, it's simply called **`plot`**. This function first calls the function that removes the old lines, then calls the function that calculates the position of all the points, and finally calls the function that draws all the lines.

That's pretty much it really. If you like then you can alter this to add a GUI as I have with **`base.swf`**. This is basically just a wrapper with some pre-built functions on it that lets you input and plot your own functions without having to go deep into the code. Check out the FLA for some ideas on how to do this, it's mostly just code attached to buttons, but you'll also need to make a couple of changes to the main code, add some equations to plot, and add another parameter to the graph function. You'll see these changes in **`base.fla`**.

To add even more depth to the terrain generated you could also use the Color object. By making the lines that connect points with small z-positions a little darker you could make it seem as if the crevices are getting little light, where as the tops of the hills are of a brighter shade and getting plenty of light.

Here are some parameters to try for the graph function, this covers the first nine parameters, and I've left the last two – the x and y origin – the same so that the origin is always the center of the screen. These go on the plotting layer, or in the appropriate boxes if you are using **`base.fla`** as a start point:

```
x_max, x_min, y_max, y_min, num_points_x, num_points_y, zoom, rotate_x, rotate_y

1.5, -1.5, 1.5, -1.5, 30, 30, 175, 90, 0
2, -2, 2, -2, 30, 30, 50, -90, 0
180, -180, 180, -180, 30, 30, 1, -20, 0
3, -3, 3, -3, 30, 30, 70, -35, 0
20, -20, 20, -20, 20, 20, 5, -60, 0
10, -10, 10, -10, 15, 15, 15, -45, 20
```

Try different combinations of these with different surface models to get some interesting results. Good luck.

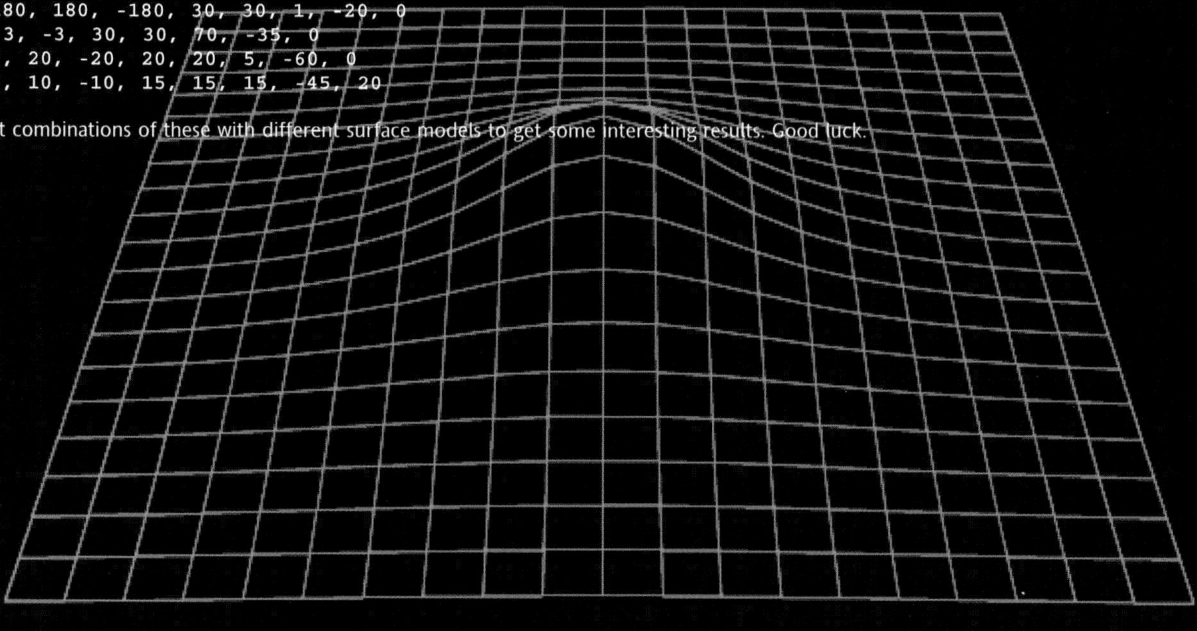

TANGENTS

www.potatoland.org/

www.flong.com

www.kettering.edu/~drussell/demos.html

www.parasolpress.com/lewitt_2.html

www.turux.org

www.spacefuture.com/archive/inhabiting_artificial_gravity.shtml

www.sodaplay.com

http://dbn.media.mit.edu

www.georgehart.com/sculpture/sculpture.html

www.asthana.co.uk

http://flash.onego.ru

www.signwave.co.uk

www-groups.dcs.st-andrews.ac.uk/~history/Java/index.html

www.jodi.org

www.muzeumsztuki.lodz.pl/images/bridget_riley.htm

www.globalink.net/~artboy/P/riley.html

www.numeral.com/appletsoftware/online.html

www.noodlebox.com/bitsandpieces/main.htm

www-ai.ijs.si/eliza/eliza.html

www.red3d.com/cwr/boids/

www.rhizome.org

http://mathworld.wolfram.com/LogarithmicSpiral.html

www.serv.net/Java/SineRule.html

www.tygh.co.uk/tan/tan.htm

http://acg.media.mit.edu

www.re-move.org

www.roberpenner.com

www.modifyme.com

www.wireframe.co.za

http://cleoag.shockteam.com/sw3d

www.dextro.org

www.sylloge.com/5k/entries/176/1.html

www.numeral.com/artwork.html

www.red3d.com/cwr/steer

http://acg.media.mit.edu/people/golan

http://astronomy.swin.edu.au/pbourke/fractals/fracintro

http://users.shore.net/~ndm/symbols/symbols.html

www.mcs.surrey.ac.uk/Personal/R.Knott/Fibonacci/phi3DGeom.html

www.kevlindev.com/samples/life/index.htm

www.moonstar.com/~nedmay/chromat/fibonaci.htm

www.xmx54.dial.pipex.com

www.easylife.org/386dx

www.nst.ing.tu-bs.de/schaukasten/fourier/en_idx.html

www.jhu.edu/~signals/fourier2

www-groups.dcs.st-andrews.ac.uk/~history/Curves/Curves.html

www.math.ubc.ca/~feldman/demos/pendulum.html

http://mathworld.wolfram.com/animations.html

www.rhizome.org/object.rhiz?2793

www.kevlindev.com/samples/ants/index.htm

http://surface.yugop.com

www.echotap.com

www.noodlebox.com/classic/window.html

www.auto-illustrator.com

www.math.ubc.ca/~feldman/demos/demo9.html